The Power of Pentecost or the Fullness of the Spirit

By Dr. John R. Rice

SWORD of the LORD
PUBLISHERS

Printed and Bound in the United States of America

TABLE OF CONTENTS

INTRODUCTION

Seventeen years of labor on one book has now come to an end, and the manuscript is ready for the printer! In 1932 I first wrote a book-sized manuscript on the fullness of the Spirit. I felt sure then of the principal doctrines. But I felt unsure of myself as being fit to write on such a holy theme. I felt then, and feel now, that I needed the long years of waiting on God and proving Him, and of proving that these things are so by seeing multitudes of men and women brought to Christ. No other book I have written has taken more than a small fraction of the labor and study and prayer and heart-searching that have been spent on this one. Therefore with a good deal of trembling and concern, and with earnest prayer, I send it forth. Oh, may the breath of Heaven be upon its testimony and teaching!

If the doctrine taught in this book seems strange—the doctrine that the mighty power of Pentecost is available for Christians today, that the fullness of the Spirit primarily brings soul-winning power, that this mighty power may be had by prevailing prayer, that it does not need to be evidenced by speaking in tongues and that it is not the same as sanctification or the eradication of the carnal nature—this doctrine is not new. As you will see later by their own plain testimonies, Spurgeon, Moody, Finney, Torrey, Chapman, Billy Sunday, L. R. Scarborough, and many others all believed essentially the same thing as taught in this book on the power of the Holy Spirit for soul winning. The ultra-dispensational teaching of Darby, the Plymouth Brethren, and the "Bible teachers" has, among many fundamental Christians, increased as a fad and has supplanted the teaching of Moody and Torrey and Spurgeon. But it should be noted that these men who believe that the fullness of the Spirit comes only as a sovereign act of God, that no one should seek the power of Pentecost nor pray for the fullness of the Spirit, do not follow the well-known teaching of the great soul winners. This is a fad that will pass away, I believe. At any rate, these "Bible teachers" who use less Scripture than the evangelists, who have never held great revivals, are not speaking from their own personal experience as did Spurgeon, Moody, Torrey, Chapman, Billy Sunday, and their kind. The doctrine in this book is not new. You may like the new better, but remember that the teaching here given is the old orthodoxy of the mighty soul winners of the centuries.

And let me, who am the least of God's soul winners, give my

humble testimony. I know that on me the power of the Holy Spirit has
rested. I have seen His miracles changing lives and communities. I
know that I have seen drunkards made sober, harlots made pure, infidels made into believers, sinners made into saints. Hundreds of them,
yes, thousands of them, have been wonderfully transformed. I would be
wicked and sin exceedingly if I did not acknowledge that whatever
God in His mercy has wrought through my poor ministry was done
through a special anointing and enduement of the Holy Spirit. I cannot say less. I dare not deny the miracles of grace that I have seen happen through my ministry, person to person and before congregations,
large and small. How much I have sinned against God in not waiting
before Him more and in not depending on Him with more abandon to
do His mighty works in my ministry!

To all my brethren in the ministry I humbly submit that what I am
speaking about here is the only antidote for the worldliness which has
come in like a flood. It is the only antidote for modernism, that wicked
rebellion against Christ and His Word, that infidelity in pulpit and pew
so prevalent these days. What we need is not simply the arguments of
men, even of the best and wisest men. What we need is a demonstration of the power of God upon His ministers and His witnesses. Oh,
may God give it to us all! Many long for revival and pray for revival.
As solemnly as I know how I urge that there cannot possibly be any
great revival except by a mighty moving of the Holy Spirit as God's
people seek His power and wait upon Him for His enduement from on
high. And I believe that revival is the only hope of survival for Bible
Christianity in the churches. O God, send upon us the power of
Pentecost that we may see the revival for which we have so long prayed
and for which we now devoutly yearn!

Some of my beloved brethren who speak in tongues may be grieved
that I find in the Bible no teaching that speaking in tongues is the necessary evidence of the fullness of the Holy Spirit. I write with love and
fellowship for these brethren. And let us all make sure that none of us
criticize those who believe in the mighty power of the Holy Spirit and
seek this power, because of some minor differences, unless we ourselves
are as eager as they for God's fullness. What right has any man who
never prays to be filled with the Spirit of God, never teaches Christians
to seek God's mighty power—what right has such a man, I say, to criticize those who long for God's fullness, because perhaps they speak in
tongues or wish the eradication of the carnal nature? I want to name
myself a brother, one in hope and prayers and tears and aim, with all

those who seek the fullness of God's power. If I seem to be critical in this book, I hope that such brethren who differ with me will remember that I am building up and not destroying. I am urging upon every Christian everywhere to claim his inheritance and have the power of Pentecost for himself. I am a friend, not an enemy, of those who seek God's power, whether they call this power a baptism or a filling or a gift or anointing or sanctification or "second blessing." I will not agree with them on some details, but I do insist that we Christians need, more than anything else in this world, the power of God upon us to do the work of God. Will readers who differ yet count me as a friend and help me to teach Christians everywhere to restore New Testament Christianity to the world by having the power of Pentecost to carry out the Great Commission?

May I urge upon every reader that this book ought to be read with much prayer and waiting upon God. The author and much that he says may be unworthy, but the subject is worthy the most honest heart, the most serious facing of the problem. And as you pray, make sure that you let God have His way and that as you go through the book God will go through you and make you what He wants you to be. I pray not that the reader may come out at the end of the book convinced but may come out consumed! I pray not that you may come out to affirm the doctrine but to be aflame with power. May you not lay down the book with praise but with passion and power. I yearn that this book will make not passive saints but powerful soul winners. Remember that in this book you must come face-to-face, not primarily with a theological doctrine or dogma, but with the problem of your life and whatever lack it may have in a passion for souls and in the fullness of God's power.

In the Name that is above every name in Heaven and earth, and for power to do His work, yours,

JOHN R. RICE
March 1949

Chapter 1

The Lost Secret—Power

"And, behold, I send the promise of my Father upon you: but tarry ye in the city of Jerusalem, until ye be endued with power from on high."—Luke 24:49.

"But ye shall receive power, after that the Holy Ghost is come upon you: and ye shall be witnesses unto me both in Jerusalem, and in all Judæa, and in Samaria, and unto the uttermost part of the earth."—Acts 1:8.

"And with great power gave the apostles witness of the resurrection of the Lord Jesus: and great grace was upon them all."—Acts 4:33.

I. Present-Day Barrenness of the Church

It was in the summer of 1928 that I drove along a highway in western Texas toward the little town of Peacock. I had been called for revival services. The pastor had written me that a terrible drought gripped the land. For four months there had been no rain. The sun beat down pitilessly. The situation was like that described by Dr. B. H. Carroll in his testimony, "My Infidelity and What Became of It":

> I have witnessed a drought in Texas. The earth was iron and the heavens brass. Dust clouded the thoroughfares and choked the travelers. Watercourses ran dry, grass scorched and crackled, corn leaves twisted and wilted, stock died around the last water holes, the ground cracked in fissures, and the song of birds died out in parched throats. Men despaired. The whole earth prayed: "Rain, rain, rain! O Heaven, send rain!" Suddenly a cloud rises above the horizon and floats into vision like an angel of hope. It spreads a cool shade over the burning and glowing earth. Expectation gives life to desire. The lowing herds look up. The shriveled flowers open their tiny cups. The corn leaves untwist and rustle with gladness. And just when all trusting, suffering life opens her confiding heart to the promise of relief, the cloud, the cheating cloud, like a heartless coquette, gathers her drapery about her and floats scornfully away, leaving the angry sun free to dart his fires of death into the open heart of all suffering life.

So it was that summer day when I drove into West Texas to begin revival services. As we entered the drought-stricken area, signs of distress began to appear. Even in years of good rainfall, the land was too arid for corn. Now the substitute sorghum grain crops were burned and seared and withered to within a few inches of the ground, though it was yet midsummer. Much of the pastureland was as barren of grass as a roadway. What grass appeared was now as brown as in dead of winter, though we were in the midst of summer.

As we drove along in an open car, our nostrils were assailed more than once with the horrible stench of a starved cow or horse dead by the roadside. We passed one and then another deserted farm with boards nailed over the doors and windows, the barns and pastures empty. Farmers and their families had gone elsewhere to eke out a living, through these bitter months, by day labor. In the little town where I came to lead in revival services we found that drinking water had to be shipped in by railroad tank cars. The livelihood, the health, the happiness, the manner of life of thousands of people were menaced by the terrifying drought. Oh, for the rain!

After some days of hearing earnest preaching, a group of contrite and penitent people were ready to come together with fervent prayer for rain. They confessed their worldliness, their sins which had brought God's wrath upon them. Because of our awful sense of need, we waited on God, pleading with Him for rain to water the land. And thank God, in less than twenty-four hours a mighty rain came.

But all around us we Christians see and experience a drought worse than that. There is a famine but not of bread. Dearth is all around us, yet there are little alarm, little burden, little crying unto God for a rain of revival.

The church clerk of a large congregation talked to me the other day about the record for the last year. It is the largest congregation in its city. It is claimed to be both the most active church and the most orthodox in the area. It sends out a dozen or two of missionaries and supports them. Its pastor is a strong Bible preacher, evangelical, scholarly, warmhearted. It has the largest percentage of clean, devoted Christians of any large church I know. The church has an unusually high proportion of ministers and missionaries in its membership. Yet the church clerk said that last year there were only four new converts received for baptism and those four were very small children out of devoted Christian homes. Then the church clerk said with trembling lips, "No one seemed to think that was very bad!"

That church is representative of a thousand other churches that are, in the main, sound in doctrine—churches with godly and orthodox pastors, churches of sincere Christians. Yet they are churches without the power of God!

Oh, the church of Jesus Christ has lost her glory! Ichabod, "the glory is departed," is written over the doors of our stately houses of worship. Our churches, in the language of Scripture, have 'miscarrying wombs and dry breasts.' Preachers have largely become pleasing palaverers and not powerful prophets.

A gray-haired minister with twenty-five years in the pulpit told me that he had never won a single soul to Christ in personal conversation! "Do you think God intended every one of us to plead with individuals? I would not know how to begin!" he said.

Literally thousands of congregations last year did not have one single convert. Thousands of ministers in America did not win one soul. Whole denominations failed to win enough people to make up for the loss in membership by death. The drought of death is upon our country, upon our churches, upon our ministry, upon individual Christians. Few there be who know it; fewer still who care enough to wait upon God and plead for His power.

It is said that since the war less than one percent of British young people have any contact whatever with the churches. In America we face a loss increasingly similar. Whole areas of life and thought are utterly untouched by the influence of the church. Christians founded and supported the great universities in our country; our public education was once very definitely influenced by Christian principles. Now not one person in a hundred could name the Ten Commandments, which are the basis of all morality. People do not know the Beatitudes, do not know the Lord's Prayer, do not even know John 3:16. The vast majority in America have no idea what is the Gospel, what is God's plan of salvation! At least three-fourths of our college graduates are infidels, if not atheists. Lawlessness multiplies every year, particularly among young people. Two out of five marriages end in divorce, and the rate is rapidly increasing. Virginity is laughed at nearly as widely as Christianity is.

Our country is a heathen nation. The percentage of born-again Christians is steadily decreasing. Never since the great revival beginning with Charles G. Finney has the percentage of Christians run so low. The churches beat a continual retreat. We cannot win even the children of Christians, those who grow up in Christian homes and in the Sunday schools.

II. Our Trouble—We Lack the Power of God

The trouble is that we do not have the power of God!

We cannot keep Christians, and many of us cannot keep ourselves, from the degrading worldliness all about us. Shame on us all for the church people who drink and curse and fill their minds with the lewdness of the movies and the trash of dirty novels and magazines, who imbibe the morals of the barnyard from their companions and from the influence of America's tainted, ungodly civilization. It is because we do not have the power of God upon us.

We have lost the power of God, so we cannot keep those under our care from the damning blight, the unbelief, and the false guesses of the pseudoscientists in schools and colleges and places of public influence.

We have lost the power of God, so we cannot keep our converts from being led off into human cults and isms wholly foreign to Bible Christianity—Christian Science, Jehovah's Witnesses, Unity, the "I AM" movement, spiritualism, theosophy, or even "Father Divine's" group.

We have no power; therefore, in our denominations we cannot convert or outvote or oust the infidels, the deniers of Christ's deity, the scoffers at the virgin birth, the atoning blood, the bodily resurrection, the inspired Bible.

Our first great need is not church union. Twelve cylinders in a car are no better than four if there is no spark from the battery or no gas in the tank!

The first need of the church is not popularity and favor with men. Most of us now, even if the world loved us and would listen to us, do not have the power of God to win them to Christ.

The first need of Christians today is not training. We have the brains, the culture, the personality in the pulpits of our land. But sinners do not tremble and repent. Saints do not fall in confession and holy rededication before God. Drunkards are not made sober. Harlots are not made pure. Infidels are not made believers. It is not training but power that we lack and need!

We have hundreds of Christian periodicals. Christian books roll continuously from the printing presses. Radios publish the Gospel to every city apartment, village cottage or farmhouse in America. Neither the Everglades of Florida, the blistering deserts of Arizona, nor the arctic wilds of Alaska can get away from the radio Gospel. Tracts are given out by the millions. Yet there is little of revival. Most of our preaching, most of our singing, most of our testimony, most of our praying, most of our living are without power. We do not have the breath of God upon us. Heaven is shut up so that there is little spiritual rain. God has turned His face away from us! Oh, the crying shame and sin and defeat and ruin and death of our powerless lives!

When showers of revival do come in isolated sections, it is a strange phenomenon to the world today. Modernists scoff at revival as mass hysteria which will entirely disappear in an enlightened people. Ultra-dispensationalists write learned discourses on why the reported revivals must be frauds, the evangelists charlatans, the converts hypocrites. And hungry-hearted Christians can hardly believe what their eyes see and their hearts feel!

All over America a whole generation has grown up, people who never saw a great revival. In Buffalo, New York, after our great revival campaign, a minister told me with glorified face, amid tears: "I have seen what I never hoped to see in this world! For years I prayed for a revival, and then I gave it up. I thought I should never see the day when hundreds of hardened sinners would turn to Christ in a great revival and have their lives utterly transformed, claiming Christ openly and setting out to live for Him."

In Durham, North Carolina, a pastor cooperating in the revival campaign, after seeing about thirty people wonderfully converted to Christ in one service and seeing similar scenes night after night, said publicly something like the following: "I thank God for this revival, not only for the folks that are saved, but that the people of my church may see again manifested the power of the Gospel and the power of the Holy Spirit. A whole generation has passed since our city has seen this kind of revival." When God in His mercy does send a breath of revival, the great spiritual dearth everywhere is made all the more glaringly apparent by the contrast.

I would to God that every Christian in America would wake up to the awfulness of our powerless state. God has turned His back upon His people because of our sins! The power of the Holy Spirit is not manifest in most of our churches, on most of us preachers, on most of us Christians. O God, send a revival of Holy Spirit power!

We Christian workers are like the son of the prophet. He had a borrowed ax, and alas, as he chopped, the head flew off and sank in the stream. Our ministry, too, is borrowed. "Naught have I gotten but what I received." But we have lost the axhead, the power of the Holy Spirit, the cutting edge to the preached Word. *Then* the young son of the prophet was dismayed and turned lamenting to Elisha. *Then* the prophet of God knew how to get back the lost axhead. *Today,* to our shame be it said, most of us try to chop along with an ax handle but no axhead of power. And most of us do not know any Elisha, any mighty man of God to whom we may turn for instructions. O God, raise up anointed evangelists to show American Christians their need and to call us back to the fullness of the Holy Spirit!

III. Our Powerlessness Contrasted With Christ's Promises

This drab barrenness, this powerlessness and fruitlessness—is that all that God has for His people? Must Christians be as lights hid under a bushel, as salt that has lost its savor? No! God never intended that His children should be fruitless and barren. Powerless Christianity is not normal Christianity. No Christian need go without winning souls. Christ Himself is our guarantee that every one of us may have the fullness of power to win souls.

Jesus Himself is the One who gives power to win souls, and He has given us many great and precious promises about the divine enabling for this holy task.

John the Baptist announced, "I indeed baptize you with water; but one mightier than I cometh, the latchet of whose shoes I am not worthy to unloose: he shall baptize you with the Holy Ghost and with fire" (Luke 3:16). Jesus is the One who baptizes with the Holy Ghost, the One who sends the Holy Spirit in power upon His people. Peter tells us how the fullness of the Spirit at Pentecost came. "This Jesus hath God raised up, whereof we all are witnesses. Therefore being by the right hand of God exalted, and having received of the Father the promise of the Holy Ghost, he hath shed forth this, which ye now see and hear" (Acts 2:32, 33).

Many, many times the Lord Jesus made special promises to His disciples about the power from Heaven. In the tenth chapter of Luke we find the record of how He sent the seventy before Him to witness and prepare the way for His coming to various cities and towns. So weighty were their words to be that even these new converts, leaving a city which would not hear them, should shake the very dust of the city off their feet. Jesus declared that it should be more tolerable in the judgment for Sodom than for any city that failed to hear the empowered witnessing of the seventy lambs sent out among wolves. The seventy went; wonderful blessings attended their ministry. And we are told of their return:

"And the seventy returned again with joy, saying, Lord, even the devils are subject unto us through thy name. And he said unto them, I beheld Satan as lightning fall from heaven. Behold, I give unto you power to tread on serpents and scorpions,

and over all the power of the enemy: and nothing shall by any means hurt you."—
Luke 10:17–19.

These are wonderful promises. These young converts, sent out to be witnesses, were to be able to tread on serpents and scorpions and over all the power of the enemy; and they cast devils out of sinners.

Do you believe that the Lord Jesus would give such promises and pour out such power on those who did His bidding then and leave us, His children now doing His work, without His power and presence? No indeed! He gave to the disciples and to us many promises of His continued presence and power for those who did His will.

In John 7:37,38 Jesus gave a wonderful promise:

"In the last day, that great day of the feast, Jesus stood and cried, saying, If any man thirst, let him come unto me, and drink. He that believeth on me, as the scripture hath said, out of his belly shall flow rivers of living water."

Here is a promise for the time then future. After Jesus was risen from the dead, His disciples, and not only those then His disciples but all that should believe on Him, had an unceasing, unfailing source of power promised. "He that believeth on me, as the scripture hath said, out of his belly [his innermost being] shall flow rivers of living water." And by this river, this life-giving stream flowing out from a Christian's heart and life, Jesus meant the fullness of the Holy Spirit. *The Word*

If we are only empty cisterns, or if we are stagnant pools, we do not have what Jesus promised us! We are not obtaining our full birthright! We are not living up to our privileges! Every Christian should be a living fountain of the water of life. The Holy Spirit, within us and flowing from us, should bring life to those about us, just as an artesian well brings life to the desert. So Jesus promised for those who should believe on Him. It is a promise for every Christian, the promise of fullness of power.

The night before Jesus was crucified, instead of seeking comfort for Himself, He comforted the disciples. After telling them, "Let not your heart be troubled," Jesus made them exceeding great and precious promises. Jesus said: "Verily, verily, I say unto you, He that believeth on me, the works that I do shall he do also; and greater works than these shall he do; because I go unto my Father" (John 14:12).

Here is a promise so great that few will believe it. Jesus Himself did *True* all His mighty works in the power of the Holy Spirit. Now He tells the disciples that they may do exactly the same kind of work as He did. He does not make a single exception. He does not say that some of His

From works to Miracles

miracles were too stupendous to be done by the hands of others. He does not say that the raising of the dead or the healing of the sick or the cleansing of the leper or the conversion of the drunkard and the harlot and infidel were too much for these disciples. No, He said plainly, "He that believeth on me, the works that I do shall he do also." And then He added that they should do even greater works, since His life was cut short and His public ministry ended at the crucifixion.

Here is a startling teaching, but it is true. Jesus promised that the marvels, the power, the wonder of His own ministry might be repeated in the lives of multitudes of all who believed in Him. Jesus was never barren. He was never powerless. He was never defeated. He was never even discouraged by the circumstances. There was a life-changing marvel in His speech, in every contact He made. The mighty power of God His Father, through the Holy Spirit, poured through His life. Every touch of His hand, every tone of His voice was freighted with the power of the Holy Spirit. And that miraculous power could be reproduced, He promised, in the lives of His disciples!

Of course Jesus never meant that anybody else could die on the cross and atone for men's sins, as He did. No one else was the virgin-born Saviour, God incarnate, one with the Father, as He was. But He did plainly promise that the same power of the Holy Spirit that attended His walk and talk and ministry day by day could attend the service and testimony of others who followed Him and believed in Him. O Christian, believe it! God has for you blessings you have never claimed, power you have never used, an enduement you have never sought and found!

And lest one should think that this promise was only for the twelve, or only for the Christians of apostolic times, Jesus made the promise clear. It is to him "that believeth on me" that Jesus promised, "The works that I do shall he do also." Those who trust in Christ may have His fullness of power and may reproduce some of the marvels of His soul-winning power.

Again, the same night that Jesus was betrayed, He gave the disciples the promise of John 15:5: "I am the vine, ye are the branches: He that abideth in me, and I in him, the same bringeth forth much fruit: for without me ye can do nothing."

Are you bearing much fruit? Are you winning many souls? If not, then surely you have someway missed the blessing here promised for all who abide in Christ!

After Jesus rose from the dead, He reiterated this promise of soul-winning power for His disciples. And this time the promise was more definite than ever: He was promising the fullness of the Holy Spirit in order that His disciples might carry out the Great Commission and win souls.

This blessed promise is given just before Jesus ascended to Heaven in Luke 24:46–49:

"Thus it is written, and thus it behoved Christ to suffer, and to rise from the dead the third day: And that repentance and remission of sins should be preached in his name among all nations, beginning at Jerusalem. And ye are witnesses of these things. And, behold, I send the promise of my Father upon you: but tarry ye in the city of Jerusalem, until ye be endued with power from on high."

The gospel message that men should repent and have their sins forgiven must be preached in all nations, Jesus said. These same disciples were the witnesses of His life and ministry and death and resurrection; hence, they were to set out to get the Gospel to every creature.

"But wait!" said Jesus. They were not to go powerless. They were not to go empty. They dared not depend on human learning or talent or personality to make their message effective. They must tarry in Jerusalem until they should be "endued with power from on high"!

After the Gospel of Luke was finished, again Luke took up his pen to tell the story of the marvelous, Spirit-filled ministry of the disciples and some of their converts, in the Book of Acts. Again the Spirit of God gave him the words, and his writings were Holy Writ, the very Word of God. And the very first thing he records is the promise and command of Jesus:

"And, being assembled together with them, commanded them that they should not depart from Jerusalem, but wait for the promise of the Father, which, saith he, ye have heard of me. For John truly baptized with water; but ye shall be baptized with the Holy Ghost not many days hence."—Acts 1:4,5.

Then Jesus put in definite, unmistakable terms the promise, "But ye shall receive power, after that the Holy Ghost is come upon you: and ye shall be witnesses unto me both in Jerusalem, and in all Judæa, and in Samaria, and unto the uttermost part of the earth" (Acts 1:8). The power promised was a definite coming upon them of the Holy Spirit. Its result was to be definite, beyond any argument. They would be soul-winning witnesses for Christ when the Holy Spirit should come upon them, bringing His mighty power.

In Matthew 28:19,20 Jesus promises to all His disciples faithfully carrying out the Great Commission, "Lo, I am with you alway, unto the end of the world." The promise was not just to the twelv to believers in all the world and to the end of the age. The promise is to every Christian who obeys Christ in taking the Gospel to every creature and teaching the converts to obey Christ. But in the light of other statements Christ made about the same matter, we know the meaning of the promise that Christ will be with His people. For what? To comfort them? Yes, but that is not first. To give them wisdom? Yes, but that is not the most important. Would He be with them, through His Holy Spirit, to guide them into all truth? Yes, that is promised, but that is not the main promise Jesus made here. Christ promised, "Lo, I am with you alway," meaning primarily that through His Holy Spirit He would be with the disciples in mighty power to carry out His Great Commission. *True*

In the light of Christ's dear promises and the fullness He has freely offered His people who wait upon Him, to be endued with power from on high, how shameful, how sinful and how needless are the barrenness and fruitlessness and powerlessness of His people today!

In view of the promises of Christ, any Christian who is content not to have the soul-winning power of the Holy Spirit upon him lives in complacent sin, with God's dear face turned away from him.

May God give to all who read this a holy unrest, a distress of soul, an unquenchable thirst for the power of God. For God has promised, "For I will pour water upon him that is thirsty, and floods upon the dry ground: I will pour my spirit upon thy seed, and my blessing upon thine offspring" (Isa. 44:3).

IV. How Different Is Modern Christianity From That of the Apostolic Age!

Christianity is a Bible religion. It reached its fullest revelation and development in the New Testament. Christianity is not true Christianity, not complete Christianity, if it does not reproduce the salvation, the joy, the power and victory over sin, the progress and making of converts of New Testament times.

No Bible-believing Christian would think of denying what I am saying. It seems too trite to need repeating here. But surely we need to come back and face this solemn issue: we should reproduce Bible Christianity in our lives. We should see in this day the same kind of results that New Testament Christianity produced.

Any religion that is not based upon the New Testament is not Christianity. Any religion that does not hold up Christ, the same Saviour, does not demand the same new birth on condition of the same penitent faith, is certainly not Christianity. Then we must rightly conclude that after one has trusted in Christ, after one has this same Saviour, this same new birth, this same indwelling Holy Spirit, and is become a new creature as were believers in New Testament times, one should certainly manifest the same power New Testament Christians exemplified!

If any doctrine varies from New Testament doctrine, then it is off-color, it is inadequate, and it certainly does not truly represent Christianity. And likewise, the life that does not have the power New Testament Christians had is off-color and inadequate Christianity. The ministry of the Gospel which does not have the power of God upon it as so many preachers had in Bible times is not the New Testament type of preaching.

Oh, to demonstrate first-century Christianity again in this twentieth century! Oh, to see again the same vibrant, joyous, supernatural power in the lives of Christians! Oh, to see multitudes converted, to see whole communities, whole empires transformed by the triumphant, conquering revivals that took place under the preaching of Peter and Paul and Barnabas and other New Testament Christians!

It is one kind of modernism, one kind of infidelity, that rejects New Testament *doctrine*. How sinful, how wicked, how barren, how full of the poison of Hell, is that wicked unbelief that rejects the authority of the Bible, the deity of Christ, salvation by the blood! But we ought to say frankly that it is another kind of infidelity, and perhaps equally deadly, which gives lip service to the *doctrines* of the New Testament but does not reproduce the life and power and fruitfulness of New Testament Christianity! What does it matter whether people go to Hell because modernists have robbed them of any confidence in the Bible or whether they go to Hell because their loved ones have no power, no supernatural influence, no anointing from God to win souls, to change lives, to draw the unsaved to Christ! The results are the same. The sins that bring the same results are not far apart in wickedness!

Consider what happened at Pentecost.

"These all continued with one accord in prayer and supplication" (Acts 1:14). How strange, how unlike present-day churches!

"The multitude came together, and were confounded" (Acts 2:6). Mighty crowds hearing the Gospel with profound concern! How different from our empty churches and the indifference and disgust which the multitudes feel for the church and its ministry!

"Now when they heard this, they were pricked in their heart, and said unto Peter and to the rest of the apostles, Men and brethren, what shall we do?" (Acts 2:37). Conviction! Broken hearts! Inquiring the way of salvation!

"Then they that gladly received his word were baptized: and the same day there were added unto them about three thousand souls" (Acts 2:41). Three thousand saved and baptized in one day! Today in the most evangelistic denominations in America it takes about twenty persons one year to win one soul. In many denominations there is a net loss in membership every year, and in literally thousands of congregations not a single convert is won to Christ in a year! Is this Bible Christianity? Do you marvel that the gainsaying world has no interest in our churches, in our ministry, in our Christian profession when these are so fruitless compared with Bible Christianity?

Consider the ministry of Peter and John. The lame man healed in the gate of the temple—wonderfully, miraculously healed! (Acts 3:1–11). Preaching the Word of God with power to the assembled multitudes in temple courts and streets! Being jailed, beaten, yet 'filling Jerusalem' with their doctrine and charging the blood of Jesus Christ against the Jewish rulers! The leaders of the city marveling at the boldness of Peter and John, perceiving that they were unlearned and ignorant men! Peter and John praying with the Christians until "the place was shaken where they were assembled together; and they were all filled with the Holy Ghost, and they spake the word of God with boldness." Multitudes believing, chief priests being converted! Persecution raging in the midst of the revival, yet thousands upon thousands of people being saved! So was the ministry of Peter and John.

Consider Philip, a deacon, going down to Samaria and conducting there a revival that shook the whole city. "The people with one accord gave heed unto those things which Philip spake, hearing and seeing the miracles which he did," with unclean spirits cast out, the sick and lame healed, and great joy in the whole city! (Acts 8:5–8).

Consider Stephen, preaching with such power that the chief priests could not resist the wisdom and Spirit with which he spoke. Consider his facing the multitude, filled with the Holy Ghost, knowing that it meant his death, and yet preaching boldly, "Ye stiffnecked and uncircumcised in heart and ears, ye do always resist the Holy Ghost: as your fathers did, so do ye"! (Acts 7:51). Consider how Stephen so preached that "they were cut to the heart"; so convicted into a frenzy over their sins that they rushed on him, gnashed on him with their teeth, and furiously drove him from the city to stone him. Now see Stephen's face shining like that of an angel as the stones crush his skull and beat him into a bloody mass in the street while he looks up and sees Jesus and smiles! Remember that bloody Saul could never get away from the face of dying Stephen until he was converted.

And consider the results that followed the ministry of Paul. Never mind the danger, the persecution, the stonings, the scourgings, the shipwrecks, the fights with wild beasts. Never mind the perils of the deep, the perils of his own countrymen. Where, oh, where are the men today whose ministries light a prairie fire even in heathendom in every community where they stop to preach! Oh, for one man or two men like Paul and Barnabas or Paul and Silas to do for America or Russia or China or India what Paul did for the Roman Empire! Fellow ministers, can you and I claim to reproduce the power of New Testament Christianity, the fruitfulness, the supernatural evidence of transformed lives and hearts and homes and cities which followed the men of God in Bible times? How far have we fallen!

What a triumphant attitude, what a certainty of blessing, what an overpowering confidence that the Gospel could not fail, marked these men. Hear the divinely inspired words of Paul: "I can do all things through Christ which strengtheneth me" (Phil. 4:13). The certitude of power! The boldness of a divine enabling, a Holy Spirit anointing! God worked with New Testament preachers like Paul!

win souls march on with the Gospel

When Paul planned to go to Rome, the center of the world, the seat of the empire, he did not tremble. He had no inferiority complex. He had no doubt of the result. Writing to those at Rome he said, "And I am sure that, when I come unto you, I shall come in the fulness of the blessing of the gospel of Christ" (Rom. 15:29). Oh, that God will give to preachers who read this page, at whatever cost of prayer and tears and self-crucifixion and revolution in their lives, such a holy confidence, such a divine certitude of power as Paul had when he faced Rome! Paul was sure that he would come "in the fulness of the blessing of the gospel of Christ." Does that certitude mark your ministry and mine? If not, there is a horrible lack, a declension, a degeneracy that ought to put us on our faces in shame until the boldness and power and fruitfulness of New Testament Christianity is reproduced in our lives and ministries!

Again hear the typical comment, a comment inspired by the Holy Spirit Himself and now sanctified for us as Holy Writ, the very Word of God: "Now thanks be unto God, which always causeth us to triumph in Christ, and maketh manifest the savour of his knowledge by us in every place" (II Cor. 2:14). Paul was grateful to God because He "always causeth us to triumph in Christ." Everywhere Paul went there was triumph, victory! It was incidental and inconsequential that Paul was often in jail, that there were chains on his hands or feet, that he was stoned and left for dead or went hungry or cold or was hated and slandered and despised. Never mind about those things, for Paul himself did not think them of any consequence. But whatever of the incidental things like persecutions and poverty and pain might come, Paul was always certain of one thing: always, always he would triumph!

And Paul did not mean that he would suffer martyrdom and be content. The triumph Paul spoke about was that sinners were cut to the heart, that men in high places and low were conquered for Jesus Christ. Whether it were a slave girl fortuneteller at Philippi; or the runaway slave, Onesimus, whom Paul won in Rome; or deputy Sergius Paulus on an island of Cyprus, converted under Paul's preaching; or the soldiers of the prætorian guard whom he won in Cæsar's palace basement prison in Rome ("they that are of Cæsar's household"); or whether it were Felix the governor who trembled when Paul stood before him; or King Agrippa who said, "Almost thou persuadest me to be a Christian," it was just the same: men were cut and burned and saved or damned by the preaching of Paul! There was the breath of Heaven; there was the sword of God; there was a regenerating miracle in every sermon Paul preached, in every contact Paul made!

Sadly enough, most of us deny the power thereof. We do not reproduce the manifestations, the fruitfulness of New Testament Christianity! We do not want revival and the saving of souls as Bible Christians wanted revival and the saving of souls. Therefore, we do not pay God's price and do not have the fruitfulness of New Testament Christianity.

Here is the background of most of our cults. Here is the excuse for most of our denominational divisions. The Methodist group left the Episcopal denomination and founded another. What they really needed was not a new denomination but new power. Thank God they got the power. They did not materially change in doctrine from the Church of England background.

Today in America the Wesleyan Methodists, the Free Methodists, and the Nazarenes have come out of Methodism to found new denominations. They did not materially change in doctrine. Indeed, they are much nearer the doctrine of Wesley and the early Methodist church than is the modern Methodist church itself. But they came out because they felt the overmastering urge for a new visitation of God's power!

Those who have followed the Pentecostal movement and the Holiness movement closely will agree, I think, that the formalism, the coldness, the fruitlessness and deadness of the old denominations have caused multitudes to turn from them as from a plague, as from the Black Death, to newer, stranger denominations. People were often conscious of some fanaticism in the new movements, but fanaticism was better than the death, the barrenness, of churches which had no more revivals!

Even the very worst of the false cults have had their growth primarily at the cost of older denominations which had lost their zeal, lost their holy attraction, lost their fruit-bearing power.

Multiplied thousands have gone into so-called Christian Science or Jehovah's Witnesses or other false cults because their hearts were never satisfied with any demonstration of New Testament power in the older churches to which they would more normally have been attracted had other things been equal.

Even modernism—that insidious and wicked and shameless Christ-rejecting and Bible-denying sin that only by intentional and deliberate deceit calls itself Christianity at all—that modernism, I say, which has stolen control of most of the large denominations in America, has been made possible by a decline in power, by the loss of the fervor and zeal and power of New Testament Christianity. Oh, we need plain Bible teaching. We need apologetics to prove that Christianity and the Bible are true. We ought to be set for a 'defense of the faith,' as the Scripture commands. We ought to expose the utter immorality of those who seek the salaries and honors of the Christian ministry when they are Christ-rejecting infidels in their hearts. But all the argument in the world cannot keep us from losing the hearts and confidence of the people if we do not have the power of God. The best antidote for modernism is a great revival. D. L. Moody stopped more infidelity, answered more pseudoscientific heresy, turned more university men to Christ than the greatest scientists with a Ph.D. who ever lived. The antidote for modernism is the power of God upon Christians, the power of a great revival, the soul-saving, life-changing, city-sweeping power of a great revival!

The modernist denies the doctrines of New Testament Christianity. But the modernist is not much convicted of his shameful deceit as long as the fundamentalist does not reproduce the power and results of New Testament Christianity.

V. How Different Is Present-Day Christianity From That of the Great Revivals!

On Wednesday morning, August 13, 1727, a Moravian Brethren congregation was assembled at Herrnhut, Austria, on the estate of young Count Zinzendorf. The mighty power of the Holy Spirit came upon that congregation. Count Zinzendorf was only twenty-seven, and most of the others averaged about the same age. But out of that small congregation of laymen came ministers and missionaries, deacons, presbyters and bishops. And there started the great Moravian mission movement. Dr. Warneck, the German historian of Protestant missions, says, "This small church in twenty years called into being more missions than the whole evangelical church has done in two centuries." Through Moravian Brethren, God first convicted John Wesley that he was unsaved. Then Peter Boehler, of the Moravian Brethren, first showed John Wesley how to be saved by faith in Christ, and so with Charles Wesley. Fruit-bearing power was shown in the Moravian revival.

So it was in the Wesleyan revival. The Wesleyan revival saved England from a revolution like the one in France. The freedom, the culture, the benevolences, even our governments and education and our traditions in England and America were all largely colored by the great Wesleyan revival. If one doubts that, he has but to read the proof in that remarkable book, *This Freedom—Whence?* by Dr. John Wesley Bready (American Tract Society). In England, where the established church clergy did not believe the Bible, where crime, licentiousness, corruption in government and home and business abounded on every side, the Wesleyan revival turned the nation back toward God. And it had much of the same effect in America. Why do not our churches and our preachers and our own lives manifest the same power today?

Where is the power that sent David Brainerd out to win the Indian natives? There were times when he prayed all day alone in the snowy, wintry forest, bringing down the power of God so that sometimes when only a drunken interpreter was available, the mighty power of God fell and whole villages were converted to Christ.

Where is the power that went everywhere with Charles G. Finney? In his autobiography (page 183) Finney tells about going to a place called New York Mills, and there going through the mill while people were busy at their looms, or attending to the mules and other implements of work. He tells how the workers observed him and became agitated, convicted:

They saw me coming, and were evidently much excited. One of them was trying to mend a broken thread, and I observed that her hands trembled so that she could not mend it. I approached slowly, looking on each side at the machinery, as I passed; but observed that this girl grew more and more agitated, and could not proceed with her work. When I came within eight or ten feet of her, I looked solemnly at her. She observed it, and was quite overcome, and sunk down, and burst into tears. The impression caught almost like powder, and in a few moments nearly all in the room were in tears. This feeling spread through the factory. Mr. W_____, the owner of the establishment, was present, and seeing the state of things, he said to the superintendent, "Stop the mill, and let the people attend to religion; for it is more important that our souls should be saved than that this factory run." The gate was immediately shut down, and the factory stopped; but where should we assemble? The superintendent suggested that the mule room was large; and, the mules being run up, we could assemble there. We did so, and a more powerful meeting I scarcely ever attended. It went on with great power. The building was large, and had many people in it, from the garret to the cellar. The revival went through the mill with astonishing power, and in the course of a few days nearly all in the mill were hopefully converted.

But the same kind of results were shown with the lawyers in the city of Rochester as with the humble mill people. Everywhere there was a convicting, sin-killing, life-transforming, soul-saving power on Charles G. Finney ever after that day when he was wonderfully baptized in the Holy Spirit. Where is such power now?

Let me remind you again of the power of D. L. Moody. Moody was not a learned man. He had never finished what we could call a grammar school education. But, oh, the breath of Heaven that came upon him in Wall Street, New York, one day! Oh, the mighty results as he 'lifted two continents toward God' and won a million souls to Christ! Who can ever sum up the mighty influence of D. L. Moody, his influence on the Bible schools, on the mission fields, on the thousands of pastors, missionaries and evangelists who went out to give their lives in soul-winning service because of him! Where, oh, where in our modern churches is the power which D. L. Moody manifested?

Where is the power that was on Torrey in his great campaigns in America, in Australia, in England and around the world? Where is the power that was on Charlie Alexander and J. Wilbur Chapman? Where is the power that was on Billy Sunday so that great cities were shaken in his campaigns? We have fallen! We have fallen! The trouble with modern Christianity is that it lacks the breath of Heaven, the power of God, the holy anointing, the supernatural enabling, that are the marks of New Testament Christianity!

VI. Present-Day Christians Are Like Certain Bible Characters in Powerlessness

In Genesis, chapter 32, we are told how Jacob started to meet Esau, his brother who had sworn to kill him. Esau was coming to meet him with four hundred armed men, with hatred burning in his heart because of very real wrongs suffered at Jacob's hand long before. But Jacob knew he was helpless and powerless. He dared not go to meet Esau until he had waited beyond the brook Jabbok and wrestled all night with the angel of God. Oh, that people today would realize how helpless and how powerless they are!

So it was with Lot down in Sodom. Though the city would be destroyed at daybreak, when Lot went to the homes of his sons-in-law "he seemed as one that mocked unto his sons in law." They did not believe his message; they were not impressed with his faith; they felt no moving of divine power in his entreaty. They stayed in their homes and were consumed with the fire and brimstone from Heaven! And just so, many of us find that we have blood on our hands. Our loved ones scoff at our Christianity because we have no power with which to convince them and convert them.

Samson, the judge of Israel, felt upon him the mighty power of the Spirit of God. With the power of the Holy Spirit he could kill a thousand men with the jawbone of an ass or lift off the gates of a city and carry them to a mountaintop! No man could bind him; no man could conquer him. But when Samson slept with his head on the lap of Delilah, his compromise and sin at last grieved away the Holy Spirit. And when Samson disloyally revealed to Delilah the secret of his strength, that his Nazarite locks were the outward sign of his surrender to God, these seven locks of his hair were cut off, and he was powerless. They put out his eyes and put him at a donkey's work, pulling the mill, and at last brought him to make sport in the temple of their god! How many of us today are blinded and bound and mocked by a world that no longer sees any supernatural manifestation in our lives! Many of us, like Samson, have lost the power of God. Samson, first awaking on the lap of Delilah with his hair cut off, "wist not that the LORD was departed from him." So with us! Many of us do not face our sin, our shame, our poverty, our barrenness! Many of us are too well content, criminally content, to win no souls, to change no lives, to demonstrate no power of God!

When Jesus came down from the Mount of Transfiguration, He found a great commotion. A father had brought his devil-possessed boy to the nine disciples who did not go to the Mount of Transfiguration. They had been unable to heal him. And the poor father, discouraged by the powerlessness of the disciples, said to Jesus, "If thou canst do any thing, have compassion on us, and help us" (Mark 9:22). Jesus healed the son of the doubting, trembling, weeping, believing father, and then when He was alone with the disciples had to face with them their own powerlessness. "Why could not we cast him out?" they asked. They seemed to know that they had misrepresented Jesus Christ, that their powerlessness had cast doubt upon the power of Christ Himself! Oh, that we too would feel our lack and be convicted and ashamed over our powerlessness and come to Christ to find the secret of it! And He would tell us too, no doubt, "This kind can come forth by nothing, but by prayer and fasting." At any rate, we may be sure that if we do not have the miracle-working, supernatural power of the Holy Spirit upon us, we cannot do the work of Christ and cannot represent Christ authentically.

Oh, the lost secret! Oh, barren churches! Oh, homes divided, Christians at ease, sinners unconvicted and callous and arrogant! What all of us need above everything else under Heaven is a visitation of the power of God!

May the power of Pentecost come on our churches. May it come upon every earnest minister. May it come upon every Bible-believing Christian who has loved ones unsaved. May God restore the lost power as Elisha the prophet restored the lost axhead to the sons of the prophets! May God restore to us the lost secret, the secret of the soul-winning power of Pentecost!

Chapter 2

The Usual Work of the Holy Spirit

Other Ministries of the Holy Spirit Done for Every Christian, Not Including the Fullness of the Spirit, the Anointing or the Enduement With Power for Soul Winning

"And I will pray the Father, and he shall give you another Comforter, that he may abide with you for ever; Even the Spirit of truth; whom the world cannot receive, because it seeth him not, neither knoweth him: but ye know him; for he dwelleth with you, and shall be in you."—John 14:16,17.

The elect

"For by one Spirit are we all baptized into one body, whether we be Jews or Gentiles, whether we be bond or free; and have been all made to drink into one Spirit."—I Cor. 12:13.

The other chapters in this book are on the special enduement of power for soul-winning witness such as the disciples received when they were filled with the Holy Spirit at Pentecost. The other chapters are about this extraordinary work of the Spirit, this fullness, this filling of the Spirit, or gift of the Holy Spirit, or anointing of the Spirit, sometimes called the baptism of the Spirit. That extraordinary, unusual and special ministry of the Holy Spirit (which miraculously enables one to do the work for Christ which he is commanded to do in witnessing with power and bearing fruit for Christ) is possible for every Christian and commanded for every Christian. But we must admit that it is unusual. There are not many Christians filled with the Spirit of God as New Testament disciples were at Pentecost, as Peter and John and Paul and Philip and Barnabas and other such mighty soul winners were in Bible times. Not many Christians have power such as Finney and Moody had. The book is on the power of Pentecost or the fullness of the Holy Spirit.

souls

I. Who Is the Holy Spirit?

But first, let us get acquainted with the Holy Spirit. Let us learn about the Holy Spirit's ordinary and usual work which every Christian experiences in some degree, and every Christian should experience in a far larger degree. These ordinary or usual ministries of the Holy Spirit every Christian should realize in a much larger way than is usual.

Before we can know the mighty enduement of power from on high, wrought by the Holy Spirit as He fills us and endues us for soul winning, we need to know who the Holy Spirit is and what He does.

1. The Importance of the Holy Spirit's Work
Indicates Who He Is

How little we realize the mighty importance of the Holy Spirit!

The Holy Spirit took part in the creation of the universe: "And the Spirit of God moved upon the face of the waters" (Gen. 1:2).

The Holy Spirit was the real Author of the Bible, for "holy men of God spake as they were moved by the Holy Ghost" (II Pet. 1:21) and "the Spirit of Christ which was in them...testified beforehand the sufferings of Christ, and the glory that should follow" (I Pet. 1:11).

It is amazing how much the Holy Spirit had to do with Christ's incarnation and ministry.

The Angel Gabriel told Mary, "The Holy Ghost shall come upon thee, and the power of the Highest shall overshadow thee: therefore also that holy thing which shall be born of thee shall be called the Son of God" (Luke 1:35). So, as the Apostles' Creed declares, Christ "was conceived of the Holy Ghost."

The Holy Spirit came upon Christ at His baptism in bodily shape and endued and empowered Him for service. There was never a miracle, never a healing, never a sermon, never a soul saved by the direct ministry of Jesus Christ until He was endued with the power of the Holy Spirit when He was about thirty years old! (Luke 3:21–23). And Jesus was "full of the Holy Ghost," was "led by the Spirit," "returned in the power of the Spirit into Galilee." The Spirit of the Lord had come upon Christ; and Jesus said, "He hath anointed me to preach the gospel" (Luke 4:1,14,18).

Jesus cast out devils by the Spirit of God (Matt. 12:28).

It was by "the eternal Spirit" that Jesus offered Himself without spot to God (Heb. 9:14).

Christ was raised from the dead by the Holy Spirit (Rom. 8:11).

After His resurrection from the dead it was by the Holy Ghost that He gave commandments unto His disciples (Acts 1:2).

When Jesus returns to the earth to reign as the Branch from David's root, He will reign in the power of the Holy Spirit! (Isa. 11:1-3).

It is startling to realize the work that the Holy Spirit does for a human being. It is the Holy Spirit who convicts a sinner, the Holy

Spirit who regenerates one who trusts in Christ, the Holy Spirit who makes him a new creature. It is the Holy Spirit who comforts a Christian, who brings the witness and the assurance of salvation into his heart. It is the Holy Spirit who helps a Christian to understand the Bible, helps a Christian to pray, brings to his memory the commands of Christ. It is the Holy Spirit who works out and develops and produces the fruit of the Spirit, the Christian graces, in the Christian's life: "love, joy, peace, longsuffering, gentleness, goodness, faith, Meekness, temperance" (Gal. 5:22,23).

The Holy Spirit is called by many names, and it is important for any reader of the Bible to understand these terms and to know that they refer to the one person, the Holy Spirit, or the Spirit of God. He is sometimes called the Holy Spirit, sometimes the Holy Ghost. Both terms mean the same.

He is called "the Spirit of God." He is called "the Spirit of Christ."

He is called "the eternal Spirit."

He is called "the Spirit of truth."

He is called "the spirit of glory and of God."

He is called "the Comforter."

He is called "the spirit of adoption."

And all these and many other blessed names or titles of the Holy Spirit are needed to tell of His wonderful and perfect divine work. But every Christian should be familiar with such terms, and in reading the Bible he should seek carefully to notice every term used about the blessed Spirit of God, the Holy Spirit.

2. The Holy Spirit Is Really a Person

Dr. R. A. Torrey in that great book, *The Holy Spirit—Who He Is, and What He Does*, says that the distinctive marks or characteristics of personality of the Holy Spirit are *knowledge, feeling* and *will*.

The Holy Spirit does not have a body, except as He dwells in our physical bodies, but He is nevertheless a person, as definitely and really a personality as Christ is a personality. The Scriptures tell us that the Holy Spirit has knowledge and feeling and will. For example, I Corinthians 2:11 says that the Holy Spirit has knowledge. First Corinthians 12:11 says that the Holy Spirit divides His gifts to people, "to every man severally as he will." Romans 8:27 speaks of "the mind of the Spirit" and says that "he maketh intercession for the saints according to the will of God." The Holy Spirit has a mind, and He makes intercession for us. Romans 15:30 speaks of "the love of the

Spirit." The Holy Spirit loves us, loves as a person. Nehemiah 9:20 says, "Thou gavest also thy good spirit to instruct them." The Holy Spirit is good, and He instructs people.

Ephesians 4:30 says that the Holy Spirit may be grieved. Isaiah 63:10 shows that the Holy Spirit may be vexed. Acts 7:51 says that He can be resisted. The Holy Spirit does work that only a person can do. For example, we are told that He teaches Christians (John 14:26), that He guides us into the truth (John 16:13), that He helps our infirmities (Rom. 8:26), that He searcheth all things (I Cor. 2:10, 11).

The Holy Spirit knows and wills and feels and acts as a person, and so He is a person.

Many people thoughtlessly speak of the Holy Spirit as "it." Perhaps when the matter is called to their attention they say, "Oh, I know better." Well, in one's head one may know better, but actually one has not come to realize that the Holy Spirit is a blessed and real and familiar person, if he speaks of the Holy Spirit as an impersonal, neuter "it." No woman who loves her husband ever speaks of him as "it" because she does not feel that way about him. She knows him as a living, loving person and so calls him by the masculine pronoun. And Christians everywhere who learn to know the Holy Spirit intimately speak about Him and speak to Him with the greatest reverence and with the masculine pronoun, just as we refer to God the Father and just as we refer to our Saviour Jesus Christ, God's Son. The Holy Spirit is a blessed and wonderful person with whom the Christian should become very intimately acquainted.

In fact, the Holy Spirit is the one person of the Godhead with whom the Christian has the most intimate and daily contact. For Christ, with a glorified, resurrected body, is in Heaven, sitting at the right hand of the Father, interceding for us. But God the Holy Spirit literally lives within the body of a Christian, is with him all the time and represents the Father and represents Jesus Christ.

3. The Holy Spirit Is God, One Person of the Holy Trinity

Did I say in the paragraph above, "God the Holy Spirit"? Yes, and that is exactly who He is. The Holy Spirit is God, just as Jesus, God's Son, is God, and just as God the Father is God.

Jesus is God, deity, for He said, "I and my Father are one" (John 10:30). But Jesus declares that the Holy Spirit has this same oneness with the Father and with Christ Himself. Jesus comforted the disciples, telling them that it was expedient that He should go away so that the

Holy Spirit would come (John 16:7). And He said that when the Holy Spirit was come that thus both Jesus and the Father would come, through the Holy Spirit, and make their abode with the Christian (John 14:23).

The titles of the Holy Spirit clearly identify Him as deity. He is the Spirit of God. He is the Spirit of Christ. He is the Holy Spirit. He is the eternal Spirit. Such terms would fit no person but deity.

A number of Scriptures make it clear that there are three persons in the Godhead.

John 14:16 mentions all three in one verse. Jesus said, "And I will pray the Father, and he shall give you another Comforter, that he may abide with you for ever."

Acts 10:38 again mentions all three, as separate persons, though perfectly united, in these words: "How God anointed Jesus of Nazareth with the Holy Ghost and with power: who went about doing good, and healing all that were oppressed of the devil; for God was with him." God, Jesus, and the Holy Ghost are all mentioned in this verse.

But several times the Bible speaks of the Holy Ghost as God. One place is in Acts 10:38, mentioned above. "God anointed Jesus of Nazareth with the *Holy Ghost*," the Scripture says, and then Jesus "went about doing good, and healing all that were oppressed of the devil; for *God* was with him." Who was with Jesus? The Holy Ghost, the first part of that verse says. But the last part says, "...for *God* was with him." God the Holy Ghost was with Jesus as He went about doing good.

In Acts 10:40 the Scripture says that God raised Jesus from the dead. "Him God raised up the third day, and shewed him openly." And in Acts 2:32 Peter says likewise, "This Jesus hath God raised up, where-of we all are witnesses." And many other Scriptures say that God raised Christ. But I Peter 3:18 says that Christ was "put to death in the flesh, but quickened by the Spirit." It was the Holy Spirit who quickened or brought to life again Jesus Christ. And Romans 8:11 again tells us that God raised up Jesus, but by the Holy Spirit. You see, God the Father and God the Holy Spirit both worked together in raising Christ from the dead. The Holy Spirit is God.

Of course none of us can understand the marvelous mystery of the Trinity. But an illustration will help.

A man and his wife are said to be "one flesh." The law has often regarded a man and his wife as one and decided that the property of one belonged to the other and the responsibilities of one were the responsibilities of the other. Actually, no man and wife are perfectly united. They are different personalities and imperfect personalities. Each one is somewhat selfish, since they are human beings, and so they never perfectly merge in perfect unity and agreement. But, all praise to the Father, Son and Holy Spirit, the three persons of the Godhead agree perfectly. What one wants, the others want too. What one does, the others help do. For that reason it is perfectly proper to pray to the Father or to pray to our Lord Jesus Christ, the Son, or to pray to the Holy Spirit. Some have tried to divide the work of salvation and say, for example, that it is Christ who made atonement for sinners, it is the Holy Spirit who works regeneration in the hearts of believers, and it is God the Father who forgives and justifies. But actually Jesus Himself often spoke forgiveness and claimed that He had "power upon earth to forgive sins," and He makes it quite clear that the Holy Spirit represents both Father and Son. The humble believer need not fret if he sometimes addresses his prayer to God the Father and sometimes to the Son. If one of these three persons hears, the others hear. If one of them is pleased, the others are pleased. If one of them acts, the others act. The three are one and the one is three. I do not fully understand it, but I can believe it, since it is taught in the Word of God.

II. The Work of the Holy Spirit in Regeneration and Salvation

It was Christ who became a man, lived a sinless life among men and then died on the cross to atone for the sins of mankind. It is Christ who is our Saviour. But in the work of saving sinners it is the Holy Spirit who represents Christ and does His will. It is amazing how much the Holy Spirit does in connection with the salvation of a sinner. And all this is the usual work of the Holy Spirit, that which takes place in some measure in everybody who is saved.

1. It Is the Holy Spirit Who Convicts a Sinner and Leads Him to Turn to God

Jesus said of the Holy Spirit, "When he is come, he will reprove the world of sin, and of righteousness, and of judgment" (John 16:8). No sinner will ever be saved unless the Spirit of God moves on his heart and causes him to realize that he is a sinner. Jesus said, "No man can come to me, except the Father which hath sent me draw him" (John 6:44). And the Father draws sinners through the blessed work of the Holy Spirit.

Remember that God uses the Word to convict sinners, but the Holy Spirit and the Word of God work together. In fact, the Holy Spirit is the divine Author of the Bible, and the Word of God is "the sword of the Spirit."

Genesis 6:3 shows us that the Holy Spirit strives with men, but that He will not always strive. There are many good examples in the Bible of conviction wrought in the hearts of sinners by the Holy Spirit. When Jesus spoke from Heaven to Saul of Tarsus on the road to Damascus and said, "It is hard for thee to kick against the pricks" (Acts 9:5), He meant that the Holy Spirit had been convicting Paul and constantly pricking his conscience, showing him his sin, his need for salvation. The jailer who "came trembling, and fell down before Paul and Silas, And brought them out, and said, Sirs, what must I do to be saved?" (Acts 16:29,30) was terribly convicted by the Holy Spirit. When Paul stood before Felix and "reasoned of righteousness, temperance, and judgment to come, Felix trembled" (Acts 24:25). The trembling of Felix was the trembling of conviction. God's Holy Spirit spoke to his heart through the preaching of the Word by Paul.

From the last example it is evident that many are convicted who are never saved. There is no record that Felix ever turned to the Lord for forgiveness. But he was thoroughly convicted by the Spirit of God.

Everybody who is ever saved is moved by the Spirit of God to seek forgiveness, to see his sins and the need of salvation. That is part of the divine work of the Spirit of God in salvation. And it is the usual work of the Holy Spirit, in the sense that no one is ever saved who does not have some degree of conviction of the Holy Spirit.

2. The New Birth Is a Miracle Wrought by the Holy Spirit

How does one get to be a Christian? On man's side, one repents and trusts in Christ for forgiveness and salvation. But on God's side, a new heart is given, then the sinner is born again, as Jesus insisted to Nicodemus that one must be to see the kingdom of God (John 3:3,5). Those who are saved, thus, by a miracle, become "partakers of the divine nature" (II Pet. 1:4). One actually has a new nature, a nature like God's, is born of God, when he is saved.

Who works this miracle of regeneration in the heart of one who comes to trust Christ? It is done by the Holy Spirit! So one who is born again is "born…of the Spirit," as Jesus said in John 3:5. Titus 3:5 says that it is "not by works of righteousness which we have done, but according to his mercy he saved us, by the washing of regeneration, and renewing of the Holy Ghost." The Holy Ghost makes a new creature out of one who is saved.

It is deeply suggestive to remember that Christ Himself was conceived by the Holy Spirit in the womb of the Virgin Mary (Luke 1:35). By a miracle the Spirit of God caused the generation of the body of the God-Man. And it is by a similar miracle of grace that the Holy Spirit makes for any poor old, wicked, undone sinner a new nature; and this new nature is a part of the divine nature. Although a Christian is still a poor, frail human being with the taint and tendency of sin in him, yet he has within him the seed of God. And this new nature does not sin, for "whosoever is born of God doth not commit sin; for his seed remaineth in him: and he cannot sin, because he is born of God" (I John 3:9).

We will not here discuss all the implications of that Scripture. But I am saying that every Christian is become a partaker of the divine nature and the seed of God is in him, wrought there miraculously by the Holy Spirit at regeneration.

3. The Holy Spirit Makes the Body of a Christian His Temple and Dwells Within

We sometimes say, "I let Jesus come into my heart." That is true in a very real sense. Wherever the Holy Spirit goes, Jesus goes. The Holy Spirit manifests both the Father and the Son, as Jesus made clear in John, chapter 14. But actually Jesus has a human body. And Jesus is now in Heaven, seated beside the Father on His throne (Rev. 3:21). Jesus is our "great high priest, that is passed into the heavens" (Heb. 4:14). And He is there at the right hand of God now, ever interceding for us. So it is not *literally* true that Jesus comes into our hearts. But it is literally true that the Holy Spirit of God, representing both the Father and the Son, came into our *bodies* when we were saved and made our bodies His temple and dwells there forever. It seems that there is some slight difference in the way the Spirit of God dwells in our bodies and the way He dealt with Christians in the Old Testament. Certainly all who were ever saved were saved the same way, and all who were ever regenerated were regenerated by the Holy Spirit. But at least we may be sure that since Jesus rose from the dead and breathed on His disciples and said, "Receive ye the Holy Ghost" (John 20:22), all Christians now have the Holy Spirit abiding in them. Jesus plainly told the disciples the night before His crucifixion, "And I will pray the Father, and he shall give you another Comforter, that he may abide with you for ever; Even the Spirit of truth; whom the world cannot receive, because it seeth him not, neither knoweth him: but ye know him; for he dwelleth with you, and shall be in you" (John 14:16, 17).

Blessed, blessed Comforter who abides *with* Christians forever and, better than that, dwells *in* the Christian! Furthermore, blessed is the Christian in having such a heavenly Resident! How blessed, indeed, is the body which is the temple of God the Spirit!

It is because of this that I Corinthians 6:19,20 says: "What? know ye not that your body is the temple of the Holy Ghost which is in you, which ye have of God, and ye are not your own? For ye are bought with a price: therefore glorify God in your body, and in your spirit, which are God's."

You see, then, that every Christian's body is the temple of the Holy Ghost. Romans 8:9 says the same thing again, and so does I Corinthians 3:16,17. And this is the ordinary and usual work of the Holy Spirit in the sense that every Christian ever converted has the Spirit of God dwelling in his body.

4. The Holy Spirit Baptizes Each Christian Into the Body of Christ, Making Him a Part of the Mystical Church of the First-Born

Here is a blessed truth taught in I Corinthians 12:13: "For by one Spirit are we all baptized into one body, whether we be Jews or Gentiles, whether we be bond or free; and have been all made to drink into one Spirit." Every Christian has received the Holy Spirit into his body. The Holy Spirit has done more than this. The new convert is made a member of the body of Christ. When Jesus comes again the "general assembly and church of the firstborn, which are written in heaven" will be assembled in the air, then in the heavenly Jerusalem (I Thess. 4:17; Heb. 12:22,23). That is, everyone who was a child of God will have his body resurrected, and his spirit will be reunited with a glorified body and will be caught up together. The Christian dead will be raised, the Christian living will be changed, and together they will assemble. That called-out assembly will be properly a *church*, in New Testament language. As soon as one is saved, the Holy Spirit in some mystical way makes sure that the new convert is a part of this body and destined for that glorious rapture when Jesus comes.

When a stone is put into the wall of a building and then covered over with mortar and other stones, it is submerged or buried or covered in the wall. It is "baptized" in the wall. In that sense the Holy Spirit baptizes every new convert into the body of Christ, makes him a part of this body, the group of Christians who will be called out when Jesus comes.

Many have confused this with being baptized or overwhelmed with the Holy Spirit with such an empowering and anointing as came to the disciples at Pentecost, but we believe they are badly mistaken. To be baptized into the body of Christ simply means that one is regenerated by the Holy Spirit, has the Holy Spirit living in his body, and is now destined to be called out at the rapture of the general assembly and church of the firstborn, when Jesus comes for His own. To be filled and covered or baptized with the Holy Spirit for service is another matter, as we will prove elsewhere. But to be buried, baptized into the body of Christ, is the usual and ordinary work of the Holy Spirit, which He does for every single person ever converted. The fullness of the Spirit is another matter which many Christians never do receive, although they should. Every Christian is put into the body of Christ by the Holy Spirit.

5. The Holy Spirit Is, Himself, the Seal of Our Salvation

We have seen that the Holy Spirit is the One who convicts the sinner, regenerates one when he believes in Christ, makes the believer's body His temple and dwells therein, and makes the new convert a part, a member, of the body of Christ. In other words, the work of salvation is wrought out by the Holy Spirit.

And then the Scripture makes it clear that the Holy Spirit is Himself the seal of our salvation.

Second Corinthians 1:21,22 states this beautiful truth: "Now he which stablisheth us with you in Christ, and hath anointed us, is God; Who hath also sealed us, and given the earnest of the Spirit in our hearts." You see, God has sealed us and given us the earnest of the Spirit in our hearts. That is, the Holy Spirit Himself is the firstfruits of salvation, or the earnest of salvation. More is yet to come. We do not yet have our glorified bodies. We do not yet have the taint and trouble of sin altogether removed. We do not have our weaknesses conquered, our natures made righteous and perfect and our bodies glorified, as we will when Jesus comes. But we already have part of the change, part of the glorification. Thank God, we have the Holy Spirit living in our hearts and in our bodies! He is the seal, the firstfruits, the evidence, the token payment of our eternal and glorious redemption! And so Ephesians 4:30 says, "And grieve not the holy Spirit of God, whereby ye are sealed unto the day of redemption." Ephesians 1:13 speaks of Christ, "In whom ye also trusted, after that ye heard the word of truth, the gospel of your salvation: in whom also after that ye believed, ye were sealed with that holy Spirit of promise." When one believes in

Christ, then he is sealed as a child of God by the impartation of the Holy Spirit who comes to be with the Christian and abide with him and in him forever.

This blessed truth is taught further in Romans 8:23 which says, "But ourselves also, which have the firstfruits of the Spirit, even we ourselves groan within ourselves, waiting for the adoption, to wit, the redemption of our body." The Holy Spirit Himself is the seal, the earnest, the firstfruits of salvation. Praise the Lord, much more is coming for the child of God.

But all these things are wrought in every Christian in the world. They are not a matter of our works but a matter of grace, and all these things the Holy Spirit does for every person ever saved at the time of his salvation. He is convicted, regenerated; the Holy Spirit dwells within his body; the Holy Spirit baptizes him into the body of Christ, making him a part of this heavenly body; and the Holy Spirit is the seal of salvation.

III. The Holy Spirit's Regular Work in the Lives of All Christians

All the work of the Holy Spirit mentioned above takes place immediately when a sinner trusts Christ for salvation. And these things are all done completely, and as a matter of grace, a part of salvation, for every soul ever saved.

But there are other works of the Holy Spirit in the daily life of the Christian, other ministries of the Holy Spirit following salvation. He is the same Spirit, but He has a number of ministries in the life of the believer. These ministries continue through all the life of a Christian. And they vary somewhat in degree.

There is no varying in the way the Holy Spirit regenerates, the way He dwells in the body of a Christian, the way He puts a convert into the body of Christ and makes him a member of that body. There is no difference in the way He Himself is the seal of redemption. But as the Christian life continues, the Holy Spirit will do more for the Christian—as much as the Christian permits. We might say that every Christian goes to the same school, but some learn more than others from the same teacher. And the things mentioned here are still the usual and regular work of the Holy Spirit in the lives of all Christians.

1. The Holy Spirit Is the Comforter

In a very real way the Holy Spirit now takes the place of Jesus

Christ, being literally present with every believer. Jesus seemed to teach that it is much happier for a Christian to have the Holy Spirit abiding in his body and present to comfort him, than to have Jesus Christ Himself present in the world! For in John 16:7 Jesus said, "Nevertheless I tell you the truth; It is expedient for you that I go away: for if I go not away, the Comforter will not come unto you; but if I depart, I will send him unto you."

In John 14:16,17 Jesus said, "And I will pray the Father, and he shall give you another Comforter, that he may abide with you for ever; Even the Spirit of truth; whom the world cannot receive, because it seeth him not, neither knoweth him: but ye know him; for he dwelleth with you, and shall be in you." Jesus Himself is one Comforter. The Holy Spirit is another Comforter, the *Parakletos*, an Advocate, one called alongside to help. Oh, how sweet are the comfort, the fellowship, the companionship of the blessed Spirit of God! Every Christian has some of this blessed fellowship and comfort. Every Christian, doubtless, could have much more of this ministry of the Holy Spirit.

2. The Holy Spirit Is the Christian's Guide and Teacher and Reminder

That last night before Jesus was crucified He urged the disciples to have peace, in view of the blessed work the Holy Spirit would work in them. And Jesus said in John 14:26: "But the Comforter, which is the Holy Ghost, whom the Father will send in my name, he shall teach you all things, and bring all things to your remembrance, whatsoever I have said unto you."

Again the same night Jesus said, in John 16:12–14:

"I have yet many things to say unto you, but ye cannot bear them now. Howbeit when he, the Spirit of truth, is come, he will guide you into all truth: for he shall not speak of himself; but whatsoever he shall hear, that shall he speak: and he will shew you things to come. He shall glorify me: for he shall receive of mine, and shall shew it unto you."

Now consider those two passages. The Comforter, the Holy Ghost, "shall teach you all things, and bring all things to your remembrance, whatsoever I have said unto you," and "He will guide you into all truth," for He is the Spirit of truth.

An unsaved man cannot well understand the spiritual lessons of the Bible. "But the natural man receiveth not the things of the Spirit of God: for they are foolishness unto him: neither can he know them, because they are spiritually discerned" (I Cor. 2:14). But a Christian has a teacher, the Spirit of God Himself, to enlighten his mind. The Holy Spirit wrote the Bible, and every Christian has this same Holy Spirit abiding within him to teach him as he reads the Bible. We are prone to forget what we read. But if we submit ourselves to the Holy Spirit, He will bring to our remembrance the things that Jesus said. The best Bible teacher in the world is the Holy Spirit. Every Christian, every time he opens the Bible, should prayerfully ask the sweet Spirit of God to make clear what He wants to say through the Word of God. To the open and contrite heart, the Spirit makes clear spiritual truth.

Do you want to know more about Jesus? Then be sure that you yield yourself to the influence of the Holy Spirit when you read the Bible and when you pray. For He will receive the things of Jesus as given Him and show them unto us (John 16:14).

Some preachers do not preach what the Bible says about the Holy Spirit. Some men do not have any special anointing of the Holy Spirit, and perhaps they are embarrassed to talk about Him. Such people misinterpret John 16:13. Jesus said, "Howbeit when he, the Spirit of truth, is come, he will guide you into all truth: for he shall not speak of himself; but whatsoever he shall hear, that shall he speak: and he will shew you things to come." They say, "The Holy Spirit never speaks of Himself," as if the Holy Spirit were so modest that He would not reveal any truth about Himself! But that is not what the Scripture means nor what it says. What it really says is that the Holy Spirit does not work independently of Jesus and the Father. He speaks what is given Him to speak.

Any student of the Bible will find that the Holy Spirit who moved on the hearts of the men who wrote it, the Holy Spirit who is the real Author of the Bible, wrote much about Himself. But everything He wrote, He wrote because the Father and the Son agreed with Him that it should be written. The Holy Spirit does not work independently of Christ and the Father. He speaks about Himself and about Jesus and about the Father, but He does it as all are perfectly agreed, and He represents the others as much as Himself, Jesus said. So as the Holy Spirit guides one in understanding the Scripture, one can know just as much as if he could sit down with Jesus and hear the dear Saviour Himself explain the Word of God. For the Holy Spirit tells us just what Jesus would tell us. He is our teacher and guide!

3. The Holy Spirit Is Our Prayer Helper

A beautiful lesson is given to us in Romans 8:26,27:

"Likewise the Spirit also helpeth our infirmities: for we know not what we should pray for as we ought: but the Spirit itself maketh intercession for us with groanings which cannot be uttered. And he that searcheth the hearts knoweth what is the mind of the Spirit, because he maketh intercession for the saints according to the will of God."

How infirm we are in the matter of prayer! We do not even know what we ought to pray for. The frailty of our flesh, our coldness, our halfheartedness, our unbelief, all hinder us in prayer. But the blessed Holy Spirit helps our infirmities. While we "know not what we should pray for as we ought," yet "the Spirit itself [this should be translated *himself*] maketh intercession for us with groanings which cannot be uttered." The Holy Spirit not only helps us pray, but He prays for us and makes intercession for us. What a wonderful thought it is that Jesus in Heaven is praying for us and the Holy Spirit here living in our bodies is praying for us! How bold we ought to be in prayer! How strong should be our faith! And the Holy Spirit always knows what is right, what will please God, and how to pray according to the Father's will.

With this in mind, Ephesians 6:18 commands us to be "praying always with all prayer and supplication in the Spirit." We should be careful to follow the leading of the Holy Spirit in prayer. We should be earnest in prayer as the Spirit moves our hearts to pray. And how blessed it is when the Holy Spirit who is Himself "the spirit of grace and of supplications" (Zech. 12:10) does His blessed work in making us desire to wait on God in prevailing prayer!

4. The Holy Spirit Gives Assurance of Salvation

Another work which the Holy Spirit in some measure does for every Christian, and longs to do more perfectly, is to give assurance of salvation. In Romans 8:15,16 we are told:

"For ye have not received the spirit of bondage again to fear; but ye have received the Spirit of adoption, whereby we cry, Abba, Father. The Spirit itself beareth witness with our spirit, that we are the children of God."

The Holy Spirit loves to make the believer sure that God is his own beloved Father. The Holy Spirit loves to give assurance to the child of God that his sins are forgiven. This blessed work of the Holy Spirit varies. In my own case, when I trusted Christ as a nine-year-old boy, that very day sweet assurance came to my heart that I was a child of God. Later I was discouraged; I fell into sin, I did not know the Bible, and there were three years during which I often thought I was unsaved. But all those three years I had in me the witness that I loved God and wanted to please Him, even though I was not always sure I was accepted. Then one day I found the blessed promise in John 5:24, and the Holy Spirit made it clear to me once and forever that I was a child of God and would not come into condemnation.

And this moment, as I write, I have the sweet assurance, the Holy Spirit speaking in my heart, that I am a child of God.

Every Christian who is willing to take God's Word for it (the Word of which the Holy Spirit is author), and who will follow the leading of the Holy Spirit in daily life so he can hear what the Holy Spirit says, will receive sweet assurance that his sins are forgiven, his soul is saved.

5. The Holy Spirit Works in the Christian the Fruit of the Spirit, the Christian Graces

Every Christian has the Holy Spirit abiding in him; and the blessed Holy Spirit, in some measure, as we let Him have His way, is a Comforter and Guide and Reminder and Prayer Helper of every Christian. Now does the abiding Holy Spirit grow any Christian graces in the Christian? Does not this constant association with the Holy Spirit have blessed fruit in the Christian life? Yes! In Galatians 5:22,23 the fruit of the Spirit is named as follows: "But the fruit of the Spirit is love, joy, peace, longsuffering, gentleness, goodness, faith, Meekness, temperance: against such there is no law."

Unconverted people naturally tend toward the works of the flesh which are listed in that same fifth chapter of Galatians as "adultery, fornication, uncleanness, lasciviousness, Idolatry, witchcraft, hatred, variance, emulations, wrath, strife, seditions, heresies, Envyings, murders, drunkenness, revellings, and such like" (Gal. 5:19–21). When an unconverted man sins, it is the most natural thing in the world. But, thank God, a Christian has a new nature; and the abiding Holy Spirit will, as we allow Him to have His way, grow these blessed Christian graces in the Christian—love, joy, peace, long-suffering, gentleness, goodness, faith, meekness, temperance.

Of course there is a great variance in the development of Christians. Some Christians grow in grace more than others. Some Christians exhibit more of these outward evidences of the Holy Spirit's work than do other Christians. But in some degree these blessings are given every Christian, and these results are wrought in every Christian's life. These are the inward fruit of the Spirit.

Please note this is a usual ministry of the Holy Spirit and that in some degree these results are worked out in every Christian's life, in every born-again person. These are not the same as the fullness of the Spirit, the special enduement of power from on high. These are simply the ordinary Christian graces by which the Holy Spirit can make a Christian extraordinary in contrast to the unsaved. But we must remember that these Christian graces of character are not yet the highest work of the Holy Spirit. Jesus had all these Christian graces before He ever went to the Jordan River to be baptized of John and before the Holy Spirit came upon Him in visible form like a dove. Jesus had all these Christian graces before He was anointed to preach the Gospel.

There is good reason to believe that the eleven disciples, and other Christians with them, had a large measure of these Christian graces while they tarried and prayed, waiting for the mighty power of God which came at Pentecost.

Everything in this chapter concerning the ordinary work of the Holy Spirit had already been done in the lives of those who were commanded to tarry until they were endued with power from on high. They already had love. They already had joy. They already had peace. Already they were willing to suffer for Jesus and had been greatly revived and strengthened after His resurrection, with His forty days of teaching and enlightening. The Holy Spirit had worked all these usual blessings which He ministers to every Christian, in some degree, in the lives of all those who waited in the Upper Room for the unusual and extraordinary blessing, the fullness of the Holy Spirit.

It will help greatly in the understanding of the power of Pentecost, the fullness of the Spirit, if we keep separate in our minds these ordinary and usual ministries of the Spirit which He works in every Christian life on the one hand, and remember the unusual, supernatural, miraculous power of the Holy Spirit for soul winning which He gave to the apostles and others at Pentecost and offers now to Christians who are willing to pay the price for this power. Every Christian does have in some sense the blessings mentioned in this chapter. We do well to make much of these ministries of the Holy Spirit and to let the Holy Spirit completely master our lives and change our characters and rejoice our hearts and lift our burdens and guide our footsteps and give us victory in prayer. We do well to let Him grow in us the abundant fruit of the Spirit, the Christian graces. But we must then remember that we still are not fit to work for Christ, not fit to carry out His Great Commission and are not able to win souls unless He gives us a supernatural enduement of power, the unusual and extraordinary work of the Holy Spirit which all Christians may have, but some, sad to say, never have.

Chapter 3

Jesus, Filled With the Holy Ghost

"That word, I say, ye know, which was published throughout all Judæa, and begun from Galilee, after the baptism which John preached; How God anointed Jesus of Nazareth with the Holy Ghost and with power: who went about doing good, and healing all that were oppressed of the devil; for God was with him."—Acts 10:37,38.

The Lord Jesus Himself had the mighty power of Pentecost! The above Scripture, Acts 10:37,38, tells us how the Holy Ghost came upon Him, after His baptism by John the Baptist: "How God anointed Jesus of Nazareth with the Holy Ghost and with power." Jesus did all His ministry, all His preaching, all His healings, all His miracles, all His soul winning, in the power of the Holy Spirit!

What condescension, that the Lord of Glory should become a man and voluntarily take on Himself the humiliation and frailty and temptations of mankind! Philippians 2:5–8 says:

"Let this mind be in you, which was also in Christ Jesus: who, being in the form of God, thought it not robbery to be equal with God: But made himself of no reputation, and took upon him the form of a servant, and was made in the likeness of men: And being found in fashion as a man, he humbled himself, and became obedient unto death, even the death of the cross."

In Heaven the dear Lord Jesus was in the form of God and equal with God. Just a glimpse of His majesty was shown on the Mount of Transfiguration when He was transfigured before the disciples. Long after Christ's ascension, John the beloved, on the isle of Patmos, saw Jesus "in the midst of the seven candlesticks one like unto the Son of man, clothed with a garment down to the foot, and girt about the paps with a golden girdle. His head and his hairs were white like wool, as white as snow; and his eyes were as a flame of fire; And his feet like unto fine brass, as if they burned in a furnace; and his voice as the sound of many waters. And he had in his right hand seven stars: and out of his mouth went a sharp twoedged sword: and his countenance was as the sun shineth in his strength" (Rev. 1:13–16). How did John greet the Saviour, the same Saviour upon whose bosom he had once so familiarly laid his head? John tells us: "And when I saw him, I fell at his feet as dead. And he laid his right hand upon me, saying unto me,

Fear not; I am the first and the last: I am he that liveth, and was dead; and, behold, I am alive for evermore, Amen; and have the keys of hell and of death" (Rev. 1:17,18).

What a contrast between the Saviour in His glory in Heaven and the Saviour on earth when He had laid aside the garments of His glory and taken on Himself the form of a servant! The power with which the Lord Jesus created the worlds, He did not manifest on earth. He made Himself of no reputation and took upon Himself the form of a servant and was made in the likeness of men. Of all the wonderful works that Jesus did, He did not a one of them in His power as deity, His power as the Son of God. These works were all done as a Spirit-filled *man!* They were done in the power of the *third* person of the Trinity, the power of the Holy Spirit, such as other men can have, not in the power of the *second* person of the Trinity. The Lord Jesus left His own native power and the manifestation of His glory in Heaven. The power that He exercised was the same power that other men may have, the power of the Holy Spirit.

So, "God anointed Jesus of Nazareth with the Holy Ghost and with power: who went about doing good, and healing all that were oppressed of the devil; for God was with him," we are told.

I. Many Scriptures Clearly Teach That Jesus Was Filled With the Holy Spirit and Did All His Service and Ministry in the Power of the Spirit

It is surprising how many times the Scriptures discuss how the Lord Jesus, our Saviour, was filled with the Holy Spirit. There is a very clearly taught doctrine in both the Old and the New Testaments that the Saviour in His preaching and teaching and miracles was filled with the Holy Spirit and that all His work was done in the power of the Holy Spirit.

1. The Prophet Isaiah Three Times Mentions That Jesus Would Be Filled With the Holy Spirit

Isaiah 42:1–4 mentions Christ, the servant of Jehovah, as filled with the Holy Spirit:

"*Behold my servant, whom I uphold; mine elect, in whom my soul delighteth; I have put my spirit upon him: he shall bring forth judgment to the Gentiles. He shall not cry, nor lift up, nor cause his voice to be heard in the street. A bruised reed shall he not break, and the smoking flax shall he not quench: he shall bring forth judgment unto truth. He shall not fail nor be discouraged, till he have set judgment in the earth: and the isles shall wait for his law."*

All the ministry of the Lord Jesus on earth and His later return and reign seem to be included in the promise here. God says, "I have put my spirit upon him."

Isaiah 61:1,2 mentions this same pouring out of the Holy Spirit upon Christ for His public ministry:

"The Spirit of the Lord GOD is upon me; because the LORD hath anointed me to preach good tidings unto the meek; he hath sent me to bind up the brokenhearted, to proclaim liberty to the captives, and the opening of the prison to them that are bound; To proclaim the acceptable year of the LORD, and the day of vengeance of our God; to comfort all that mourn."

It is noteworthy that the Lord Jesus found this very passage and read it in the synagogue at Nazareth of Galilee after He had been filled with the Holy Spirit at His baptism by John in the Jordan River and then had returned to Nazareth.

Luke 4:16–21 tells us how Jesus read this Scripture in the synagogue and said to His hearers: "This day is this scripture fulfilled in your ears"! But we should note that Jesus stopped the quotation in the middle of Isaiah 61:2 and did not read the last half of the verse. "The day of vengeance of our God" had not yet come. But Jesus was already "anointed...to preach the gospel to the poor," as Luke 4:18 quotes the passage from Isaiah.

This passage clearly teaches that the power of the Holy Spirit would be upon Jesus, not only in His personal ministry while He was on earth, but also later in His return and His judging of the nations and in His reign.

In Isaiah 11:1–3 we have this teaching very clearly again, that when Christ returns to reign on the earth, He will reign in the power of the Holy Spirit. That Scripture says:

"And there shall come forth a rod out of the stem of Jesse, and a Branch shall grow out of his roots: And the spirit of the LORD shall rest upon him, the spirit of wisdom and understanding, the spirit of counsel and might, the spirit of knowledge and of the fear of the LORD; And shall make him of quick understanding in the fear of the LORD: and he shall not judge after the sight of his eyes, neither reprove after the hearing of his ears."

Christ Himself is the sprout from the trunk of Jesse's tree and the branch that grew out of the royal line, which was temporarily cut off from the throne of David. The Scripture says that "the spirit of the

LORD shall rest upon him, the spirit of wisdom and understanding, the spirit of counsel and might, the spirit of knowledge and of the fear of the LORD." It is by this Holy Spirit that Christ will reign perfectly and gloriously on the earth in the millennial kingdom.

But the anointing of Jesus, or the pouring out of the Spirit upon Him, took place when He prayed, standing in the Jordan River after having been baptized by John the Baptist.

2. Old Testament Types Clearly Taught That the Coming Messiah Would Do His Work in the Power of the Holy Spirit

The Lord Jesus is beautifully pictured in the tabernacle furniture and offerings of the Old Testament ceremonial law. We remember that God had filled Bezaleel "with the spirit of God, in wisdom, in understanding, and in knowledge, and in all manner of workmanship," so he could adequately prepare the tabernacle furniture to picture the Messiah, the Saviour (Exod. 35:30–35).

Exodus 37:17–24 tells of the making of the golden "candlestick" of the Tabernacle. As one entered the sanctuary, the outer room of the Tabernacle, on the left-hand side was this golden "candlestick." On the right was the table of the shewbread. Both of them represented Christ. The "candlestick" represented Christ, the Light of the World. The shewbread represented Christ as the Bread of Life.

But actually the "candlestick" was not a candlestick at all—it was a lampstand! Instead of burning candles, it burned olive oil in seven lamps. These fonts were kept filled with olive oil continually, and the light of this golden lampstand was never to go out.

Is not this lampstand a beautiful picture of the Saviour? The number seven pictures the divine perfection of Jesus Christ. It was made of a talent of pure gold, and gold is used many times for deity, as wood is often used for humanity. But the oil pictures the Holy Spirit. Just as the priests and kings of the Old Testament were anointed with oil as a token that the Spirit of God was upon them to do the service of God, so the oil here means the Holy Spirit. So Christ, the Light of the World, in His earthly ministry shone by the power of the Holy Spirit!

Again, some of the offerings in Old Testament times pictured Christ as anointed with the Holy Spirit. All the offerings pictured Christ. The Passover lamb pictured Christ. First Corinthians 5:7 says, "Even Christ our passover is sacrificed for us." John the Baptist said, "Behold the Lamb of God, which taketh away the sin of the world" (John 1:29).

Abraham told his son Isaac, "My son, God will provide himself a lamb for a burnt-offering" (Gen. 22:8), and he there certainly referred to the Lord Jesus. The bullock offered in sacrifice represented Christ, the burden-bearing Saviour. The scapegoat pictured Christ carrying away our sin and our humiliation and shame from the face of God. The white pigeons pictured the pure and sinless One dying for the guilty, and the mourning turtledove pictured Christ as a Man of sorrows and acquainted with grief. All the sacrifices certainly pictured Jesus Christ.

Leviticus 2:4–7 tells of the meat offering (literally the "food offering"):

> "And if thou bring an oblation of a meat-offering baken in the oven, it shall be unleavened cakes of fine flour mingled with oil, or unleavened wafers anointed with oil. And if thy oblation be a meat-offering baken in a pan, it shall be of fine flour unleavened, mingled with oil. Thou shalt part it in pieces, and pour oil thereon: it is a meat-offering. And if thy oblation be a meat-offering baken in the fryingpan, it shall be made of fine flour with oil."

In this offering the fine flour pictured Christ, the crushed Saviour, bruised and beaten for us. The cakes were made unleavened; for leaven is a type of sin, and Jesus had no sin. But the fine flour was mingled with oil, and the unleavened wafers were anointed with oil. Because even the pure and holy Saviour had so emptied Himself of the manifestation of His power and glory, He could not acceptably do the work of the Father except through the special anointing of the Holy Spirit.

In the same chapter, verses 14–16 tell about the firstfruits of green ears of corn (grain) or grain beaten out of full ears:

> "And if thou offer a meat-offering of thy firstfruits unto the LORD, thou shalt offer for the meat-offering of thy firstfruits green ears of corn dried by the fire, even corn beaten out of full ears. And thou shalt put oil upon it, and lay frankincense thereon: it is a meat-offering. And the priest shall burn the memorial of it, part of the beaten corn thereof, and part of the oil thereof, with all the frankincense thereof: it is an offering made by fire unto the LORD."

It is a very beautiful and tender thing to see how the bruised grain pictures Jesus. He was wholly given up to all the suffering and abuse that sin could ever deserve. He was bruised corn. He was flour, ground very fine. But the holy and beautiful and sinless Lamb of God needed the anointing oil. That is, He needed the Holy Spirit of God upon Him. The frankincense in this gift, which was the incense offered to deity, was accompanied by the oil which pictured the Holy Spirit. The Saviour was the sinless and perfect Son of God. He was God in human form. But He did His work in the power of the Holy Spirit. Thus it is clearly foretold in the Old Testament that the Lord Jesus would accomplish His ministry in the power of the Holy Spirit. We would not leave any impression that Jesus was less than very God. "His name shall be called Wonderful, Counsellor, The mighty God, The everlasting Father" (Isa. 9:6). But His sinlessness is shown in this offering because the bread was unleavened bread. He is shown as atoning for our sins in the oven fires of God's wrath on sin, which Christ suffered for us on the cross. He is the fine flour; ground and beaten and broken to the finest particles, it pictures the Saviour who had no will of His own but gave Himself up wholly to the will of the Father and to take the place of men, in bearing our sins and our punishment. But this holy and sinless Saviour could not adequately serve the heavenly Father except in the power of the Holy Spirit! What a lesson for our poor, proud and self-confident hearts!

But again we remember that the men who were types of the coming Messiah were themselves anointed with olive oil, as Christ would be anointed with the Holy Spirit.

Aaron, the high priest of Israel, was anointed with holy oil. In Leviticus 8:12 we are told how Moses took the anointing oil, "And he poured of the anointing oil upon Aaron's head, and anointed him." The meaning clearly is that Aaron was to act for God and to be filled with the Spirit of God. But Aaron was in some sense a type of our own High Priest, the Lord Jesus Christ who was anointed with the Holy Spirit.

Samuel was sent from God to anoint David to be king. After Saul was disobedient, "Then Samuel took the horn of oil, and anointed him in the midst of his brethren: and the Spirit of the LORD came upon David from that day forward" (I Sam. 16:13). David was anointed to serve God, and the outward sign of olive oil upon his head represented a far more important anointing, the pouring out of the Spirit of God upon David which came at the same time and never left him!

But Christ is "the seed of David." Christ is "the king of the Jews." Christ Himself is the greater David, mentioned in Ezekiel 34:23,24. So it seems to many Bible interpreters. The anointing oil upon David, and the Holy Spirit fullness that came upon David for his ministry, is only a foretaste of the fullness of the Holy Spirit which was to come on the Lord Jesus Christ, David's greater Son!

3. New Testament Scriptures Repeatedly Refer to the Fact That the Lord Jesus Did His Mighty Works in the Power of the Holy Spirit

We want to quote again the passage with which we started this chapter: "How God anointed Jesus of Nazareth with the Holy Ghost and with power: who went about doing good, and healing all that were oppressed of the devil; for God was with him" (Acts 10:38). Here the three persons of the Godhead are mentioned. God the Father anointed Jesus, the second person of the Trinity, with the Holy Ghost, the third person of the Trinity. Jesus went about doing good, for God the Holy Ghost was with Him, and this took place after John baptized Him in the river Jordan, as the preceding verse tells us.

Hebrews 9:14 tells us how the Saviour unflinchingly faced the cross. There we are told that Christ "through the eternal Spirit offered himself without spot to God." If any man ever has trouble facing the daily crucifixion of self and the giving up of his fondest desires, ever has trouble facing the direst persecution, then he must remember that the Lord Jesus faced His ordeal through the eternal Spirit—that is, through the power of the Holy Spirit who filled Him.

In Acts 1:2 we are told that Jesus was taken up to Heaven, "after that he through the Holy Ghost had given commandments unto the apostles whom he had chosen." The Lord Jesus, even the resurrected Saviour, the glorified Saviour, gave commandments through the power of the Holy Spirit to the apostles whom He had chosen!

What a strange teaching this was to me when I first discovered it in the Bible! I was amazed to find that in all His ministry on earth Jesus never won a soul, never worked a miracle, never preached a sermon, except in the power of the Holy Spirit! He faced the crucifixion in the power of the Spirit. He gave commandments to His apostles after His resurrection in the power of the Spirit! When Jesus returns to reign on the earth, He will reign in the mighty power of the Holy Spirit!

4. The Coming of the Holy Spirit in Power Upon Jesus at His Baptism Is Clearly Described

God made much of the fact that the Lord Jesus would be made known to the public by the coming of the Holy Spirit in visible form upon Him. It is rather strange that John the Baptist did not know that Jesus was the Messiah. Remember that John's mother and the mother of Jesus were cousins. John's mother, Elisabeth, had had revealed to her from God that the baby Mary bore would be the Messiah. But John the Baptist evidently did not know this. He tells us that he did not know that Jesus was the Saviour until the Holy Spirit came upon Him in John's presence like a dove, to abide upon Him continually. That was the witness that God had promised John the Baptist by which he should identify the Messiah, whose forerunner he was.

This part of the story is told in John 1:29–34 as follows:

"The next day John seeth Jesus coming unto him, and saith, Behold the Lamb of God, which taketh away the sin of the world. This is he of whom I said, After me cometh a man which is preferred before me: for he was before me. And I knew him not: but that he should be made manifest to Israel, therefore am I come baptizing with water. And John bare record, saying, I saw the Spirit descending from heaven like a dove, and it abode upon him. And I knew him not: but he that sent me to baptize with water, the same said unto me, Upon whom thou shalt see the Spirit descending, and remaining on him, the same is he which baptizeth with the Holy Ghost. And I saw, and bare record that this is the Son of God."

John had been telling about One coming after him whose shoelaces John was not worthy to untie. He had been telling of this wonderful Lamb of God who would take away the sin of the world. But when Jesus came to be baptized, John felt unworthy to baptize Him. Although he did not know that Jesus was the Messiah, he must have known how holy and blameless Jesus was. Matthew 3:13–15 tells us: "Then cometh Jesus from Galilee to Jordan unto John, to be baptized of him. But John forbad him, saying, I have need to be baptized of thee, and comest thou to me? And Jesus answering said unto him, Suffer it to be so now: for thus it becometh us to fulfil all righteousness. Then he suffered him." John the Baptist had known Jesus as his cousin, the purest and holiest man he ever knew, the only man he knew in whom there was not a hint of sin. John felt himself unworthy to baptize Jesus. But now, at Jesus' command, John baptized Him. Then the Spirit of God came upon Him in visible form like a dove, and John declared that this was indeed the Messiah! This was the One whom God had promised to send! This was the One who should fill others with the Holy Spirit as He Himself was filled with the Spirit now!

But for our purposes here, the story of how Jesus was filled with the Holy Spirit is best made clear in Luke 3:21–23:

"Now when all the people were baptized, it came to pass, that Jesus also being baptized, and praying, the heaven was opened, And the Holy Ghost descended in a bodily shape like a dove upon him, and a voice came from heaven, which said, Thou art my beloved Son; in thee I am well pleased. And Jesus himself began to be about thirty years of age, being (as was supposed) the son of Joseph, which was the son of Heli."

Jesus was baptized and praying, and the Holy Spirit came visibly upon Him. God's voice from Heaven said, "Thou art my beloved Son; in thee I am well pleased."

At what age did this happen to Jesus? When He was "about thirty years of age."

Jesus was now thirty years old. He had lived a perfect, sinless life. He had never grieved the Father, not in one particular. He was blameless as no one who ever lived was blameless. The Lord Jesus had loved the Word of God. He attended the synagogue. His personal relationships were without any lack, any failure, any sin. Not a thought of His ever grieved His heavenly Father. He was as pure and holy and sinless in those first thirty years of His life as God the Father in Heaven was sinless and perfect. Yet Jesus had never preached a sermon, had never worked a miracle, had never won a soul! All this waited until Jesus was filled with the Holy Spirit! After His baptism He returned to Galilee; and there at Cana of Galilee, as recorded in the second chapter of John, Jesus did "this beginning of miracles."

The anointing of Jesus with the Holy Spirit was no passing thing. The Holy Spirit came upon Him, "descending from heaven like a dove, and it abode upon him" (John 1:32). The Holy Spirit never left the Lord Jesus.

Immediately after the passage telling how Jesus was filled with the Holy Spirit in Luke 3:21,22, we have the genealogy of Jesus. Then the fourth chapter starts with these words, "And Jesus being full of the Holy Ghost returned from Jordan, and was led by the Spirit into the wilderness."

After His temptation was finished, we are told, "And Jesus returned in the power of the Spirit into Galilee" (Luke 4:14).

Then Jesus came into the synagogue at Nazareth where He had been brought up and went, as was His custom, into the synagogue on the Sabbath day and stood up to read the Word of God which He loved so well. They handed Him the scroll with the writings of the Prophet Isaiah, and He looked until He found Isaiah 61:1,2 and read:

"The Spirit of the Lord is upon me, because he hath anointed me to preach the gospel to the poor; he hath sent me to heal the brokenhearted, to preach deliverance to the captives, and recovering of sight to the blind, to set at liberty them that are bruised, To preach the acceptable year of the Lord."—Luke 4:18,19.

Then Jesus closed the book and sat down, "And he began to say unto them, This day is this scripture fulfilled in your ears."

The Saviour was known to these people at Nazareth. It was His regular custom to attend the synagogue, to read the Scriptures. He worked in the carpenter shop and was called a carpenter. As far as we know, He supported the family or helped to support the family, since Joseph was now evidently dead. But Jesus had never been like this! He had been holy and blameless and good, but He had never spoken with such power, with such a message from God! People had never been convicted of their sins as they had heard Jesus speak, before this. They had never felt their need of salvation. The Spirit of God had not stirred their hearts before. But now, "All bare him witness, and wondered at the gracious words which proceeded out of his mouth. And they said, Is not this Joseph's son?" (Luke 4:22).

So the Saviour began His Spirit-filled ministry. Everything that Jesus did, He did in the mighty power of the Spirit of God.

John 3:34 tells us that Jesus was given the Holy Spirit without limit: "...for God giveth not the Spirit by measure unto him."

II. The Lord Jesus Is the Perfect Pattern for Christians in the Fullness of the Spirit

The Lord Jesus is the perfect pattern for Christians in everything. In this matter of the fullness of the Holy Spirit, the mighty power of God, He is our pattern too.

Of course no unconverted person has the power to follow Jesus and be like Jesus and imitate Jesus. Before one takes Jesus as an example, he needs to take Him as his Saviour. Men need saving before they need teaching. People need to be born again before they set out to live for God. People need salvation before they need consecration. People cannot follow Jesus in winning souls until they have been won themselves. So the modernists are wholly wrong when they teach poor, unconverted, lost people with unregenerate hearts to try to live "the Jesus way." No one can live like Jesus until he becomes like Jesus in his heart by a supernatural work of God's grace. One must be made into a child of God before he has any right to follow the pattern of Jesus, the only begotten Son of God, our elder Brother. Yet it is certainly true that every Christian, everyone who has been born into the family of God, should set out to follow Jesus and pattern after Him. We should want what Jesus wants, work as He worked, pray as He prayed, and have the power which He exercised.

1. The Incarnation Itself Was Intended to Make Jesus Like Men, the Perfect Man

When Jesus was scourged and stood before the Roman governor with a platted crown of thorns and a purple robe, Pilate did not say,

"Behold the God." Christ the Lord is God incarnate. Pilate would have been right if he had said, "Behold God!" But instead of that, Pilate said, "Behold the man!" (John 19:5). For Jesus is really Emmanuel, "God with us." Jesus is a man.

How plain the Scripture makes it! Jesus was born of a human mother, nursed at a mother's breast. He grew up in a home of human poverty. Strangely enough, we are told that Jesus "increased in wisdom and stature, and in favour with God and man" (Luke 2:52). Jesus delighted to be called "the Son of man," and nearly always He called Himself by that title. He did not hesitate to declare that He and the Father are one (John 10:30). He did not hesitate to declare that all judgment was given unto the Son and that He came from Heaven. Yet He continually stressed the fact that He was man, that He was the Son of man. In His incarnation, the Lord Jesus took on Himself the form of a man. He became flesh as we are flesh. He "was in all points tempted like as we are, yet without sin" (Heb. 4:15). Jesus was as truly man as He was truly God. He was the perfect man.

How often we are commanded to be like Him! "Let this mind be in you, which was also in Christ Jesus" (Phil. 2:5). We are commanded to "walk in love, as Christ also hath loved us" (Eph. 5:2).

Hebrews 12:1,2 tells us that we are to run our race with patience, laying aside the sin of unbelief which doth so easily beset us, "looking unto Jesus the author and finisher of our faith; who for the joy that was set before him endured the cross, despising the shame, and is set down at the right hand of the throne of God." How strange that we are to run our race as Jesus ran His; we are to have faith as Jesus had faith; we are to look to the future reward as Jesus did! First John 4:17 says a strange and marvelous thing: "Herein is our love made perfect, that we may have boldness in the day of judgment: because as he is, so are we in this world." As Jesus is, so are we, even in this present world!

That is what the incarnation of Jesus meant. He became a man so He could be a fit Saviour and a fit pattern for men. Where we failed, Jesus did not fail. Where we sinned, He was sinless. But now that He has taken our place and borne our sins, He enables us to be like Himself.

We are even told what the final plan of God is, in letting Jesus come to earth and be a man and die as a man for our sins. His purpose is that at last all of us might be "conformed to the image of his Son, that he might be the firstborn among many brethren" (Rom. 8:29). Jesus is the Son of God, and we are also sons of God. Jesus was conceived of the Holy Ghost, and so also we have been born of the Spirit and have been made partakers of the divine nature. Jesus now has a glorified resurrection body. But we are taught to "look for the Saviour, the Lord Jesus Christ: Who shall change our vile body, that it may be fashioned like unto his glorious body" (Phil. 3:20,21). Oh, glorious day when Jesus comes to make us perfectly and beautifully like Himself, the sinless sons of God!

2. At His Baptism Jesus Publicly Announced Himself the Example and Pattern of Christians

Jesus came to be my pattern. But of course I was born with a sinful nature and Jesus was not. I needed to repent and Jesus did not. I needed to be born again and Jesus did not. So nothing that I did or could do on the other side of my regeneration could be following Jesus. Only when I have trusted Christ as my Saviour and when the Holy Spirit has made me a new creature and made me a partaker of the divine nature can I follow the example of Jesus.

This is made clear in the baptism of Jesus. The first duty of a Christian after accepting Christ as Saviour is to claim Him openly and be baptized. That is the way the Great Commission puts it. "Go ye therefore, and teach all nations, baptizing them..." (Matt. 28:19). "He that believeth and is baptized" (Mark 16:16) is the divine order. It is expected, in the New Testament, that those who trust Christ for salvation should be baptized in public profession of their faith, and that immediately. The examples of New Testament Christians are remarkable for the way they follow this pattern. People would get saved and then immediately would want to be baptized.

So when Jesus was thirty years old, ready to begin His ministry as soon as the Spirit of God should come upon Him in great power, He came to the Jordan River where John was baptizing others and there sought to be baptized.

"Then cometh Jesus from Galilee to Jordan unto John, to be baptized of him. But John forbad him, saying, I have need to be baptized of thee, and comest thou to me? And Jesus answering said unto him, Suffer it to be so now: for thus it becometh us to fulfil all righteousness. Then he suffered him."—Matt. 3:13–15.

Note that little word in Matthew 3:15. Jesus said, "Thus it becometh us to fulfil all righteousness." Whom did Jesus mean by that plural pronoun, "us"? I believe that Jesus meant Himself and every convert, everyone who would ever take Him as Saviour. It was fitting for Jesus to be baptized as a public proclamation of His coming death, burial and resurrection. All the righteousness of God was to be fulfilled by the Lord Jesus Christ. Every demand of the law was to be met. All or man's sins were to be paid for. So the baptism of Jesus, foretelling His death, burial and resurrection, in some sense typified all righteousness.

But it was not for Jesus alone, this beautiful ordinance! It was for "us"! It was for Jesus and others. Every Christian, then, should start out with his baptism, and then all the rest of his life, follow the example of the Lord Jesus, our pattern.

We ought to be baptized as Jesus was baptized, following His example. Then we ought to have the fullness of the Holy Spirit upon us as Jesus had, and live as Jesus lived, and work as Jesus worked. I know that He is perfect and we are imperfect. I know that He is the sinless Lamb of God and we are poor sinning mortals. Yet there is a clear Bible teaching that every Christian should set out to follow Jesus, should count himself dead because Jesus died, and alive because Jesus is alive, and count himself in every possible sense obligated to follow in the footsteps of Jesus.

3. Jesus Was Filled With the Holy Spirit to Make Himself the More Perfect Pattern for His People

How many people have delighted to say that Jesus proved Himself to be the Son of God by His miracles! But they are mistaken. If miracles would prove that Jesus was the Son of God, that He is God incarnate, then miracles would prove that Elijah and Elisha and Paul and Peter and Stephen were likewise God incarnate, for they too worked miracles! In the public ministry of Jesus the miracles were no more remarkable, I dare say, than the miracles that took place in the life of Moses. It is true that Jesus cleansed the leper, but so did Elisha heal Naaman the Syrian. It is true that Jesus stilled the storm on the Sea of Galilee, but no one could say that that is a greater miracle than Joshua's having the sun to stand still in its relation to the earth! Jesus raised from the dead the widow's son of Nain and a little twelve-year-old girl. But Peter too was used of God to raise Dorcas from the dead (Acts 9:40). Miracles certainly proved that God was with these prophets, but it did not prove that they were God incarnate as Jesus was.

The miracles of Jesus were not given to prove that He was God's Son. They did prove that God was with Him, but He Himself often insisted that the miracles should not be told. He gave one sign only that should be the positive sign of His deity; that was His resurrection from the dead. Scribes and Pharisees came to Jesus, asking for a sign:

"But he answered and said unto them, An evil and adulterous generation seeketh after a sign; and there shall no sign be given to it, but the sign of the prophet Jonas: For as Jonas was three days and three nights in the whale's belly; so shall the Son of man be three days and three nights in the heart of the earth."—Matt. 12:39,40.

I think we are justified in concluding that Jesus intended us to count nothing else the sign of His deity but His resurrection from the dead, which fulfilled all the prophecies and proved Him to be what He claimed to be—God's own Son come in human flesh.

The truth is that Christ did not work these miracles in His power as deity. Remember that Jesus is God. When He was here on earth He was God in human form. But He had left the manifestation of His glory in Heaven. He had taken on Himself the form of a servant. Jesus had so emptied Himself that for thirty years He lived on earth without working a miracle, without healing a leper or opening blind eyes or preaching a sermon or winning a soul! For Jesus had determined to come as a man, to be a perfect man, and to be an example for all who should trust Him. Hence, He must give up the advantage which He had over us and take our weakness and take our limitations. If Jesus were to be our example, then He must use only the power which we could have, and He must win only by the means which we ourselves could use too. The Saviour therefore gave up the use of His power as the Son of God, the mighty power by which He created the worlds and holds them in their orbits in the skies. He was content to use only the power of the Holy Spirit, as we must do. So we are told in Acts 10:38, "How God anointed Jesus of Nazareth with the Holy Ghost and with power: who went about doing good, and healing all that were oppressed of the devil; for God was with him."

I am often tempted. Satan is the enemy of my soul. He continually tries to overcome me. He does not want me to live a Christian life. He wants my thoughts to be unholy, my purposes selfish, my plans foolish. He wants my work for Christ to be powerless. Oh, how can I overcome this enemy of my soul? How can I defeat Satan? Every Christian faces this problem of a personal Devil.

Well, thank God, Jesus faced this problem for me first and showed me how to meet it. The very first thing after Jesus was filled with the Holy Spirit, we are told, "And Jesus being full of the Holy Ghost returned from Jordan, and was led by the Spirit into the wilderness, Being forty days tempted of the devil. And in those days he did eat nothing: and when they were ended, he afterward hungered" (Luke 4:1,2). It pleases my heart to feel that Jesus may have said to Himself,

"John Rice will come this way one time. He will face Satan. Satan may attack him when he is hungry, or when he is sick, or when he is weak. So I will fast forty days and be as weak as any man ever needs to be when he faces Satan." So the Spirit-filled Saviour, after He had fasted so that He would be as needy, as humanly helpless as any man ever would be, met Satan and defeated him.

The first temptation was about bread, for Jesus was desperately hungry. But Jesus bethought Himself to answer Satan with Scripture. And He did not try to find a Scripture that would fit Him, the Son of God, only. Rather, He sought a Scripture that would do for Jesus and me and all other Christians alike. He said, "It is written, Man shall not live by bread alone, but by every word that proceedeth out of the mouth of God" (Matt. 4:4). Jesus was quoting from Deuteronomy 8:3. Thank God, He defeated Satan with a Scripture that is just as good for me as it is for anybody else! Jesus put Himself on the plane of a poor, frail man and showed me how, with the Word of God and the power of the Holy Spirit, one may defeat the enemy of our souls.

Jesus did much of the work of an evangelist. But when God calls *me* to do His work, how pitifully helpless I would be if I had a work to do that could only be done by a God, since I am only a frail human being. If Jesus had, in His power and His deity, power that I do not have and cannot have; if Jesus as the Son of God, I say, in His own power as God, should preach sermons and deal with sinners and win them and then should tell me that I must do the same thing in my human power, I would shrink, I would tremble, I would despair. I would have a right to say, "It is not fair! God asks of me the impossible! How can I, a man, do what only a God can do?" But, thank God, Jesus has showed us that the blessed Holy Spirit endued Him and empowered Him so that He could do what would be otherwise humanly impossible, and we may have the same power of the Holy Spirit for the same work.

Don't you see why Jesus was filled with the Holy Spirit and did nothing in His public ministry without this holy enduement from on high? Jesus, in order to be our pattern, our example, must have the weakness of a man but be wonderfully endued with the power of the Holy Spirit of God, which power we also may have for the same purpose.

Let us frankly face the matter: the Lord Jesus has commanded us to do exactly the same kind of work that He did on earth! There is no way to avoid that plain fact.

In John 14:12 Jesus said, "Verily, verily, I say unto you, He that believeth on me, the works that I do shall he do also; and greater works than these shall he do; because I go unto my Father." The very works that Jesus did we who believe on Him are to do also. And since Jesus had His ministry cut short by death after some three and a half short years, then we who live longer should do even greater works than He did! Such is the plain statement of the Word of God.

Jesus, in His High Priestly Prayer in John 17:18, said to the Father, "As thou hast sent me into the world, even so have I also sent them into the world." The Father sent Jesus into the world to make a way for the salvation of sinners and then to preach the Gospel and win them. But Jesus has sent us into the world in exactly the same way!

When Jesus rose from the dead He pressed this duty upon the disciples. He met them and showed them His hands and feet; He rejoiced their hearts and took away their doubts and fears. "Then said Jesus to them again, Peace be unto you: as my Father hath sent me, even so send I you. And when he had said this, he breathed on them, and saith unto them, Receive ye the Holy Ghost" (John 20:21,22). Just exactly as the Father sent Jesus, so Jesus sent the disciples, and so He sends us today. He breathed on the disciples, and the Holy Spirit came into their bodies to dwell. This was only a foretaste of the wonderful power of Pentecost that would be theirs. Jesus had the power of God upon Him. We can have the power of God upon us. Jesus was filled with the Holy Spirit and did His mighty works in that marvelous, miraculous enduement of power. We can be filled with the Holy Spirit too and can do the same kind of work as Jesus did.

Yes, I tremble, as I hope you do when you face this fact. How weak, how unworthy, and how far short of the pattern I am. Yet we dare not deny that Jesus has commanded us to do the work that He did.

The first verse in the Book of Acts says a strange thing: "The former treatise have I made, O Theophilus, of all that Jesus began both to do and teach." Luke, who wrote the Gospel of Luke and addressed it to Theophilus, addresses the Book of Acts to the same Christian man, a lover of God. And he says that "the former treatise," the Gospel of Luke, told "of all that Jesus BEGAN both to do and teach, Until the day in which he was taken up." Now if the Gospel of Luke tells how Jesus *began*, what does the Book of Acts tell?

Dr. A. T. Pierson has said that Jesus began the work in the Gospels and that the Holy Spirit continued the work in the Book of Acts. But I think he missed the point of what the Holy Spirit is saying to us here. What God is telling us here through Luke's pen is that the Book of Luke tells of the wonderful work that a Spirit-filled Saviour worked.

Jesus began the work in the power of the Holy Spirit. Now the Book of Acts tells how His disciples did exactly the same kind of work, preached the same kind of sermons, saw as wonderful conversions as Jesus ever saw, in the same power of the same Holy Spirit. Jesus began His work in the power of the Holy Spirit. The apostles continued the same kind of ministry in the same manifestation of the Holy Spirit. We are expected, by God's grace, to carry on in their train and in their footsteps and the footsteps of Jesus, in the same power of the Holy Spirit!

Do you see, then, why Jesus elected to leave in Heaven His glorious power as the Creator, and all the manifestation of His glory and might, and to humble Himself and empty Himself and take on Himself the form of a man? Do you see that He did all this so all His work could then be done in the power of the Holy Spirit and He could be a pattern for us? As Jesus was filled with the Holy Spirit and served His Father, so may we, and so should we, be filled with the Holy Spirit to do the work left for us to do.

III. Wonderful Lessons for Us in the Power of Pentecost Upon Jesus

Since the Lord Jesus was filled with the Holy Spirit and did all His ministry in the mighty power and manifestation of the Holy Spirit, then there are some great lessons that press hard upon our hearts in this connection. I urge you very prayerfully and lovingly to search your heart and ask the Spirit of God to teach you as we meditate for a bit upon these lessons.

1. The Fullness of the Spirit Upon Jesus Makes Clear What This Supernatural Enduement Is Like

Do you want to know what people will do if they are filled with the Holy Spirit? Then go and see what Jesus did. Do you want to know how they will act? Then go and see how Jesus acted. Do you want to know what outward manifestations are necessary when one is filled with the Holy Spirit? Then see what manifestations, if any, attended the coming of the Holy Spirit upon Jesus, and do not require any manifestations that are not shown there.

First, to be filled with the Holy Spirit does not mean having the carnal nature eradicated. It does not mean cleansing from sin. It does not mean sanctification. The dear Lord Jesus had no sin. He had no evil to burn away. He did not need any cleansing. So the fullness of the Spirit does not mean cleansing, does not mean purification, does not mean sanctification. God's people do need cleansing and may have it. But the fullness of the Spirit is something else. Jesus is our pattern in this matter, and the fullness of the Spirit did not mean that Jesus was cleansed or purified or sanctified by this experience. The fullness of the Spirit means something else.

Jesus, when He was filled with the Holy Spirit, did not talk with tongues as an outward manifestation. There was no sound of a cyclone, a rushing mighty wind, as at Pentecost. There were no visible tongues like as of fire resting upon Him. Why should Jesus talk with tongues? All these present were Jews, all understood the same language, and Jesus did not talk in any foreign language and did not need to. That is never given in the Bible as a sign of the fullness of the Holy Spirit. And if Jesus did not need that evidence, then neither do we who are commanded to follow His example.

The Saviour did not have the Holy Spirit come upon Him just as an ecstasy, a matter of His own personal enjoyment. I am sure His heart was glad. I am sure He was pleased to hear the Father's voice from Heaven commending Him. But that voice from Heaven was chiefly for the onlookers. That visible manifestation of the Holy Spirit, like a dove lighting upon Him, was for John the Baptist and for others who saw it. Jesus surely knew, without the outward sign, that the Spirit of God came upon Him and that the Father was pleased with Him. I do not say that there is no joy in the fullness of the Holy Spirit. Ephesians 5:18–20 commands us to be filled with the Spirit and to make melody in our hearts to the Lord, giving thanks to God. There is always joy in being in the center of God's will, in having God's power, in doing His work, and in seeing the blessed fruit of His Gospel. But you may be sure that there was no selfish purpose in the mind of the Lord Jesus when He was filled with the Holy Spirit. He was not simply seeking "an experience." He did not simply want something to brag about, saying, "I am sanctified," or, "Now I have My baptism." Jesus was simply endued with power to do the work the Father had for Him to do. And so we should also be filled with the Spirit for that same simple purpose.

2. The Lord Jesus Was Filled With the Holy Spirit for the Purpose of Winning Souls

Surely, surely every person who read this knows that God's purpose in sending Jesus into the world was to save sinners. "This is a faithful saying, and worthy of all acceptation, that Christ Jesus came into the world to save sinners; of whom I am chief," said Paul (I Tim. 1:15). Jesus Himself said, "For the Son of man is come to seek and to save that which was lost" (Luke 19:10). Even now, we are told, "Joy shall be in heaven over one sinner that repenteth, more than over ninety and nine just persons, which need no repentance" (Luke 15:7). We know what was in the mind of the Lord Jesus when He came into this world. He came to save sinners! His anointing was for this purpose. He received a divine enabling, a divine enduement for the work God had given Him to do. The Lord Jesus received the same blessing that the disciples at Pentecost received. They tarried until they were endued with power from on high to preach the Gospel. They claimed the promise, "But ye shall receive power, after that the Holy Ghost is come upon you: and ye shall be witnesses unto me both in Jerusalem, and in all Judæa, and in Samaria, and unto the uttermost part of the earth" (Acts 1:8). Oh, keep the main thing in mind! Jesus wanted to save sinners, and that is what His holy enduement was for.

3. If the Lord Jesus Needed to Be Filled With the Holy Spirit, How Much More Do We!

Jesus waited thirty years, homesick for Heaven, I think; but He never started a revival, never preached a sermon, never set out to do the task for which He had come to earth, until He was anointed for it. Then He entered into the synagogue at Nazareth where He had attended so many times in these thirty years past and read to them the Scriptures:

"The Spirit of the Lord is upon me, because he hath anointed me to preach the gospel to the poor; he hath sent me to heal the brokenhearted, to preach deliverance to the captives, and recovering of sight to the blind, to set at liberty them that are bruised."—Luke 4:18.

How His face must have lighted up and His eyes glowed as He said, "This day is this scripture fulfilled in your ears"! (Luke 4:21). Jesus would not preach until He was anointed to preach! Jesus was never content to try to do supernatural work without supernatural power.

If that pure and holy Jesus needed to be filled with the Spirit and was not fit to preach, not equipped to preach, until He had a holy anointing from God, oh, how presumptuous are all of us who put our unholy feet into the pulpit and stand before congregations to preach the riches of Christ without an anointing from Heaven! I wonder that God does not kill some men, as He slew Nadab and Abihu, the sons of Aaron who carried strange fire into the Tabernacle instead of allowing God to give the miraculous fire from Heaven.

I do not say that anybody should stop trying to preach the Gospel.

I would not discourage any Sunday school teacher from trying next Sunday to win souls to Christ. I would not discourage any personal worker from trying earnestly to bring friends and loved ones to a decision for Christ, whether you have the supernatural power you know you ought to have or not. Oh, but I would go with such a cry and such a burden in my soul that God could not long let me go alone, without His mighty power! I believe that God never requires any Christian to do anything for which He will not supply the power, if we wait on Him and pay His price. And if Jesus needed to be filled with the Spirit, how wicked and presumptuous must our hearts appear before God when we have no burden for God's fullness, when we go on day after day in the ordinary powerless routine of so-called "Christian service" with no supernatural fruits, no mighty movings of the Holy Spirit, no souls snatched from the burning. If Jesus Christ needed to be filled with the Spirit, then every Christian who serves God needs, surely, a blessed anointing of the Holy Spirit in power.

4. The Conditions Jesus Met for the Power of Pentecost Are the Same Conditions Always Required

What were the conditions when Jesus was filled with the Holy Spirit? "Now when all the people were baptized, it came to pass, that Jesus also being baptized, and praying, the heaven was opened, And the Holy Ghost descended in a bodily shape like a dove upon him" (Luke 3:21,22). First, Jesus was baptized, and then He prayed. Those two things indicate the two great conditions required for the fullness of the Holy Spirit.

Elsewhere we will deal in detail with the conditions God requires. Here we can only briefly indicate that Jesus met these same conditions. First, He gave Himself, obedient to death, to get sinners saved. In Acts 5:32 we are told in the words of Peter, "And we are his witnesses of these things; and so is also the Holy Ghost, whom God hath given to them that obey him." The disciples before Pentecost were commanded to tarry until they were endued with power from on high, to carry the Gospel to all the world. They had given themselves up to this task commanded of them. They were willing to live or die to win souls, and this obedience of heart to God's soul-winning plan prepared them to tarry until they were endued with power from on high.

So Jesus, when He was baptized, gave Himself up to die for the saving of souls. When He came into the world, we are told He said to the Father, "Lo, I come...to do thy will, O God" (Heb. 10:5-7). The Lord Jesus, at His baptism, offered Himself up to die and to live for the saving of souls. He dedicated Himself to the task, so He had a right to ask the Father for the power He needed to complete the task.

Then when Jesus was baptized, indicating His perfect separation to the will of the Lord, His giving Himself wholly to do the will of God, He prayed. Prayer is the second requirement for the fullness of the Holy Spirit. In Luke 11:13 Jesus said, "If ye then, being evil, know how to give good gifts unto your children: how much more shall your heavenly Father give the Holy Spirit to them that ask him?" God gives the Holy Spirit, in His soul-winning fullness, to those who ask Him; that is, to those who *keep on* asking, for the word "ask" is used in the tense that indicates continued asking. Jesus prayed for the fullness of the Spirit, and that mighty power of the Spirit came upon Him.

Jesus did not need to pray as long as the disciples did, waiting in the Upper Room before Pentecost. You see, there is no indecision, no divided motive, with Jesus. So He did not need to pray so long as we often need to pray. Once, indeed, Jesus went into a mountain and prayed all night (Luke 6:12). In the Garden of Gethsemane He prayed three times, saying the same words, pleading that the cup might pass over until the morrow, the proper time for His death. And He was heard, we are told. When Jesus prayed at His baptism for the fullness of the Holy Spirit, we may well suppose that His heart had already been crying out for this fullness of God's power upon Him.

How long must we wait before God to be filled with the Holy Spirit? Well, Jesus told the disciples, "Tarry...until ye be endued with power from on high" (Luke 24:49). So we should wait and plead and pray as long as necessary. With Jesus, in this case, it did not take long.

Nor did Jesus ever fail in the fullness of the Holy Spirit's power upon Him. He was filled without measure from that moment on.

I have often thought of a rain barrel that sat at the corner of our house in West Texas. It was a dry and arid country. There were no wells to furnish water. Earthen tanks or ponds collected the water, and then some was hauled to our cisterns. But the women were always anxious to have rainwater for shampoos and for washing clothes. But when a rain came, sometimes after months of drought, the old rain barrel would have big cracks. Much of the water would leak out before the oak staves of the barrel soaked up enough water to tighten themselves and stop the leaks. We poor, frail Christians have so many leaks! We do not stay filled with the Spirit. Probably I should more properly say that we do not have the constant flow of the Holy Spirit into our lives, and so we do not stay full of His power. But Jesus did! Always Jesus was filled with the Spirit, from that day forward.

If Jesus needed to pray to be filled with the Spirit, surely we, too, ought to pray!

Now may the God and Father of our Lord Jesus Christ teach us to follow His steps. May we learn to follow in the steps of the Saviour in seeking God's fullness and having the power of the Holy Spirit upon us as our Saviour had.

Chapter 4
Misunderstood Pentecost

"And that repentance and remission of sins should be preached in his name among all nations....but tarry ye in the city of Jerusalem, until ye be endued with power from on high."—Luke 24:47–49.

"But ye shall receive power, after that the Holy Ghost is come upon you: and ye shall be witnesses unto me both in Jerusalem, and in all Judæa, and in Samaria, and unto the uttermost part of the earth."—Acts 1:8.

"And they were all filled with the Holy Ghost, and began to speak."

"...and the same day there were added unto them about three thousand souls."—Acts 2:4, 41.

Read them again! Read those Scriptures quoted above again, and you will see that at Pentecost what really happened was that the power of the Holy Spirit came on the disciples so that they could carry out the Great Commission and win souls, as Jesus had commanded them to do. That is the true meaning of Pentecost. It was a time when God's Holy Spirit came in power upon Christians who longed to be able to carry out the work God had commanded them to do. And the Holy Spirit came upon them and enabled them. Three thousand people came to Christ that day and were baptized, and Pentecost was the beginning of a world-shaking upheaval, spiritually, that extended over the world in a hundred years.

I. The One Key That Explains Pentecost

A friend of mine has a little figure of a dog made of colored pieces of plastic which, fitted together a certain way, fold together as one piece and make the form of a Scottish terrier for a watch charm. The whole secret is in one piece. If one piece be snapped out of place, the small plastic figure comes to pieces entirely, and all its parts are understood. Put back together, this one piece snapped into place holds it in its proper form. Likewise, the pieces of Pentecost all fit together and are held together by one key piece. There is one key to the understanding of the wonderful happenings at Pentecost. That key is the fact that the disciples simply waited on God until they were endued with power from on high to be soul-winning witnesses for Him. They had the commission; now they waited for the power to carry it out. And they received the power, had a multitude saved and began their evangelization of the world. No one can understand the meaning of

Pentecost who does not use this key fact, so clearly stated in the Scriptures.

But do Bible teachers and Christian leaders simply take this Bible account at face value and regard Pentecost as the pouring out of God's power upon those who would do His will in soul winning? Indeed, most of them do not! There is probably no part of the Bible on which honorable and good, believing men have differed more widely.

We are reminded of a businessman who advertised for an office boy. A number of applicants appeared, and he sat down with the boys and told them a story something like this:

"Boys, I am going to tell you a story. When I am through, you can ask me any questions that you like. Then I will try to pick out one of you for my office boy.

"Once a farmer had been greatly troubled by the loss of his chickens. Each night some wild creature got in the open door of his hen house, killed a chicken, and carried it away. The farmer resolved to catch the intruder. So, loading his shotgun and lighting his lantern, he waited in the night for the first squawk of a chicken in fear. When the noise began, with lantern and gun he rushed to the chicken house. But he had trouble. First, the light in the lantern went out in the wind. He held it inside his coat and finally lighted it, after many trials. His dog was barking furiously. Rushing toward the commotion at the chicken house, the farmer stumbled over the pig and sprawled headlong on the ground! Retrieving his lantern, he put his head in the door of the chicken house and held the lantern aloft. A frightened rooster squawked and leaped first to the farmer's bare head and then out into the night. But in the light of the lantern the farmer saw the nocturnal prowler. A large wood owl held one of his hens with claw and beak. Setting down the lantern, the farmer blazed away with his shotgun. He accidentally pulled both triggers, and both barrels of the gun went off at once. The recoil of the gun knocked him over backwards. The heavy load of shot killed three hens and blew a hole in the side of the chicken house. The farmer's dog barked excitedly, and neighbors from all sides began to arrive to see what had happened.

"That is the end of the story. Now, boys, are there any questions you want to ask?"

One boy asked, "Were the chickens white leghorn chickens?"

Another boy asked, "What was the name of the farmer's dog which was barking?"

Other boys asked about the neighbors, about what time of night it was, about the farmer's name. And as they asked questions, one little fellow got more and more concerned. Finally he piped up with this question: "Say, Mister! Did he hit the owl? That is what he started to do. Mister, did he really get the owl?"

Strangely and sadly, people read the marvelous second chapter of Acts and have their minds all absorbed with speaking in tongues, with the origin of the church, with a supposed new dispensation, with some theory of sanctification, or some other matter of relatively minor importance, never noticing, many times, whether the disciples got that for which they were waiting on God—the power of the Holy Spirit to help them carry out the Great Commission! And it is said that the businessman hired the office boy who could keep his mind on the main business at hand and look for the principal result. How sad it is that God's people are divided on a lot of secondary matters and so have missed the great principal point that God has for us in the events of Pentecost!

One of the greatest tragedies that has happened in the whole realm of Christian doctrine is the misunderstanding of the meaning of Pentecost which is so widespread among Christians today. Nearly all Bible scholars will agree that the second chapter of Acts is the most important chapter in the Book of Acts. Pentecost itself was the most important event in the more than nineteen hundred years since the ascension of Jesus Christ. Pentecost was the initial fulfillment of the great prophecy of Joel, that "in the last days, saith God, I will pour out of my Spirit upon all flesh: and your sons and your daughters shall prophesy, and...whosoever shall call on the name of the Lord shall be saved" (Acts 2:17,21 from Joel 2:28,32). Peter, by divine inspiration, said frankly, "This is that which was spoken by the prophet Joel," and quoted this prophecy. So Pentecost was the beginning of "the last days" in which the Gospel should be preached in power over all the world so that all who would believe in Christ should be saved. R BS

Jesus Himself, after plainly giving the disciples the command of the Great Commission to preach the Gospel in all nations and to the end of the world, commanded the disciples to wait and not begin the work of the Great Commission until the power of Pentecost should come upon them. And it is obvious from the record that there were no sermons preached, no souls saved, no definite beginning made in taking the Gospel to all the world after the resurrection of Christ, until Pentecost. In Acts 11:15, Peter, telling of the conversion of Cornelius and his house, about eight years after Pentecost, plainly called

Pentecost "at the beginning," that is, the beginning of the great era of carrying the Gospel to the whole world.

Pentecost was the first time Christianity got a strong foothold on this earth. Multitudes had heard John the Baptist preach, and we may well believe that multitudes were genuinely converted to Christ, trusting Him for salvation and repenting of their sins. But John the Baptist's ministry had waned; he himself had been imprisoned and then beheaded. The Lord Jesus preached to great multitudes, but soon the multitudes turned away and followed Him no more. "Will ye also go away?" Jesus asked His disciples. Then came the events preliminary to the crucifixion, when Judas betrayed Him, Peter denied Him, and all the disciples forsook Him and fled. There were only one hundred twenty present at the pre-pentecostal prayer meeting, at the close of the ten days. Acts 1:13 and 14 indicate that there were only twenty or twenty-five at the beginning of that prayer meeting. But at Pentecost "they that gladly received his word were baptized: and the same day there were added unto them about three thousand souls" (Acts 2:41). From day to day other hundreds and other thousands were saved and joined to the assemblies of Christians. Soon the Roman Empire was lighted at a thousand points by the gospel witness and hundreds of thousands were born into the kingdom of God. Pentecost was the very beginning of the triumph of the Gospel of Christ and the most important single event in all the history of the church after the ascension of Jesus Christ.

Yet it now turns out that there has been such difference of opinion about the meaning of Pentecost that many preachers never speak of it; the second chapter of Acts is not often discussed in most groups of Christians, and the doctrine of the blessed Holy Spirit Himself and His power and what He did for Christians at Pentecost is counted a controversial doctrine and so is a subject which is taboo in most congregations! How sad the misapprehensions and misunderstandings of the wonderful blessing that came at Pentecost!

It would be one of the finest blessings that could happen for every Christian if he would set out to meditate day and night for a season on this second chapter of Acts and let the marvelous teaching there grip his soul. I discovered this wonderful chapter when I was fifteen years old in my home in a little spiritually neglected cow town in West Texas. I read that wonderful chapter over and over, and my heart was exalted. For days I saw visions like the young men whom Joel wrote about. I feel that a part of the moving of the Holy Spirit upon my heart in those days remains in my ministry yet. I thought then, and I solemnly think now, that the most blessed thing that could ever happen in this world is the kind of revival God gave at Pentecost, when God's power came upon God's people so that they could speak as the Spirit gave utterance to win three thousand souls in one day! And to this day I do not see how anybody can be so much concerned about the incidental matters at Pentecost—the preaching of the Gospel in various languages to people who heard and understood these Christians speaking in their own tongues wherein they were born, the sound of a cyclonic wind, or the abstract possibility of a new dispensation or the origin of the church—when three thousand souls were saved. How anybody can think that these secondary and abstract and incidental matters are to be compared in importance with the salvation of three thousand souls kept out of Hell forever is more than I can see! I am convinced that if we get the viewpoint of Jesus Christ concerning the worth of a soul, that we can then more accurately gauge the meaning of Pentecost in the light of the Scriptures. I am certain in my own heart that the salvation of any single soul at Pentecost was more important than anything else that happened there besides the saving of other souls.

With the importance of Pentecost in mind, I have felt a need to explain away some of the misunderstandings of the meaning of Pentecost, so that believers in Christ may come to see what Jesus had in mind in having the disciples wait for the blessed outpouring of His Spirit which came there, and to see that we too, like they, could be equipped for the marvelous soul-winning service which He has in mind for us as He had for them.

I believe that the misunderstanding of the Bible emphasis of Pentecost has resulted from the following:

First, an overemphasis on speaking with tongues and opposition to this teaching.

Second, an overemphasis and a mistaken teaching about a new dispensation which is supposed to have begun at Pentecost.

Third, the teaching that Pentecost is the birthday of the church, obscuring the Bible emphasis on soul-winning power.

Fourth, the teaching that at Pentecost the disciples were sanctified, with the eradication of the carnal, sinful nature.

II. Speaking in Tongues at Pentecost Was Incidental, Secondary, Not Important to the Principal Meaning of Pentecost

Three startling miracles occurred at Pentecost in connection with

the wonderful fullness of the Holy Spirit which came upon God's waiting people. They were these: first, "a sound from heaven as of a rushing
mighty wind, and it filled all the house where they were sitting"; second,
"there appeared unto them cloven tongues like as of fire, and it sat upon
each of them"; third, those who were filled with the Holy Spirit "began
to speak with other tongues, as the Spirit gave them utterance." These
were all miracles, all wonderful outward manifestations. However, all
were secondary and incidental to the one great promised blessing, the
power of the Holy Spirit to make the disciples able to win souls and carry
out the Great Commission which Jesus gave them.

It is a part of our frail and tainted human nature that we seize on
the incidentals instead of the essentials, that we are more concerned
about outward form than inward power. It is natural for human beings
to stress baptism, or the mass, or confirmation, or confession to a priest
instead of repentance toward God and faith in our Lord Jesus Christ.
So in the study of Pentecost a thousand eager hearts have seized zeal-
ously on the incidental and secondary manifestations and have thus
obscured and missed the blessed meaning of Pentecost. It is difficult to
reproduce the sound of a cyclone, so zealous converts do not claim that
that is the meaning of Pentecost. Since visible tongues like as of fire
sitting on people's heads or shoulders cannot be easily imitated, people
give little importance to the tongues of flame which came when the
disciples were filled with the Holy Spirit at Pentecost. But speaking in
tongues has been taken up by many groups of people as if it were the
principal thing that happened at Pentecost. Many others whose hearts
are really hungry for the fullness of the Holy Spirit and who properly
make much of the need for the fullness of the Spirit of God, the need
to be filled with the Spirit of God, yet make speaking with tongues an
absolute essential to this pentecostal blessing. And by calling this
speaking with tongues "the initial evidence of the baptism with the
Holy Ghost," such people focus attention upon the speaking in
tongues, not the soul-winning power. So to countless millions of people it has come to pass that "Pentecostalism" means speaking with
tongues, not soul winning.

Let me say here very earnestly that some groups of people called
Pentecostalists have put many denominations to shame by their honest attempt to follow the Bible completely, to follow the pattern of
New Testament Christian life, to have for themselves what the apostles and other Christians received at Pentecost. In that they have done
well, and many others of us have done very badly. I think it certainly

must please the dear Lord Jesus better for one to seek with the whole heart to be filled with the Holy Spirit, even with some misunderstanding of the details of the Bible teaching about the fullness of the Holy Spirit, than to be unconcerned about the matter. Let me say in brotherly kindness that I do not agree with my brethren within the Pentecostal movement that speaking in tongues is the initial Bible evidence of the fullness of the Holy Spirit. But I do agree with them that every Christian needs to be filled with the Holy Spirit and that this wonderful life-transforming enduement with power from on high is the privilege of every Christian. And it is my conviction, as deep as my soul, that it is a fearful sin for Christians to be indifferent on this matter of the fullness of the Holy Spirit. I believe that those who are wrong about the tongues question are not nearly so far wrong as those who are wrong about the need for and a concern for the fullness of the Holy Spirit.

Therefore, let no one think that these words are an attack upon a dearly beloved people who may differ with me on the question of speaking with tongues. A hot heart which is wrong on the question of tongues is not nearly so bad as a cold heart which is right on speaking with tongues but wrong on the power of the Holy Spirit. And if I appear to criticize my Pentecostal friends on this matter of speaking in tongues, let me say earnestly that if they were altogether wrong on this matter, they would not have so much to apologize for as denominations with many leaders who do not believe the Bible is true, who do not believe in the blood of Christ, who do not believe in the miracles, who do not believe in trying to reproduce New Testament Christianity by the power of the Holy Spirit in lives today. To be wrong on speaking with tongues is not nearly so bad as to be wrong on many other things. I think our great danger is not "wildfire" but *no* fire!

However, I must say that I believe the emphasis which many good people have put on speaking with tongues in the second chapter of Acts has beclouded the true issue, has kept people from understanding Pentecost, and has done much harm to the cause of Christ. With that in mind, let us consider briefly some facts about the speaking in tongues which is mentioned in the second chapter of Acts as having taken place at Pentecost, and you will see that it is an incidental and secondary matter, not the main matter at all.

1. Speaking in Tongues Was Simply a Means to the Great End at Pentecost

Many Christians have gotten the idea that in Bible times the gift of tongues allowed a Christian to speak in some unknown language, not known among men, and that he spoke for his own delight, without any practical usage. Even the eminent G. Campbell Morgan, though against the tongues movement, was misled as to the meaning of tongues, thinking that such speaking was always a matter "of delight and of ecstasy." He says, "These voices, these tongues, were the utterances of ecstatic gladness, in adoration and in praise." He says further, "Tongues were given, and they were to be used in addressing God." We will go into this matter fully at another place, but here it is sufficient to say that the Greek word *glossa*, here translated "tongues," is used fifty times in the New Testament. It is used repeatedly for human tongues; for example, that word is used for the tongue of the rich man in Hell, for the tongue of the man who could not speak until Jesus touched his tongue. It is used repeatedly for foreign languages. *It is never used in the entire New Testament for some ecstatic language to be addressed to God alone.* That is a foolish thought that is not taken from the second chapter of Acts at all, but based on a misunderstanding of I Corinthians 14, as we will later show.

Why were the Christians at Pentecost given the power to speak in tongues? That is very simply explained in the text itself. "And there were dwelling at Jerusalem Jews, devout men, out of every nation under heaven" (Acts 2:5). These Jews, who came from many other countries, spoke various languages. So God gave to these Christians at Pentecost the power to speak in the languages of "Parthians, and Medes, and Elamites, and the dwellers in Mesopotamia, and in Judæa, and Cappadocia, in Pontus, and Asia, Phrygia, and Pamphylia, in Egypt, and in the parts of Libya about Cyrene, and strangers of Rome, Jews and proselytes, Cretes and Arabians" (Acts 2:9–11). And these people, when they heard the Gospel, said, "We do hear them speak in our tongues the wonderful works of God." They said also, "And how hear we every man in our own tongue, wherein we were born?" (Acts 2:8). The Christians at Pentecost who spoke to the Parthians spoke to them in their own language in which they were born. Those who spoke to the Medes spoke to them in their own language in which they were born. And so it was with the Romans who understood Latin, the Arabs who understood the Arabian language, etc. There is not a hint here of some kind of ecstatic language which was given for the pleasure of those who spoke, nor of a worship of God not understood by men. Not at all!

If a Chinese man were before me with a hungry heart and God

should tell me to preach the Gospel to him, what would I do? Suppose that there was no one who could translate into Chinese and the Chinese man could not understand any English. If God would give me the power to preach the Gospel to him in his own language in which he was born, and if he were to hear it and understand it and be turned to God, that would be exactly what happened at Pentecost.

The important thing was not whether they spoke in the language of the Parthians or the Medes or the Cretes or the Arabians or others; the important thing was that they spoke in the power of God to lost sinners and told them of the wonderful works of God in the death and resurrection of His Son, to save sinners. Every honest reader surely can see that the speaking in tongues was simply a means to an end. The speaking in tongues was not the main thing.

2. The Saviour Said Nothing About Speaking in Tongues When He Commanded the Disciples to Wait Until They Were Endued With Power From on High

The wonderful fullness of the Holy Spirit, or baptism with the Spirit, or pouring out of the Spirit, or gift of the Spirit which came at Pentecost (all these Bible terms are used about that same blessing), was foretold long ahead of time. It is significant that in every one of the four Gospels the words of John the Baptist are quoted, saying, "I indeed baptize you with water unto repentance: but he that cometh after me...shall baptize you with the Holy Ghost" (Matt. 3:11; see also Mark 1:8; Luke 3:16; John 1:26,33). It is evident that John made this statement, or similar ones, many times. And the Holy Ghost had the writers of the Gospels put it down these four times as a matter of great importance.

In none of these cases did John the Baptist even mention or infer that the fullness of the Spirit would involve speaking with tongues. The speaking with tongues, with the sound of a rushing mighty wind and with the visible tongues like as of fire, were all incidental and secondary miracles that were not essential to the real blessing which was sought.

In Luke 24:49 Jesus said: "And, behold, I send the promise of my Father upon you: but tarry ye in the city of Jerusalem, until ye be endued with power from on high." But Jesus said nothing to them about expecting to speak with tongues. He did not tell them that speaking in tongues was the evidence of the fullness of the Holy Spirit. He ignored the matter, just as He did other incidental things that should happen at Pentecost.

Acts 1:4, 5 tells us again of the command and promise of Jesus concerning the Holy Spirit:

"And, being assembled together with them, [Jesus] commanded them that they should not depart from Jerusalem, but wait for the promise of the Father, which, saith he, ye have heard of me. For John truly baptized with water; but ye shall be baptized with the Holy Ghost not many days hence."

The fullness of the Spirit was a matter long promised, "the promise of the Father" often referred to. Now, Jesus tells them, in a few days these disciples "shall be baptized with the Holy Ghost." Yet not a word is said about speaking with tongues nor the other incidental miracles that were to occur at Pentecost. They were not important. The disciples were not to wait for them. The disciples were to lay no stress upon them. They were to tarry until they were baptized with the Holy Ghost.

But how would the disciples know when they were baptized with the Holy Ghost? What would be the evidence? Naturally they inquired further as to the meaning. And Jesus explained Himself further in Acts 1:8. This is the evidence they were promised: "But ye shall receive power, after that the Holy Ghost is come upon you: and ye shall be witnesses unto me both in Jerusalem, and in all Judæa, and in Samaria, and unto the uttermost part of the earth."

Don't you see, then, that speaking in tongues at Pentecost was an incidental and minor matter, a simple means to an end? The important thing was that they were to have the power of God upon them and were to be God's witnesses in winning souls. What a mistake it is for us to put the cart before the horse, to major on minors, to let the tail wag the dog, in our interpretation of what happened at Pentecost!

3. We Are Clearly Told Elsewhere That Speaking in Tongues Is Incidental and Secondary, a Lesser Gift

We do not have room here to answer all the questions that arise concerning speaking with tongues. I cannot in the short space of this chapter say all that needs to be said about speaking with tongues. That will come in a later chapter. But certain principles are plainly stated which will help us to know that speaking in tongues was incidental and had no large part in the meaning of Pentecost.

First, God put speaking in tongues as the very last of the gifts mentioned in I Corinthians 12:28: "And God hath set some in the church, first apostles, secondarily prophets, thirdly teachers, after that miracles, then gifts of healings, helps, governments, diversities of tongues." Every word of God is pure. All the Bible is exactly right. God put diversities of tongues as the very last and least important of the gifts, just as the gift of an apostle, given first, was most important.

Second, the Bible clearly infers that all do not speak with tongues and should not. First Corinthians 12:30 says, "Have all the gifts of healing? do all speak with tongues? do all interpret?" The answer obviously intended is no. Speaking in tongues was not intended for every Christian.

Third, Paul himself, by divine inspiration, plainly said that speaking in tongues is infinitely less important than giving a clear testimony for Jesus. In I Corinthians 14:19 Paul says: "Yet in the church I had rather speak five words with my understanding, that by my voice I might teach others also, than ten thousand words in an unknown tongue."

More teaching on this important subject will come later, but surely this is enough to show honest Christians everywhere that it is better to speak five words with the understanding than ten thousand words in an unknown tongue. And one who puts much stress on the speaking with tongues certainly misses the wonderful meaning that God has for us in Pentecost. And that meaning is that God's people simply tarried there with prayer and supplication until they were filled with the Holy Spirit and had power to witness for Him in Jerusalem, in all Judaea, in Samaria, and unto the uttermost part of the earth. And we too can have the same power as these Christians had at the "specimen day," as D. L. Moody called it, of revival at Pentecost.

4. Bible Teachers Retreating Before the Tongues Movement Have Explained Away Pentecost and Missed Its Blessed Meaning

There can be no doubt that the fanaticism of the tongues movement and the arbitrary insistence of many misguided people that every Christian should talk in tongues and that speaking in tongues is the evidence of the baptism of the Holy Spirit have done great harm and have led people to misinterpret the meaning of Pentecost. But we must also say that much of the Bible teaching on the question of Pentecost and the power of the Holy Spirit in recent years has been colored unduly by a retreat before the tongues people. Many Bible teachers were not willing to face the implications of Pentecost. Many did not have, themselves, the power of Pentecost, such as that which fell upon great evangelists—Charles G. Finney, D. L. Moody, R. A. Torrey, J. Wilbur Chapman, and others. Yet Pentecostal people and the tongues people pressed the matter all the time. A revulsion of feeling took place among leaders of Christian thought, and it became popular to explain away Pentecost. Pentecost was the technical beginning of a new dispensation, people said. Pentecost, therefore, could never be repeated. It was simply the origin of the Christian church. All of us were already baptized in the Holy Spirit, at least potentially, and therefore we did not need to have more. It was stressed by a thousand writers and preachers that "the Holy Spirit never speaks of Himself," which is a violent misunderstanding and perversion of John 16:13 where Jesus said that the Holy Spirit would speak only what He was given to speak from the Father. Christians were taught that it was foolish to wait before God and pray for the fullness of the Spirit. Since Pentecost, said these worldly-wise Bible teachers, that was never in order. The teachings of Darby were substituted for the great doctrinal position of D. L. Moody and R. A. Torrey. The Bible teachers who never had revivals, never knew the power of Pentecost for themselves and rarely won souls, became the spokesmen in doctrine where once the soul winners—Spurgeon, Wesley, Whitefield, Finney, Moody, Torrey—had been heard. The tide of revival ebbed away as men ceased to plead for and ceased to expect the power of the Holy Spirit. To get away from the Pentecostal teaching, people retreated from any teaching on Holy Spirit power.

Oh, the dearth, the famine, the spiritual wilderness, the powerlessness resulting from this retreat from the clear Bible teaching on the power of the Holy Spirit!

Beloved reader, suppose someone has laid more stress on speaking in tongues than is proper or right; surely it is even worse for us to ignore the clear teaching of the Word of God about the power of the Holy Spirit! Surely, if the tongues people have been wrong about Pentecost, that does not excuse us for disobeying and neglecting the clear commands of the Scripture to be filled with the Spirit.

By God's grace, I will not give up a thing that is promised to New Testament Christians! If some teach baptism essential to salvation, I will not go with them, but I will still teach people to be baptized as Jesus and Paul did. If some make the Lord's Supper into a mass and put forgiveness into the hands of a priest, I will not go with them; but I will still teach Christians that Jesus said, "This do in remembrance of me." I cannot throw away part of the Bible because somebody has misinterpreted it! So I cannot, I must not, turn my back upon the marvelous teaching of Pentecost, that Christians must be filled with the Holy Spirit if they are to do the work of God acceptably, even though some have gone to fanatical extremes concerning the doctrine of the Holy Spirit.

III. Pentecost Was NOT the Beginning of a New Dispensation

Many preachers and teachers, including this author, have sometimes spoken of "this dispensation of the Holy Spirit." That is a misleading statement. Actually, no new dispensation began at Pentecost. And the reason this is a dangerous mistake is that it leads people away from understanding the meaning of Pentecost. People who think of Pentecost as simply the technical beginning of a new dispensation miss the lesson God gives us there. A dispensational event, long past, has no special message for us, they think. Hence, they do not learn to wait on God for soul-winning and revival power as did the apostles and others before Pentecost. Being absorbed in a false meaning for Pentecost, they miss the true meaning.

It is true that Pentecost is the beginning of the fulfillment of the prophecy of Joel:

"And it shall come to pass in the last days, saith God, I will pour out of my Spirit upon all flesh: and your sons and your daughters shall prophesy, and your young men shall see visions, and your old men shall dream dreams: And on my servants and on my handmaidens I will pour out in those days of my Spirit; and they shall prophesy: And I will shew wonders in heaven above, and signs in the earth beneath; blood, and fire, and vapour of smoke: The sun shall be turned into darkness, and the moon into blood, before that great and notable day of the Lord come: And it shall come to pass, that whosoever shall call on the name of the Lord shall be saved."— Acts 2:17-21.

Peter said, "This is that which was spoken by the prophet Joel," and quoted the above passage. It is true, in a sense, that the great time of the spread of the Gospel over the whole world began at Pentecost. But it is not true that at Pentecost a new dispensation began, a new way of work by the Holy Spirit.

1. Pentecost Is Not the First Time That Christians Were Filled With the Holy Ghost

At Pentecost "they were all filled with the Holy Ghost," says Acts 2:4. And through the Book of Acts we have repeated statements that

Christians were filled with the Holy Spirit. (See Acts 4:8, Acts 4:31, Acts 6:5, Acts 7:55, Acts 9:17, Acts 11:24.) With this in mind, the revered Dr. A. T. Pierson expressed the feeling of many when he commented on the first verse in the Book of Acts. There Luke says, "The former treatise have I made, O Theophilus, of all that Jesus began both to do and teach." And Dr. Pierson said that in the Gospels Jesus *began* the work; in the Book of Acts the Holy Spirit *continued* it. But he missed the point of that passage. The clear teaching of the context and of other Scripture passages is that Jesus did all His work through the power of the Holy Spirit and that when He was taken away, the disciples could do exactly the same kind of work through the same power of the Holy Spirit. Jesus said in John 14:12, "He that believeth on me, the works that I do shall he do also; and greater works than these shall he do; because I go unto my Father." If you have thought that people were not filled with the Holy Spirit before Pentecost, then you should remember Luke 1:15 where the angel said that John the Baptist should "be filled with the Holy Ghost, even from his mother's womb." And the purpose was exactly the same as the purpose of Pentecost, for the following verse says, "And many of the children of Israel shall he turn to the Lord their God." The ministry of John the Baptist had exactly the same power as Peter's ministry and the ministry of others later, at Pentecost.

In Luke 1:41 we are told that "Elisabeth was filled with the Holy Ghost," and in Luke 1:67 we are told that "Zacharias was filled with the Holy Ghost." In Luke 3:22 we are told that "the Holy Ghost descended in a bodily shape like a dove" upon Jesus at His baptism. Luke 4:1 says, "And Jesus being full of the Holy Ghost returned from Jordan." Luke 4:14 says, "And Jesus returned in the power of the Spirit into Galilee." Jesus preached in the synagogue from the text in Isaiah 61:1 which says, "The Spirit of the Lord GOD is upon me; because the LORD hath anointed me to preach...," and then said, "This day is this scripture fulfilled in your ears" (Luke 4:16–21).

It is obvious from these Scriptures that the fullness of the Spirit was upon John the Baptist, upon Elisabeth, upon Zacharias, and upon Jesus during the days preceding Pentecost.

But in the same passage that tells us that John the Baptist would be filled with the Holy Ghost from his mother's womb and that he should turn many of the children of Israel to the Lord their God, the next verse tells us that John the Baptist had exactly the same Spirit and power as Elijah: "And he shall go before him in the spirit and power of

Elias, to turn the hearts of the fathers to the children, and the disobedient to the wisdom of the just; to make ready a people prepared for the
Lord" (Luke 1:17). Elijah and Old Testament prophets were filled with
the Holy Spirit long before Pentecost. And we are expressly told in
Exodus 35:30,31: "See, the LORD hath called by name Bezaleel the son
of Uri, the son of Hur, of the tribe of Judah; And he hath filled him
with the spirit of God." The fullness of the Spirit, then, which the
waiting disciples received at Pentecost, did not inaugurate a new dispensation in that sense. People had been filled with the Holy Spirit
many times before. Being filled with the Holy Spirit was not a new
thing in the world.

Pentecost began the great era of revivals. But there had been
revivals before, like those with Elijah on Mount Carmel, of John the
Baptist at the river Jordan, like the revivals under Ezra and Josiah.

It is true that Pentecost was the beginning of the last days when
"whosoever shall call on the name of the Lord shall be saved," according to Joel's prophecy. But we must not think that no one was saved
before this time. Even in the matter of the fullness of the Spirit and
power for soul winning, Pentecost did not inaugurate a new dispensation. It was simply a time when people of God waited upon Him until
He graciously filled them with power to carry out His command of winning souls.

2. Pentecost Was Not the Beginning of the Indwelling of the Holy Spirit in Bodies of Christians

There is a widespread belief that the Holy Spirit descended at
Pentecost and there moved into the bodies of Christians and that
therefore a new dispensation in regard to the Holy Spirit began at
Pentecost. But this impression is a mistaken one, as I believe you will
easily see from the Scriptures.

It is true that once the Holy Spirit was *with* Christians and that now
He is *in* Christians. That is what Jesus said about the Holy Spirit in
John 14:16,17:

*"And I will pray the Father, and he shall give you another Comforter, that he
may abide with you for ever; Even the Spirit of truth; whom the world cannot
receive, because it seeth him not, neither knoweth him: but ye know him; for he
dwelleth with you, and shall be in you."*

The Holy Spirit then dwelled *with* the disciples, and Jesus said that
later the Holy Spirit should be *in* the disciples. At a certain time the
Holy Spirit came in to abide *in* the bodies of Christians.

This is a blessed truth that Christians ought never to forget. First Corinthians 6:19,20 says:

"What? know ye not that your body is the temple of the Holy Ghost which is in you, which ye have of God, and ye are not your own? For ye are bought with a price: therefore glorify God in your body, and in your spirit, which are God's."

Second Corinthians 6:16 says, "And what agreement hath the temple of God with idols? for ye are the temple of the living God."

First Corinthians 3:16 says, "Know ye not that ye are the temple of God, and that the Spirit of God dwelleth in you?"

And Romans 8:9,10 has a beautiful statement:

"But ye are not in the flesh, but in the Spirit, if so be that the Spirit of God dwell in you. Now if any man have not the Spirit of Christ, he is none of his. And if Christ be in you, the body is dead because of sin; but the Spirit is life because of righteousness."

We can thank God for this wonderful truth, that now the Spirit of God dwells in the body of every Christian. BUT THIS DISPENSATIONAL CHANGE DID NOT BEGIN AT PENTECOST!

The clear teaching of the Word of God is that the new dispensation (when the Holy Spirit should dwell in the body of every believer) began the day Jesus rose from the dead. Jesus Himself promised this in John 7:37–39:

"In the last day, that great day of the feast, Jesus stood and cried, saying, If any man thirst, let him come unto me, and drink. He that believeth on me, as the scripture hath said, out of his belly shall flow rivers of living water. (But this spake he of the Spirit, which they that believe on him should receive: for the Holy Ghost was not yet given; because that Jesus was not yet glorified.)"

The Holy Spirit was to come into people's bodies and make His headquarters there. He should flow out in His fullness from the innermost beings of Christians like a stream of thirst-quenching water. But the giving of the Holy Spirit, in the sense of His indwelling, in the sense of His making His headquarters in the human body and working out from the human body, was delayed. "For the Holy Ghost was not yet given; because that Jesus was not yet glorified." When the Lord Jesus was glorified—that is, raised from the dead in a glorified body— then the Holy Spirit was to be given to live in the bodies of Christians.

As the Gospel of John records this promise, the same Gospel records its fulfillment. In John 20:19–22 we are told how, the day Jesus rose from the dead, He appeared to the disciples and breathed on them and said, "Receive ye the Holy Ghost." Jesus breathed on them there, and they received the Holy Ghost.

In the Bible, remember that the Greek word for *Spirit* and the word for *wind* or *breath* are the same. Jesus literally breathed upon these disciples the Holy Spirit of God. They received Him, and He, the third person of the Trinity, came into their bodies to dwell.

It is quite clear, then, that the dispensational change, when the Holy Spirit, instead of being *with* Christians, lived *in* Christians, took place the day Jesus rose from the dead, when the disciples received the Holy Ghost to live in their bodies. It was only about four days after Jesus had promised in John 14 that the Holy Spirit would abide in them, that "he dwelleth *with* you, and shall be *in* you" (John 14:16,17). We may properly understand that when the Holy Spirit came into the bodies of these apostles to dwell, He came into the bodies of all the other Christians in the world. And from that day to this, at the time one is converted, born again, his body becomes the temple of the Holy Spirit. This same Holy Spirit who regenerates the soul moves in and makes the body His habitation, His temple. But that dispensational change took place the day Jesus rose from the dead, and not at Pentecost!

When Jesus told the disciples, "And, behold, I send the promise of my Father upon you: but tarry ye in the city of Jerusalem, until ye be endued with power from on high" (Luke 24:49), He did not mean that they were to wait for the indwelling presence of the Holy Spirit. Already He dwelt in their bodies. Jesus had already breathed upon them and said, "Receive ye the Holy Ghost." The Holy Spirit was already with them to comfort them, to guide them into the truth. He was an abiding Person, living in their bodies. And yet they needed to wait for the fullness of power, power to make them soul winners, power for revival, power to carry out the command of the Great Commission Jesus had given them.

It is a great mistake to dismiss Pentecost as simply being the inauguration of a new dispensation. It was not that. It was a great revival when God's people were endued with power from on high to win souls.

When the eleven disciples, the women who had stayed near Jesus, His mother and His half brothers waited in the Upper Room before Pentecost, it is said, "These all continued with one accord in prayer and supplication" (Acts 1:14). But they were not waiting simply for a new dispensation to start! They were not waiting for some technical change in the way God deals with men. They were waiting for power—

the power that would make them witnesses in Jerusalem, in all Judaea, and in Samaria, and unto the uttermost part of the earth—to make them effective soul winners.

IV. The Teaching That "Pentecost Is the Birthday of the Church" Wholly Misrepresents the Meaning of Pentecost

Multiplied thousands of Christian people have been taught that "Pentecost is the birthday of the church." They have been taught that at Pentecost the group of Christians were molded into one unit, one organism, and the church, the mystical body of Christ, began. Now the date for the beginning of the church is not given in the Bible and is perhaps not a matter of much importance. Certainly I would not raise a quarrel with my brethren who see the matter differently than I; I would not even argue the matter except for a very great harm that has resulted from this false teaching, because when people think about Pentecost they think of it only as the technical beginning of the body of Christ, the church. If the church is already begun, it will never originate again, and so, they think, the blessing of Pentecost can never be repeated. They therefore entirely miss the teaching of the Scriptures, that Pentecost was a model revival ("a specimen revival," D. L. Moody called it) in which God's people, at the beginning of this great era of preaching the Gospel to all the world, waited on God until they were empowered from on high and then with that power won three thousand souls in a day. I am distressed not simply because people think the church began at Pentecost. I am distressed because they thus miss the clear teaching of the Word of God that it is impossible for a Christian to win souls without the power of the Holy Spirit. The lesson of Pentecost, that God's children can wait on Him and have His power, is missed because people see other things in the events at Pentecost than those the Bible itself emphasizes. But I believe that several facts faced honestly and prayerfully here will show open-minded Christians that to talk about Pentecost as the birthday of the church is wholly missing the point of the Scriptures.

1. The Bible Nowhere Says That the Church Began at Pentecost

Suppose some honest Christian will not be persuaded that the church did not begin at Pentecost. All right; let us not quarrel about the matter. If you insist on believing that the church began at Pentecost, I will not be distressed, provided you take the Bible attitude about the matter and say nothing about it. In all the discussions about Pentecost—when John the Baptist foretold it, when Jesus commanded the disciples to tarry for it, when the prayer meeting itself is described, and later when Pentecost really came and marvelous results were obtained—there was not a single verse of Scripture that said that Pentecost would be the birthday of the church. When John the Baptist said, 'One cometh after me who shall baptize you with the Holy Ghost,' he said nothing about the origin of the church. When Jesus said, "Tarry ye in the city of Jerusalem, until ye be endued with power from on high," He said nothing about the origin of the body of Christ. In the first chapter of Acts, when the command of Jesus and the Great Commission are recounted again, no word is said to warn them that the church would begin. Rather, Jesus commanded them, "Wait for the promise of the Father, which...ye have heard of me. For John truly baptized with water; but ye shall be baptized with the Holy Ghost not many days hence" (Acts 1:4,5). And again He said: "But ye shall receive power, after that the Holy Ghost is come upon you: and ye shall be witnesses unto me both in Jerusalem, and in all Judæa, and in Samaria, and unto the uttermost part of the earth" (Acts 1:8).

The second chapter of Acts describes the events at Pentecost—the blessed oneness of heart of the disciples, the tongues like fire resting upon them, the miraculous gift that allowed them to speak to sixteen different nationalities in the languages of people who were present so that they heard in their own languages the wonderful works of God. There we are told of the sermon of Peter, his warning that people should repent, his promise that this same gift was 'for all that are afar, as many as the Lord should call.' There we are told of the blessed results, with some three thousand joining with the Christians that day and being baptized. We are told of the joyous fellowship and the continued blessing. But not a word is said about the church being born at Pentecost!

Throughout the rest of the New Testament, many references are made to Pentecost, or to those early days of the church. But no word is said about the church beginning at that date.

Now the sensible way for a Christian to act on such a matter is to put the emphasis where the Bible puts it. If the Bible does not speak of Pentecost as the birthday of the church, then it is a false emphasis, a misapplication of Scripture and certain to obscure the meaning of what God has said, if we talk much about a church being born at Pentecost when the Bible itself says nothing about it.

Paul has much to say about the church in his epistles. Where does Paul ever say that the church began at Pentecost? He does not say it! Then suppose we be Pauline in our emphasis and methods—all of us Christians—and talk about the same things he talks about when we discuss the church and Pentecost! The Bible never, in a single verse, says nor even clearly implies that the church began at Pentecost. Practically all the talk of the Bible about Pentecost is of the coming of power to win souls and the precious, glorious result of that soul-winning power upon the testimony of Spirit-filled Christians. Let us put the emphasis where the Bible puts it! If the Bible does not talk about the church beginning at Pentecost, then let us likewise avoid such talk.

2. "Baptized Into One Body" in I Corinthians 12:12,13 Has No Reference to Pentecost and the Origin of the Church

The Plymouth Brethren have done great service in stimulating study of the Bible. Darby and other leaders among this denomination (which does not like to be called a denomination) have turned many people to studying the Word of God. For this we thank God. They have heavily emphasized the truth that all saved people are in the body of Christ and that membership in any earthly denomination or human organization does not save, does not help save. But it is only fair to say that these dear people have stimulated the ultradispensational view-point and that their teaching has tended toward division and toward great overemphasis of some truths to the neglect of others. As I under-stand the teachings of Darby and the Plymouth Brethren, these dear people have widely stressed the teaching that the church began at Pentecost; that it is entirely a new thing, unknown before that time; that it is a mystery revealed to Paul alone of New Testament writers. And the tendency has been for many of the Brethren assemblies to contend that their assemblies alone adequately represent the church of Jesus Christ on earth.

This teaching that the church began at Pentecost is often based on I Corinthians 12:12,13, which reads as follows:

"For as the body is one, and hath many members, and all the members of that one body, being many, are one body: so also is Christ. For by one Spirit are we all baptized into one body, whether we be Jews or Gentiles, whether we be bond or free; and have been all made to drink into one Spirit."

Certainly the body is one. All Christians are members of Christ's mystical body. One who is saved thus becomes a member of the body of Christ. It is the Holy Spirit who makes the new convert a child of God, imparts the divine nature, makes him a part of the mystical body of Christ which will be caught up to meet the Saviour at His coming. All this is taught or implied in these verses.

But does the Scripture here refer to the origin of the body of Christ? I insist that it does not. Does the Scripture here teach that that body began at Pentecost? To ask the question is almost to answer it. I insist that it does not.

Notice part of verse 13: "For by one Spirit are we all baptized into one body." The one connection between this Scripture and Pentecost is that two important words are used here, "baptized" and "Spirit," which were also used in discussing Pentecost. Here people are baptized by the Spirit into one body. At Pentecost, we are told in Acts 1:5, the disciples were baptized into the Spirit Himself (there called the Holy Ghost).

Compare Acts 1:5 with I Corinthians 12:13, and you will see that being baptized in the Holy Spirit at Pentecost and baptized by the Spirit into the body of Christ are two different baptisms.

Acts 1:5 says, "...but ye shall be baptized with the Holy Ghost not many days hence." This referred to the fullness of the Spirit for soul-winning power at Pentecost. The disciples were to be overwhelmed, covered with the Holy Spirit, and hence baptized in the Holy Ghost, at Pentecost.

First Corinthians 12:13: "For by one Spirit are we all baptized into one body."

The two phrases are much alike: "baptized with the Holy Ghost" and "by one Spirit...baptized into one body." In the Greek New Testament, as originally written, the phrases are even more alike, because the preposition in the two phrases, "*with* the Holy Ghost" and "*by* one Spirit," in each case is the Greek word *en*. So Plymouth Brethren Bible teachers and many others following them thought that I Corinthians 12:13 referred to the same baptism of the Holy Spirit as Acts 1:5. They thought that the two baptisms mentioned in Acts 1:5 and I Corinthians 12:13 were the same baptism. But I believe we can show that they are wrong for several reasons:

1. First, the translators of the King James Version of the Bible thought they should be translated differently. Acts 1:5 is "baptized with the Holy Ghost." First Corinthians 12:13 has it, "For by one Spirit are we all baptized into one body." One is not wise to laugh off the united

agreement of the many noble and scholarly men who made the Authorized or King James translation of the Bible.

2. A newer version, largely translated by modernists, the Revised Standard Version, now says, "By one Spirit" in I Corinthians 12:13. The pressure of opinion was so great that in the American Standard Revision the translation was changed to, "For IN one Spirit are we all baptized into one body." Hence, many Bible teachers, particularly followers of J. N. Darby and Bullinger, who did not believe in a definite enduement of power for soul winning and particularly were anxious to combat the Pentecostal movement and the tongues heresy, insisted that the Holy Spirit in I Corinthians 12:13 was not mentioned as the agent by whom Christians were put into the body of Christ, but that that Scripture simply referred to being baptized in the Holy Ghost as at Pentecost. Hence, they believed that in a potential sense every Christian of the future was baptized in the Holy Spirit at Pentecost and that no such enduement should be sought now. They said that the translation, "Baptized by one Spirit" in I Corinthians 12:13, as in the Authorized Version, was not a proper translation.

We do not recommend the Revised Standard Version. We do not trust unconverted men, modernists, to translate accurately certain passages which are questioned generally by unbelievers. But we believe the RSV translators were unbiased in translating I Corinthians 12:12,13 from the Greek word en to "by" in the English language. And in this new translation the eminent scholars change the wording of I Corinthians 12:13 back to the wording of the Authorized Version, in this disputed matter. The new translation reads, "For by one Spirit." In other words, I Corinthians really says and really means that the Holy Spirit is the agent who buries a new convert into the body of Christ, making him a part of the same.

And now most of the world's most eminent Bible scholarship agrees, along with the King James Version translators, that in I Corinthians 12:13 the Holy Spirit is mentioned as an agent of the baptism into the body of Christ, while in Acts 1:5 the Holy Spirit is the element in which Christ submerges and covers the Christian with power for soul winning. The baptism by the Spirit into the body of Christ, mentioned in I Corinthians 12:13, is not the baptism in the Spirit which occurred at Pentecost.

3. Famous Greek authorities clearly hold that the Greek preposition en is often properly translated in English as "by." THAYER'S Greek-English Lexicon of the New Testament, the greatest of all, defines en thus:

"*en*, a preposition taking the dative after it...Eng. *in, on, at, with, by, among.*" Thayer has a long discussion of this word and says, "Akin is its use...of the instrument or means by or with which anything is accomplished...where we say *with, by means of, by (through)*." Many examples from the New Testament Greek are given to prove the point that *en* would properly be translated dative of the instrument, means, or agency.

Dr. A. T. Robertson, famous Greek scholar, in his monumental Greek grammar, gives a number of examples of the use of the preposition *en* in Greek which, he says, "are fairly equivalent to the purely instrumental case." Then he says, "But there are real instances enough," and he gives a number of examples.

My Donnegan *Greek-English Lexicon*, over one hundred years old, says that "*en* means 'through,' 'by means of,' or 'with,' when a means, or cause is assigned, this especially in Pind., also in Thuc., where in other cases a dat. alone."

So the translators of the King James Version, the translators of the newest Revised Standard Version, with other leading Greek authorities, show that it is proper to translate I Corinthians 12:13 as saying "*by* one Spirit." The Holy Spirit there is the agent who submerges a Christian into the body of Christ, making him a part of the body which will be called out at the rapture.

4. A careful study of the way the Greek proposition *en* is used in the New Testament shows that it must be translated "by" in many cases. It is the preposition of agency. Bible examples are more important than anybody's opinion.

For example, in Matthew 12:24, the Pharisees said, "This fellow doth not cast out devils, but by Beelzebub the prince of the devils." "By" is here a translation of the Greek word *en*.

In Matthew 12:27 Jesus answered, "And if I by Beelzebub cast out devils, by whom do your children cast them out?" The word "by" in both cases in this verse is a translation of *en*. The word "by" in Matthew 12:28 is used likewise.

In Mark 3:22, *en* is translated "by," in the matter of casting out devils.

There are numerous other examples:

Matthew 17:21: "Howbeit this kind goeth not out but *by* prayer and fasting."

Mark 12:36: "David himself said *by* the Holy Ghost...."

Luke 4:1, speaking of Jesus, says that He "was led *by* the Spirit into the wilderness."

In Acts 13:39 the Scripture says, "And *by* him all that believe are justified from all things, from which ye could not be justified *by* the law of Moses." Believing sinners are justified by Jesus Christ.

Galatians 3:11: "But that no man is justified *by* the law in the sight of God...."

Ephesians 3:5: "...as it is now revealed unto his holy apostles and prophets *by* the *Spirit*."

In all these quoted verses above, the word "by" is a translation of the Greek preposition *en*.

Young's *Analytical Concordance,* in listing the 142 times that the preposition *en* is translated "by" in the King James Version, gives the following meaning for the Greek word *en:* "in, by, with."

Thirty-seven times in our Bible the Greek preposition *en* is translated "through." Here Young's *Analytical Concordance* again defines this Greek word *en* as "in, by, with, among." And these translations "through" usually mean "by," or "by the agency of." See "through" in Matthew 9:34, Luke 10:17, Luke 11:15, Luke 11:18. See "sanctify them through thy truth" in John 17:17. See "that believing ye might have life through his name" in John 20:31. See "preached through Jesus the resurrection" in Acts 4:2. See "alive unto God through Jesus Christ our Lord" in Romans 6:11.

It is certainly proper then, you see, to translate the Greek word *en* as "by" or "through." With that in mind, you see why the translators of the King James Version of the Bible have translated thus: "For *by* one Spirit are we all baptized into one body."

In I Corinthians 12:13 we are told that all Christians have been placed *by* the Holy Spirit into the body of Christ. But at Pentecost, Jesus said in Acts 1:5, the disciples should be baptized *in* the Holy Ghost—that is, covered, overwhelmed with His mighty enduement of power.

But one soon sees by comparison that the two Scriptures are not talking about the same thing. Similarity in terms may be misunderstood if one does not take a little heed to the exact wording.

In Mark 1:8, John said of Jesus, "I indeed have baptized you with water: but he shall baptize you with the Holy Ghost." In Acts 1:5 Jesus said, "For John truly baptized with water; but ye shall be baptized with the Holy Ghost not many days hence." First Corinthians 12:13 says,

"For by one Spirit are we all baptized into one body." Two verses talk about two baptisms. The other verse talks about another baptism. Here are three kinds of baptism pictured:

(a) *John* baptized converts in water.

(b) *Jesus* baptized the disciples in the Holy Spirit at Pentecost.

(c) The *Holy Spirit* baptized the Christians at Corinth into the body of Christ.

In these three kinds of baptism there are three agents who did the baptizing: In (a), John the Baptist did the baptizing. In (b), Jesus did the baptizing. In (c), it is the Holy Spirit Himself who acts as the agent to take the newborn child of God and put him into the body of Christ.

To be immersed, or covered, or buried, or overwhelmed in water, physically is one kind of baptism. To be immersed, or buried, or covered, or overwhelmed with the Holy Spirit poured out upon a Christian is another kind of baptism. To be immersed, or covered, or buried into the body of Christ, becoming a part of that body, never to be taken out, is still another kind of baptism. You see, the baptism into the body of Christ did not happen at Pentecost except for those saved that day. It was not the same as the baptism in the Holy Spirit.

First Peter 2:5 says, "Ye also, as lively stones, are built up a spiritual house, an holy priesthood." The Holy Spirit is building a house out of living stones. The house is the mystical body of Christ, the church. It is built as converts, born-again people, born of the Spirit, are being made partakers of the divine nature. Every one of these converts, at the moment of his salvation, is built into the wall, surrounded, covered— that is, baptized into the wall. Every Christian is put into the body of Christ by the Holy Spirit. That does not refer to what happened at Pentecost. It simply refers to what happens to every repenting sinner when he is born again and is made a part of the body of Christ by the work of the Holy Spirit. Notice the difference: the Holy Spirit is the agent who regenerates a sinner and makes him a part of the body of Christ at the time of regeneration, but Christ is the agent who poured out the Holy Spirit upon His people at Pentecost, filling them, overflowing them, covering them in the Holy Spirit to empower them for service. It is a serious mistake to confuse what happened at Pentecost, when Christ baptized people with the Holy Spirit, with what happened to the Corinthian believers as described in I Corinthians 12:12, 13, when the Holy Spirit made Christians and put them into the body of Christ, making them a part of this living house, this mystical body of Christ.

Aside from the fact that the Bible is speaking in I Corinthians

12:12,13 of an entirely different baptism than that which occurred at Pentecost, the persons addressed and the time mentioned obviously do not refer to Pentecost. First Corinthians is primarily addressed "unto the church of God which is at Corinth" (I Cor. 1:2). None of these Christians, as far as we know, had been present at Pentecost, which had occurred some twenty-five years earlier—before they were ever converted, before even Paul the apostle, who had first established the church at Corinth and won souls there, had himself been saved. So when Paul said, "For by one Spirit are we all baptized into one body," he did not refer to anything that happened at Pentecost. None of these people were present at Pentecost. And those of us to whom the epistle is secondarily addressed were not at Pentecost. All of us who are saved people have been baptized into the body of Christ, but for me that did not happen at Pentecost. For the reader it did not happen at Pentecost, just as for the Christian at Corinth it had not happened at Pentecost.

Someone has said that "*potentially*, every Christian was baptized in the Spirit at Pentecost." That is a doctrine not anywhere stated in the Bible and certainly not stated in I Corinthians 12:13. The danger of such a teaching is that it leaves us feeling that whatever Pentecost meant, we have already gotten all the benefits from it that we can ever get—we cannot have the blessing those Christians had because the blessing of Pentecost can never be repeated. The doctrine that all Christians were potentially baptized into the body of Christ at Pentecost, long before they were born, robs us of the blessing that we might get from the Scripture and makes us miss the point that Jesus Himself stressed. Before starting out to preach the Gospel to every creature, the disciples were to tarry in Jerusalem until they received power from on high. That is what Jesus plainly said in Luke 24:46–49. The disciples were to receive power when the Holy Spirit came upon them, and they were to be witnesses unto Him in Jerusalem, in all Judaea and unto the uttermost part of the earth. That is what Jesus Himself expressly promised in Acts 1:8. When the power of the Holy Spirit came at Pentecost, we are expressly told that then these Spirit-filled disciples spake for the Lord as the Spirit gave them utterance (whatever the language) and three thousand people were converted and the great worldwide, soul-winning ministry of the church was well and auspiciously begun. How foolish, how harmful, and I would almost say how inexcusable, for us to miss the clear teaching that Jesus gave about the meaning of Pentecost, while trying to establish the fact that the church was all baptized in the Spirit potentially and that the church was thus formed and organized or originated at Pentecost! Actually, the Bible says nothing like that. The Bible does not say that the church originated at Pentecost. The Bible does plainly say that the disciples there received soul-winning power.

3. The Church Was Not "a Wholly New Thing," Not the Mystery Revealed to Paul, So Was Not Begun at Pentecost

The Scofield Reference Bible is the best reference Bible in the world. I use it constantly. I have been greatly helped by many of the notes. However, on this matter the Scofield Reference Bible, I believe, is in error, following the teachings of Darby. Ephesians, chapter 3, in the Scofield Bible is given the heading "The church a mystery hidden from past ages." And then at the bottom of the page there is a footnote on Ephesians 3:6 which says:

"That the Gentiles were to be saved was no mystery (Rom. 9:24–33; 10:19–21). The mystery 'hid in God' was the divine purpose to make of Jew and Gentile a wholly new thing—'the church, which is his [Christ's] body,' formed by the baptism with the Holy Spirit (I Cor. 12:12,13) and in which the earthly distinction of Jew and Gentile disappears (Eph. 2:14,15; Col. 3:10,11). The revelation of this mystery, which was foretold but not explained by Christ (Mt. 16:18), was committed to Paul. In his writings alone we find the doctrine, position, walk, and destiny of the church."

But was the church a wholly new thing? Was it never revealed before Paul? Was it never begun before Pentecost? As humbly as I may, and begging the forbearance of the godly men with whom I differ, I think I can show that these notes, patterned after the teachings of Darby and the Plymouth Brethren, are mistaken.

Ephesians, chapter 3, does speak of a mystery. What was it? Read verses 1 to 6:

"For this cause I Paul, the prisoner of Jesus Christ for you Gentiles, If ye have heard of the dispensation of the grace of God which is given me to you-ward: How that by revelation he made known unto me the mystery; (as I wrote afore in few words, Whereby, when ye read, ye may understand my knowledge in the mystery of Christ) Which in other ages was not made known unto the sons of men, as it is now revealed unto his holy apostles and prophets by the Spirit; That the Gentiles should be fellowheirs, and of the same body, and partakers of his promise in Christ by the gospel."

Read those verses carefully. Verse 2 says a dispensation of the grace of God was given to Paul to preach, that God gave Paul a revelation and made known to him a certain mystery which in ages past was not revealed but is now revealed. Note, however, that the mystery was not revealed to Paul alone. "It is now revealed unto his holy apostles and prophets by the Spirit," says verse 5. Not only Paul, but all the twelve apostles, all the prophets of New Testament times, all those who had heard Christ explain the Scriptures, understood the mystery which Paul was given to preach and teach at Ephesus, since he first carried the Gospel there and was the apostle to the Gentiles.

And what was the mystery? Was the mystery "a wholly new thing— 'the church, which is his [Christ's] body,'" as the note in the Scofield Bible says? No, that is not what the Scripture says. The mystery is described in Ephesians 3:6 as follows: "That the Gentiles should be fellowheirs, and of the same body, and partakers of his promise in Christ by the gospel."

There was no mystery that there would be a body of people saved, made Christ's own and eventually taken up by Christ to be with Him forever. (That is what is meant by the church.) That was no mystery. The mystery was "that the Gentiles should be fellowheirs, and of the same body" as the Jews, "partakers of his promise in Christ by the gospel." It is true that some Gentiles were saved in the Old Testament times. It is true that Old Testament prophets made it quite clear that the whole earth should eventually be full of the knowledge of the Lord and that Gentiles should turn to the Lord. But it is equally clear that the Jews never understood this and never believed that Gentiles would be taken into the fellowship of Christ on exactly the same basis as the Jews. The mystery was that Gentiles would be converted and be on exactly the same footing as Jews and that in Christ there would be neither male nor female, bond nor free, Jew nor Gentile.

And since Paul was the apostle to the Gentiles, it was given to him primarily to teach this fact, that the Gentiles were received on exactly the same basis as the Jews and made partakers of the same promise of the Gospel which all the apostles knew about, which all the prophets of the Old Testament times knew about.

What was made clear in the Old Testament was that Christ would be one day the King of the Jews and reign at Jerusalem and that His kingdom should cover the earth. But there are many evidences that that kingdom will be largely a Jewish kingdom. Christ, of the seed of David, will sit on David's throne at Jerusalem. The twelve apostles will sit on twelve thrones judging the twelve tribes of Israel (Matt. 19:28). Then the "law shall go forth of Zion, and the word of the LORD from

Jerusalem" (Micah 4:2). It was not made clear in the Old Testament that there would be a long interval before Christ returned to reign, after His first coming. It was not made quite clear that the saints would be caught out to meet Christ in the air. Hence, the state of things during all this age when Christ is rejected of the world and the state of things when we are caught up into the air to meet Him—that Gentiles are equal to Jews when converted and all are alike in the same body of Christ, the church—that was the mystery not revealed in times past but revealed in the New Testament to all the apostles and prophets by Jesus Christ. Gentiles were now to hear the Gospel like Jews, be in the same body. That was a mystery Paul was now explaining to his converts at Ephesus. They, like converted Jews, were members of the body of Christ.

There is no evidence, then, that the church began at Pentecost as a new thing.

In the letter to the Ephesians, Paul had much to say about the beautiful, thrilling fact that the Gentiles who once were far off were now made nigh by the blood of Christ. But read Ephesians 2:11–22. There the Apostle Paul, by divine inspiration, is speaking of the church as clearly as in the following third chapter. And there the Scripture makes quite clear his meaning. Verse 12 says that the Gentiles were before "without Christ, being aliens from the commonwealth of Israel, and strangers from the covenants of promise, having no hope, and without God in the world." The Scripture is not saying that there were none before who were in the body of Christ, taken close to His heart, possessing His life, the body of which He was the head. No, no! Ephesians 2:12 is simply saying that it had not before been made clear that Gentiles—heathen, despised Gentiles—were now to be made as near as the beloved Jews, the chosen of God. Verse 13 says, "But now in Christ Jesus ye who sometimes were far off are made nigh by the blood of Christ."

Ephesians 2:16–18 says:

"And that he might reconcile both unto God in one body by the cross, having slain the enmity thereby: And came and preached peace to you which were afar off, and to them that were nigh. For through him we both have access by one Spirit unto the Father."

The great new lesson here is not that there is a body, but the great, joyful news is that Gentiles who trust in Christ are now made nigh and the enmity between Jews and Gentiles is slain by the cross. Gentiles who once were far off and Jews that are nigh are thus made one when they come by one Spirit unto the Father. Both are together in the same body. That is the mystery now made clear: Gentiles are now in the same body before thought of as a Jewish body.

At Pentecost many were saved, but it was not especially made clear there that Gentiles had the same privileges, stood on the same footing as Jews. That was not the issue at Pentecost. In fact, not until years later, when Peter went to Cornelius (and nearly got pitched out of the Jerusalem church on his ear for being presumptuous, until he explained how God had forced him to take the Gospel to the Gentiles), was this matter made clear, that Gentiles were in the church exactly like Jews. To say that Pentecost was "the birthday of the church" does not at all explain what happened there. And, in my humble opinion, there are no Scriptures that justify such a statement.

4. The Church, the Body of Christ, Is Made Up of All Those Who Were Ever Saved, Both Old Testament and New Testament Saints, and Began Long Before Pentecost

From the above Scriptures, surely you have seen that the body of Christ is not just a new thing first revealed to Paul, not just a new thing which began at Pentecost. The one hundred twenty who were in the Upper Room when the great blessing of Pentecost came were already Christ's. They were already His forever. They were already the temples of the Holy Spirit. They were already united in heart, of "one accord," as the Scripture a number of times says (Acts 1:14; Acts 2:1; Acts 2:46, etc.). It seems rather foolish to claim that if one of these disciples, waiting in the Upper Room as the Lord commanded, continuing steadfastly with the others in prayer and supplication, had died the day before Pentecost, he would not have been in the church, the body of Christ. A Christian who was saved was just as much saved before Pentecost as after it. One saved in the Old Testament was saved the same way as in the New Testament. Peter, in Acts 10:43, makes it clear that people were saved just alike in all dispensations and in all generations and that every prophet agrees on this. "To him give all the prophets witness, that through his name whosoever believeth in him shall receive remission of sins."

What does "the church" mean? The word church is a translation of the Greek word ekklesia. That word means a called-out assembly. For example, the nation Israel, called out of Egypt and assembled in the wilderness at Mount Sinai, is called "the church in the wilderness" in Acts 7:38. Israel, a called-out assembly, was literally a church.

New Testament congregations of Christians—that is, called out of their homes and, in a figurative sense, called out of the world and assembled together—were called "churches" in the New Testament.

In Acts 19 there are three startling uses of this Greek word *ekklesia* which is everywhere else in the New Testament translated "church." But there, in Acts 19:32,39,41, the word is translated "assembly" and in these three cases refers to the mob assembled to kill the Apostle Paul and his companions! That mob was not composed of Christians, but they were a called-out assembly. So they were called by the Greek word *ekklesia*, which means a called-out assembly.

The word *ekklesia*, which in every other occurrence in the New Testament is translated "church," does not mean an assembly of a particular kind of people. Israel at Mount Sinai was a church, though it included saved people and lost people, good and bad. But they were a called-out group assembled together. That assembly or mob called out at Ephesus to kill the Christian leaders because they preached against the worship of the goddess Diana, whose shrines the silversmiths there made—that group of people was also a called-out assembly. You see, the word *church* simply refers to a called-out assembly of people.

We should remember that the word *church* in the Bible never means a denomination. The term is always used of a local assembly of people, except when it refers to a great future called-out assembly, including all the saints called out to meet Christ at the rapture. When the Lord Jesus calls all His own up into the air to meet Him at His coming, then that will be a called-out assembly; and so the Bible speaks of this group, including all the saved people of all ages, past and present and future, as a *church*.

Hebrews 12:22–24 speaks in detail of this called-out assembly, those who will meet together with Jesus in the air and be taken with Him into glory. After saying that the believer does not come to Mount Sinai and is not under the law, this Scripture says:

"But ye are come unto mount Sion, and unto the city of the living God, the heavenly Jerusalem, and to an innumerable company of angels, To the general assembly and church of the firstborn, which are written in heaven, and to God the Judge of all, and to the spirits of just men made perfect, And to Jesus the mediator of the new covenant, and to the blood of sprinkling, that speaketh better things than that of Abel."

Notice that Christians are to come *"to the general assembly and church of the firstborn, which are written in heaven, and to God the Judge of all, and to the spirits of just men made perfect, And to Jesus the* mediator of the new covenant, and to the blood of sprinkling, that speaketh better things than that of Abel." It is obvious that the Lord speaks of the whole assembly that will be gathered in Heaven. Since they will be called out of this world and assembled together there, they are properly called "the general assembly and church of the firstborn." And this is the group "which are written in heaven." This is the group which includes all "the spirits of just men made perfect," the Scripture says here.

Surely such an assembly will contain all the saints of God, all those who ever put their trust in the blood. Here will be righteous Abel who by faith offered a more excellent sacrifice. Abel knew about the Saviour and trusted Him and was saved. He is one of "the spirits of just men made perfect." He is one of those "which are written in heaven." Enoch will be there, who walked with God and God took him. So will Noah and those saved with him in the ark. Abraham, who saw Christ's day and was glad, will certainly be there. Moses will be there. David will be there. Elijah and Elisha will surely be there. So will everyone who ever put his trust in the coming Messiah or in a Saviour already come—everyone who has his name written in Heaven.

When the Lord Jesus comes, "the dead in Christ shall rise first," says I Thessalonians 4:16. That surely will include Old Testament saints as well as New Testament saints. Then we Christians who are alive and remain shall be caught up together with them to meet the Lord in the air. And all this vast called-out assembly which will gather in the New Jerusalem in Heaven is called "the church of the firstborn." This is the body of Christ. And it did not begin at Pentecost. It surely began the first time a soul trusted in God for forgiveness and salvation and was made into a child of God, made into a new creature and destined to meet with us in Heaven.

Did Jesus Himself build the church? In Matthew 16:18 we have this well-known statement by the Saviour: "And I say also unto thee, That thou art Peter, and upon this rock I will build my church; and the gates of hell shall not prevail against it." Certainly the Lord Jesus had no thought here of promising that He would build a human denomination, including some saved, some lost, some believers and some modernist infidels, wearing the name of some particular sect. No, no! Jesus had in mind this body, including all the saints, all believers of all ages.

How, then, could Jesus say, "I WILL build my church"? Did that mean that the church was future when Jesus told Peter that He, Christ, would build upon Himself a church?

Instead of an entirely future meaning, what Jesus really said is, "I will be building My church," that is, that bit by bit, adding one convert and then another, the Lord Jesus would continually build His church. The word used by Jesus here in Matthew 16:18, "I will build," is *oikodomeo*, which simply means "to build a house" (Young's *Analytical Concordance*) and is used many times in the New Testament for building a house, a city, a tower, a sepulchre. And it means the slow, arduous process of building one stone upon another, one stone upon another. The term is never used for an instantaneous matter like the coming of the Holy Spirit at Pentecost. The verb necessarily implies a process. And so, bit by bit, Christ is building His church as new converts are added to it. Long before this, others had built upon this one foundation, Jesus Christ the foundation stone and cornerstone (who will also be the capstone). Before this, people had been made part of this great assembly and church of the firstborn written in Heaven who would assemble in the heavenly Jerusalem at the rapture of the saints. And now Jesus was saying that all those who should be saved, He would continue to build upon Himself into a holy temple, a body, a church.

This one-by-one building of the church, the body of Christ, that group which is to be called out into the wonderful assembly in Heaven, is discussed in Ephesians 2:19–22. Read these verses carefully:

"Now therefore ye are no more strangers and foreigners, but fellowcitizens with the saints, and of the household of God; And are built upon the foundation of the apostles and prophets, Jesus Christ himself being the chief corner stone; In whom all the building fitly framed together groweth unto an holy temple in the Lord: In whom ye also are builded together for an habitation of God through the Spirit."

You see, we are built "upon the foundation of the apostles and prophets." Others were in the body of Christ before us Gentiles. And these prophets—were they not Old Testament prophets and leaders for God?

But specially notice that this building continually grows, "Jesus Christ himself being the chief corner stone; In whom all the building fitly framed together groweth unto an holy temple in the Lord." Every time a soul is saved, the body of Christ grows. The temple grows. The building progresses and grows. And all of us Christians "are builded together for an habitation of God through the Spirit."

This constant growth of the body of Christ, His church, is clearly taught in I Peter 2:5, mentioned before: "Ye also, as lively stones, are

built up a spiritual house, an holy priesthood, to offer up spiritual sacrifices, acceptable to God by Jesus Christ." You see, the building is still
growing. And here in my Scofield Bible is a marginal note. For "are
built up" the margin gives "are being built up." And that verifies the
way I have explained the statement of Jesus in Matthew 16:18, "I will
be building My church."

It is well to notice also that the Apostle Peter wrote this "church
truth," as did the author of the Book of Hebrews and the Apostle Paul.

In I Corinthians 12:12,13, when Paul told the people at Corinth
that they were all baptized by one Spirit into one body, he simply
meant that when they were converted each one was built into the wall
of this growing building. Each one was a living stone, put into the wall,
there submerged, covered, buried with others in becoming a part of this
holy temple which God is building, this house of God through the
Spirit, this body of which He is the head, His church. When they were
converted they were made a part of this great assembly which will be
called out at the rapture and assembled in Heaven.

Do you not see, then, that all who are saved in all ages will have to
be called out together and assembled in Heaven together and be a part
together of "the church, which is His body," the "general assembly and
church of the firstborn, which are written in heaven"? And if all the
Old Testament saints are to be in this called-out assembly, then the
building was first started when the first soul was ever saved. Every person who ever came to know forgiveness and regeneration and salvation, everyone who ever was made a partaker of the divine nature and
became the Lord's, then and there became a part of this body which
Christ is still building.

Evidently this is why the Bible never discusses "the origin of the
church." It was not some great dispensational happening. It did not
occur at Pentecost. The origin of the church was really the beginning
of the salvation of sinners. One cannot divorce the fact of salvation
and the fact of membership in the body of Christ. Everyone saved will
be raptured. "We shall not all sleep, but we shall all be changed, In a
moment, in the twinkling of an eye" (I Cor. 15:51,52). All of God's
own will be raised and changed and collected at the same time. There
will be no distinction between Old Testament saints and New
Testament saints in the rapture. All will be assembled together in
Heaven when Jesus comes. And all that assembly is called the "church
of the firstborn." They are all the same called-out assembly. And that
assembly, that church, that body of Christ, did not begin at Pentecost.

I would give no special importance to the matter of whether the church began at Pentecost, except that people who are blinded by this misunderstanding of Pentecost lose the clear teaching of the Bible that at Pentecost Christians were simply filled with the Holy Spirit and prepared to win souls as Jesus had commanded them to do and that the blessing of Pentecost is held forth as a sample for the rest of us to experience and follow. We too are to be filled with the Spirit of God; and then with the power of God we are to witness in our Jerusalem, in all our Judaea, in Samaria and unto the uttermost part of the world. How tragic, how sad, to miss the meaning of Pentecost by thinking of some technical, theoretical, dispensational change taught by Darby and Plymouth Brethren and the ultradispensationalists. How sad to miss the power of Pentecost and the lesson of Pentecost which this generation of Christians has so widely missed and so greatly needs!

V. The Blessing of Pentecost Was Not What Is Called "Sanctification," Was Not "Christian Perfection," Was Not the Eradication of the Carnal Nature

Some dear, good people make much of an experience which they call sanctification, in which they think that the carnal nature is eradicated, the sin principle is destroyed and burned out. They often call this, after John Wesley's term, "Christian perfection." They often claim to be sinless. These are often very good, earnest, devout people, and we have no quarrel with them. There is a Bible sanctification. There is a Bible holiness which all Christians should follow after. We do not believe that it is the eradication of the carnal nature. We do not understand the Scriptures to teach that by one crisis experience this side of Christ's coming or this side of death a person is made sinless and, in a Christian sense, perfect. Yet we believe in holy living, we believe in daily victory and joy, and we would not for a moment make light of the earnest longings of people who want to please Jesus Christ in everything. I know that I myself long unceasingly to please Him and to be all that He wants me to be. And I know that I can thank Him for daily grace, daily wonderful victory and daily cleansing as I obey Him in daily confessing and forsaking of my sins. We have no fight to make with those who strive after holiness. Thank God for every soul who longs to be pure and good. That ought to be the attitude of all of us, surely. None of us should excuse sin. None of us should ever be complacent about our failures and the ways we come short of the glory of God.

But there is an idea abroad with many good people that at Pentecost the disciples received a personal experience of sanctification, that at Pentecost they were purified and the carnal nature was burned out and destroyed, the root and principle of sin eliminated. Some people so believe, but a study of the Word of God will prove that they are mistaken. That is not what happened at Pentecost.

Jesus did not say to the apostles, "Tarry ye in the city of Jerusalem until ye be sanctified." Rather, He said, "Tarry ye in the city of Jerusalem, until ye be endued with power from on high," and He specified that it would be power to be witnesses for Him—that is, to preach repentance and remission of sins in His name among all nations (Luke 24:47–49). We Bible Christians must teach what Jesus taught. He did not say that at Pentecost the disciples would be sanctified.

Again the matter is taken up in Acts 1:4,5. Jesus, "being assembled together with them, commanded them that they should not depart from Jerusalem, but wait for the promise of the Father, which, saith he, ye have heard of me. For John truly baptized with water; but ye shall be baptized with the Holy Ghost not many days hence." Note carefully that no mention is made here of sanctification or the eradication of the carnal nature.

The disciples wanted to know what Jesus meant, and so He explained it in Acts 1:8, just following: "But ye shall receive power, after that the Holy Ghost is come upon you: and ye shall be witnesses unto me both in Jerusalem, and in all Judæa, and in Samaria, and unto the uttermost part of the earth."

What were the disciples to receive when the Holy Ghost came upon them? They were to receive power! Power that would make them witnesses in Jerusalem, Judaea, Samaria and in the whole world! Nothing is said here about sanctification nor about any special experience of cleansing and purification for themselves.

Now study the account of what happened at Pentecost, as given in the second chapter of Acts. "And they were all filled with the Holy Ghost, and began to speak with other tongues [regular languages of other nationalities], as the Spirit gave them utterance." They spoke the Gospel in the languages of the Parthians, Medes, Elamites, etc., a total of some sixteen different nationalities, and every one of them heard the Gospel in his own tongue wherein he was born. Then Peter preached a sermon explaining what happened at Pentecost, and three thousand people were saved. And he said not one word about these Christians' being sanctified or purified or having sin eradicated at

Pentecost. It simply did not happen there. It is never mentioned in connection with Pentecost in the Bible.

The Bible often speaks of people's being filled with the Holy Spirit. We are told that John the Baptist was "filled with the Holy Ghost, even from his mother's womb" (Luke 1:15). But nothing is said of his sanctification. We are told how the whole group was filled with the Holy Ghost *after* Pentecost, in Acts 4:31, yet no mention is made of sanctification or of a special purification. Acts, chapter 6, tells of the Spirit-filled deacons. Acts 9:17 tells how Paul was filled with the Holy Ghost. Acts 11:24 speaks of Barnabas as filled with the Holy Ghost. Yet none of these Scriptures even hint that being filled with the Holy Spirit involved what is often called sanctification or the eradication of the sinful nature. That simply did not happen at Pentecost. Pentecost means something else, not sanctification.

The Lord Jesus Himself was filled with the Holy Ghost at His baptism, according to Luke 3:21,22. Does any reader believe that Jesus was up to that time sinful and that then He was sanctified and purged and the sinful nature eradicated? Surely no one can believe that about the sinless, immaculate Son of God. So, being filled with the Spirit does not mean sanctification. It does not mean the eradication of the carnal nature.

Once when I was preaching on this matter a man called my attention to Acts 15:8,9, where the Scriptures say: "And God, which knoweth the hearts, bare them witness, giving them the Holy Ghost, even as he did unto us; And put no difference between us and them, purifying their hearts by faith."

But I noticed then, as you will by reading those verses again, that "purifying their hearts by faith" refers to the salvation which had come to the Gentiles. In verse 11 following, Peter says, "But we believe that through the grace of the Lord Jesus Christ we shall be saved, even as they." A purifying of the heart when one is born again is one thing; and the eradication of the carnal nature entirely, so that one has no sin principle in him, no taint of Adam's sin, is an entirely different matter.

Let us accept the fact made plain by the Scriptures, then; at Pentecost the disciples were not "sanctified," they were not made perfect, they were not made sinless, they did not have the carnal nature eradicated. That is not what was promised. That is not what they received. That is not what they waited for and not what they got. They were promised the power of the Holy Spirit. They waited upon God until they were filled with the Spirit and had the promised power.

Then they witnessed for the Lord, and three thousand were saved. That is the meaning of Pentecost.

And I think that I ought to say here that every other blessing that the Spirit of God can give to a Christian, after salvation, is less than this one great blessing. The Spirit of God convicts sinners. Then when sinners repent and trust Christ, the Holy Spirit regenerates them, makes them new creatures. They are thus "born of...the Spirit" (John 3:5). They have the Holy Spirit abiding in them, dwelling in their bodies. The Holy Spirit also is a Comforter. The Holy Spirit also guides Christians into truth. The Holy Spirit also helps us pray with groanings that cannot be uttered. The Holy Spirit works in the Christian character, as one walks in Him and abides in Christ, the Christian graces— the fruit of the Spirit: "love, joy, peace, longsuffering, gentleness, goodness, faith, Meekness, temperance" (Gal. 5:22,23). But all these are different from what came at Pentecost. There at Pentecost Christians were filled with the Holy Spirit and empowered to carry out the commands of Jesus in the Great Commission. They were made fit to be witnesses—powerful, soul-winning witnesses for Christ.

Many Christians talk about consecration. We are for it.

Many Christians talk about separation. We believe in it—that is, in a careful avoidance of worldly things that grieve the Spirit of God and hinder a Christian's testimony.

Christians speak about "the deeper life." We are for that too.

Bible teachers often speak about "the crucified life." We believe that every Christian ought to die daily and be crucified with Christ.

Christians speak about holiness. They speak about sanctification. They speak about the baptism in the Holy Spirit. We are for all of these, if you will allow us to mean by these terms what we believe is the Bible meaning for them. But we believe that for any Christian to lay claim to any of these blessings when he is not willing to pay God's price for power to win souls, and is thus a disobedient child of God on the main matter of soul winning, is a sinful disgrace. We believe that Christian's claim is false. We believe that he has missed entirely the great blessing of Pentecost which gives power to win souls.

VI. Pentecost Was Not Simply a Growth in Christian Grace

We have said that it is a mistake to teach that Pentecost was simply the beginning of a new dispensation, the dispensation of the Holy Spirit.

We have said that it is a misunderstanding of the meaning of Pentecost to say that that date was the birthday of the church.

We have said that the great blessing which the Holy Spirit brought at Pentecost was not sanctification or the eradication of the sin nature.

Now we want to show you some other things that did not specially happen at Pentecost.

We have shown that the dispensational change occurred the day Jesus rose from the dead. Then He, in His glorified body, appeared to the disciples and breathed on them and said, "Receive ye the Holy Ghost." This was a fulfillment of what He promised them in John 7:37–39. So before Jesus commanded the disciples to tarry in Jerusalem until they should be endued with power from on high, they already had the Holy Spirit dwelling in their bodies. You see, the indwelling of the Holy Spirit and the special empowering of the Holy Spirit—the fullness of the Spirit for soul winning—are different ministries of the same Spirit.

John 14:16, 17 makes clear that the comfort of the Holy Spirit came to the disciples long before Pentecost. The night before He was crucified, Jesus said:

> *"And I will pray the Father, and he shall give you another Comforter, that he may abide with you for ever; Even the Spirit of truth; whom the world cannot receive, because it seeth him not, neither knoweth him: but ye know him; for he dwelleth with you, and shall be in you."*

The same Holy Spirit who then was *with* them and later should dwell *in* them was to abide with them as a Comforter.

John 14:26, in the same discussion by the Saviour, tells us: "But the Comforter, which is the Holy Ghost, whom the Father will send in my name, he shall teach you all things, and bring all things to your remembrance, whatsoever I have said unto you." The teaching ministry of the Holy Spirit, making plain the words of God and the will of Christ, came to the disciples when the Holy Spirit came in to dwell as their living, abiding Comforter. All this happened before Pentecost. In John 16:13 Jesus promised these disciples that same night: "Howbeit when he, the Spirit of truth, is come, he will guide you into all truth: for he shall not speak of himself [that is, He will not speak the things that He Himself originates. He will speak the things given Him by the Father and by Christ]; but whatsoever he shall hear, that shall he speak: and he will shew you things to come." You see, the Holy Spirit, who guides into the truth, was already abiding in the disciples before Pentecost.

Let us go back to that farewell meeting with Jesus and the disciples as recorded in Luke 24, just before Jesus ascended to Heaven. In that same chapter where He, in verse 49, commanded them to tarry in the city of Jerusalem until they be endued with power from on high, we are told. "Then opened he their understanding, that they might under-stand the scriptures" (vs. 45). Just before He commanded the disciples to wait at Jerusalem for power, He opened their understanding so that they understood all the things "written in the law of Moses, and in the prophets, and in the psalms" concerning Himself (vs. 44). These men who waited at Jerusalem for the blessing of Pentecost already under-stood the Bible. They already had the guidance and teaching and wit-ness of the Holy Spirit in their own hearts. They were not waiting for the indwelling of the Spirit nor His comfort nor His teaching nor His guidance; they were waiting for the fullness of His power to make them soul winners.

Now let us go back to the day Jesus rose from the dead and breathed on the disciples and they received the Holy Spirit in their bodies. In John 20:19–23 the story is given:

"Then the same day at evening, being the first day of the week, when the doors were shut where the disciples were assembled for fear of the Jews, came Jesus and stood in the midst, and saith unto them, Peace be unto you. And when he had so said, he shewed unto them his hands and his side. Then were the disciples glad, when they saw the Lord. Then said Jesus to them again, Peace be unto you: as my Father hath sent me, even so send I you. And when he had said this, he breathed on them, and saith unto them, Receive ye the Holy Ghost: Whose soever sins ye remit, they are remitted unto them; and whose soever sins ye retain, they are retained."

That was, at first, the saddest bunch of Christians ever gathered in one place! Jesus had died! They were discouraged. They were more than discouraged; they were in despair! Then Jesus appeared to them and said, "Peace be unto you." And to prove that He was their own Saviour, He showed them His hands and His side. "Then were the dis-ciples glad, when they saw the Lord." The saddest group of Christians the world ever saw were changed in a few breathless moments into the gladdest, most joyous Christians! No wonder Jesus said, "Peace be unto you." Their fears, their doubts, their unrest all fled away. How revived, how blessed they were!

And we are told a little later in the same chapter how Thomas, a week later, saw Jesus and heard the same sweet words, "Peace be unto you," and, convinced of the genuineness of the Saviour's resurrection with a physical body, he fell down happily, wondrously comforted and tremulously said, "My Lord and my God"! You see, the disciples did not need to wait for Pentecost for gladness and a sense of forgiveness for all the unbelief and backsliding they had experienced. These were all blotted out when they saw Jesus.

The twenty-first chapter of John tells how Simon Peter was taken back into full communion on the seashore and how he was commanded to get about the Lord's business of feeding the sheep. And all of this was before the disciples were commanded to tarry in Jerusalem until they be endued with power from on high.

In John 20:23, after Jesus had breathed on the disciples and said, "Receive ye the Holy Ghost," He gave them this wonderful authority, "Whose soever sins ye remit, they are remitted unto them; and whose soever sins ye retain, they are retained." Whatever authority the disciples had they were given on that marvelous day when Jesus rose from the dead and appeared to them and when the Holy Spirit was breathed upon them and they received Him, the third person of the Trinity, to dwell in their bodies.

You see, then, that the disciples did not wait at Pentecost for joy and ecstasy. They already had that.

You see, then, that the disciples did not wait until the Holy Spirit should comfort them. Already they had been comforted. They had heard Jesus say, "Peace be unto you," and they were glad.

You see, then, that the disciples did not wait for Pentecost to be forgiven of their backslidings, their failures, their doubts. Thomas and Peter and the quarreling, divided group were forgiven and cleansed and united so that they could wait "with one accord," pleading with God for the power of the Holy Spirit to make them soul winners.

There is a fearful taint in human nature of which all of us must beware. There is a constant tendency in the very best of us to take the outward form as more important than the inward fact. All over the world honest preachers have to guard against those who would think more of church membership than of regeneration; against those who would put baptism, rites of the church and good works as the way to salvation, instead of the blood. Christians are tempted to be satisfied with a pharisaical righteousness of some *dos* and *don'ts*, instead of the deep holiness of heart and the passion for souls and for the will of God which should characterize us. I say, all of us need to beware of this perverseness of our carnal natures that makes us seek the outward instead of the inward, the temporal instead of the eternal, the incidental instead of the all-important things.

And so, when we approach the Bible account of Pentecost we are tempted to be absorbed with the question of tongues. Don't do it! That is *not* the meaning of Pentecost. We are tempted to be sidetracked with some teaching about the origin of the church. Don't do it! That is not the meaning of Pentecost. We are tempted to be intrigued with a technical doctrine about the Holy Spirit coming in to dwell. Don't do it! The Holy Spirit does dwell in the Christian's body, but that did not begin at Pentecost, and that is not the meaning of Pentecost. We are tempted, when thinking of Pentecost, to talk about some great ecstasy, some joy for ourselves, some "experience," some feeling that we can relate to others and often repeat. Don't do it! That is not what was promised; that is not what the disciples waited for; that is not what they got. They waited for power and they got power—power that would make them witnesses, power that would make them soul winners, power that would help them to carry out the Great Commission Jesus had just given them! What they waited for, what they were promised, and what they got was the mighty power of God upon them to make them soul winners. O God, give us a heart to see this meaning of Pentecost and to seek and to find for ourselves the same power that New Testament Christians received there!

Chapter 5

Spirit-Filled Means Empowered Witnessing

"But ye shall receive power, after that the Holy Ghost is come upon you: and ye shall be witnesses unto me both in Jerusalem, and in all Judæa, and in Samaria, and unto the uttermost part of the earth."—Acts 1:8.

In this chapter we shall show beyond any possibility of a doubt that to be Spirit-filled means not anything else but to be empowered for witnessing and soul winning. The Holy Spirit may give various gifts when He comes in power, but always when He fills a Christian, it is for soul-winning witnessing and service. It is an incidental matter whether Spirit-filled Christians talked in foreign languages to those who heard them. Once, at Pentecost, Spirit-filled Christians were enabled to preach the Gospel to foreign-born Jews in the languages of the countries in which they were born. Other times Spirit-filled Christians did not speak in foreign languages at all. But always in the Bible Spirit-filled people witnessed for Christ and were empowered for service and soul winning. Once in the Bible Spirit-filled Christians heard a sound of a rushing mighty wind. Then, too, tongues like as of fire visibly sat upon them. Another time Spirit-filled Christians felt the place shaken where they were gathered. In other cases there was no such outward physical manifestation. But always in the Bible Spirit-filled Christians were empowered for service and testimony, particularly prepared for soul winning. First, the Lord Jesus Himself plainly said that this would be true. Second, the examples given us before Pentecost show that supernatural power for service and testimony was always given when one was filled with the Spirit. And, third, the examples in the Book of Acts show the same thing.

I. The Lord Jesus Expressly Promised Soul-Winning Power for All Who Are Filled With the Holy Spirit

One who believes the Bible and takes it at simple face value need have no doubt about the meaning of Pentecost. Men's difficulties on this subject are primarily because they do not listen carefully and take at face value what Jesus Christ Himself said about it.

1. That Promise Was Given to the Apostles
With the Great Commission

In the Great Commission which Jesus gave His disciples before He ascended to Heaven after His resurrection, our Lord plainly command-ed that the Gospel must be preached to every creature, that the apos-tles and the converts they would win and other Christians to be won down through the ages should preach the Gospel among all nations, even to the end of the age. As recorded in the Gospel of Luke, the Great Commission given by our Saviour plainly says that they were to wait for the power of the Holy Spirit in order to carry out the Great Commission and to witness to all the world with supernatural power.

Let us read very carefully the Great Commission as given in Luke 24:46–49:

"Thus it is written, and thus it behoved Christ to suffer, and to rise from the dead the third day: And that repentance and remission of sins should be preached in his name among all nations, beginning at Jerusalem. And ye are witnesses of these things. And, behold, I send the promise of my Father upon you: but tarry ye in the city of Jerusalem, until ye be endued with power from on high."

If you analyze this passage carefully you will see, first, that the Lord Jesus is commanding "that repentance and remission of sins should be preached in his name among all nations, beginning at Jerusalem." Second, you will see that these disciples to whom He is speaking are the witnesses who are to begin the work, taking the Gospel to every creature. Third, for this purpose the power of the Holy Spirit was to come upon them.

It is as plain as the nose on one's face that the enduement of power from on high which came at Pentecost was given to enable people to witness for Jesus, preaching and teaching repentance and forgiveness of sins to sinners all over the world, beginning at Jerusalem.

One statement of the Bible should be enough for a Christian. But there is another statement certainly just as explicit as this, given in Acts 1:8. Remember that the Gospel of Luke and the Book of Acts have much in common. Both were written by the same man, Luke, under divine inspiration. Both were addressed to the same man, Theophilus. The Book of Acts in its first few verses gives a brief résumé of the Book of Luke. The Book of Luke presents Jesus as "the Son of man," as the pattern of a Christian. The Book of Luke says more about the fullness of the Holy Spirit than do any others of the Gospels. The Book of Luke is intended to be followed by the Book of Acts. So Acts 1:8 repeats the clear statement that the Holy Spirit's coming upon the disciples at Pentecost was intended to empower them for soul winning and witnessing.

Jesus had just commanded the disciples "that they should not depart from Jerusalem, but wait for the promise of the Father, which, saith he, ye have heard of me. For John truly baptized with water; but ye shall be baptized with the Holy Ghost not many days hence" (Acts 1:4,5). There is no misunderstanding the setting. Then Jesus explains, "But ye shall receive power, after that the Holy Ghost is come upon you: and ye shall be witnesses unto me both in Jerusalem, and in all Judæa, and in Samaria, and unto the uttermost part of the earth" (Acts 1:8).

Jesus did not say that the disciples would receive tongues, or sanctification, or see the origin of the church, or feel a great ecstasy of joy; no, not any of these! Jesus said that these disciples should receive *power* after that the Holy Ghost should come upon them at Pentecost! And power for what? Power to be witnesses: "And ye shall be witnesses unto me both in Jerusalem, and in all Judæa, and in Samaria, and unto the uttermost part of the earth." No honest Christian can misunderstand the meaning of the Lord Jesus here. The coming of the Holy Spirit upon the disciples at Pentecost was to empower them for soul-winning witnessing.

2. Since the Great Commission Is for Us, So Also Is the Promised Power for Soul Winning

But what the fullness of the Holy Spirit meant to the disciples who heard Jesus give these commands and these promises is exactly the same as the fullness of the Holy Spirit will mean for us. *For the clear promise of Jesus in Luke 24:46–49 and in Acts 1:8 is in the Great Commission, to last to the end of the age!* The Great Commission given by the Saviour in Luke 24:47, "That repentance and remission of sins should be preached in his name among all nations," certainly could not be fulfilled by the apostles alone. The apostles and others of the one hundred twenty who were filled with the Holy Spirit at Pentecost did go to *many* nations, but not to *all* nations. The Great Commission is for the whole church of Christ and all through this age. And only the whole church of Christ can perfectly fulfill this command of the Lord Jesus about taking the Gospel to all nations. And that means that in our day when the Holy Spirit comes upon us, we will receive power for witnessing, just as the disciples received power for witnessing in their day. The Great Commission is as clearly for Christians today as it was for Christians who waited for Pentecost over nineteen hundred years ago.

Acts 1:8 also clearly speaks to the whole church of Jesus Christ, to all the Christians of this age: "But ye shall receive power, after that the Holy Ghost is come upon you: and ye shall be witnesses unto me both in Jerusalem, and in all Judæa, and in Samaria, and unto the uttermost part of the earth." It was utterly impossible for the one hundred twenty who were empowered for witnessing at Pentecost to complete the work of this Great Commission. They could not take it to every hamlet, to every village, to every home, to every person, as Jesus commanded them to do. They made a good start. But what I am proving is that Acts 1:8 fits us as well as it fitted the disciples in the New Testament. That means that the fullness of the Spirit today will mean soul-winning power on our witnessing, just as it meant that to them.

3. Dr. R. A. Torrey Has Wonderfully Stated This Truth, That to Be Filled With the Spirit Means Power for Soul-Winning Witnessing

In the splendid book *The Holy Spirit—Who He Is, and What He Does*, by the late Dr. R. A. Torrey, published in 1927, the year before his death, Dr. Torrey has a statement which we want to quote. Dr. Torrey uses the term "the baptism with the Holy Spirit." He meant, just as Jesus meant in Acts 1:5, the fullness of the Spirit which came at Pentecost. Dr. Torrey's term is a scriptural term, but we want to make sure that he is not misunderstood. The following great statement is by Dr. Torrey:

> 3. In the third place, *the baptism with the Holy Spirit is a work of the Holy Spirit always connected with and primarily for the purpose of testimony and service.* This is evident from the passage where our Lord Jesus made the original promise of the baptism with the Holy Spirit, Acts 1:8: "But ye *shall receive power,* after that the Holy Ghost is come upon you: and *ye shall be witnesses* unto me both in Jerusalem, and in all Judaea, and in Samaria, and unto the uttermost part of the earth."... *There is not one single passage in the Bible, either in the Old Testament or the New Testament, where the Baptism with the Holy Spirit is spoken of, where it is not connected with testimony or service.* I made this statement some years ago in speaking to a large class of theological students. At the close of the lecture two students came up to me and said, Did we understand you to say, Mr. Torrey, that there was not a single passage in the Bible, where the Baptism with the Holy Spirit is mentioned, where it is not connected with testimony or service?" "Yes," I replied, "that is exactly what I said." "Well," they said, "we doubt it." I replied, "You have a perfect right to doubt it, but now go and search your Bible and bring me, if you can, one single passage in the Bible where the

Baptism with the Holy Spirit is definitely mentioned or referred to, where it is not connected with testimony or service." They went to work to search for the passage. I think they must be searching for it yet, for they have never brought it to me; and they never will, for it is not to be found anywhere in the Bible. I have gone through my Bible on this subject, time and time again since I made that remark to those students, and without the slightest fear of successful contradiction I repeat the statement already made, that there is not a single passage in the Old Testament or New Testament where the Baptism with the Holy Spirit is spoken of or referred to where it is not connected with testimony or service.

The Baptism with the Holy Spirit is not primarily for the purpose of making us individually holy. Please note carefully my words and grasp exactly what I say. I do not say that it is not the work of the Holy Spirit to make us holy, for it is His work to make us holy, and it is only through His work that any one of us can become holy. I do say, however, that it is not *the primary purpose* of the *Baptism* with the Holy Spirit to make us holy. *The primary purpose of the Baptism with the Holy Spirit is to equip us and fit us for service.* This will become still clearer when we come to study the next part of our subject: the Results of the Baptism with the Holy Spirit.

Neither is it the primary purpose of the Baptism with the Holy Spirit to make us personally happy. Note again carefully what I say. I do not say that the Baptism with the Holy Spirit will not make us happy, if we receive it. I have never known anyone yet who was "baptized with the Holy Spirit" into whose heart a new and more wonderful joy did not come, but I am saying that *this is not the primary purpose of the Baptism with the Holy Spirit.* The primary purpose of the Baptism with the Holy Spirit is not to make us happy but to make us useful for God. I am glad that this is so, for while ecstasies are all right in their place, and while I know something about them in my own experience, yet in a world such as you and I live in, where there is this awful tide of men, women, and children sweeping on unsaved to a hopeless eternity, I would rather go my entire life through without one single touch of ecstasy or rapture, and have power to do my part to stem this awful tide and save at least some, than to have indescribable raptures every day of my life and have no power to save the lost.

I wish to be very clear and very emphatic at this point, for here is where a multitude of people in our day are going astray. Men and women go off to "Bible Conferences," to "meetings for the deepening of the spiritual life," and to "tarrying meetings," and all that sort of thing, and they come back and tell you what a wonderful experience they have had, what raptures they have passed through, and how they have been "baptized with the Holy Spirit," and I have watched care-fully a good many of these people; and many of them are of no more use to their pastors or their churches than they were before. And some of them are of far less use than they were before and are sometimes a positive nuisance. They have no more love for souls than they had before, make no more effort for the salvation of the lost than they did before, and win no more souls to Christ than they did before; and I am therefore sure that whatever experience they may have received they have not had the Baptism with the Holy Spirit along the lines so plain-ly laid down in God's own Word. So I repeat it again, THE BAPTISM WITH THE HOLY SPIRIT IS ALWAYS CONNECTED WITH, AND IS PRIMARILY FOR THE PURPOSE OF EQUIPMENT FOR TESTIMONY AND SERVICE: IT IS TO MAKE US USEFUL FOR GOD IN THE SALVATION OF SOULS AND NOT MERELY TO MAKE US HAPPY.

Every honest student, after reading the scriptural proof we will give below, must agree with what Dr. Torrey says, that to be filled with the Holy Spirit, or baptized with the Holy Spirit, or endued with power from on high, or to have the Holy Spirit poured on one, as at Pentecost, means that one will have the power of God upon his wit-nessing and soul-winning efforts.

In other words, one could properly say that one who is filled with the Holy Spirit wins souls. One who does not win souls is not filled with the Holy Spirit. And all who win souls in any degree do it by some measure of the power of the Holy Spirit.

II. People Filled With the Holy Spirit Before Pentecost Witnessed for God With Power

It would be an easy matter to go through the Old Testament and find Scripture after Scripture showing that Old Testament prophets, when the Spirit of God came upon them, witnessed for God with power. And that enduement of power on Old Testament prophets, on David, on some of the judges, was the same enduement of power as came at Pentecost and is mentioned in other places in the New Testament. But here it seems wise to use the examples in the Bible where Christians are said to be "filled with the Spirit" or "filled with the Holy Ghost" before Pentecost. One of these cases is in the Old Testament, and four others are in the Gospel of Luke. In each case peo-ple who were "filled with the Spirit" or "filled with the Holy Ghost" witnessed for the Lord with power.

1. Bezaleel, Who Worked on the Tabernacle and Its Furniture in the Wilderness, Was "Filled...With the Spirit of God"

In Exodus 35:30,31 we are told:

"And Moses said unto the children of Israel, See, the LORD hath called by name Bezaleel the son of Uri, the son of Hur, of the tribe of Judah; And he hath filled him with the spirit of God, in wisdom, in understanding, and in knowledge, and in all manner of workmanship."

Aholiab and others helped Bezaleel. But Bezaleel was particularly "filled...with the spirit of God" for the work.

At first glance one would not think that this Tabernacle was a gospel testimony for God. It is service, truly; but was the work of Bezaleel in building the Tabernacle and its furniture and preparing the garments of the priesthood really a testimony to Christ and to the plan of salvation? Assuredly it was!

The Tabernacle in the wilderness is one of the clearest pictures of Christ. The outer covering of the Tabernacle was of badger skins, dull and drab, for Christ has no form nor comeliness to the outsiders who do not know His beauty. Another covering underneath was of rams' skins dyed red, which surely was meant to symbolize the blood of Jesus Christ which atoned for our sins. And under that was a white linen cover which pictured the beauty and sinless righteousness of the Lord Jesus, manifest only to those who know Him.

The upright boards of the Tabernacle, of shittim wood, represented the humanity of Christ. The solid covering of the boards with gold pictured the deity of Christ. The tenons on the ends of these boards rested in sockets of silver, and this silver was the redemption money paid in for the redemption of all the men of Israel. Surely, surely it pictured Christ our Redeemer, buying men out of sin. In the Tabernacle the golden lampstand pictured Christ, the Light of the World. The table of shewbread pictured Christ, the Bread of Life. The great brass altar out in front pictured Christ bearing the judgment and wrath of God for us, brought it to mind every time a lamb was slain, or a bullock, or a red heifer, or a scapegoat! All about the Tabernacle and its furniture and its services reminds us of Jesus Christ and of salvation by the blood! How foolish it would have been to expect any man to plan and supervise the construction of all this wonderful wealth of material, with every item of it picturing something about Jesus and salvation, unless the one so engaged were filled with the Spirit of God to give him wisdom and power on this testimony! One who reads C. H. Mackintosh on the Pentateuch or *Christ in the Pentateuch*, by J. B. Tidwell, will find wonderful help here. Bezaleel was filled with the Spirit of God for a soul-winning testimony.

2. John the Baptist Was "Filled With the Holy Ghost," That Is, Soul-Winning Power

Zacharias, the priest, and his wife, Elisabeth, had earnestly prayed for a son. God sent an angel to tell Zacharias the glad news, as he was in the temple of the Lord in regular service. This is the message the angel gave:

"Fear not, Zacharias: for thy prayer is heard; and thy wife Elisabeth shall bear thee a son, and thou shalt call his name John. And thou shalt have joy and gladness; and many shall rejoice at his birth. For he shall be great in the sight of the Lord, and shall drink neither wine nor strong drink; and he shall be filled with the Holy Ghost, even from his mother's womb. And many of the children of Israel shall he turn to the Lord their God."—Luke 1:13–16.

John the Baptist was to "be filled with the Holy Ghost, even from his mother's womb." "Filled with the Holy Ghost" is exactly the same term used of the disciples at Pentecost in Acts 2:4. And what were the results when John the Baptist was filled with the Holy Ghost? What would be the evidence? What would the fullness of the Holy Spirit do in John? We are answered in Luke 1:16: "And many of the children of Israel shall he turn to the Lord their God." John the Baptist, filled with the Holy Spirit, turned many, many souls to God. He had soul-winning power.

Throughout the Gospel of Luke and the Book of Acts, wherever people were filled with the Holy Spirit, you will find an "and"—that is, something else is to happen when people are filled with the Holy Spirit. Being filled with the Spirit is never an end in itself. It is always for soul-winning witness in power.

3. Elisabeth Also Was Filled With the Holy Ghost and Witnessed for Christ

In the first chapter of Luke we learn how Elisabeth, the mother of John the Baptist, was herself filled with the Holy Ghost.

"And it came to pass, that, when Elisabeth heard the salutation of Mary, the babe leaped in her womb; and Elisabeth was filled with the Holy Ghost: And she spake out with a loud voice, and said, Blessed art thou among women, and blessed is the fruit of thy womb."—Luke 1:41, 42.

Elisabeth was "filled with the Holy Ghost." Again, it is exactly the same term as used in Acts 2:4 about the enduement with power at Pentecost. And Elisabeth, we find, when she was filled with the Holy Ghost, "spake out with a loud voice" and gave testimony to the coming Saviour to be born of the Virgin Mary! Study the passage carefully, including Luke 1:43–45, and you will see that here were a divinely given prophecy and a supernatural power on Elisabeth's testimony for Jesus.

4. Zacharias, Too, Was Filled With the Holy Ghost and Witnessed With Power

In the same first chapter of Luke, verse 67 tells us, "And his father Zacharias was filled with the Holy Ghost, and prophesied."

A wonderful prophecy is given. By that we mean that it was a Spirit-filled exhortation and revelation, given in the power of God. In this case it was about the coming Saviour, the Messiah. John, Zacharias' own baby boy, was to be the forerunner of the Saviour, and the Spirit of God gave testimony to all who were nearby through the prophesying of the Spirit-filled Zacharias.

It is here well to remember that at Pentecost those who preached the Gospel and spoke for Christ were prophesying, in the Bible sense. For Peter plainly said that this was the fulfillment of the words of Joel: "And on my servants and on my handmaidens I will pour out in those days of my Spirit; and they shall prophesy" (Acts 2:18). Zacharias was filled with the Holy Spirit exactly as they were, and he witnessed with power. In him was fulfilled the promise that Jesus would later give to His disciples in Acts 1:8: "But ye shall receive power, after that the Holy Ghost is come upon you: and ye shall be witnesses unto me...."

5. Jesus, Filled With the Spirit, Began His Supernatural Ministry

In Luke 3:21,22 we learn how when Jesus was baptized "the Holy Ghost descended in a bodily shape like a dove upon him." Then Jesus was filled with the Holy Spirit, though the term "filled with the Spirit" or "filled with the Holy Ghost" is not used in those particular verses. But such a term is used immediately following that in Luke 4:1: "And Jesus being full of the Holy Ghost returned from Jordan, and was led by the Spirit into the wilderness."

Jesus was full of the Holy Ghost. That is exactly what happened to the disciples at Pentecost. The Spirit of God came on them, and they were full of the Holy Ghost. Then the same fourth chapter of Luke tells how Jesus "returned in the power of the Spirit into Galilee" and began His public ministry, and His fame went through all the region. And Jesus told the people, "The Spirit of the Lord is upon me, because he hath anointed me to preach the gospel to the poor; he hath sent me to heal the brokenhearted, to preach deliverance to the captives, and recovering of sight to the blind, to set at liberty them that are bruised" (Luke 4:18). Jesus was filled with the Spirit just as the apostles were later filled with the Spirit at Pentecost, and the same results were shown in His life and ministry as He promised the disciples. He began His witnessing and doing the soul-winning work of His Father in mighty power, supernatural power.

It is immediately clear that John the Baptist, Zacharias, Elisabeth and the Lord Jesus were filled with the Holy Ghost just as people were filled with the Holy Ghost in the Book of Acts. And in every case they began to witness with power, the enduement of power from on high. They began their soul-winning efforts with supernatural help from God. That is what the fullness of the Spirit brings! To be filled with the Spirit means to be empowered for witnessing.

III. In the Book of Acts, Wherever People Were "Filled With the Holy Ghost," They Witnessed With Power

In the Book of Acts six times the phrase 'filled with the Holy Ghost' is used. In every case except one we are explicitly told that those filled with the Holy Spirit witnessed for God. In the single exception, Acts 13:52 tells us of the disciples at Antioch of Pisidia, "And the disciples were filled with joy, and with the Holy Ghost." We may be sure that they too received power and witnessed for the Lord when the Holy Ghost came upon them. But how remarkable that in five out of six cases in the Book of Acts we are particularly told that those who were filled with the Holy Ghost witnessed for Christ!

Four other times in the Book of Acts the slightly different phrase 'full of the Holy Ghost' is used. Two of these times the phrase 'full of the Holy Ghost' is used about the deacons in the sixth chapter of Acts, and there are three separate instances where people in the Book of Acts are reported to have been "full of the Holy Ghost." And in every single case we are told about their soul-winning testimony!

In other words, in nine out of ten times where the Book of Acts expressly says that people were filled with the Holy Ghost or full of the

Holy Ghost, we are told that they witnessed for Christ. Since the Lord Jesus promised that this would happen, that one should receive power and witness for Him when the Holy Ghost came upon him, we would know it were true if the result were not mentioned in a single one of the ten times. But fortunately the Bible, line upon line, presses upon our hearts this great truth that when the Spirit of God comes upon people He gives them soul-winning testimony!

1. At Pentecost People "Filled With the Holy Ghost" Began to Witness for Christ

In Acts 2:4 we read, "And they were all filled with the Holy Ghost, and began to speak with other tongues, as the Spirit gave them utterance." Never mind the tongues. The message was just the same in effect, though given in different languages. The important thing is that everyone filled with the Holy Spirit began to speak for God as the Holy Spirit showed him what to say. In other words, he had power from God on his testimony and began to use this power in soul winning. And so on the day of Pentecost we are told that "they that gladly received his word were baptized: and the same day there were added unto them about three thousand souls" (Acts 2:41).

Pentecost is certainly set as a model case, in some ways a typical case, of a revival when God's people, filled with the Holy Ghost, set out to win souls for Him. And it is important to see the one main thing Jesus had promised would happen when people were filled with the Holy Spirit came at Pentecost just the same as at other times. One misses the point of Pentecost entirely if he does not see that here people, filled with the Holy Spirit, set out to keep the command of Jesus and carry the Gospel to everybody they could reach, beginning at Jerusalem.

2. Peter, After Pentecost, Was Filled With the Holy Ghost Again for Powerful Witnessing

In Acts 4:8 we find this interesting statement, "Then Peter, filled with the Holy Ghost, said unto them, Ye rulers of the people, and elders of Israel...."

And then follows a wonderful message about the Lord Jesus whom they had rejected, the only name given under Heaven whereby we must be saved. Peter at Pentecost, filled with the Holy Spirit, witnessed with power. A few days later, filled again with the Holy Spirit, he witnessed with power. At Pentecost or after Pentecost, exactly the same thing happens when people are filled with the Holy Spirit. They receive power and witness for Jesus. One who does not witness, or one who witnesses without power, is not filled with the Holy Spirit.

3. The Whole Group of Disciples Were Filled Again, As at Pentecost, With Similar Results

In Acts 4:31 we have a remarkable case to study. It is remarkable, first, because it is a report of how the same group who were filled with the Holy Spirit at Pentecost were filled again just a little later. It is remarkable, second, because exactly the same nine words are used, "And they were all filled with the Holy Ghost." Now read Acts 4:31. It tells the story of how Peter and John, being released from prison, came and told the other Christians their story, and all prayed together. And then, "when they had prayed, the place was shaken where they were assembled together; and they were all filled with the Holy Ghost, and they spake the word of God with boldness."

Many lessons could be noted from this verse. For one thing, those who were filled with the Holy Spirit before, and witnessed, needed to be filled again for new power in witnessing. Again, exactly the same thing happened here, essentially, as happened at Pentecost. Exactly the same nine words are used to describe it. The outward manifestations were not the same as at Pentecost. In one case there were a sound of a mighty rushing wind and visible tongues like as of fire, and foreign languages, while in the other case there was an earthquake. But essentially exactly the same thing happened. In both cases God gave great power on His disciples for witnessing. These, filled with the Holy Ghost anew, "spake the word of God with boldness." And verse 33, just following, says, "And with great power gave the apostles witness of the resurrection of the Lord Jesus: and great grace was upon them all." And the fifth chapter, immediately following, tells of the miraculous death of Ananias and Sapphira and how "by the hands of the apostles were many signs and wonders wrought among the people," and then it tells us this heartening and beautiful truth: "And believers were the more added to the Lord, multitudes both of men and women."

When people are filled with the Holy Spirit, then they have great boldness to speak the Word of God. Then they have power upon their witness for Jesus! Then believers are added to the Lord! Oh, for God to fill His people again with the Holy Spirit so we may be bold, so we may speak out with power, so many people may be turned from their sins to trust Christ!

4. Stephen, Filled With the Holy Spirit, Witnessed in Mighty Power

In the sixth chapter of Acts we find that the apostles saw the need for deacons, and the people were urged to look out seven men full of the Holy Ghost and wisdom whom the apostles might appoint over the business of the care of the poor. Then Acts 6:5–8 tells us:

"And the saying pleased the whole multitude: and they chose Stephen, a man full of faith and of the Holy Ghost, and Philip, and Prochorus, and Nicanor, and Timon, and Parmenas, and Nicolas a proselyte of Antioch: Whom they set before the apostles: and when they had prayed, they laid their hands on them. And the word of God increased; and the number of the disciples multiplied in Jerusalem greatly; and a great company of the priests were obedient to the faith. And Stephen, full of faith and power, did great wonders and miracles among the people."

What happened when Stephen and other godly deacons were full of the Holy Ghost? Then "the word of God increased; and the number of the disciples multiplied in Jerusalem greatly." And again, "Stephen, full of faith and power, did great wonders and miracles among the people." Here is the power and here is the witnessing, resulting in souls saved! And that is what happens when people are really filled with the Holy Spirit.

In Acts 7:55 we are told of Stephen's being full of the Holy Ghost again: "But he, being full of the Holy Ghost, looked up stedfastly into heaven, and saw the glory of God, and Jesus standing on the right hand of God." Stephen is on trial for his life. He has just preached a wonderful story of God's dealing with Israel. And now, full of the Holy Ghost, what will Stephen do? Why, he will testify for Christ, of course, and that with great power! The following verses tell us how Stephen reported, "Behold, I see the heavens opened, and the Son of man standing on the right hand of God." And as they stoned him, Stephen called upon God, saying, "Lord Jesus, receive my spirit," and then, broken and dying, he kneeled down and cried with a loud voice, "Lord, lay not this sin to their charge." The Spirit-filled Stephen died. He fell asleep.

But were there no results, no souls saved, this last time that Stephen was full of the Holy Ghost and gave his dying message? Should we not expect that there would be some work of power, some soul-saving result when Stephen, filled with the Holy Ghost, witnessed for Christ the last time? Yes, and I believe we do have the evidence of the best results that Stephen ever got. For the next chapter tells how "Saul was consenting unto his death," and Saul then went on in his hatred of Christians, after seeing Stephen die. But he could never get away from it. In the ninth chapter of Acts we are told that on the road to Damascus he was still 'kicking against the pricks,' fighting the conviction that was on him, never getting any peace. Oh, no doubt, again and again he could see Stephen's dying face, as the face of an angel, and hear the Spirit-filled testimony that God had hooked onto his soul with grips of steel! And so Saul was converted out on the road to Damascus. That does not mean that without any human instrument Saul turned to God and became Paul the apostle. Rather, God had used the message of dying Stephen, Spirit-filled Stephen, to convict and save Paul the apostle. And when we get to Heaven much of the credit of what Paul the apostle did will go to the man who died for Jesus while he witnessed, full of the Holy Spirit, before the young man Saul who kept the clothes of those who stoned Stephen.

5. Paul the Apostle, Too, Filled With the Holy Spirit, Began His Powerful Ministry

In Acts the ninth chapter, we learn of the conversion of Paul on the road to Damascus. Then after Paul had fasted and prayed three days and nights, Ananias came to him. And Acts 9:17 tells us:

"And Ananias went his way, and entered into the house; and putting his hands on him said, Brother Saul, the Lord, even Jesus, that appeared unto thee in the way as thou camest, hath sent me, that thou mightest receive thy sight, and be filled with the Holy Ghost."

Paul, the new convert, was "filled with the Holy Ghost." This is the same term used of the disciples at Pentecost in Acts 2:4. And what happened with Saul? The following verse says, "And immediately there fell from his eyes as it had been scales: and he received sight forthwith, and arose, and was baptized." And verse 20, immediately following, says, "And straightway he preached Christ in the synagogues, that he is the Son of God." What astonishment to hear the infidel, the murderer of Christians, now himself preaching the Gospel in power! When Saul was filled with the Spirit he began bold and powerful witnessing for Jesus. And there is no other explanation for the ministry of the Apostle Paul than this simple fact: he was "filled with the Holy Ghost"!

But Paul was filled with the Holy Spirit more than once. And each time the results were the same soul-winning power. In Acts, chapter 13, we are told of the first missionary journey and how it began with Barnabas and Saul "sent forth by the Holy Ghost." At Paphos they came to preach the Gospel to Sergius Paulus, the deputy of the country. Elymas the sorcerer withstood them and sought to turn away Sergius Paulus from trusting Christ. Here was need for the power of God, if they were to win the lost man they sought to win. And, as we should expect, Saul was filled afresh with the Holy Spirit, rebuked the sorcerer with power, and the deputy was saved. Acts 13:9–12 tells this thrilling story:

> "Then Saul, (who also is called Paul,) filled with the Holy Ghost, set his eyes on him, And said, O full of all subtilty and all mischief, thou child of the devil, thou enemy of all righteousness, wilt thou not cease to pervert the right ways of the Lord? And now, behold, the hand of the Lord is upon thee, and thou shalt be blind, not seeing the sun for a season. And immediately there fell on him a mist and a darkness; and he went about seeking some to lead him by the hand. Then the deputy, when he saw what was done, believed, being astonished at the doctrine of the Lord."

Saul was "filled with the Holy Ghost," he spoke out boldly for God, the sorcerer was struck blind, and Sergius Paulus believed.

We are to infer that always those who are Spirit-filled will speak for God boldly, that God's power will be present on the witnessing, and that if the ministry gift of miracles is present, as it was here, it will be for the express purpose of winning souls. The fullness of the Spirit, in the case of Paul, meant empowered witnessing for soul winning. And any ministry gifts which are a manifestation of the fullness of the Spirit, like the tongues at Pentecost, the miraculous death of Ananias and Sapphira at the word of Spirit-filled Peter, or the miraculous blindness of Elymas at the word of Saul who was filled with the Spirit, are for soul-winning evidence, to give power to the Word preached.

6. Barnabas, Too, Filled With the Holy Ghost, Won Many Souls

Barnabas is one of the sweet characters of the New Testament. He was not self-seeking. He was willing to play second fiddle to Paul. He was a great soul winner. And Barnabas too was full of the Holy Ghost, and that was the secret for his power.

In Acts 11:24 we have this clear statement about Barnabas and the soul-winning power given him by the Holy Ghost: "For he was a good man, and full of the Holy Ghost and of faith: and much people was added unto the Lord."

There is a simple and brief statement. Barnabas was "full of the Holy Ghost," and almost as a matter of fact, as a matter that was inevitable, a matter which must naturally follow, we are told, "and much people was added unto the Lord."

When God's preachers are filled with the Holy Ghost, they will win many souls. When God's laypeople are filled with the Holy Ghost, they too will win souls; for Jesus promised, "Ye shall receive power, after that the Holy Ghost is come upon you: and ye shall be witnesses unto me both in Jerusalem, and in all Judæa, and in Samaria, and unto the uttermost part of the earth."

Here are the instances we have before Pentecost. Bezaleel, in the Old Testament, filled with the Holy Spirit, was enabled by miraculous power to make the Tabernacle coverings and furniture and altars and the clothing of the priest witness to the saving grace of the Lord Jesus Christ who was yet to come. John the Baptist, filled with the Holy Ghost, turned many of the people of Israel to the Lord their God. Elisabeth, filled with the Holy Ghost, spoke with a loud voice a wonderful testimony about the coming Saviour. Zacharias, filled with the Holy Ghost, prophesied about the coming Jesus and witnessed in a loud voice to all the people who gathered to hear him. Jesus, too, filled with the Holy Spirit, did all His marvelous ministry on earth.

In the Book of Acts we found it the same way. At Pentecost people were filled with the Holy Spirit and witnessed with soul-saving power. Peter was filled with the Holy Spirit and witnessed and won souls. Stephen was full of the Holy Ghost and spoke with great power, and multitudes of believers were added to the Lord. Paul the apostle was filled with the Holy Ghost and began his marvelous ministry. Later, when filled afresh, such powerful results continued. Barnabas was full of the Holy Ghost, and "much people" was added to the Lord.

No honest reader of the Scriptures on this subject can avoid the clear conclusion that to be filled with the Holy Spirit means to have soul-winning power on our testimony!

Are you filled with the Holy Spirit? Well, if you are, you will be having this Bible evidence and fruit; you will have the power of God upon you as you witness for Him and win souls. God grant that all His people may seek and may find this blessing, this power, this enduement, to make them powerful witnesses.

You may speak with tongues, but you are not filled with the Holy Spirit unless you have power to win souls!

You may have had a great "experience" with ecstasy, but you are not filled with the Holy Spirit after the Bible fashion unless you have soul-winning power like Bible Christians had when filled with the Holy Spirit.

You may claim to be "sanctified," but if you do not have soul-winning power you are not filled with the Holy Spirit! Oh, be satisfied with nothing less than the power of God to help you win souls! For to be Spirit-filled means, always, empowered witnessing.

Chapter 6

Bible Terminology for the Power of Pentecost

"...*but tarry ye in the city of Jerusalem, until ye be* endued with power from on high."—Luke 24:49.

"*And they were all* filled with the Holy Ghost."—Acts 2:4.

"...*ye shall be* baptized with the Holy Ghost *not many days hence.*" —Acts 1:5.

"*But this is that which was spoken by the prophet Joel;...* I will pour out of my Spirit."—Acts 2:16,17.

"...*on the Gentiles also was poured out* the gift of the Holy Ghost." —Acts 10:45.

"*Then laid they their hands on them, and they* received the Holy Ghost." —Acts 8:17.

What shall we call that which happened to the disciples at Pentecost? Shall we say that the waiting disciples got "the second blessing"? Shall we say that they got "a second work of grace"? Shall we say that at Pentecost the apostles and others who waited were "sanctified"? Certainly we ought to find some acceptable terminology that is true to the Scriptures when we discuss the power that came at Pentecost upon the waiting disciples. We ought to use terms that mean what God meant when He talked about the blessing He gave at Pentecost, and we ought to use terms that are descriptive and accurate. Much harm has been done, we are sure, by Christians talking about the Pentecostal experience without using correct terms.

I believe the simplest and best way is to use the terms which the Bible uses about what happened at Pentecost. We are always safer when we are on Bible ground. We are always wise to use Bible terminology about matters which the Bible clearly discusses.

Some terms widely used about what happened at Pentecost are misleading human terms with which we ought to dispense. We will be less likely to teach heresy, will be more likely to understand what the Bible says, will be much more likely to be able to agree about the power of Pentecost if we use Bible terms for what we are talking about. The term "the second blessing," used about the power of Pentecost, is misleading. There is a sense, of course, in which the fullness of the Holy Spirit is an entirely different blessing from salvation. So in some sense it is a second blessing. That is, if one is saved and then immediately thereafter, before he gets any other blessing, he gets filled with the Spirit of God, then it is a second blessing. But there are many, many other blessings, and not only two. And Pentecost was not simply the second blessing the Christians at Pentecost had received.

Another weakness of this term is that it is not descriptive. It does not define what happens. One can read into the term "the second blessing" whatever he himself may mean or wish to mean by the term. Hence, such a term, which is not a Bible term and which is misleading, would better be avoided.

Was the supernatural enduement which came at Pentecost "a second definite work of grace"? Well, the term sounds good. All the great blessings which God gives are matters of His grace and favor. I believe that the Christians at Pentecost did have, and we today may have, a very definite filling with the Spirit, so definite that we may know whether or not we have been filled with the Spirit. But again, the term "a second definite work of grace" is not a Bible term. And it is made to mean whatever people who use it may want it to mean. Generally, those who use this terminology mean that a Christian may have a second regenerative work, or a miraculous change in his nature, wrought by the Holy Spirit, whereby the sinful carnal nature is "eradicated" or burned out and the "sin principle" is destroyed. Sometimes the term is used by those who do not have this special meaning, but at any rate, the term is subject to all the frailties that human beings have; it is not a Bible term, and so is misleading and inadequate.

I do not believe in "a second definite work of grace," if you mean that another work of grace has been wrought upon my soul, which is a permanent change in nature like that which came at regeneration. I do not believe that Christians have the carnal nature eradicated, the sin principle destroyed, the carnal tendency burned out, by the Holy Spirit in a second definite work of grace. "A second definite work of grace" —that term is misleading, and I believe one should not use it for what happened at Pentecost, for the divine enduement of power which Christians had then and which Christians may have now.

Were the disciples who waited at Pentecost "sanctified"? Were they there made holy? Now, I believe in sanctification. I believe in holiness. And I believe that the blessed Spirit of God uses the Word of God and uses other means to sanctify us. I am not referring to sinless perfection. I am not referring to the eradication of the carnal nature. I do not believe that Christians now, in the flesh, have the carnal nature eradicated. I do believe in Bible holiness, and I think that all Christians should earnestly follow after holiness, in the Bible sense, and use means appointed in the Scriptures for sanctification. But what happened at Pentecost was not sanctification! The disciples were not there made holy. They were not there purified. They did not have the carnal nature taken out. Nothing like that is mentioned in the Bible account of Pentecost.

Every Christian in some sense is purified and sanctified at the moment of regeneration. Hebrews 10:14 plainly says, "For by one offering he hath perfected for ever them that are sanctified." And verse 10 before that in the same chapter says, "By the which will we are sanctified through the offering of the body of Jesus Christ once for all." The Spirit of God does sanctify us, in some sense, when we are converted. In Acts 15:9 we are told that God put no difference between the Jews and the Gentiles, "purifying their hearts by faith." But these disciples at Pentecost were already set apart for God, already had their hearts purified by faith. Certainly all the Scriptures referring to Pentecost can be searched without finding once that God used the term "sanctification" for the blessing He gave the disciples who waited in the Upper Room until the day of Pentecost was fully come. We ought not to confuse the issue, then, by using the term "sanctification" when speaking of the fullness of the Holy Spirit which the disciples received at Pentecost or which Christians today receive when they are endued with supernatural power for service and witnessing.

Since we see the difficulties into which men fall by using human and misleading terminology, let us study carefully the terms which the Bible, the blessed Word of God, uses about the blessing which came at Pentecost. We will find that at least five terms were very clearly used about what happened to the disciples at Pentecost. These terms are: (1) "endued with power from on high," (2) "filled with the Holy Ghost," (3) "baptized with the Holy Ghost," (4) "I will pour out of my Spirit," (5) "the gift of the Holy Ghost." These terms are clearly used about the one identical blessing. Since it is Bible terminology which we seek, let us reverently examine the way the Lord Jesus and the inspired writers of the Bible talked about the blessing that came at Pentecost.

I. At Pentecost the Waiting Disciples Were "Endued With Power From on High"

Jesus said to His disciples, "...but tarry ye in the city of Jerusalem, until ye be endued with power from on high" (Luke 24:49). This terminology, "endued with power from on high," is important for several reasons. First, it was given by Jesus Christ Himself to the disciples in telling them what they were to wait for. This terminology was used by the Saviour before Pentecost came and before the power of God came upon the disciples. They needed explicit language. They needed to know what to expect. Jesus described the blessing they were to receive as an enduement of power from on high.

Again, in the first chapter of Acts we have a discussion of the commandment Jesus gave His apostles, to wait in Jerusalem for the promise of the Father. Again He told them exactly what should come. "But ye shall receive power," He said, "after that the Holy Ghost is come upon you: and ye shall be witnesses unto me both in Jerusalem, and in all Judæa, and in Samaria, and unto the uttermost part of the earth" (Acts 1:8). Again Jesus said, as clearly as it was possible for Him to say it, that the disciples would receive power after the Holy Spirit came upon them, supernatural power for witnessing in His name.

Similar terminology is used in Acts 4:31. The disciples had just been again "all filled with the Holy Ghost" as at Pentecost. And in verse 33, following that, the Scripture says, "And with great power gave the apostles witness of the resurrection of the Lord Jesus: and great grace was upon them all." Again we are told that there was a supernatural enduement of power when they were filled with the Holy Spirit.

This reference to an enduement of power from on high when people were filled with the Holy Spirit appears again in Acts, chapter 6. The people had elected some deacons "full of the Holy Ghost and wisdom." Among them was Stephen, "a man full of faith and of the Holy Ghost" (Acts 6:5). Then verse 8 tells us, "And Stephen, full of faith and power, did great wonders and miracles among the people." Stephen was endued with power from on high. Verse 10 tells us, "And they were not able to resist the wisdom and the spirit by which he spake."

We mention the term "power from on high" first of the Bible terms because it is a descriptive term. It is actually a definition of what happened. The term is literal, not figurative. It is practical and clear. To have the power of Pentecost, or to have what the disciples had at Pentecost, means simply that people must be endued with power from on high for service and witnessing.

There are other terms about the blessing of Pentecost. But let everybody who would understand the scriptural meaning of Pentecost set up this rule for himself: No terminology about Pentecost is accurate and truthful if it does not fit as a synonym for this terminology, "endued with power from on high." Any term that means something besides an enduement of power from on high is not correct biblical terminology about the blessing of Pentecost.

It is all right to speak of being "filled with the Spirit" if you mean endued with power from on high. It is all right to speak of being 'baptized with the Spirit' if you make it quite clear that you mean endued with power from on high. It is all right to speak of the pouring out of the Holy Spirit upon people if you mean that they were endued with power from on high. It is all right to speak of the gift of the Holy Ghost if you mean the enduement of power from on high. *But it is wrong to use any terminology about what happened to the disciples at Pentecost if that terminology means anything but an enduement of power from on high.* This terminology is given as a divine definition from the lips of the Lord Jesus Himself. We must not vary from the meaning that Jesus gave in these words to the Pentecostal experience.

II. At Pentecost the Disciples Were "Filled With the Holy Ghost"

Acts 2:4 describes the blessing that came on the disciples at Pentecost in these words, "And they were all filled with the Holy Ghost." The Scripture here does not speak of the indwelling of the Holy Spirit. Jesus had breathed upon them about fifty days before and said to them, "Receive ye the Holy Ghost" (John 20:22). The Holy Spirit, the day Jesus rose from the dead, had come into their bodies to dwell. But these disciples, whose bodies were already the home of the Holy Spirit, now were filled with Him.

This term, "filled with the Holy Ghost," is the term more often used in the Bible than any other about the enduement of power which came at Pentecost. Consider the following examples, besides Acts 2:4:

In Acts 4:8 we are told, "Then Peter, filled with the Holy Ghost, said unto them..." The context makes it clear that Peter here received a divine enduement which enabled him to witness for Christ with great power to the rulers and elders of Israel.

In Acts 4:31 we are told how the same Christians who had been filled before, were filled again. Strikingly enough, the same nine words as are used in Acts 2:4 are used again in Acts 4:31. These nine words are "and they were all filled with the Holy Ghost." Again it was a supernatural enduement of power from on high that they received.

The first deacons chosen were required to be men "full of the Holy Ghost" (Acts 6:3). Stephen was a man "full of faith and of the Holy Ghost" (Acts 6:5). When Stephen was about to be stoned to death, he preached to the crowd that included Saul of Tarsus. Acts 7:55 tells us that "he, being full of the Holy Ghost," saw the glory of God and Jesus in Heaven and then gave his wonderful testimony that cut Saul of Tarsus to the heart so that he could never get away from his conviction until he was saved.

In Acts 9:17 we are told that Ananias came to the new convert, Saul of Tarsus, that he might receive his sight, "and be filled with the Holy Ghost." Verses 20 and 22, following, tell of the beginning of Paul's powerful ministry.

Of Barnabas, the missionary companion of Paul, we are told, "For he was a good man, and full of the Holy Ghost and of faith: and much people was added unto the Lord" (Acts 11:24).

On his missionary journey, Paul at Paphos faced Elymas the sorcerer who opposed him. "Then Saul, (who also is called Paul,) filled with the Holy Ghost, set his eyes on him, And said..." (Acts 13:9,10). Paul, filled afresh with the Holy Spirit, spoke with power and proclaimed divine judgment upon the opposer.

At Antioch of Pisidia great opposition was raised to the preaching of Paul and Barnabas, and they were expelled out of that country and went to Iconium. But many souls had been saved; and Acts 13:52 tells us, "And the disciples were filled with joy, and with the Holy Ghost."

"Filled with the Spirit" is the term most often used of the power of Pentecost.

Another good reason for using the term "filled with the Holy Ghost" or "filled with the Holy Spirit" is that in Ephesians 5:18 all Christians of today are commanded, "Be not drunk with wine, wherein is excess; but be filled with the Spirit." All of us know that in the Bible "the Holy Spirit" and "the Holy Ghost" mean the same Spirit of God. Both are translations of the same Greek words. We are commanded to be filled with the Spirit, or to be filled with the Holy Ghost, just as were Bible Christians.

It is my usual practice to use the term "filled with the Holy Spirit" (or "filled with the Holy Ghost") more often than other terms because it is the one most frequently used in the Bible.

"Filled with the Holy Ghost" means exactly the same as "endued with power from on high."

III. At Pentecost Those Waiting in the Upper Room Were "Baptized With the Holy Ghost"

One of the things the Lord Jesus clearly promised to the disciples who were waiting to be endued with power from on high was, "For John truly baptized with water; but ye shall be baptized with the Holy Ghost not many days hence" (Acts 1:5). It was in explanation of this same statement that He said, "But ye shall receive power, after that the Holy Ghost is come upon you: and ye shall be witnesses unto me" (Acts 1:8). The enduement of power and the baptism in the Holy Ghost were the same thing. They are different terms for the same blessing. To be baptized in the Holy Ghost means to be endued with power from on high.

1. The Term "Baptized With the Holy Ghost" Should Be Used as a Synonym for Pentecostal Power

If we want to understand the meaning of "baptized with the Holy Ghost," we must remember that Jesus used this term in Acts 1:5 as a synonym for being endued with power from on high, as He Himself explained in Acts 1:8. In one verse He promised, "Ye shall be baptized with the Holy Ghost not many days hence." Three verses later He explained that this baptism with the Holy Ghost did not refer to His second coming nor the restoration of the kingdom of Israel; "But," said He, "ye shall receive power, after that the Holy Ghost is come upon you: and ye shall be witnesses unto me...." "Ye shall be baptized with the Holy Ghost not many days hence," He said. Only by reading into the Bible account of Pentecost things that God did not put in it can you make this promise mean anything else but a synonym for an enduement of power from on high. Baptized with the Holy Ghost is the terminology that Jesus Christ Himself used about what would happen at Pentecost when the disciples were endued with power from on high.

We have no right to say that Jesus meant He would begin the church at Pentecost when He said, "Ye shall be baptized with the Holy Ghost not many days hence." If Jesus had meant that the Holy Spirit would, at Pentecost, baptize them into the body of Christ, He could have said so. But He did not say so. In fact, these disciples were already saved and were already in the body of Christ which will be called out at the rapture. They were already members of that "general assembly and church of the firstborn, which are written in heaven" (Heb.

12:23). To confuse Acts 1:5 with I Corinthians 12:13 as if they were talking about the same thing shows lack of careful scholarship and investigation. Jesus did not mean that these disciples at Pentecost would be put into the body of Christ by the Holy Spirit, baptized into that body, buried or submerged into that body and made a part of it. No, they were already made members of this body of Christ, were already submerged or covered or baptized into the body of Christ. But at Pentecost they were to be buried or submerged or covered in the mighty power of the Holy Spirit from God.

Many people these days avoid the term 'baptism in the Holy Ghost.' But it is a Bible term. It is a term that Jesus Christ Himself used about the enduement of power from on high which came at Pentecost. If Jesus Christ used it for that enduement, we have a right to use it also.

Not only did Jesus use that terminology, but long before, that terminology had been used by John the Baptist. In Matthew 3:11 we hear John the Baptist saying, "I indeed baptize you with water unto repentance: but he that cometh after me is mightier than I, whose shoes I am not worthy to bear: he shall baptize you with the Holy Ghost, and with fire." Three or four years before Pentecost John had told the multitudes that they should look for one who would baptize them with the Holy Ghost.

This teaching of John the Baptist, that the Lord Jesus would later baptize many with the Holy Ghost, must be held very important, for it is mentioned in all four of the Gospels. In Mark 1:8 John the Baptist is quoted as saying, "I indeed have baptized you with water: but he shall baptize you with the Holy Ghost." In Luke 3:16 we are told, "John answered, saying unto them all, I indeed baptize you with water; but one mightier than I cometh, the latchet of whose shoes I am not worthy to unloose: he shall baptize you with the Holy Ghost and with fire." In John 1:33 we are told, "And I knew him not: but he that sent me to baptize with water, the same said unto me, Upon whom thou shalt see the Spirit descending, and remaining on him, the same is he which baptizeth with the Holy Ghost."

No reverent Bible student can lightly regard the fact that in every one of the four Gospels John the Baptist is recorded as having said to all those who heard him that the Lord Jesus would baptize with the Holy Ghost. The phrase 'baptize with the Holy Ghost' is a Bible term. It was widely used in the ministry of John the Baptist. In fact, this statement of John had become so widespread that Jesus Himself seems to have been quoting John the Baptist in Acts 1:5 when He said, "For John truly baptized with water; but ye shall be baptized with the Holy

Ghost not many days hence." Jesus was deliberately using and endorsing a term which had very wide currency already.

2. Why the Term "Baptized With the Holy Ghost" Is Now in Reproach

There are two reasons why many godly people have been discouraged from using this Bible terminology, "baptized with the Holy Ghost."

First, the term has been seriously abused and misused. To thousands of people the term simply means talking in tongues. In the minds of the public it is connected with many kinds of religious extravagance and fanaticism. Many people who devoutly hold to a doctrine of being "baptized with the Holy Ghost," as they say, never once understood that that terminology referred to an enduement of power from on high. Many people have told me that they were "baptized with the Holy Ghost according to Acts 2:4," when they simply meant that they had had a religious ecstasy, an emotional period of excitement, and that they had talked in some language or tongue, or what they thought was a language, unknown to themselves. Many such people have told me they were "baptized with the Holy Ghost" who had never won a single soul to Christ nor ever seriously tried to do so! It is fair to say, then, that our beloved friends of the Pentecostal movement have sometimes brought great reproach on this term, "baptized with the Holy Ghost." It is a Bible term, and we ought to redeem it from the abuse and misuse into which it has fallen.

In this same connection, people who teach that they have been "wholly sanctified" by a baptism of the Holy Ghost, that they have had the carnal nature eradicated by a baptism of the Holy Ghost, have helped to bring reproach on the term. To thousands of the best Christians the term "baptized with the Holy Ghost" has a connotation of fanaticism and false claims and spurious emotional excitement.

I do not say that those who have misunderstood and misused the term "baptized with the Holy Ghost" are not good Christians. I do not say that they have not received great blessings of the Holy Spirit or that many of them have not been truly, wonderfully endued with power from on high. But I say that the terminology has often been mistaken and that the terminology has been abused by many in these movements so that the term "baptized with the Holy Ghost" to many people means talking in tongues or extravagant claims of sinlessness. The terminology is Bible terminology, nevertheless, for what happened at Pentecost, and we have a right to use Bible terminology.

Besides the abuse which the term has received by those who use it much, it has become unpopular to use the term "baptized with the Holy Ghost" because of the teaching of John Nelson Darby and other Plymouth Brethren teachers which has infiltrated fundamental ranks very, very widely. This teaching that Pentecost was simply the technical beginning of the church, that Pentecost can never be repeated, that all Christians were potentially baptized into the body of Christ at Pentecost and that therefore no Christian need ever seek to be baptized with the Holy Ghost, has brought the term into great disfavor. This teaching has been very largely reproduced in the notes of the Scofield Bible. In the notes on Acts 2:4 Dr. Scofield says in part, "Every believer is born of the Spirit...indwelt by the Spirit, whose presence makes the believer's body a temple...and baptized by the Spirit." This teaching that Pentecost was the technical beginning of the church, that it can never be repeated, that all Christians are now baptized in the Holy Spirit, and that no Christian should ever pray for the baptism of the Holy Spirit or otherwise seek that baptism, has infiltrated into practically all the orthodox and fundamental Bible institutes and has been promulgated by the Bible teachers who are influenced by the Scofield Bible and by Moody Bible Institute.

The Scofield Reference Bible is the best reference Bible in the world, the one I constantly use. The Bible institutes and the Bible teachers who have been influenced by Darby are among the soundest and most orthodox Christians in most particulars concerning the inspiration of the Bible, the deity of Christ, the blood atonement, and salvation by faith. Among the Bible believers in America, they are one of the strongest influences for fundamental Christianity. That they have been led wrong on this matter is an unspeakable tragedy. It has resulted in playing down all the Bible teaching about Pentecost. It has led to the discouraging of anybody who prayed for the power of Pentecost. It has deliberately discouraged the term "baptized with the Holy Ghost." Particularly orthodox Christians have been generally on the defensive against the extremes of Pentecostalism and the tongues groups. So we have a whole generation of fundamental Christian people who have been taught that they already have the Holy Spirit, that they are already baptized with the Holy Spirit, that they should not pray for the Holy Spirit, and that they should not use the term "baptized with the Holy Ghost" about any enduement of power from Heaven.

If these fundamental people who are influenced by Darby and the Plymouth Brethren group had simply discouraged the term "baptized with the Holy Ghost" and earnestly taught others to seek the power of the Holy Spirit, to seek with all their hearts to be "endued with power from on high" in order to be witnesses for Christ, the result would not have been so bad. But in truth, the same group that teaches people that all Christians are now baptized in the Holy Ghost, that every Christian has all of the Holy Spirit that he can have, also discourages the seeking of the Holy Spirit in power. They discourage prayer for an enduement from Heaven. The result has been the decline of revivals. The result has been a generation of Christians with little emphasis on the Holy Spirit.

There can be no doubt but that the decline in revivals, the growth of modernism and formalism in the churches, the worldliness among church members can largely be traced to this lack of properly balanced emphasis upon the Holy Spirit enduement which Christians should have, following the pattern of New Testament Christians. Without emphasis on the Holy Spirit, there is no revival. Without emphasis on the Holy Spirit and His enduement of power, there is a tendency toward worldliness and away from Christian separation. There is a tendency away from soul winning. There is a tendency to minimize evangelism and magnify abstract Bible teaching. Without an emphasis upon the Holy Spirit, there is a tendency away from preaching against sin and a tendency toward preaching to please people instead of to arouse them and convict them.

If the Pentecostal groups and the sanctification groups have brought reproach on the term "baptized with the Holy Ghost," which Jesus Himself used about the enduement of power which came upon certain disciples at Pentecost, then likewise the ultradispensationalists who follow Darby and Plymouth Brethren teachers have also brought reproach upon the term and have been guilty of teaching hungry Christians to despise the terminology and the promise of Jesus Christ, "Ye shall be baptized with the Holy Ghost."

3. Why Did Jesus Use the Term "Baptized With the Holy Ghost"?

What does the term "baptized with the Holy Ghost" mean? We know that Jesus used the term to refer to the enduement with power from on high. But why did He use such language?

"Baptize" was a very familiar term in common use among God's people in the life of Christ. John the Baptist had come baptizing in the river Jordan. Multitudes from all over Judaea and Jerusalem went out to him and were baptized of him in Jordan, confessing their sins. The ministry of John the Baptist had profoundly shaken the entire Jewish nation. It is fair to assume, and surely we must assume, that multiplied thousands of these who were baptized genuinely repented, turning from their sins to God and trusting in the Messiah, the Lamb of God whom John the Baptist preached. There was nothing wrong with the baptism of John. It was the baptism that Jesus Himself took gladly. It was the only baptism in water that the twelve apostles ever received. It was exactly the same kind of baptism which is taught in the Great Commission—that is, the baptism of a penitent believer in Christ as a public profession of his faith. John did not baptize people in order to save them, nor was there a particle of difference in the plan of salvation which John preached and the plan of salvation which Jesus preached. Compare the Gospel as preached by John in John 3:36 with that preached by Jesus in the same chapter! When Jesus began His public ministry, the crowds flocked to hear Him, and the startling statement was made "that Jesus made and baptized more disciples than John, (Though Jesus himself baptized not, but his disciples)" (John 4:1,2). So practically everybody in the country of the Jews knew about baptism and was accustomed to using the term for the immersion of a penitent believer in water.

What does baptism mean? It means an immersion, a burial, the submerging of an object. New Testament and Christian baptism means the burial of a new convert in water, picturing the burial and resurrection of Jesus Christ, as we are plainly told in Romans 6:3–5. I say that baptism simply means that an object is submerged or covered or buried or overwhelmed in some element. Jesus was overwhelmed with sufferings, and He referred to it as a baptism (Luke 12:50). The children of Israel, passing through the Red Sea with a wall of water on each side and covered with the cloud of God above them and around them, are said to have been "all baptized unto Moses in the cloud and in the sea" (I Cor. 10:2). So, using a very familiar term, Jesus made it into a figure of what would happen when the Holy Spirit should come upon the disciples at Pentecost. He said that they would be overwhelmed, buried, covered, submerged in the Holy Spirit, or "baptized with the Holy Ghost."

Literal, physical Christian baptism, of course, is the immersion of a believer's body in water. Certainly when Jesus said, "Ye shall be baptized with the Holy Ghost not many days hence," He did not mean that God the Father would put the Holy Spirit into a literal pitcher and physically pour the Holy Spirit upon the disciples until they were literally, physically covered, buried. Jesus was using a figure of speech. So we may properly say that the term "baptized with the Holy Ghost" is a figurative term. Literal baptism everywhere in the Bible is baptism in water. The Bible does not even usually say "water baptism," as we often do. If the Bible says a man was baptized and says no more about it, we understand that it was literal, physical baptism, not a figurative baptism such as the disciples had at Pentecost when they were overwhelmed and submerged and covered with the Spirit of God. For instance, in Ephesians 4:5 "one baptism" means "the same baptism" and refers, I believe, to baptism in water.

Is there any difference in the meaning of "filled with the Holy Ghost" and "baptized with the Holy Ghost"? Do the two terms mean the same thing? There might be a shade of difference in degree. For example, a cup might be filled with water and not be surrounded by water. Or a cup may be set in a dishpan and may be filled with water and also surrounded by water. It is possible to imagine that the very highest degree of power, the greatest degree of mastery of an individual by the Holy Spirit, is better pictured by the term "baptized with the Holy Ghost" than by the term "filled with the Spirit." But for all practical purposes the terms are the same. Certainly Jesus used the term "baptized with the Holy Ghost" about the same thing which is described in Acts 2:4 as "they were all filled with the Holy Ghost." When Jesus promised the blessing, He called it "baptized with the Holy Ghost." When it came, Acts 2:4 calls it "filled with the Holy Ghost." We have no right to make any important distinction when the Bible mentions none at all.

4. Should We Today Use the Term "Baptized With the Holy Ghost"?

Is it proper and right for a preacher of the Gospel now to use the term "baptized with the Holy Ghost"? It is a Bible term, a term used by John the Baptist and used by the Lord Jesus Himself, about the enduement of power that came at Pentecost. Now, should I use this Bible term in discussing the fullness of the Spirit, as Jesus used it?

Here a word of caution is necessary. Every Christian must not only speak the truth, but he must also be understood correctly. Every man is accountable not only for what he actually says but also for what people understand him to say. So if I teach people that they ought to be "baptized with the Holy Ghost" and they understand me to teach something which is unscriptural and wrong, then I have been at fault. I have no right to use terminology in a way that teaches something which is not true to the Word of God. Even to use Bible terms in a way that will be misunderstood and will tend to encourage false doctrine would be a mistake. So if I use the term "baptized with the Holy Ghost" I must make sure that people understand what I mean. If I use the term "baptized with the Holy Ghost," I must explain my meaning. Usually I find it better to use the term "filled with the Holy Ghost" or "filled with the Spirit," both of which are Bible terms, terms used much more often in the Bible and with the same meaning that I would give to the term "baptized with the Holy Ghost." The term used most in the Bible would properly be the term that Christians should use most today.

Dr. R. A. Torrey, who taught much on the Holy Spirit and was himself wonderfully endued with the power of God for soul winning, in one of his books on the baptism of the Spirit suggests that a Christian might call his first great enduement with power "the baptism with the Holy Ghost" and that other and later enduements might be called "fillings of the Holy Spirit." I believe that the beloved Dr. Torrey was trying to avoid undue criticism, and there is some merit to what he says. Yet I am not convinced that when Acts 2:4 says, "And they were all filled with the Holy Ghost," that should be called "baptized with the Holy Ghost," and that when the same crowd "were all filled with the Holy Ghost" in Acts 4:31 and exactly the same nine words are used to describe the event, the second event should not be called the same name as the first. If one filling of the Holy Spirit was a baptism, I do not see why another filling with the Holy Spirit would not be a baptism.

A misunderstanding of the term "baptized with the Holy Ghost" springs from a very widely spread current misunderstanding of baptism itself. The Catholic church, up until about the thirteenth century, baptized always by immersion, as did first-century Christians, and early Catholic church buildings still standing have the large baptistries then used for the immersion of adults. The Catholic church had already begun to baptize infants, and then they began to use sprinkling or pouring instead of immersion with adults also. These facts may be found in the *Catholic Encyclopedia*, and a fuller discussion in the author's book *Bible Baptism*.

Now, it naturally turns out that to Catholic writers and theologians the scriptural meaning of baptism is lost. They do not understand that baptism is the immersion of the believer as a profession of his faith in the Saviour who died for him, was buried and rose again. They do not understand that baptism pictures the believer's death to sin and his being raised up to live in newness of life. So without any reference to the original meaning of the Greek word *baptizo*, Catholics simply think of baptism as an initiation into the church. *And practically the whole Protestant world has absorbed this Catholic perversion of the term!* But the term "baptism" does not mean initiation, and never did in the Bible. Baptism means to immerse, to plunge, to cover, to overwhelm, to dip. It does not mean initiation. So there is no logical reason why a person could not be baptized with the Holy Ghost a second time as well as the first time. Certain it is that the disciples were "all filled with the Holy Ghost" in Acts 2:4 and again they were "all filled with the Holy Ghost" in Acts 4:31. It is equally certain that to be filled with the Holy Ghost at Pentecost was the same as baptized with the Holy Ghost. When a Christian is overwhelmed with the Holy Spirit, one may properly say he is baptized with the Holy Spirit.

But certainly this much is clear to us. In the Bible the enduement of power was usually called being filled with the Holy Ghost. Christians would probably be wise to use such terms as are used most in the Bible. Certainly, beyond any shadow of doubt, any man who uses the term "filled with the Holy Ghost" or the term "baptized with the Holy Ghost" ought to make it clear that he means what the Bible means. He ought not to leave the impression that he means talking in tongues, if he does not mean that. He ought not to leave the impression that he means the eradication of the carnal nature, if he does not mean that. Any man who preaches or teaches the Word of God is accountable to God to use language so it will be clearly understood and so he will not in effect teach false doctrine while using scriptural terms. So if you use the term "baptized with the Holy Ghost," explain what you mean!

Yet I could not honestly leave this topic without saying a greatly needed word. That is that down all the Christian centuries until the last few decades, Christian leaders, great preachers and evangelists and great Bible teachers have been almost unanimous in using the term "baptized with the Holy Ghost" to mean an enduement of mighty power from God. People must be left free to use this Bible term as it has always been used by the best Christians of the ages.

5. Greatest Soul Winners and Bible Teachers Have Called Pentecostal Power "Baptism With the Holy Ghost"

Moody frankly called the power of Pentecost "the baptism of the Holy Spirit." In the book *Moody, His Words, Works, and Workers*, is a long article by Moody with the heading "The Baptism of the Holy

Spirit for Service"; and he said, "...there is no use of sending out men who are not baptized for service."

C. I. Scofield used this term also, "baptized with the Holy Spirit," as a synonym for soul-winning power. At the funeral of Moody, Dr. Scofield gave a short address in which he said:

> The secrets of Dwight L. Moody's power were: First, in a definite experience of Christ's saving grace. He had passed out of death into life, and he knew it. Secondly, he believed in the divine authority of the Scriptures. The Bible was to him the voice of God, and he made it resound as such in the consciences of men. Thirdly, he was baptized with the Holy Spirit, and he knew it. It was to him as definite an experience as his conversion.

Dr. R. A. Torrey had a book copyrighted in 1895 and 1897 on *The Baptism With the Holy Spirit*. He used the term all the way through that book to mean a special enduement of power for Christian service and witnessing. Again in the year before he died, Dr. R. A. Torrey had published and copyrighted a book *The Holy Spirit, Who He Is, and What He Does*, in which he used the same terminology.

But Dr. R. A. Torrey used the term "baptized with the Holy Ghost" just as D. L. Moody did. Torrey worked with Mr. Moody. Again and again by special request of D. L. Moody, Dr. Torrey gave his lecture on "The Baptism With the Holy Ghost." And Moody continually urged people to seek to be baptized with the Holy Ghost. He himself frankly said that after two years of earnest burden on this matter he had received a mighty baptism with the Holy Ghost.

The teaching of Torrey and of Moody was the original teaching of Moody Bible Institute. It was the teaching of the evangelists that were associated with them.

Charles G. Finney frankly and repeatedly used the term "a baptism of the Holy Ghost." In Finney's autobiography, he tells of his own experience as follows:

> As I went in and shut the door after me, it seemed as if I met the Lord Jesus Christ face to face....He said nothing, but looked at me in such a manner as to break me right down at His feet. I wept aloud like a child, and made such confessions as I could with my choked utterance....As I turned and was about to take a seat by the fire, I received a mighty baptism of the Holy Ghost....No words can express the wonderful love that was shed abroad in my heart. I wept with joy and love.

In his *Lectures on Revivals*, Finney said: "Every step of progress in the Christian life is taken by a fresh and fuller appropriation of Christ by faith, a fuller baptism of the Holy Spirit."

Spurgeon spoke of people being baptized with the Holy Ghost when he meant endued with power from on high. J. B. Gambrell, B. H. Carroll and L. R. Scarborough, mighty soul-winning leaders among Southern Baptists, used similar terminology and did it in print many times. As a boy I read editorials by J. B. Gambrell in the *Baptist Standard* in which he said that the crying need of the churches everywhere was for Christians to be baptized with the Holy Ghost. He meant what practically all the great soul winners and orthodox Christian leaders in the world meant in those days by the terminology.

In recent decades many Johnny-come-latelies have derided the terminology "baptized with the Holy Ghost." A recent article by a godly man, a dear friend of mine, said that Dr. R. A. Torrey "was mistaken in his terms." Who is there who is fit to say that Dr. Torrey was mistaken in his terms? Dr. R. A. Torrey was one of the greatest Bible teachers America ever saw. He was a thorough scholar, with two degrees from Yale and work in two German universities. Besides that, he had unusual fitness to speak on the matter of the power of the Holy Spirit because beyond any controversy he himself was endued with the mighty power from on high. He himself exemplified the power of the Holy Spirit. Why should some sophisticated Bible teacher who never had any great manifestation of the Holy Spirit upon him, never had a mighty revival, never turned thousands of sinners to Christ—why should any such man feel himself so thoroughly capable of setting Dr. R. A. Torrey, D. L. Moody, Charles G. Finney and the other great soul winners right on their teaching about the Holy Spirit?

Consider for a moment a parable. A certain man set out for a city in a far country. Of two men he asked advice. The first adviser had never been to the city. In fact, he told the inquiring wayfarer that there was some doubt whether the city now existed. Very probably, he thought, it had once existed but had later disappeared entirely. The guidebook, indeed, said such a city existed and gave instructions; but that part of the guidebook, he thought, was now out of date. He had never been along the road, but he gave learned advice to the pilgrim as to every turn he should take if he would reach the city. But in fact he doubted if the city now existed and thought the wayfarer was wasting his time to seek it.

The other adviser said plainly, "I know there is such a city. I have been there myself. I know every step of the road because I have traveled it, and I will tell you the way to the city you seek. I have proved the instructions in the guidebook still apply. Then go forward boldly; you will find it even as I have told you."

Now to which of these advisers should the wayfaring man listen? The first adviser is the "Bible teacher." All over America many godly Bible teachers, good men, devoted men, Bible-believing men, say that now there is no more baptism with the Holy Ghost except what people receive when they are converted. They tell young Christians who long to have all the power and blessing that God has for them that they ought not to pray for the Holy Spirit, that to "tarry" will likely lead to fanaticism. They say that the baptism of the Holy Ghost was finished entirely at Pentecost when the church and all future Christians were in some mystical manner "potentially baptized in the Holy Ghost." But these Bible teachers do not claim themselves to have been wonderfully endued with power from on high for witnessing. They have had no great revivals. They have seen no marvelous manifestations of the Holy Spirit. They represent the adviser who had never been to the city and yet with very learned language discussed the road with the inquiring pilgrim.

The other adviser represents the great evangelists. The great evangelists and soul winners, almost without exception, teach that there is a definite enduement with power from on high which Christians should seek. They beseech us earnestly to pray for the fullness of the Spirit. They often call that heavenly anointing and heavenly enduement "the baptism with the Holy Ghost." I maintain that on this matter the men whom God has blessed, the men whom God has honored, the men in whom God has demonstrated the mighty Pentecostal enduement, are more trustworthy advisers than those men who have never paid the price for the fullness of power, have never had great revivals, have never won multitudes to Jesus. The evangelists—Moody and Torrey and Chapman and Spurgeon and the like, the great soul winners who were endued with power from on high themselves—are more worthy of our respect on this matter than all the Bible teachers who follow Darby and the ultradispensationalists but who themselves never experienced the mighty manifestation of the power of God.

Here I pause to nail down an unworthy and untrue rumor. Dr. R. A. Torrey was, as the reader will know, the most influential force in the establishment of Bible institutes in America. He organized Moody Bible Institute and, working with D. L. Moody, inaugurated the Bible institute curriculum. He likewise helped to found and establish the Los Angeles Bible Institute. So Dr. R. A. Torrey's teaching on the Holy

Spirit has been a focal point of attack by the followers of Darby and others who would discourage people from seeking to be filled with the Holy Spirit as a special enduement of power from on high. These people who have opposed the teaching of D. L. Moody and R. A. Torrey have whispered it about that "Dr. Torrey changed his conviction about the Holy Spirit before he died. If Dr. Torrey had it to do over he would change all his teaching about the baptism of the Holy Spirit."

Every reader can very easily find out for himself that there is no truth in such a charge. A man who has gone to Heaven can usually not speak for himself to defend himself from misquotation and misrepresentation. Fortunately Dr. R. A. Torrey can defend himself. Here is how Dr. Torrey shows that he never changed his mind about the fullness of the Holy Spirit or the baptism with the Holy Ghost. In 1895 Dr. R. A. Torrey wrote a book *The Baptism With the Holy Spirit*. It was copyrighted in 1895 and 1897. Dr. R. A. Torrey at that time was thirty-nine years of age, a mature Christian leader. In that book Dr. R. A. Torrey plainly said that he himself had been baptized with the Holy Ghost, that the baptism with the Holy Ghost was so definite that every Christian might know from the Bible whether or not he had received it, and that every Christian should be baptized with the Holy Ghost.

But did Dr. Torrey change his mind? No, Dr. Torrey became world-famous as an evangelist. He went around the world, and hundreds of thousands of souls were turned to Christ under his ministry. Then he returned to the United States. He was now an old man. He helped to establish the Bible Institute of Los Angeles. He wrote many books. He held revival campaigns. He preached in Bible conferences all over America. Then as an old man he wrote another book on the Holy Spirit. It is *The Holy Spirit, Who He Is, and What He Does*, and is still published by Fleming Revell. (The same publishers published his other volume.) In this book Dr. Torrey goes over the same ground as the volume written many, many years before. Again Dr. Torrey says that he himself had been baptized with the Holy Ghost. Again he says that the baptism of the Holy Ghost is so definite that every Christian may know whether or not he has received it. He says that the baptism with the Holy Ghost in every case in the Bible was for an enduement of power for service and witnessing. He says again that every Christian should be baptized with the Holy Ghost. The book was published in 1927. Dr. Torrey was then seventy-one years old, and in 1928 Dr. Torrey died. One year before he died, Dr. Torrey restated, in great detail, his teaching on the Holy Spirit.

Now for anybody to try to say that Dr. Torrey changed his position in later years and did not believe and did not preach what he before had taught, with D. L. Moody, betrays ignorance of the facts. Do not believe what anybody tells you if he hints that Dr. Torrey changed his position on the Holy Spirit in later years. Read for yourself what Dr. Torrey has to say in 1895 and then thirty-two years later, in 1927, in the book published just before his death.

It is true that Dr. Torrey, after the Pentecostal movement led many to seeking tongues, was very careful in his statements to explain that he did not mean, by the baptism of the Holy Ghost, what Pentecostal groups meant. He frequently said that it did not matter so much if there were differences in terminology, just so people really received the fullness of the Spirit and the enduement of power from on high. Dr. Torrey was not making a fetish of certain language. He was willing to use different terms to be clearly understood. But Dr. Torrey did not change his position on the baptism of the Spirit or the fullness of the Spirit. Any who think he did change ought to read for themselves Dr. Torrey's statements and see that they have been misled.

Let us bring back the Bible terminology on the subject of the Holy Spirit. Let us again, when necessary, use the term "baptized with the Holy Ghost" as the great soul winners down through the years used it. But let us make sure that the public understands what we mean, and let us make sure that we use the term as a synonym for "endued with power from on high," as Jesus Himself used it.

IV. At Pentecost God's Spirit Was "Poured Out" Upon Christians

On the day of Pentecost, after the marvelous power of God was manifested and the one hundred twenty who had waited in the Upper Room were all filled with the Holy Spirit, Peter stood up and explained what had happened to them.

"For these are not drunken, as ye suppose, seeing it is but the third hour of the day. But this is that which was spoken by the prophet Joel; And it shall come to pass in the last days, saith God, I will pour out of my Spirit upon all flesh: and your sons and your daughters shall prophesy, and your young men shall see visions, and your old men shall dream dreams: And on my servants and on my handmaidens I will pour out in those days of my Spirit; and they shall prophesy."—Acts 2:15–18.

It is proper, then, to say that at Pentecost God poured out His Spirit upon Christians. The pouring out of the Holy Spirit upon Christians means the same as the enduement of power from on high, means the same as being filled with the Spirit, means the same as the baptism with the Holy Ghost.

This picturesque figure of speech, calling the enduement of Holy Spirit power the pouring out of the Holy Spirit upon people, is a familiar one in the Old Testament Scriptures:

"For I will pour water upon him that is thirsty, and floods upon the dry ground: I will pour my spirit upon thy seed, and my blessing upon thine offspring: And they shall spring up as among the grass, as willows by the water courses."—Isa. 44:3,4.

Also, in Isaiah 32:15 Israel is warned that the land will one day be desolate and neglected "until the spirit be poured upon us from on high"—that is, when Israel as a nation is restored, it will be brought about by the coming of the Holy Spirit in great power upon the remnant of Jews who turn to God. This is partly the same promise as Joel 2:28,29 which Peter quoted at Pentecost.

In Proverbs 1:23 we are told how Wisdom, as deity personified, cries, "Turn you at my reproof: behold, I will pour out my spirit unto you...."

In the Old Testament God often says that He will pour out His wrath, or His indignation; and sometimes He promises to pour out His blessings.

There are many other Scriptures which say that the Spirit of the Lord "came upon" people. Note the following passages:

"And I will take of the spirit which is upon thee [Moses], and will put it upon them."—Num. 11:17.

"When the spirit rested upon them, they prophesied."—Num. 11:25.

"...the spirit rested upon them...and they prophesied."—Num. 11:26.

"And Moses said...would God that all the LORD's people were prophets, and that the LORD would put his spirit upon them!"—Num. 11:29.

"And the Spirit of God came upon Saul."—I Sam. 11:6.

"And the Spirit of the LORD came upon David from that day forward."—I Sam. 16:13.

In the Book of Judges we are told that the Spirit of the Lord came upon Jephthah and upon Samson.

Second Chronicles 15:1 says, "And the Spirit of God came upon Azariah."

About the Lord Jesus it was said, "The Spirit of the Lord GOD is upon me"(Isa. 61:1).

Again in Isaiah 42:1 it was said, "I have put my spirit upon him," referring to the Lord Jesus.

We are told in the Gospels that John saw the Holy Spirit "descending upon" Jesus.

All these Scriptures which speak of the Holy Spirit's being *on* people refer not to the indwelling of the Holy Spirit and not to regeneration, but to a special enduement of power. So the terminology used about Pentecost fits in with the usual Bible terminology about the enduement of power from on high.

It is probable that the picture of God pouring out the Holy Spirit upon His people follows the pattern of pouring anointing oil upon priests and kings, when God endued them with wisdom and power for His service. The anointing oil was a symbol of the Spirit of God. In fact, in one passage referring to the Lord Jesus, the same verse says, "The Spirit of the Lord GOD is upon me; because the LORD hath anointed me to preach" (Isa. 61:1, quoted in Luke 4:18). The Holy Spirit coming upon one in divine enduement of power is called an anointing. As David was anointed to be king, as Aaron was anointed to be high priest, so God anoints His servants with the Holy Spirit. The pouring out of the Holy Spirit is evidently intended to remind us of this special symbol of the Holy Spirit used throughout the Old Testament and sometimes in the New Testament.

An amusing and interesting question has been asked which might be answered here, both because it is interesting and because it sheds light on the meaning of the terms used at Pentecost. Someone has said that if the pouring out of the Spirit upon people and the baptism of the Holy Spirit are the same thing, then baptism in water should be by pouring and not by immersion! If baptism is an immersion, a burial, an overwhelming, then how could it be by pouring?

That question is answered by a simple illustration. Suppose a cup is put in the dishpan and the faucet is turned on so that the water runs into the cup. There is the "pouring out" of the water upon the cup. Then the cup becomes "filled" as the disciples were filled with the Spirit at Pentecost. Then as the water continues to run, the cup is baptized, covered, immersed, buried in the water. So God poured out His Spirit upon Christians at Pentecost until they were filled and covered and surrounded with the Holy Spirit. The three terms used about the Holy Spirit at Pentecost all fit together. The pouring out of the Holy Spirit and the fullness of the Spirit and the baptism with the Spirit were the same blessing. All of these terms refer to the enduement of power from on high.

V. The Power of Pentecost Was Called "the Gift of the Holy Ghost"

When Peter preached his wonderful sermon on the day of Pentecost many were pricked in their hearts "and said unto Peter and to the rest of the apostles, Men and brethren, what shall we do?" They wanted not only salvation but also the fullness of the Spirit which was obviously manifested before them this day. They wanted to be saved, and then they wanted power to witness for Jesus. Peter's answer is given in Acts 2:38: "Then Peter said unto them, Repent, and be baptized every one of you in the name of Jesus Christ for the remission of sins, and ye shall receive the gift of the Holy Ghost."

It is important to see that two subjects are under consideration in this verse. The first subject is salvation. Those who repented were saved. Those who after they were saved went on to be baptized, publicly and wholly dedicating themselves to the crucified life, the witnessing, soul-winning life, would also receive "the gift of the Holy Ghost."

We cannot at this moment take time to prove that baptism is not here mentioned as necessary to salvation. The author's sixty-four-page pamphlet, *Bible Baptism*, will be found to answer that question clearly from the Scriptures. Here we simply state the fact that Acts 2:38 teaches that people who have repented should then be baptized "for the remission of sins" which they have already received. That is, baptism refers to and announces the remission of one's sins which has been obtained by penitent faith. Nor can we, in this chapter, discuss in detail the conditions for the enduement of power from on high. That will come later. But it seems obvious that Peter is here promising these inquirers that they too can have the same gift of the Holy Spirit which the hundred twenty received that day. In other words, "the gift of the Holy Ghost" means the enduement of power, the fullness of the Spirit, the baptism with the Holy Ghost, the pouring out of the Holy Spirit, which many Christians received at Pentecost.

It is further made clear that "the gift of the Holy Ghost" means the fullness of the Holy Spirit or the enduement of power from on high, by the use of the term in Acts 10:44-48. That Scripture, telling about how Cornelius and his household were saved and filled with the Holy Spirit, says:

"While Peter yet spake these words, the Holy Ghost fell on all them which heard the word. And they of the circumcision which believed were astonished, as many as came with Peter, because that on the Gentiles also was poured out the gift of the Holy Ghost. For they heard them speak with tongues, and magnify God. Then

answered Peter, Can any man forbid water, that these should not be baptized, which have received the Holy Ghost as well as we? And he commanded them to be baptized in the name of the Lord. Then prayed they him to tarry certain days."

In verse 44 we are told that "the Holy Ghost fell on" Cornelius and his household. That sounds like the pouring out of the Spirit upon the disciples at Pentecost.

But verse 45 is even more explicit: "...because that on the Gentiles also was poured out the gift of the Holy Ghost." Notice that little word "also." The gift of the Holy Ghost was poured out on Cornelius. But the same gift of the Holy Ghost had been poured out before on the disciples at Pentecost! That is clearly the meaning.

Peter admits as much when he says, "These...have received the Holy Ghost as well as we." Cornelius and his household received "the gift of the Holy Ghost." But Peter says that that was the same gift which he and others had received at Pentecost.

Again in Acts 11:15–17, when Peter was explaining to the apostles and leaders at Jerusalem his visit to Cornelius, he said: "And as I began to speak, the Holy Ghost fell on them, as on us at the beginning. Then remembered I the word of the Lord, how that he said, John indeed baptized with water; but ye shall be baptized with the Holy Ghost. Forasmuch then as God gave them the like gift as he did unto us, who believed on the Lord Jesus Christ; what was I, that I could withstand God?"

The Holy Spirit fell on Cornelius and his household as was promised when the apostles were at the beginning—that is, at Pentecost.

Then Peter says that he remembered that Jesus had promised His disciples, "Ye shall be baptized with the Holy Ghost." This "gift of the Holy Ghost" which Cornelius received in Acts 10:45 was the baptism with the Holy Spirit.

In verse 17 of chapter 11 Peter said that Cornelius received the like gift as other Christians had received, the gift of the Holy Ghost. That refers not to salvation, though it convinced Peter that Cornelius and his household were saved. The gift of the Holy Ghost is not salvation, but the enduement of power from on high which others received at Pentecost.

In Acts 8:20 Peter calls the fullness of the Holy Spirit "the gift of God."

The Scripture here is not speaking of the various gifts which the Holy Spirit Himself gives to those whom He fills: the gift of prophecy, or of healing, or of miracles, or of tongues. Here the gift is the Holy Spirit Himself, given in power on a Christian to enable him to win souls.

VI. Those Endued With Power From on High Were Said to Have "Received the Holy Ghost"

Since the fullness of the Holy Spirit, as given at Pentecost, is called "the gift of the Holy Spirit," it is but a step further to say that those who received this supernatural enduement of power "received the Holy Ghost." And several Scriptures, speaking about this enduement of power, call it receiving the Holy Ghost.

When "the Holy Ghost fell on all them which heard the word" and "on the Gentiles also was poured out the gift of the Holy Ghost," then Peter said about Cornelius and his household that they "have received the Holy Ghost as well as we" (Acts 10:47). If God gives "the gift of the Holy Ghost," then Christians upon whom He is poured out in power "receive the Holy Ghost." And Peter was here clearly speaking about the experience of Cornelius and his household as being identically the same as others received at Pentecost.

In Samaria, Philip the deacon had preached Christ and had a blessed revival. But the converts there were not filled with the Holy Spirit. They had been saved, but they needed this power from on high. God had reason to exalt the apostles and teach the converts to look to His appointed apostles for leadership and authority, particularly until the New Testament should be written. So the apostles sent Peter and John to pray for these new converts that they might receive the Holy Ghost. The story is told in Acts 8:14–17 as follows:

> *"Now when the apostles which were at Jerusalem heard that Samaria had received the word of God, they sent unto them Peter and John: Who, when they were come down, prayed for them, that they might receive the Holy Ghost: (For as yet he was fallen upon none of them: only they were baptized in the name of the Lord Jesus.) Then laid they their hands on them, and they received the Holy Ghost."*

Note that here are people who have already received the Word of God, have already believed and are baptized. They are Christians, certainly; yet they need something else besides salvation. They need the mighty power of God to make them soul winners, to help them witness for Christ. It is explained that "as yet he [the Holy Spirit] was fallen upon none of them." This is language like that of Joel about Pentecost. The Bible, when it speaks of the Holy Spirit's coming upon people, always means in a special enduement of power; so it means here. To receive this enduement of power of the Holy Spirit was called simply to "receive the Holy Ghost."

It is certainly true that these converts already had the Holy Spirit abiding in their bodies before Peter and John came. They had been regenerated when they believed, and the regeneration was wrought by the Holy Spirit. There is a sense in which they had already received the Holy Spirit, as every Christian had. How much the dispensationalists, who might think that these new converts were not yet in the body of Christ, and who speak so wisely of a "transitional period," have muddied the waters here! One who believes in Christ is saved. That is true through all the Bible. One who is saved is a member of the body of Christ and has the Holy Spirit dwelling in his body. That is certainly true of every Christian since the day Jesus rose from the dead and was glorified and, appearing to His disciples, breathed on them and commanded them, "Receive ye the Holy Ghost." But to have the Holy Spirit in regeneration is one thing. To have His open, public manifestation, His fullness, His anointing, His divine enduement of power, is another and vastly different thing. Here these new converts received the Holy Ghost in His fullness. We have a right, then, to speak of Christians receiving the Holy Ghost, referring to the fullness of the Holy Spirit. That is a Bible usage.

In Acts 19:2 we have this term, "received the Holy Ghost," used again. It is used in a question. Paul said to a dozen disciples at Ephesus, "Have ye received the Holy Ghost since ye believed?"

Here the note in the Scofield Bible has led many wrong. Dr. Scofield says, "Paul was evidently impressed by the absence of spirituality and power in these so-called disciples. Their answer brought out the fact that they were Jewish proselytes, disciples of John the Baptist, looking forward to a coming King, not Christians looking backward to an accomplished redemption." But the Scofield Reference Bible, often so helpful, here is on dangerous ground. What right has any man to say "so-called disciples" when the Bible says "disciples"? That is making light of the plain statement of the Word of God. Since the Bible says they were disciples, then Bible believers must accept it that they were disciples. Not only so, but they had believed in Christ and had been baptized on their profession of faith. Apollos, to whom the context points as the one who won these converts, had been "instructed in the way of the Lord; and being fervent in the spirit, he spake and taught diligently the things of the Lord, knowing only the baptism of John" (Acts 18:25). Apollos had received his instruction principally from John the Baptist. He had probably been absent at his home in Alexandria at the time of Pentecost and so did not fully understand about the fullness of the Spirit. He could not teach the doctrine of the fullness of the Spirit, though he himself was "fervent in the spirit," that is, empowered by the Holy Spirit to win souls.

To these converts who had believed and been baptized under the able and spiritual and fervent preaching of Apollos, Paul said, "Have ye received the Holy Ghost since ye believed?" Then he explained to them that when they were baptized, that itself should have involved the kind of holy dedication and surrender to the Lord's will and obedience to the Lord's command as would have led them to be filled with the Holy Spirit, had they fully understood baptism. We are told, "And when Paul had laid his hands upon them, the Holy Ghost came on them; and they spake with tongues, and prophesied" (Acts 19:6). "The Holy Ghost came on them." That is the same enduement of power that came at Pentecost. That is the same power that was on Christ when it was said that "the Spirit of the Lord is upon me" (Luke 4:18). And these Spirit-filled men upon whom the Holy Ghost came, prophesied—that is, they had the supernatural gift which the Holy Spirit often gives people to witness with mighty power. They did this witnessing in more than one language, though we are not told whether the languages were the supernatural gift of tongues or whether they naturally spoke several languages and each one praised the Lord and witnessed in his own language. But there can be no doubt that here was a supernatural enduement of *power* like that at Pentecost. It is possible that the speaking in tongues is here mentioned because of the similarity to the account given of the blessing at Pentecost. Certainly we are intended to understand that these were filled with the Spirit.

That being true, we know that by the question, "Have ye received the Holy Ghost?" Paul meant, "Have you been endued with power from on high?"

In John 7:39 and in John 20:22 the Scripture speaks of receiving the Holy Ghost, when it seems to refer clearly to the indwelling of the Holy Spirit which was to begin when Jesus rose from the dead and was glorified. Note John 20:21,22: "Then said Jesus to them again, Peace be unto you: as my Father hath sent me, even so send I you. And when he had said this, he breathed on them, and saith unto them, Receive ye the Holy Ghost." Since Jesus a little later expressly commanded the disciples to tarry at Jerusalem until they were endued with power from on high, we certainly may infer that the disciples did not here receive the power from on high they must yet await. Yet when Jesus breathed upon them and commanded them, "Receive ye the Holy Ghost," I believe that we must fairly infer that they did receive the Holy Spirit into their bodies. I believe that here was truly fulfilled, at least in part, the promise Jesus gave in John 7:37–39. Jesus said:

"If any man thirst, let him come unto me, and drink. He that believeth on me, as the scripture hath said, out of his belly shall flow rivers of living water. (But this spake he of the Spirit, which they that believe on him should receive: for the Holy Ghost was not yet given; because that Jesus was not yet glorified.)"

There are two parts of that promise. One is that the Holy Spirit should make His headquarters in the bodies of Christians and should flow out from Christians and that His power would radiate from Christians. The indwelling is the first promise. The second promise is that the power of the Holy Spirit would be manifested in these Christians in whose bodies the Spirit dwelt.

So we conclude that when Jesus rose from the dead and said to the disciples, "Receive ye the Holy Ghost," His words were both an announcement and a command. I think He then announced the indwelling of the Spirit and that when Jesus there breathed on His disciples, the Holy Spirit literally came in to dwell. But we are certain that there is a command that these same disciples should later receive the Holy Spirit in His fullness of power. It was for this that they were to tarry at Jerusalem. And they were to do the work that Jesus had done, for Jesus said, "As my Father hath sent me, even so send I you."

We conclude that before the Holy Spirit came into the bodies of Christians to dwell, the term 'receiving the Holy Spirit' would partly refer to His indwelling. But certainly in every case the fullness of the Spirit is meant.

In Luke 11:13 Jesus said, "...how much more shall your heavenly Father give the Holy Spirit to them that ask him?" The context shows that Jesus is speaking about a Christian's having bread for sinners, about a Christian's having power from Heaven to win others.

With these things in mind, we can say that to receive the Holy Spirit is a term used for the enduement of power from on high, though it is not frequently used in the Bible and though there are complications which might make it misunderstood unless we clearly explain that the term refers to the fullness of the Spirit, the enduement of power from Heaven.

Summing up, the following terms are all used about what happened to Christians at Pentecost:

(1) They were "endued with power from on high." They 'received power after that the Holy Ghost came upon them, and they were witnesses.' This is a definition which Jesus Himself gave, and all the other terminology regarding the power of Pentecost must mean an enduement of power from on high.

(2) At Pentecost the disciples were "filled with the Holy Ghost." This term, "filled with the Spirit," or "filled with the Holy Ghost," is used many times in the Bible and is the term used in the command for Christians today, in Ephesians 5:18. It is the most commonly used term for the power of Pentecost.

(3) The disciples at Pentecost were "baptized with the Holy Ghost." That is the term Jesus used, the term John the Baptist had repeatedly used. It is a Bible term and has been understood by the greatest soul winners and Bible teachers through many centuries to refer to the special enduement of power. The term has been somewhat confused by its use by the tongues people and by eradicationists, and its use has been discouraged by the ultradispensationalists particularly. But it is a Bible term used by the Saviour Himself about the power of Pentecost. So we have a right to say that Christians need to be "baptized with the Holy Ghost," but we should be careful to define what we mean since the term has been misused so much.

(4) At Pentecost God poured out His Spirit upon the waiting disciples. So we may properly say that the Holy Spirit came upon Christians at Pentecost and that He comes upon Christians today for the same reason, to give them an enduement of power for witnessing.

(5) The power of Pentecost is called also "the gift of the Holy Ghost."

(6) The power of Pentecost is also called "receiving the Holy Ghost."

If one wants to be clearly understood and to be true to the Bible, he probably should not use the terms "the second blessing" or "a second definite work of grace," referring to the power of Pentecost. But he should teach that Christians need to be "endued with power from on high"; that Christians need to be "filled with the Spirit."

Chapter 7

The Fullness of the Holy Spirit and the Ministry Gifts in Old Testament and New

"For to one is given by the Spirit the word of wisdom; to another the word of knowledge by the same Spirit; To another faith by the same Spirit; to another the gifts of healing by the same Spirit; To another the working of miracles; to another prophecy; to another discerning of spirits; to another divers kinds of tongues; to another the interpretation of tongues."—I Cor. 12:8–10.

"And God hath set some in the church, first apostles, secondarily prophets, thirdly teachers, after that miracles, then gifts of healings, helps, governments, diversities of tongues."—I Cor. 12:28.

One chapter in the New Testament gives detailed information about spiritual gifts which the Holy Spirit divides to different people for the ministry or service of Christ. We call them "the ministry gifts." That chapter is I Corinthians, chapter 12. These gifts, given by the Holy Spirit to individual Christians, are named twice, once in verses 8 to 10 above, and again in verse 28.

You will see that the two lists are not exactly alike. Apostles are mentioned in verse 28, but not in verses 8 to 10. It is quite evident that apostles would have a number of the gifts mentioned in the first list.

In verse 28 the Lord evidently names the gifts in the order of importance, for He says, "...first apostles, secondarily prophets, thirdly teachers, after that miracles, then gifts of healings, helps, governments, diversities of tongues." God expressly says that the apostles are first, that prophets are secondary in importance, teachers are third in importance, and other gifts following, evidently in order of importance. As apostles are first in importance, then gifts of tongues are least in importance.

But in I Corinthians 12:8–10 God does not claim to put them in order of importance. More likely, He puts them in order of frequency. "For to one is given by the Spirit the word of wisdom; to another the word of knowledge by the same Spirit; To another faith by the same Spirit." These are evidently the most frequent gifts. These first three do not involve miracles, at least not what we generally call miracles. And after them in frequency come healing, miracles, prophecy, discerning of spirits, and, last of all, divers kinds of languages and the interpretation or translation of languages.

As tongues or languages are last in importance (vs. 28), they are also last in order of frequency (vs. 10). Hence, we are not surprised to find that only one clear case of the miraculous gift of tongues, that is at Pentecost, is described in the Bible. Tongues are mentioned elsewhere, meaning foreign languages, but there is no other particular case of the miraculous *gift* of tongues mentioned, as far as we can clearly know. Acts 10:46 mentions that Cornelius and his household spoke with tongues. Acts 19:6 tells that a dozen other Christians at Ephesus spoke with foreign languages. It is not said that either was the miraculous gift of tongues.

The gifts of an apostle, called, as were the twelve and later the Apostle Paul, to speak with divine authority in the setting up of the New Testament doctrine and practice and the setting up of the local churches, were the most important gifts. I believe that the same gifts of an apostle were given to those who were divinely inspired to write parts of the Bible. In fact, a number of the apostles—Matthew, John, Paul, Peter and James—were inspired to write parts of the New Testament.

These ministry gifts which the Holy Spirit gives to individual Christians for the service of Christ interest us profoundly. The following questions about them will indicate the matter dealt with in this chapter:

First, are these ministry gifts given indiscriminately to every Christian, as some other works of the Holy Spirit are given to every Christian? For example, it is certain that the Holy Spirit dwells in the body of every Christian (Rom. 8:9; I Cor. 6:19,20). The Holy Spirit has regenerated every Christian and made him a part of the body of Christ and in some degree is the Comforter and the Guide and the Witness and Seal of salvation and the Prayer-helper of every Christian. These are the ordinary and usual works of the Holy Spirit which every Christian experiences in some degree. Now, are the ministry gifts mentioned in I Corinthians, chapter 12, the ordinary and usual work of the Holy Spirit, or are they extraordinary enduements and enablings such as many Christians never have and such as come only when people are filled with the Holy Spirit? I think we can clearly prove that these ministry gifts are the unusual and extraordinary manifestations of the Holy Spirit in people who are filled with the Holy Spirit, with a supernatural enduement of power for service.

Second, were the Old Testament prophets, who spoke for God and sometimes worked miracles and prophesied, filled with the Holy Spirit as New Testament Christians sometimes were? Did they have these same ministry gifts of I Corinthians 12? Beyond any doubt we feel we can prove that they did have these same ministry gifts and were filled with the Holy Spirit just as New Testament Christians were at Pentecost and on some other occasions.

I. The Ministry Gifts Were Always the Manifestation of the Fullness of the Holy Spirit

At Pentecost, we are told, those one hundred and twenty waiting in the Upper Room were "all filled with the Holy Ghost." The term "filled with the Holy Ghost," or "filled with the Spirit," is a common term in the New Testament for a supernatural enduement of power for service. There are a number of evidences that only when filled with the Holy Spirit did Christians have these supernatural manifestations, the ministry gifts. And in the churches today we might have the same wonderful manifestations of the power of God—the gifts of the Holy Spirit to equip men for service, with prophecy and miracles and healings, as promised—if all God's people were taught to seek God's face and meet God's requirements to be filled with the Holy Spirit in Bible fashion. But we believe that these ministry gifts are never given except as Christians are filled with the Holy Spirit.

1. The Example of the Lord Jesus Christ Proves the Ministry Gifts Are Simply Manifestations of the Fullness of the Spirit

The Lord Jesus is our Example. He said to His disciples the day He rose from the dead, "As my Father hath sent me, even so send I you" (John 20:21).

In His High Priestly Prayer the night before He was crucified, Jesus identified all Christians with Himself in these wonderful words:

"They are not of the world, even as I am not of the world. Sanctify them through thy truth: thy word is truth. As thou hast sent me into the world, even so have I also sent them into the world."—John 17:16–18.

Just as the Father sent Jesus, so He sends us Christians into the world.

The same night Jesus had told the disciples He was going away but that the work which He did, Christians should do also. "Verily, verily, I say unto you, He that believeth on me, the works that I do shall he do also; and greater works than these shall he do; because I go unto my Father" (John 14:12).

It is clear that we take the place of Jesus Christ in this world. We are to preach as He would preach. We are to have the mind of Christ and do the work of Christ. We are to do even greater works than He did, because His personal ministry was cut short.

And since we are to do the work that Jesus did, we must have the power that Jesus had. We have shown elsewhere that Jesus, our dear Saviour, was filled with the Holy Spirit wonderfully at His baptism in the river Jordan (Luke 3:21,22). When we read the fourth chapter of Luke we will find that Jesus, after the Holy Spirit came upon Him, set out to do the work of His public ministry. He was "full of the Holy Ghost," was "led by the Spirit" (Luke 4:1). He "returned in the power of the Spirit into Galilee" (Luke 4:14). Then He read the text in Isaiah 61:1, "The Spirit of the Lord is upon me, because he hath anointed me to preach the gospel to the poor" (Luke 4:18). And then He said, "This day is this scripture fulfilled in your ears" (Luke 4:21).

Before this time Jesus had never worked a miracle, never preached a sermon, never healed a sick person, never cleansed a leper, never won a soul! Now, filled with the Holy Spirit, He began His mighty ministry. In Acts 10:38 Peter said, "How God anointed Jesus of Nazareth with the Holy Ghost and with power: who went about doing good, and healing all that were oppressed of the devil; for God was with him." You see, the ministry of the Lord Jesus was in the power of the Holy Spirit, which power He received when the Holy Spirit came upon Him visibly like a dove, following His baptism in the river Jordan.

Now notice this carefully: the Lord Jesus never manifested any of the ministry gifts until after He was endued with power, filled with the Holy Spirit. Jesus was pure. He was sinless. He was perfectly pleasing to God before He was filled with the Spirit. But He worked no miracles; He brought no revelations from God; He healed no sick. He could not be said to have the gift of prophecy, nor the gift of healing, nor the gift of miracles, nor any of the ministry gifts, until He was filled with the Holy Spirit.

Thus, it seems we may rightly declare that the ministry gifts are the manifestations of the fullness of the Holy Spirit and that they never appear except in people filled with the Holy Ghost.

2. Speaking With Tongues at Pentecost Was a Ministry Gift Following the Fullness of the Holy Spirit

Speaking with tongues or the gift of tongues is the least of the ministry gifts, we understand, from the order in which it is mentioned in

I Corinthians 12:28. Yet it is clearly mentioned as one of the ministry gifts. And it is important to notice that this ministry gift appeared at Pentecost after the fullness of the Holy Spirit. In Acts 2:4 we read, "And they were all filled with the Holy Ghost, and began to speak with other tongues, as the Spirit gave them utterance." It was not a babble of sounds, but it was the miraculous gift of speaking to others in their own foreign languages so they could hear the Gospel. That gift appeared only when these disciples were filled with the Holy Spirit. May we not say, then, that the ministry gifts are the manifestations of the fullness of the Holy Spirit? I believe that is a fair conclusion from the use of tongues or foreign languages by the gift of the Spirit at Pentecost.

3. The Gift of Prophecy at Pentecost Came Only After the Fullness of the Spirit

What happened at Pentecost? A number of things happened. But one thing that happened was that a certain prophecy from Joel 2:28, 29 was fulfilled. Peter, standing up on the day of Pentecost to explain the phenomenon that had taken place, said the following:

"But this is that which was spoken by the prophet Joel; And it shall come to pass in the last days, saith God, I will pour out of my Spirit upon all flesh: and your sons and your daughters shall prophesy, and your young men shall see visions, and your old men shall dream dreams: And on my servants and on my handmaidens I will pour out in those days of my Spirit; and they shall prophesy."—Acts 2:16–18.

He quoted more of Joel's prophecy, but the above quotation is sufficient for our purpose. Joel had foretold, by the inspiration of the Holy Spirit, that "in the last days, saith God, I will pour out of my Spirit upon all flesh: and your sons and your daughters shall prophesy." And again, "And on my servants and on my handmaidens I will pour out in those days of my Spirit; and they shall prophesy." Now Peter says, by divine inspiration, that Joel's prophecy is fulfilled at least in part. Here are people filled with the Holy Spirit as Joel said, and they prophesy!

So when the people preached the Gospel and witnessed for Christ, filled with the Holy Spirit, they were prophesying. It is only incidental that some of them prophesied in foreign languages. But the important thing is that they did prophesy; that is, they spoke for Christ by divine revelation and by divine enabling, and this was called prophesying, and it came, we are told, as a result of the pouring out of the Holy Spirit upon Christian people.

Clearly we have a right to say that prophecy in this case was a manifestation of the fullness of the Spirit upon Christians.

When we study the prophecy of Joel further, we find that "the last days" which began at Pentecost are still in existence, and the promise of Joel for the pouring out of the Holy Spirit is good for the whole age. The wonders in the heavens and in the earth—blood and fire and pillars of smoke, the sun turned into darkness—and the term "the great and notable day of the Lord" indicate that even down to the closing days of this age and the Great Tribulation time, this promise is true. And immediately following, the first verses of the third chapter of Joel tell about the restoration of a remnant of the nation Israel, the gathering of the nations to the battle of Armageddon, etc. It is quite clear, then, that the pouring out of the Holy Spirit, causing God's people to prophesy or to witness for Him with a divine revelation and enabling, is to continue during this age, as God's people meet God's requirements for His fullness. So the ministry gifts mentioned in I Corinthians 12 are obviously the manifestations of the fullness of the Spirit.

4. The Gift of Miracles Likewise Is Given Only as a Manifestation of the Fullness of the Holy Spirit

First Corinthians 12:10 and 28 both name miracles as a special gift of the Holy Spirit for service and witnessing. It is a ministry gift. Doubtless we should expect that when people are filled with the Holy Spirit, sometimes, as the Holy Spirit Himself divides severally as He will the gifts to different people, some miracles will appear. But they will never appear except as people are filled with the Holy Spirit.

Of course miracles were never frequent. Elijah raised one from the dead. Elisha raised another. Paul raised one, and Peter one. Most of the great apostles and prophets named in the Bible never raised anybody from the dead. Miracles were never frequent. They would not be frequent now if many, many of God's people were filled with the Holy Spirit. But we may be sure that they would never appear except as a manifestation of the fullness of the Holy Spirit.

Notice in the Book of Acts how miracles followed the fullness of the Spirit. The second chapter of Acts is filled with miracles which occurred on the day of Pentecost. There was a sound of a cyclonic, mighty wind. There were the visible tongues like as of fire sitting on Christians. There was the miraculous gift of tongues. These miracles were obviously accompaniments and manifestations of the fullness of the Holy Spirit.

But when we read on we discover that these same Spirit-filled people saw other miracles. The third chapter of Acts tells of the wonderful healing of a man who had been lame for more than forty years, all his life. One cannot avoid seeing that that miracle happened because Peter and John were filled with the Holy Ghost.

In Acts 4:31 another filling of the Holy Spirit and another miracle are mentioned together. "And when they had prayed, the place was shaken where they were assembled together; and they were all filled with the Holy Ghost, and they spake the word of God with boldness." The earthquake and the fullness of the Spirit came together. The earthquake was evidently a miraculous manifestation of the Holy Spirit.

And it is important to see that the disciples, praying in the preceding verse for the power of the Holy Spirit to come upon them afresh, asked that God would stretch forth His hand to heal, "and that signs and wonders may be done by the name of thy holy child Jesus" (Acts 4:30). They asked for miracles, and the fullness of the Holy Spirit came, and with it the manifestation of miracles.

In the following chapter, Ananias and Sapphira were struck dead (Acts 5:5–10). And then, "by the hands of the apostles were many signs and wonders wrought among the people" (Acts 5:12). And many sick were healed, and unclean spirits were cast out (Acts 5:16).

Acts 6:5 tells us of the deacon "Stephen, a man full of faith and of the Holy Ghost"; and then verse 8 tells us, "And Stephen, full of faith and power, did great wonders and miracles among the people."

The miracles followed the fullness of the Holy Spirit.

Let us remember that miracles had happened before Pentecost. But people were filled with the Holy Spirit before Pentecost too. Even the twelve apostles, eleven of whom were filled with the Holy Ghost later at Pentecost, had been commanded by the Saviour, "Heal the sick, cleanse the lepers, raise the dead, cast out devils" (Matt. 10:8). And the seventy others, also sent out by the Saviour into cities and towns whither He Himself would later come, returned with joy, reporting miracles. Luke 10:17 says, "And the seventy returned again with joy, saying, Lord, even the devils are subject unto us through thy name." Then Jesus told them, "Behold, I give unto you power to tread on serpents and scorpions, and over all the power of the enemy: and nothing shall by any means hurt you" (Luke 10:19). Yet the Saviour told these seventy that the miracles were not the important thing, but they were to rejoice rather that their names were written in Heaven.

So, although the same disciples had been used of God to work miracles before, from the way miracles occurred in the Book of Acts only as a manifestation of the fullness of the Holy Spirit, we can properly expect that always they occurred only as the manifestation of being filled with the Spirit of God. Ministry gifts, then, are not the usual and ordinary work of the Holy Spirit which every Christian has. Rather, the ministry gifts are the unusual and extraordinary gifts which people have only when filled with the Holy Spirit.

First Corinthians 12:7 says, "But the manifestation of the Spirit is given to every man to profit withal." God wants every Christian to have not only the Holy Spirit abiding in him and the comfort and guidance and daily help of the Spirit, but the fullness of the Spirit and the *manifestation* of the Spirit. Every Christian has the Holy Spirit within him. But not every Christian has the supernatural manifestation of the Spirit in these ministry gifts. But he could have! The gifts are offered and the manifestation is promised to everyone who will meet God's requirements. The ministry gifts are extraordinary— not in that they could not be had, some of them, by every Christian (as the Spirit Himself should decide), but in that they usually are not had because God's people are usually not filled with the Holy Spirit.

As an earnest student of revivals and evangelism for many, many years, I have been deeply impressed with the fact that God's miraculous manifestations frequently appear in great revival movements. Where there was a mighty moving of the Holy Spirit, then some of God's ministry gifts have often appeared.

Charles G. Finney in his autobiography tells of the miraculous cure of an insane woman (p. 110); of a woman who was instantly given the power to read the Word of God, though she had never learned to read (p. 75); and of the sudden death of two railing opposers of his work, in a fashion that seemed to have been God's miraculous interposition (pp. 65 and 166). The account of Finney's revivals leaves one with the impression that it would not be surprising for God to show Himself in any miraculous manifestation in the midst of such fullness of the Spirit and such mighty power.

In the marvelous work of D. L. Moody there were evidences of the ministry gifts of the Holy Spirit too. Moody was always anxious that no extreme reports should be given about the revivals, but others have told of remarkable, supernatural events in connection with Mr. Moody's Spirit-filled work. For example, the Honorable John V. Farwell, in his book published by Moody Press, *Early Recollections of Dwight L. Moody*, tells the wonderful story of a man with a hip disease from his early youth who was wonderfully healed instantly, when he was thirty-eight years old. Mr. Farwell said he and Moody were witnesses to the miraculous healing.

The Spirit-filled ministry of John Wesley was accompanied by remarkable, miraculous manifestations. In Wesley's Journal, on September 19, 1750, he records the healing of his brother in answer to the prayer of several. The healing was not ascribed to medicine but it is clearly inferred that God simply touched his body and gave him rest and strength.

On May 8, 1741, Wesley recorded his own serious illness and the fact that the Scripture, "These signs shall follow them that believe," from Mark 16:17, came strongly to his mind and he called on Jesus aloud. Instantly the pain vanished, the fever left, by God's mercy.

On March 17, 1746, Wesley records that his horse "was so exceeding lame" and that "my head ached more than it had done for some months." Then very sensibly he records what God did in these words: "(What I here aver is the naked fact: let every man account for it as he sees good.) I then thought, 'Cannot God heal either man or beast, by any means, or without any?' Immediately my weariness and head-ache ceased, and my horse's lameness in the same instant. Nor did he halt any more either that day or the next. A very odd accident this also!"

Wesley records the healing of insanity in answer to prayer and many other evidences of supernatural working of the Spirit of God.

In the little book, *I Cried, He Answered*, published by Moody Press, are many incidents of remarkable answers to prayer, assembled by Henry W. Adams, Norman H. Camp, William Norton and F. A. Steven. There is an introduction by Dr. Charles G. Trumbull, former editor of the *Sunday School Times*. One testimony is that of a student in Moody Bible Institute with a serious optic nerve trouble so that he was unable to do his work. Dr. R. A. Torrey, the Spirit-filled evangelist, had taught on the matter of healing in an Institute class. This student went to Dr. Torrey's home, was anointed and prayed for, and wonderfully healed in answer to prayer. This incident, so fully authenticated, seems to be a manifestation of the miraculous gift of the Holy Spirit which went with the fullness of the Spirit in the great revival work of Dr. Torrey.

The casting out of demons has often occurred in the midst of great revivals. Jonathan Goforth, a great Presbyterian missionary in China, in the little book *By My Spirit* has one chapter on "Evil Spirits Defeated and Cast Out in Honan." Mrs. Howard Taylor tells of the wonderful miracles wrought in response to the believing prayers of Pastor Hsi.

Hudson Taylor was once miraculously healed. And all these miraculous manifestations appeared with people who seemed to be filled with the Holy Spirit.

To the glory of Christ, I ought to say that God, on a few occasions, has shown wonderful manifestations in connection with my own work. I went to see a woman who had been sent home to die after two years in the state's tuberculosis sanitarium at Kerrville, Texas. She was instantly, marvelously healed, as I sat by her bedside and prayed. In a few days she was doing all of her housework, in a few weeks she had gained forty pounds, and four years later she was in good health, with no recurrence of the tuberculosis.

I am a witness that in Roosevelt, Oklahoma, and in Waxahachie, Texas, God struck down wicked men to instant death, men who had not listened to the Word of God and who had trifled with holy things, in great revivals.

The ministry gifts of the Holy Spirit are manifested only as people are filled with the Holy Spirit for service.

II. Old Testament Prophecies and Miracles Manifested the Same Fullness of the Holy Spirit as at Pentecost

In the New Testament, we have shown, the ministry gifts, prophecy, miracles, etc., were simply the manifestation of the fullness of the Holy Spirit. But what about the miraculous manifestations in the Old Testament? The prophecies, divinely given, the Word of the Lord brought to the people, the miracles wrought in His name—were these, too, simply the manifestations of the fullness of the Holy Spirit like that at Pentecost? Yes, they were the work of the Holy Spirit, and the Holy Spirit came upon people with power in the Old Testament just as He did at Pentecost, and just as He has often done since. And men, filled with the Spirit of God, were given miraculous manifestations in the Old Testament just as they were at Pentecost. We have no right to make a distinction between the fullness of the Holy Spirit in the Old Testament and the fullness of the Holy Spirit in the New Testament, or of the gifts which the Holy Spirit gives, dividing to each one severally as He will.

1. The Holy Spirit "Came Upon" Christians, "Filled" Them in Old Testament Times, Just As in the Book of Acts

We have already mentioned that a number of people were filled with the Holy Spirit before Pentecost in the New Testament, as record-ed in the Gospels. That is particularly true of John the Baptist (Luke 1:15), Elisabeth (Luke 1:41), Zacharias (Luke 1:67), and Jesus (Luke 3:21,22). So Pentecost is not the first time anyone was filled with the Holy Spirit. In the cases of John the Baptist, Elisabeth and Zacharias, the same term is used as in Acts 2:4, describing Pentecost—that is, "filled with the Holy Ghost." And in the case of Jesus, we are told that "the Holy Ghost descended...upon him." And we remember that at Pentecost Peter said the coming of the Holy Spirit upon them was a fulfillment of the prophecy of Joel: "...I will pour out of my Spirit," and, "On my servants and on my handmaidens I will pour out in those days of my Spirit; and they shall prophesy." So the coming of the Holy Spirit *upon* Jesus is the same as the pouring out of the Holy Spirit *upon* the disciples at Pentecost.

Many times in the Old Testament the Scripture speaks of the Holy Spirit coming upon people to endue them with power for service.

In Numbers 11:25–27 we are told that God took of the spirit that was upon Moses and gave it unto the seventy elders, and they prophesied.

We are told that "the Spirit of the LORD came upon Jephthah" to enable him to defeat the children of Ammon (Judg. 11:29).

We are told that "the Spirit of the LORD came mightily upon" Samson so that he worked miracle after miracle, with God's punish-ment on the Philistines and in the deliverance of Israel and of himself (Judg. 14:6; 14:19; 15:14).

We find that "the Spirit of God came upon" King Saul and he prophesied (I Sam. 10:6–10). Again "the Spirit of God came upon Saul" and helped him to assume leadership over all Israel and defeat the Ammonites (I Sam. 11:6).

When Samuel anointed David with oil, "the Spirit of the LORD came upon David from that day forward" (I Sam. 16:13). So David killed Goliath and became a mighty man of God.

We are told that Elisha sought and received a double portion of the Spirit that was on Elijah (II Kings 2:9–15). And Elisha continued with the same wonderful prophetic and miraculous ministry which had marked Elijah.

Note that the usual Old Testament language is that "the Spirit of the LORD came upon" men. But all these men certainly exercised the ministry gifts which were the "manifestation of the Spirit," available to all Christians as the Holy Spirit sees the need, as they are filled with the Holy Spirit of God for service. At Pentecost God poured out His

Spirit, and those upon whom the Spirit was poured prophesied and worked miracles and spoke in foreign languages and showed other of the ministry gifts. In the Old Testament, when the Spirit of God came upon people, they manifested the same ministry gifts of the Holy Spirit, prophecy and miracles, etc. So it is proper to say that the coming of the Holy Spirit upon one is the same as the fullness of the Spirit. The Holy Spirit came on the disciples at Pentecost and filled them. So either term is used for the same fullness of the Holy Spirit. About Jesus, it was prophesied in Isaiah 42:1, "I have put my spirit upon him." And Isaiah 61:1 foretold that it would be true of Jesus: "The Spirit of the Lord GOD is upon me; because the LORD hath anointed me to preach." One who had the Spirit of God upon him had the same enduement of power as that given at Pentecost, when God poured out His Spirit upon the waiting Christians and they prophesied.

However, the term "filled...with the spirit," very much like the language of Acts 2:4 about the disciples at Pentecost, is used of Bezaleel in Exodus 35:31. It was said that God had called Bezaleel for the work of preparing the Tabernacle and its furniture, "And he hath filled him with the spirit of God, in wisdom, in understanding, and in knowledge, and in all manner of workmanship."

It is true that in one particular point there seems to be a definite difference in the ministry of the Holy Spirit in the Old Testament and up to the resurrection and since that time. We believe that that difference is indicated in John 14:17 where Jesus promised that He would pray the Father and the Father would send them the Comforter to abide with them forever, "Even the Spirit of truth; whom the world cannot receive, because it seeth him not, neither knoweth him: but ye know him; FOR HE DWELLETH WITH YOU, AND SHALL BE IN YOU." The Holy Spirit, the Spirit of truth, the Comforter, up to that time dwelt *with* Christian people. But when Jesus should rise from the dead, then the Holy Spirit should be *in* them. So John 20:22 tells us how Jesus breathed upon the disciples the day of His resurrection and said unto them, "Receive ye the Holy Ghost." Since that time the Spirit of God makes His home in the bodies of Christian people. But we are not taught in the Word of God that there is otherwise a particle of difference in the way the Holy Spirit blesses and helps New Testament Christians and the way He blessed and helped Old Testament Christians.

It is very interesting to note that in I Peter 1:10,11 we are told that the Old Testament prophets "inquired and searched diligently, who prophesied of the grace that should come unto you: Searching what, or what manner of time *the Spirit of Christ which was in them* did signify, when it testified beforehand the sufferings of Christ, and the glory that should follow." Note the clear statement that the Spirit of Christ (the Holy Spirit) was *in* these Old Testament prophets! In other words, they were filled with the Spirit when they prophesied. The Holy Spirit was not only *with* them, but *in* them. There is some technical difference in the way the Spirit of God dwells in the bodies of Christians since the resurrection of Christ, but it is a change that began at Christ's resurrection, not at Pentecost, and it did not affect the way the Spirit of God anoints His servants, or fills them or comes upon them, to manifest Himself in the ministry gifts, for service.

2. Prophecy, the Most Prominent of Old Testament and New Testament Gifts of the Spirit

Joel foresaw that wonderful Pentecost revival which occurred some fifty days after the crucifixion. And what did happen at Pentecost, according to the divine revelation given through Joel? God said, "I will pour out my spirit upon all flesh," and again, "And also upon the servants and upon the handmaids in those days will I pour out my spirit" (Joel 2:28,29). The pouring out of the Holy Spirit upon God's servants would mark Pentecost and the last days, which began at Pentecost. And what would happen when the Spirit of God should be poured out upon Christians? Then "your sons and your daughters shall prophesy," and the servants and handmaids also should prophesy, as Peter quoted Joel in Acts 2:17,18. So the fullness of the Holy Spirit at Pentecost made people prophesy. The important thing at Pentecost, from the prophetic viewpoint, is not that the people of God spoke in other languages, but that they spoke as the Spirit gave them utterance. Prophecy, then, is clearly a manifestation of the fullness of the Holy Spirit. It was so called in the Old Testament when Joel prophesied this mighty occasion. It was so called in the New Testament when Peter related that the divine promise was being fulfilled. Jesus, in Acts 1:8, promised the disciples that they should receive power when the Holy Ghost was come upon them, "and ye shall be witnesses unto me." Did the disciples understand that when the Spirit of God came upon them, they would prophesy? Did they understand that their witnessing for Christ in the power of the Holy Spirit would be prophecy? Yes, if they understood what Jesus meant in Acts 1:4 and what He meant when He had Joel write down his prophecy. For both prophecies referred to what would happen when the disciples were filled with the Holy Spirit.

Spirit-filled, they prophesied; that is, they spoke as the Holy Spirit gave them wisdom and power to speak, witnessing for Jesus.

When the Spirit of the Lord came upon Old Testament prophets, they prophesied. When the Spirit of the Lord came upon the hundred and twenty at Pentecost, they too prophesied.

Prophecy is clearly regarded by the inspired writers of the Bible as the most important manifestation of the Holy Spirit, the most important ministry gift for Christians. Apostles are mentioned as having the highest gift in I Corinthians 12:28, but then we do not have any apostles today, nor do we need them, these men sent specially to speak with authority for God when the Word of God did not sufficiently cover the needs. The Bible never intimated there would be other apostles after the New Testament times. Now we have a completed Bible, a perfect and adequate reservoir of truth, perfectly furnishing the man of God for all his ministry, as far as divine authority is needed. But the second gift of prophecy is the one that all Christians are encouraged to seek. And in I Corinthians 14:31 the Christians at Corinth are plainly told, "For ye may all prophesy one by one, that all may learn, and all may be comforted." All may prophesy. And in a supposed case which Paul mentions as a proper example, we are told, "But if all prophesy, and there come in one that believeth not, or one unlearned, he is convinced of all, he is judged of all" (I Cor. 14:24). It would be perfectly proper, therefore, for every Christian to seek to prophesy.

In fact, Christians are commanded to "desire spiritual gifts, but rather that ye may prophesy" (I Cor. 14:1). On this matter, it is remarkable that Paul and Moses said almost the same thing. When the Lord took of the Holy Spirit's anointing which was on Moses and put the same blessed Holy Spirit upon the seventy elders who would help Moses rule, they prophesied. Two of the seventy had remained in camp instead of going with Moses and the other sixty-eight, to take their stand about the Tabernacle. These two also had the same remarkable enduement. "...and the spirit rested upon them; and they were of them that were written, but went not out unto the tabernacle: and they prophesied in the camp" (Num. 11:26). These men were named Eldad and Medad. A young man ran and told Moses. Joshua, jealous for the authority and power of Moses, said, "My lord Moses, forbid them"! What did Moses answer? "And Moses said unto him, Enviest thou for my sake? would God that all the LORD'S people were prophets, and that the LORD would put his spirit upon them!" (Num. 11:29). Moses wished that all the Lord's people were prophets and that God's Spirit would be upon them to enable them to prophesy.

Paul said nearly the same thing: "I would that ye all spake with tongues," that is, that they could speak to others in foreign languages as he did, "but rather that ye prophesied" (I Cor. 14:5). Paul and Moses both agreed; they wanted all God's people to prophesy, as a result of the fullness of the Spirit of God.

No such encouragement is given Christians to seek other gifts, as the gift of prophecy. What, then, does it mean to prophesy?

3. What Is This Supernatural Gift of the Spirit, Prophecy?

One who has carefully compared the references to prophecy in the Old and New Testaments will find that to prophesy in the Old Testament and to prophesy in the New Testament meant exactly the same thing. There are some very widespread ideas about prophecy which are not true to the Scriptures. Many believe that the word *prophesy* in the Old Testament does not mean the same as in the New. They believe that to prophesy meant to foretell the future in the Old Testament. In the New Testament, many believe that prophesying is simply preaching. No, prophecy is exactly the same in the Old and the New Testaments. The New Testament quotes Old Testament Scriptures about prophecy. Joel in the Old Testament and Peter in the New Testament meant the same thing when they quoted the same words, one writing in Hebrew and the other's message recorded for us in Greek. There are several ways by which we may learn what Bible prophesying meant.

First, prophesying is what the disciples did after they were filled with the Holy Spirit at Pentecost. So Joel 2:29 plainly declared, as quoted by Peter at Pentecost. So prophesying is Spirit-filled witnessing for Christ, giving a message which is directly given from God and in the power of the Holy Spirit. Speaking in foreign languages was not necessarily a part of prophecy, but speaking "as the Spirit gave them utterance" was prophecy.

The divine definition of prophecy is given in I Corinthians 14:3: "But he that prophesieth speaketh unto men to edification, and exhortation, and comfort." We are to understand that such speech comes as a special spiritual gift. One does not prophesy who speaks with natural wisdom, simply as a result of his study or when, without divine anointing, some man expounds the Word of God. No, his speech must be with a supernatural enduement of power from God, a special gift. It edifies men, it has exhortation, and it has comfort. Not all edification would be prophecy. Not all exhortation would be prophecy. Not all comfort would be prophecy, but only that given by direct enduement of God, the fullness of the Holy Spirit.

Compare that with verses 24 and 25 in the same chapter (I Cor. 14):

"But if all prophesy, and there come in one that believeth not, or one unlearned, he is convinced of all, he is judged of all: And thus are the secrets of his heart made manifest; and so falling down on his face he will worship God, and report that God is in you of a truth."

To prophesy would mean to speak with such power of God that even unbelievers would be convinced and judged and would see revealed the secrets of their hearts, and fall down before God and turn to Him. You see, prophecy is speaking with a special supernatural enablement and power, witnessing for God.

Third, we may know what New Testament prophecy meant by the way the term was used about Jesus Christ. For example, Luke 22:64 gives us a clear example of what prophecy meant: "And when they had blindfolded him, they struck him on the face, and asked him, saying, Prophesy, who is it that smote thee?"

The wicked men who buffeted Jesus in the house of the high priest, before His crucifixion, blindfolded Jesus and then slapped His face, saying, "Prophesy, who is it that smote thee?" In other words, they meant that if Jesus were really filled with the Spirit of God and were what He claimed to be, God would reveal to Him who it was that tormented Him. For Jesus to prophesy to them would be to speak to them with a message from God, showing that God had revealed to Him their sin and who it was that struck Him. Prophecy would not necessarily be a foretelling of the future, but it would certainly be a message from God to the hearts of those present, a supernaturally given message, in the power of the Holy Spirit. Prophesying would not be speaking by natural human knowledge.

Luke 7:39 gives us another true picture of the gift of a prophet. Jesus had gone to eat dinner in the house of a Pharisee. A woman who was a sinner came behind Jesus as He reclined on the couch at the table and wept over His feet and anointed Him with an alabaster box of ointment. She kissed His feet and dried them with her hair. Verse 39 says:

"Now when the Pharisee which had bidden him saw it, he spake within himself, saying, This man, if he were a prophet, would have known who and what manner of woman this is that toucheth him: for she is a sinner."

In other words, a prophet is one who has a direct revelation from God or a divine enablement to give him the message needed. The

Pharisee therefore lightly thought that if Jesus were filled with the Spirit of God and were what He claimed to be, He ought to have known that this woman was a sinner. The truth is that Jesus did know that very thing. He knew her heart and knew the message to give her. In this case again, the gift of a prophet was the supernatural anointing and enablement which prepared Jesus to speak to each individual the message needed, a message in supernatural power, a message directly from God. Spirit-filled witnessing it was.

Again, we can tell what the gift of prophecy means by the New Testament prophet, Agabus, who is twice mentioned in the New Testament as giving prophecies from God. Acts 11:28 tells us:

"And there stood up one of them named Agabus, and signified by the Spirit that there should be great dearth throughout all the world: which came to pass in the days of Claudius Cæsar."

This was a supernatural revelation. In this particular case it referred to the future. Prophecy is sometimes foretelling the future and sometimes not, but it is always a supernatural message given in the power of the Holy Spirit.

In Acts 21:11 another prophecy by this same Agabus is given:

"And when he was come unto us, he took Paul's girdle, and bound his own hands and feet, and said, Thus saith the Holy Ghost, So shall the Jews at Jerusalem bind the man that owneth this girdle, and shall deliver him into the hands of the Gentiles."

This was a message of the Holy Spirit, a divine revelation. It was in this case again a revelation of the future. But the important thing is that it was a message given by the Holy Ghost, not in the power or wisdom of men. It was not an exposition of the Bible. It was not preaching. It was composed of only one sentence. It was addressed to Paul and one or two others, not a church congregation.

It is important to note that Agabus spoke to Paul and his companions when he prophesied and was not giving an address before the church. When people slapped Jesus and asked Him to "prophesy, who is it that smote thee?" they did not mean that He was to preach a sermon. When the Pharisee said that if Jesus were a prophet, He would have known that the woman who wept over His feet was a sinner, he did not refer to the preaching of a sermon. The New Testament clearly forbids a woman to take a place of authority or leadership in the church, and says that a woman is to remain silent, and so could not preach in the official public proclamation of the Gospel to mixed congregations. But women can prophesy. That is, they may speak to individuals in the power of the Holy Spirit, if they be filled with the Spirit and have light and instruction from God as to what to say to individuals.

Incidentally, the prophetesses did not preach in either the Old Testament or the New Testament. There is no hint that Deborah preached. She gave a message from God to Barak. She judged individual cases as people brought their problems to her, and God gave her His answer to their problems by the fullness of the Holy Spirit.

So, prophecy does not mean simply preaching. It means a witness, whether public or private, in the power of the Holy Spirit, in the fullness of the Spirit; a message that God has particularly given for the ones who hear. It may be a foretelling of the future, or it may not foretell the future. But always it gives a message from God to those present and gives it in the mighty power of the Holy Spirit.

III. Old Testament Saints Met the Same Pentecostal Requirements for Fullness of the Spirit and the Ministry Gifts

In other chapters I give the detailed teaching of the Scriptures on the conditions we must meet to be filled with the Holy Spirit. I cannot in this chapter deal at length with these conditions. Yet I want to show that there were conditions which Old Testament prophets and saints met when they were filled with the Holy Spirit, just as at Pentecost and since Pentecost Christians have been required to meet certain divine conditions for the fullness of power and the gifts of the Spirit, or manifestations of the Spirit, for service.

The ultradispensationalists have done great harm in teaching that the Old Testament is out of date; that God does not deal with people now as He did in Old Testament times; that we are not to expect the same kind of blessings. It is popular with certain groups to say that repentance was necessary to salvation in the Old Testament and under the preaching of John the Baptist, but not required now. Such ultradispensational Bible teachers think they discern a difference between "Paul's gospel" and "the kingdom gospel." Those who follow John Nelson Darby and other Plymouth Brethren Bible teachers have frequently fallen into similar errors. They have taught that material blessings are promised in the Old Testament for the Jews only, and spiritual blessings for Christians in this dispensation. Some have taught that the Sermon on the Mount was more law than grace, and not suitable for Christians. Some have taught that the Lord's Prayer, the model prayer given by the Saviour, is not a proper prayer for Christians. Some have taught that John the Baptist had a different plan of salvation than that given by the Saviour. Plymouth Brethren generally have taught that the Book of Acts represents "a transitional period." They have taught that the church was born at Pentecost, "a wholly new thing," and that Pentecost therefore was simply a dispensational turning point, and that Pentecost can never be repeated. Many say it is wrong for Christians to be taught to seek the enduement of power which God gave Christians at Pentecost. They even say that the promise of Jesus in Luke 11:13, "...how much more shall your heavenly Father give the Holy Spirit to them that ask him?" is out of date. This sad way of chopping up the Bible and throwing most of the pieces away, as far as practical usefulness for Christians today is concerned, has robbed many Christians of blessings that God wanted them to have. So I feel that we need to show by the Word of God that some Old Testament Christians were filled with the Holy Spirit and had the same ministry gifts and witnessed for Christ in the same way as New Testament Christians did at Pentecost and at other times when they were filled with the Holy Spirit. Then we need to show too that Old Testament prophets and saints had to meet definite conditions for God's fullness and power, just as we must do today.

The Scofield Reference Bible is the best reference Bible in the world. The notes therein have been of measureless blessings to many thousands, including myself. Yet, I am sorry to say, the notes in the Scofield Bible often follow the teachings of Darby (who so greatly influenced the orthodox Bible teachers of the last generation) and frequently are overdispensational and wrong. In the Scofield Bible, on page 981, in a summary of the Old Testament doctrine of the Holy Spirit, part 4, the Scofield note reads:

"In the Old Testament the Spirit acts in free sovereignty, coming upon men and even upon a dumb beast as He will, nor are conditions set forth (as in the N.T.) by complying with which any one may receive the Spirit."

We are sorry to find a similar note in the Scofield Reference Bible commenting on Acts 2:4: "In the O.T....He comes upon whom He will, apparently without reference to conditions in them."

Now let us agree that in the supernatural work of God the Holy Spirit does act in free sovereignty. That is true in the New Testament as well as in the Old. Even now it is true that no man ever turns to Christ except as the Father draws him. If God does not call, a sinner will not repent. And God's divine sovereignty is manifest in this matter of the fullness of the Spirit and the ministry gifts. For we are plainly told that all these gifts are given by "the selfsame Spirit, dividing to every man severally as he will," that is, as the Holy Spirit chooses (I Cor. 12:11). We do not understand all of the great truths of divine sovereignty and infinite knowledge and God's election and choice. We do not need to understand all about them. We know that whosoever will may take of the water of life freely. We know that anybody who is willing to turn to Christ may do so and be saved. And we know that Christians are to covet the best gifts and may have them and that Christians themselves must take the blame if they are not filled with the Holy Spirit.

And exactly the same truth held in all Bible times. Old Testament saints and prophets who were filled with the Spirit and received miraculous manifestations of His power met certain requirements of God. It is a grave mistake that our ultradispensational brethren make when they say, "...nor are conditions set forth (as in the N.T.) by complying with which any one may receive the Spirit." I feel I can prove that that position is false, prove that God did have certain conditions which Old Testament prophets and saints were required to meet to have the fullness of the Spirit.

> 1. Consider Isaiah 44:3: "For I will pour water upon him
> that is thirsty, and floods upon the dry ground:
> I will pour my spirit upon thy seed, and
> my blessing upon thine offspring."

Here is a clear promise about the pouring out of the Holy Spirit. And the Holy Spirit is to be poured "upon him that is thirsty." Water here is clearly a symbol for the Holy Spirit, and the form of the verse is parallelism, a customary Hebrew form, a restatement of the same truth in different words. God promises that those whose hearts cry out for the fullness of the Spirit may have Him poured upon them.

The pouring of the Holy Spirit upon people is what happened at Pentecost. It is the fullness of the Spirit. And this fullness of the Spirit produces its own supernatural manifestations, as the Spirit chooses, to enable men to serve God with power.

What is this condition, "...him that is thirsty"? Isn't this same requirement of thirst the requirement that the disciples met as they waited in the Upper Room, pleading, with "prayer and supplication," before Pentecost? Here is an Old Testament promise of the fullness of the Spirit, but there is also a requirement: those who would have the fullness of the Spirit must thirst for Him! And the same promise is good for today. Those whose hearts cry out with a consuming thirst for power to win souls may have the Holy Spirit's enduement for that purpose.

2. Consider Psalm 126:5,6: "They that sow in tears shall reap in joy. He that goeth forth and weepeth, bearing precious seed, shall doubtless come again with rejoicing, bringing his sheaves with him."

It is clear that here is God's recipe for soul-winning power. Those who sow in tears shall reap in joy. One who goes forth with a broken heart, with the Word of God, will win souls and return happy, rejoicing, with souls saved. Now all of us know surely that conviction and regeneration are the work of the Holy Spirit. This Scripture speaks of the same problem that faced the apostles before Pentecost. They were commanded to go into all the world and preach repentance and remission of sins in the name of Christ. But Jesus said, "...but tarry ye in the city of Jerusalem, until ye be endued with power from on high." They were to win souls, but how could they do it without the supernatural enduement of power? So they tarried for the power. And here in the Old Testament we find the same theme and the same conditions. Those who would reap must sow. Those who would reap with joy must sow in tears. There must be a divine "go" in soul winning, a broken heart in soul winning, and the use of the Word of God in soul winning, here clearly taught in Psalm 126:6. The Holy Spirit is not specifically mentioned here, yet it is His work to save souls, and only by His enduement may one ever win souls. The same promise is for us today, and the same conditions must be met. If any Christian today will set out to work at soul winning, going with a broken heart and taking the Word of God, the Holy Spirit will go with him and give him power to witness and win souls, and he will come back with sheaves.

I maintain that the above Scripture shows that there were conditions to Holy Spirit power in the Old Testament exactly as there are conditions to the same Holy Spirit power and fullness in this day.

3. Consider Isaiah 40:28–31: "Hast thou not known? hast thou not heard, that the everlasting God, the LORD, the Creator of the ends of the earth, fainteth not, neither is weary? there is no searching of his understanding. He giveth power to the faint; and to them that have no might he increaseth strength. Even the youths shall faint and be weary, and the young men shall utterly

fall: But they that wait upon the LORD *shall renew their*
strength; they shall mount up with wings as eagles;
they shall run, and not be weary; and
they shall walk, and not faint."

All human power fails, says the Lord in this Scripture. "Even the
youths shall faint and be weary, and the young men shall utterly fall."
The vigor of youth, the natural strength of man, is not enough for
divine service. God's servants need a supernatural enduement. But
God "giveth power to the faint; and to them that have no might he
increaseth strength." That is a clear teaching of supernatural power,
the power of the Holy Spirit. Notice verse 31 again carefully. The
promise here is for supernatural strength: "They shall mount up with
wings as eagles." The wings here are not airplane wings. For a man to
take wings and fly literally is a miracle. If it were physically flying with
wings, it would be a physical miracle. If the miracle is spiritual, it is still
a miracle.

And to whom is this mighty power given? "They that wait upon the
LORD shall renew their strength." That is exactly what the one hundred and twenty did in the Upper Room before Pentecost. They waited on the Lord! They 'tarried in Jerusalem until they were endued with
power from on high.' The strength, the power, that God gives to those
who wait upon Him is supernatural power, the power of the Holy
Spirit. And here the same conditions are required as at Pentecost and
since Pentecost.

4. The Example of David Shows That God's Conditions
Had to Be Met for the Fullness of the
Spirit in the Old Testament

In I Samuel 16:13 we are told how Samuel anointed David to be
king and that "the Spirit of the LORD came upon David from that day
forward." We are not, in the immediate context, told of all the conditions which David met which resulted in his being filled with the Holy
Spirit. Yet a little search will indicate that David had very seriously met
the conditions which God required for a special fullness of the Spirit.

When Saul had disobeyed the Lord, then Samuel said to him, "The
LORD hath rent the kingdom of Israel from thee this day, and hath
given it to a neighbour of thine, that is better than thou" (I Sam.
15:28). Surely that means that David met certain conditions better
than Saul met them. Then in the sixteenth chapter we see Samuel in
the house of Jesse, to find among his eight sons the one which the Lord

had chosen to be king. Eliab passed by and Samuel said, "Surely the LORD'S anointed is before him." But God had not chosen Eliab. "But the LORD said unto Samuel, Look not on his countenance, or on the height of his stature; because I have refused him: for the LORD seeth not as man seeth; for man looketh on the outward appearance, but the LORD looketh on the heart." Surely that statement of the Lord can mean only one thing: David had certain qualities of heart that fitted him to be anointed with oil as king and to be filled with the Spirit of God for his duties in ruling for the Lord over Israel. It was not an arbitrary choice which God made in selecting David. God selected David because He looked upon David's heart and saw there that David met certain requirements that other men did not meet.

Let us go back a little earlier, then, when God had first told Saul that he was not acceptable. In I Samuel 13:14 the Lord said, "But now thy kingdom shall not continue: the LORD hath sought him a man after his own heart, and the LORD hath commanded him to be captain over his people, because thou hast not kept that which the LORD commanded thee." Could it be plainer? David was a man *after God's own heart!* God had sought and sought for such a man. Saul had at first tried to please God, and when he was small in his own sight and humble in God's sight, he had done good work. God's Spirit had been upon him. But David was 'a man after God's own heart.' That cannot but mean that David had met certain spiritual requirements to be filled with the Spirit of God and be used of God.

If one follows the lad David as he prepares to fight the giant Goliath and hears his brave testimony, hears how David had learned to trust the Lord in his fight with the lion and the bear, hears how David gives God the glory, he cannot help but be impressed that this lad knows the Lord well, that he has earnestly sought the Lord with all his heart. If one reads the Psalms and studies there the revealed prayer life of David, one cannot avoid the impression that David sought God earnestly and with the deepest devotion, in order to have God's fullest blessing and the power of God's Spirit upon him.

But sin came into the life of David—his sin in regard to Bath-sheba and Uriah the Hittite. The fifty-first Psalm gives us David's heartbroken prayer after that sin was fully revealed to him. And David prayed, "Cast me not away from thy presence; and take not thy holy spirit from me. Restore unto me the joy of thy salvation; and uphold me with thy free spirit. Then will I teach transgressors thy ways; and sinners shall be converted unto thee."

In this amazing prayer, notice that David feared to lose the blessed power of the Holy Spirit which had been upon him! In other words, he knew that he had failed God. Disobedience and sin might cause him to lose the power of the Holy Spirit which had been upon him. David besought the Lord, "Take not thy holy spirit from me." David then promised that if he should have restored the joy of salvation and if the Holy Spirit would still uphold him, David would teach transgressors the ways of God and sinners would be converted! Why, that sounds like New Testament Christians praying for revival, praying for God's Holy Spirit to be upon them in power so they can win souls!

Surely David's case makes it clear that there were conditions to the fullness of the Holy Spirit in Old Testament times, just as in New Testament times.

5. King Saul and Samson Are Examples of Men Who Lost the Power of the Holy Spirit Because They Did Not Keep On Meeting God's Conditions

First Samuel 10:1–13 tells us how Saul was anointed king, and then how the Spirit of the Lord came upon him and he prophesied. The long-suffering Spirit of God helped Saul much, even after disobedience and self-will. Then in I Samuel 16:14, after David has been anointed for the future kingdom, we are told, "But the Spirit of the LORD departed from Saul, and an evil spirit from the LORD troubled him." Do not say, then, that there were no conditions to be met for the fullness of the Spirit in Old Testament times. Once Saul met those conditions. Later he did not. We are not to understand that Saul was first saved and then became lost. That is not discussed. But certainly God's power was once with Saul, and then that power of the Holy Spirit was lacking.

Samson is a remarkable example of the way the Holy Spirit came upon people for service and brought His mighty miracle-working power in the Old Testament. The fourteenth, fifteenth and sixteenth chapters of Judges say again and again that "the Spirit of the LORD came upon him," or "the Spirit of the LORD came mightily upon him," and wonders were done by this Spirit-filled man of God. But sin came into the life of Samson. We are not told of all the penitent periods that must have come in the life of this man who sometimes was overcome by the flesh. But he trifled with God, played with Delilah, the heathen woman, and at last revealed to her the secret that he was a Nazarite, that he was wholly dedicated to God, and that his long hair was a mark of this consecration to God. He had broken again and again every bond with which they had tried to bind him. But when his long hair, which pictured his dedication wholly to God as a Nazarite, was cut off, then he was powerless as other men were. Delilah said, "The Philistines be upon thee, Samson." It was a sad awakening for Samson. "And he awoke out of his sleep, and said, I will go out as at other times before, and shake myself. And he wist not that the LORD was departed from him." So the Philistines put out his eyes and led him bound to the prison house. But later the house of the idol god was full of thousands of worshipers, and Samson was led out that he might make sport for them. "And Samson called unto the LORD, and said, O Lord GOD, remember me, I pray thee, and strengthen me, I pray thee, only this once, O God, that I may be at once avenged of the Philistines for my two eyes." God heard that penitent prayer and gave His mighty power to Samson again. Two middle pillars were broken down by Samson, and thousands of Philistines who were upon the roof were slain.

But we must solemnly see the warning in the example of Samson. It was the same in Old Testament times as now; men cannot trifle with God. And men cannot continue to have the mighty power of God except as they walk softly before the Lord and as they seek God's power, as Samson sought it again and found it.

No, the great spiritual laws are the same in the Old Testament as in the New. The only way anybody was ever saved in either the Old Testament or the New Testament was by faith. God heard prayer just the same in Old Testament times as in the New Testament. And those who sought to have His power and to be used of God had the fullness of the Spirit and the ministry gifts of the Spirit for service as men had them at Pentecost and have had them since. Galatians 6:7–9 is still true. And those who sow to the Spirit shall reap of the Spirit. It was so in the Old Testament times. And as Jeremiah 29:13 says, "And ye shall seek me, and find me, when ye shall search for me with all your heart." Spiritual power and blessing in Old Testament times, that mighty fullness of the Spirit, depended on certain conditions which God required men to meet then as now.

6. The Case of Elisha the Prophet Who Sought So Earnestly to Have the Same Spirit Upon Him As Was Upon His Teacher, Elijah, Shows That the Holy Spirit's Power Was for Those Who Sought It, Who Met God's Conditions

In II Kings, chapter 2, is the thrilling story of the translation of Elijah. God let it be known to Elijah and to Elisha, the younger prophet who had been his understudy and servant, that Elijah would be taken to Heaven that day. Elijah again and again besought the younger prophet, "Tarry here, I pray thee." First, said Elijah, the Lord had sent him to Bethel. Elisha went with him. The Lord sent Elijah to Jericho, and then Elisha would not stay in Jericho when Elijah was called to the Jordan. He would not leave Elijah. When asked to make any final request, he asked, "I pray thee, let a double portion of thy spirit be upon me." And he would not be denied! He insisted that he must have the power, even a double portion of the mighty power of the Spirit of God which had rested on Elijah. And when Elijah went to Heaven in the chariot of fire and a whirlwind, Elisha took up his mantle and wore it. But immediately he slapped the waters of the Jordan River with the mantle, and they parted before him as they had for Elijah. All the sons of the prophets said, "The spirit of Elijah doth rest on Elisha." They meant simply that the Holy Spirit, who had so obviously led and empowered the mighty miracle-working Elijah, now rested in power upon the younger prophet.

What pleading! What insistence! What holy seeking! That is the way Elisha was filled with the Spirit of God which had rested upon his master. That requirement is the same requirement that the disciples, who waited in the Upper Room before Pentecost, met.

Surely it is clear, then, that Old Testament saints who had the miracle-working power of the Holy Spirit and His ministry gifts upon them, met conditions like apostles and others met at Pentecost and later. In both the Old and New Testaments, then, we have evidence that only those are filled with the Spirit of God and have the manifestation of the Holy Spirit who seek God's face and meet God's requirements.

Chapter 8

Speaking With Tongues

"And they were all filled with the Holy Ghost, and began to speak with other tongues, as the Spirit gave them utterance."—Acts 2:4.

"Yet in the church I had rather speak five words with my understanding, that by my voice I might teach others also, than ten thousand words in an unknown tongue."—I Cor. 14:19.

"If therefore the whole church be come together into one place, and all speak with tongues, and there come in those that are unlearned, or unbelievers, will they not say that ye are mad?"—I Cor. 14:23.

What does the Bible teach about Christians speaking with other tongues or languages? Is speaking with tongues the Bible evidence of the baptism in the Holy Ghost? The subject of tongues is worth study because it is in the Bible. Then we need to learn what the Bible says on this subject for two great reasons, at least.

First, there is such a widespread difference of opinion, separating earnest, Bible-believing Christians, that, if possible, the truth of the matter should be sought carefully in humility and with an open mind in order that Christians may understand each other and be of one mind. It must grieve God that many people who love Him and believe the Bible think so harshly of one another and differ so radically with one another on these questions.

But the second great reason for studying the question of tongues in the Bible is even more important. I am convinced that thousands of people, by a false understanding of this subject, seek for the experience of speaking in tongues instead of seeking for the power of the Holy Spirit to win souls. And multiplied thousands of other Christians are so repulsed by what seems to them fanaticism that they are turned away from any study of the fullness of the Spirit and they do not seek and do not find the mighty power which God has promised to those who wait upon Him to be filled with the Holy Spirit. It is my earnest hope that by a careful, brotherly Bible study of this subject of speaking in tongues we may help to prepare thousands of Christians to seek and find the fullness of God's Holy Spirit, His power upon a soul-winning testimony which they otherwise might not even desire or believe possible. I want Christians to be filled with the Spirit of God. I want them to be endued with power from on high. I want them to have all the blessings that God has for them. I want Christians, myself included, to have all the power and fruitfulness that New Testament Christians had. I believe that misunderstanding of the question of speaking in tongues hinders revival and hinders soul winning. With this honest motive, then, I seek to help readers see what the Bible teaches about speaking with tongues.

I am an evangelist, both by calling and choice. My passion, my burden, is to see God's saints revived and to see the mighty power of Bible Christianity felt again in America and all the world. We do not seek here to build any denomination. We do not seek here to oppose any movement of godly people. We do not seek a quarrel with Christian brethren. Rather, we seek simply to help men understand the Word of God and to clear away the hindrances to revival, showing them what God wants them to do and what He does not want them to do; showing them what they need in order to do God's work and what they do not need.

SECTION I
My Personal Testimony

If the reader will kindly forgive the personal pronoun for a bit, I will use it to give a personal testimony. In my early ministry I saw the absolute necessity for the power of the Holy Spirit upon my life and ministry, if I were to be and do what God wanted me to be and do. I determined, at any cost under Heaven, to have the fullness of God's power. I longed to win souls. I longed to be used of God in bringing revivals. And so I promised God that I would go anywhere the quest led me, take gladly anything He gave me, pay any cost He required, if only He would fill me with His Spirit. I went into this tongues question then quite thoroughly. I attended the services of tongues preachers. I read every book on this subject that I could find, written by godly leaders of the Pentecostal movement. I was willing to talk in tongues if that was necessary to have the fullness of God. I knew there would be reproach on me if I should speak with tongues. I knew it would be a heartbreaking thing for me to leave my denomination, as, of course, I should do, if I personally experienced and then began to preach speaking in tongues as the duty of Christians and as the necessary evidence to the fullness of the Holy Spirit. As God is my witness, I faced that matter honestly, prayerfully, with many tears, with long, long hours of prayer. I studied my Bible with holy eagerness to learn what God's

Word taught on this subject. But God first showed me in the Word that speaking in tongues was not the Bible evidence of fullness of the Spirit and that it was not expected of Christians generally, and gave me perfect peace of mind on this question. I knew I had found His will. And then, praise His name, He also, in His infinite mercy, breathed upon me power from Heaven, for which my heart had cried so long, with the result that multiplied thousands of souls have been saved under my ministry.

Let no one say, then, that I shrank from having all God has for a Christian. That is not true. Let no one say that I feared the disapproval of men. I was willing to face it then, had God so led. I have since, more than once, faced the disapproval of good men to do the will of God. I deliberately took the course which lost me the friends of a lifetime, classmates in college and university and seminary, as well as Christian associates in my denomination, by taking a stand for the verbal inspiration of the Bible and against evolutionary teaching. I have repeatedly taken such a strong stand for holy living by Christians and have preached so boldly and earnestly to please God and, by His grace, to help bring revival, that I have often suffered at the hands of brethren who thought me too fanatical. Let no one say that I feared to face the consequences if I should speak in tongues. That is untrue.

Nor should anyone accuse this unworthy author of being against the fullness of the Holy Spirit. On the contrary, that fullness has been my heart's desire and, thank God, my rejoicing these many years. It has also been the repeated subject of my preaching and writing. As one of the most unworthy of Christ's servants, I say it with praise to God and a deep sense of my weakness, that I know I have been breathed upon by the Holy Spirit in power. I know that I have felt, in a degree for which I should be profoundly grateful and should not apologize, the passion and tears and holy boldness and power of the Holy Spirit which have enabled me to win many thousands of souls to Christ. Not a bit of credit, not even so large as a grain of sand, do I deserve, but a degree of blessing has rested upon my poor labors for which I must give glory to God and say that the power of His blessed Spirit has been present to make my labors fruitful. No one, therefore, can properly say either that I have not earnestly sought the will of God in this matter or that I have failed to have a measure of blessing that entitles me to speak, as humbly as I may, on this matter, what I find in the Word of God.

Someone may say, "If you have not talked in tongues, how can you tell what God requires? How can you speak without experience?" That question deserves an answer, and it is easy to give an honest one. The answer is that this matter must be settled by the Bible, not by anybody's experience. Our Mormon friends long taught that polygamy was commanded of God. But it would be foolish to suppose that I would have to try polygamy and have two or three wives at once in order to know what the Bible, the Word of God, teaches on this subject! I never "fell under the power" in a trance, yet I do not need to have that experience to see whether God's Word requires such an experience, either for salvation or for healing. I know some men who were led to trust in Christ while lost in the vast Pacific in a rubber life raft. I never had their experience, and I do not need to have that experience to find out whether the Bible requires one to be lost in a life raft before he can be saved. If the Bible tells how to be saved, that settles it without hearing strange experiences of others. I never had delirium tremens either, but I have a perfect right to learn from the Bible that drunkenness is wrong, without the experience. Bible questions are not settled by men's experiences but by the Word of God.

If one who reads these words lays aside the book without thorough study, with indignation because it does not bear out his own private opinions, then the reader does not seek the truth as earnestly as I have sought it through many years. If one accuses the writer of not sincerely seeking to find the will of God on the tongues question and of not being willing to have anything that would please God and scripturally prepare one to win souls, then the reader's attitude is not as charitable as the writer's, and that attitude may well be a bias, a preference in favor of the reader's own way instead of God's way. If any reader scornfully accuses that the author has not been filled with the Holy Spirit, not "baptized with the Holy Ghost," then I beg you to consider whether your complaint does not prove that you are missing the point of the whole matter. Poor as I am, God has enabled me to be a Spirit-filled witness, fulfilling the promise of Jesus in Acts 1:8. Tens of thousands have claimed Christ as Saviour under my poor ministry. Can any honest heart think that is of less importance to God than talking in tongues? And whatever the failures of the author, that will not excuse the reader if he did not quietly and earnestly and humbly search through this matter in the light of the Word of God. Arrogance and denominational pride and boasting over others are poor evidences of a Spirit-filled life. So I plead with the reader to study diligently the material here presented, as I have done through many years and with much toil and many tears and, thank God, with great rejoicing and victory and power. Honest, Bible-believing Christians must be willing to go back to the Bible to settle this matter of the fullness of the Spirit and what it will mean and how to have it. It cannot be settled by human experience alone, but by the Word of God.

Let us also make it clear that we retreat not one inch from the position that the whole Bible is the Word of God and everything taught in the Bible can be believed. Let us go even further and say that we believe the promises of the New Testament are for us and the blessings of New Testament times are for Christians in these modern days. I believe that the gifts of the Spirit may still be given as it pleases God. I believe there was a gift of tongues in Bible times, and there may be gifts of tongues today. We do not see many miracles, but there is nothing in the Bible to indicate that God will never work any miracles in our day. We may not see the manifestation of some of the gifts of the Spirit enumerated in I Corinthians, chapter 12. But I verily believe that as the Holy Spirit wills He may still give them, "dividing to every man severally as he will" (I Cor. 12:11).

I agree with the late Dr. W. B. Riley who, in *The Bible of the Expositor and the Evangelist*, said:

> That such a tongue existed in the New Testament experience cannot be sanely disproved; that the gifts of the New Testament time were intended for all ages is not the subject of doubt with some of us. With Gordon we affirm that it is impossible for us to look at that rich cluster of promises that hang by a single stem in Mark 16:16–18, and pluck out what suits us, declaring that the rest of them obtained only for a short time. Such treatment of the Word of God is unworthy the sincere students of the Bible. The "gift" is there, and the "gift" may be here.

Accepting every part of the Bible as the Word of God and believing that all the New Testament is for us today, I insist that we must go to the Bible, the Word of God, to settle the question of tongues. Let us not depend on our feelings or our emotions or our experiences. Let us not be unduly influenced by the marvelous experiences of which others tell us. Rather, let us go to the very Word of God and find what God has to teach about tongues.

It is a sad thing, long observed, that most of those who teach Christians to seek for an experience of speaking in tongues base their teaching primarily on what they themselves felt or did or what others they know did or felt. Human experience and human opinion are frail evidences indeed compared with the Word of God. Surely honest-hearted Christians can agree to go to the Bible and to find what the Word of God itself teaches on this question.

SECTION II
What Speaking With Tongues Meant in the Bible

The central and most important Bible passage on the tongues question is found in Acts 2:1–11. This is the most important passage for several reasons.

I. Why Acts 2:1–11 Is the Key Scripture on Tongues

It is most important because it is the first time the tongues question is discussed in the New Testament.

This passage in the second chapter of Acts is most important because it discusses the question of tongues as connected with the great revival at Pentecost, which was the beginning of world evangelization by the apostles, after the resurrection of Christ. As Pentecost was the most important event that had happened on earth since the ascension of Christ and was the beginning of "the last days" of world evangelization, prophesied in the second chapter of Joel, so the speaking in tongues in that connection would be the most important discussion on the tongues question in the New Testament.

That passage in the second chapter of Acts is most important because the speaking in tongues was on a larger scale than in either of the other two cases mentioned in the Book of Acts. Sixteen different nationalities are named as hearing in their own tongues the wonderful works of God. No event has ever happened approaching the scope of speaking in tongues like the scope of the tongues at Pentecost.

The passage in Acts 2 is the most important and central passage because there a detailed description is given of speaking in tongues. Eight or nine verses there are used telling the details of how Christians spoke in tongues in sixteen different languages by the power of the Holy Spirit. In Mark 16:17 only one verse mentions speaking in tongues. In Acts 10:46 speaking in tongues is mentioned in only the one verse describing what happened at Cornelius's household. In Acts 19:6 the one verse again tells all that is said about speaking in tongues with the disciples at Ephesus. In the twelfth chapter of I Corinthians only twenty words in four phrases deal with the tongues question. In the fourteenth chapter of I Corinthians quite a long passage discusses the use of tongues, but no particular instance is given, and practically the entire chapter is spent in reproving a heresy about tongues, and not a single person is mentioned as having the gift of tongues from God or of tongues used in a scriptural manner. The chapter is a rebuke for heresy. On the contrary, in Acts 2:4–11 we have a clear description of speaking in tongues with the power and approval of God, and what it meant.

Yet another important fact causes us to regard the passage in Acts 2:1–11 as the central and definitive passage on the question of speaking with tongues. That fact is this: only in this passage can we be sure that we have an account of the *miraculous gift* of tongues. Only here is it clearly shown that the languages were a special miracle of God.

In Acts 10:46 we are told that Peter and the six Jews who went with him to Cornelius's household heard this household of the Italian band "speak with tongues, and magnify God." But since the word "tongues" here simply means languages, it is very possible that Cornelius and his household simply gave their testimony to salvation and praised God in both the Latin and the Aramaic languages. And they could have done that without any special gift of tongues. The Scripture does say, "…that on the Gentiles also was poured out the gift of the Holy Ghost" (Acts 10:45), but the Scripture does not say that they had the miraculous gift of tongues.

Likewise, in Acts 19:6 we are simply told that some twelve men at Ephesus "spake with tongues, and prophesied." They were certainly natural languages, and the languages may have been learned as people usually learn languages in a city of many nationalities. The Bible does not say that it was the miraculous gift of tongues.

So at Pentecost alone do we certainly have the gift of tongues illustrated and described in detail, in Acts 2:1–11.

No one can understand the miraculous gift of tongues except by seeing what happened at Pentecost. It seems obvious, then, that the place to begin the study of speaking in tongues is in Acts, the second chapter, the first and central and most important passage in the Bible on the tongues question. And here we will find what speaking in tongues means in the Bible.

"*And when the day of Pentecost was fully come, they were all with one accord in one place. And suddenly there came a sound from heaven as of a rushing mighty wind, and it filled all the house where they were sitting. And there appeared unto them cloven tongues like as of fire, and it sat upon each of them. And they were all filled with the Holy Ghost, and began to speak with other tongues, as the Spirit gave them utterance. And there were dwelling at Jerusalem Jews, devout men, out of every nation under heaven. Now when this was noised abroad, the multitude came together, and were confounded, because that every man heard them speak in his own language. And they were all amazed and marvelled, saying one to another, Behold,*" *are not all these which speak Galilæans? And how hear we every man in our own tongue, wherein we were born? Parthians, and Medes, and Elamites, and the dwellers in Mesopotamia, and in Judæa, and Cappadocia, in Pontus, and Asia, Phrygia, and Pamphylia, in Egypt, and in the parts of Libya about Cyrene, and strangers of Rome, Jews and proselytes, Cretes and Arabians, we do hear them speak in our tongues the wonderful works of God."*—Acts 2:1–11.

II. A Study of This Passage Shows That the Word "Tongues" Means Regular Languages Already in Use by Some People

The Bible is very, very careful, in this second chapter of Acts, to make clear that the languages used were regular languages. "And how hear we every man in our own tongue, wherein we were born? Parthians, and Medes, and Elamites, and the dwellers in Mesopotamia, and in Judæa, and Cappadocia, in Pontus, and Asia, Phrygia, and Pamphylia, in Egypt, and in the parts of Libya about Cyrene, and strangers of Rome, Jews and proselytes, Cretes and Arabians, we do hear them speak in our tongues the wonderful works of God." The Spirit-filled Christians at Pentecost witnessed for Jesus in sixteen different languages, beginning with that of the Parthians and ending with that of the Cretes and Arabians, in the divine record.

There is nothing here spoken about an "unknown" tongue, except that some languages are simply unknown to other people who speak other languages. Here was no so-called "spiritual language," no "heavenly language." The languages used were normal human languages. This was no babble of sound unfamiliar to any human mind. It was no jabber. God simply gave the disciples power to speak in languages before unknown to them, but known to the people of the various nationalities who were present.

The word translated "tongues" in Acts 2:4 is the Greek word *glossa*. It is used in the New Testament fifty times. Sixteen times it refers to a literal, human tongue, the physical organ in the mouth. Once, in Acts 2:3, it is used of "cloven tongues like as of fire." All the other times it means languages. For example, Revelation 5:9 speaks of people "out of every kindred, and tongue, and people, and nation."

Not one time in the Bible does the word "tongues" mean something mysterious, a language unknown to mankind.

At Pentecost the tongues given by the Holy Spirit were genuine languages, and the nationalities of the people in whose languages they were allowed to speak is given.

In Acts 10:46 we are told how Cornelius and his household also were heard to "speak with tongues, and magnify God." And we know that to them was given literal, regular human languages: first, because Peter and the Jewish hearers "heard them speak...and magnify God." They heard and understood the praises of these Spirit-filled new converts. And Peter, later telling about it, said, "And as I began to speak, the Holy Ghost fell on them, as on us at the beginning" (Acts 11:15). So the tongues given to Cornelius and his household were simply regular languages like those given at Pentecost. Cornelius and his household were members of the Italian band, from Rome, and naturally spoke Latin. Peter and the Jews spoke Syriac or Aramaic. From long association, no doubt, each racial group understood some of each other's language. It is likely that both groups spoke some Greek. They could understand one another a bit. The Holy Spirit allowed the people from Rome to speak in more than one language so these Jews could know beyond any doubt that Cornelius and his household were genuinely saved. There was certainly nothing mysterious about that. Were the languages miraculously given, or did Cornelius and his household simply praise God in Latin, Greek and Aramaic, which they already used? The Bible does not say "miraculous tongues," just "tongues," or languages.

In I Corinthians 14 Paul very severely rebukes a misuse of languages among the Christians at Corinth. But he referred to definite, regular human languages. In this chapter, translators inserted the word "unknown" before the word "tongue" in many cases. The word is not in the Greek in this passage. In this chapter Paul speaks of languages that are unknown to unlearned people—that is, regular languages that certain nations speak regularly, though the language may be unknown to some others.

First Corinthians 14:2–4 is often misunderstood, so a little careful study here will clarify it in your mind.

"For he that speaketh in an unknown tongue speaketh not unto men, but unto God: for no man understandeth him; howbeit in the spirit he speaketh mysteries. But he that prophesieth speaketh unto men to edification, and exhortation, and comfort. He that speaketh in an unknown tongue edifieth himself; but he that prophesieth edifieth the church."

The Scripture simply says that if a man speaks in the church in a foreign language, God understands him but men do not. He may be saying good things, but they do nobody any good if they are spoken in a foreign language that people present do not understand. He may comfort himself, but he does not help the church.

This Scripture does not say and does not mean that the gift of tongues in the Bible meant languages known only to God. The example of Pentecost is a clear evidence that the tongues given by the Holy Spirit are regular foreign languages. And naturally, if I should speak German to an English-speaking audience that did not understand German, I would be speaking only to God, since the people would not understand me. I might enjoy it and might be blessed in it, but I would not bless others nor build them up. What God has in mind here is simply foreign languages unknown to those present.

That is made very clear further on in the fourteenth chapter of I Corinthians. Verses 23 and 24 are especially clear:

"If therefore the whole church be come together into one place, and all speak with tongues, and there come in those that are unlearned, or unbelievers, will they not say that ye are mad? But if all prophesy, and there come in one that believeth not, or one unlearned, he is convinced of all, he is judged of all."

Imagine the scene! A church service is in progress, and people speak all in various foreign languages. Some uneducated people come in—"unlearned" the Scripture calls them—who have not learned any but their own native language. If these unlearned people who do not understand the foreign languages spoken are unsaved, unbelievers, "will they not say that ye are mad?" asks the Scripture. But if the church members, instead of speaking in some foreign language that the unlearned people do not know, should all prophesy (that is, speak as the Holy Spirit fills them and leads them, but in the native tongue of those present), then the unbeliever and the unlearned man will be "convinced of all" and "judged of all." Verse 25 indicates that thus the uneducated man who did not know foreign languages and who would think the Christians were crazy if they talked in foreign languages in his presence, hearing these believers speaking by the Holy Spirit or prophesying in their own native language, would be convinced and would worship God and give a good report.

These two uses of the word "unlearned" in verse 23 and verse 24 show that the languages referred to may be learned by study, as all foreign language may. Unlearned people do not know the foreign languages that might be spoken in a church service, so it is wise to dispense with them and use the native languages of those present.

Now if speaking in tongues meant speaking in some mysterious language known only to God and not known to any group of men, no matter how much learning and education a man has, he would not know these languages. Learning would be of no effect in understanding heavenly languages. But foreign languages known among men can be learned. And the fact that these foreign languages are the kind that unlearned men would not understand indicates that it was known, regular human languages to which the Bible refers when it speaks of tongues and when the fourteenth chapter of I Corinthians speaks of 'unknown tongues.'

Remember, then, that "tongues" in the Bible simply means *languages*, usually foreign languages.

III. Speaking in Tongues in the Bible Was an Incidental and Secondary Matter Used When Necessary in Preaching to Foreigners

What did speaking in tongues mean in the Bible? That is very simple. At Pentecost it was simply a miracle that God used to enable the disciples, after they were filled with the Holy Spirit and had God's power upon their message, to preach to the many, many people of Jewish blood but natives of other countries and speaking the languages of foreign countries, and give them the Gospel.

Jesus had told the disciples, "Tarry ye in the city of Jerusalem, until ye be endued with power from on high." Tarry? Yes, they were told to delay their work of evangelization. Jesus had said to them "that repentance and remission of sins should be preached in his name among all nations, beginning at Jerusalem. And ye are witnesses of these things" (Luke 24:47,48). And then He gave them the plain command not to start any revivals, not to open any mission stations, but to wait until they were endued with power from on high. So they waited in Jerusalem. They "continued with one accord in prayer and supplication, with the women, and Mary the mother of Jesus, and with his brethren" (Acts 1:14). Then on the day of Pentecost they were all filled with the Holy Ghost. They wanted to speak for God. All about them were Jews of foreign lands who had come back to Jerusalem for the feast of Pentecost. How would they give the Gospel to these who were Jews by blood and Jews by religion, but who did not speak the language the apostles used? God simply gave them the power to preach the Gospel and give their testimony in the languages in which these other people were born.

Speaking in tongues was not given as a sign of the baptism of the Holy Spirit. Tongues are a sign to unsaved people who hear the Gospel in their own language, not a sign to Christians about anything. See I Corinthians 14:22. The gift of tongues was given these disciples as a practical measure, enabling them to take the Gospel to people of other languages, then present. The gift of tongues was not given to these disciples to give them an ecstasy, a joy, some spiritual frenzy. No, no! Nothing like that is inferred in the Scriptures. Those who teach such an idea get it from history, from books or from human experiences. They do not get it from the Bible. The Bible says nothing about a frenzy, an ecstasy, about "falling under the power" or being in a trance. These earnest Christians, now ready to win souls and breathed upon by God's Holy Spirit, were given the miraculous privilege of preaching the Gospel in the language of others who were present and needed the Gospel. That was the practical purpose of speaking in tongues.

In I Corinthians 14 Paul, by divine inspiration, takes great pains to show that speaking in tongues is utterly profitless unless those who hear understand what is spoken. In verses 6 to 9 he said:

"Now, brethren, if I come unto you speaking with tongues, what shall I profit you, except I shall speak to you either by revelation, or by knowledge, or by prophesying, or by doctrine? And even things without life giving sound, whether pipe or harp, except they give a distinction in the sounds, how shall it be known what is piped or harped? For if the trumpet give an uncertain sound, who shall prepare himself to the battle? So likewise ye, except ye utter by the tongue words easy to be understood, how shall it be known what is spoken? for ye shall speak into the air."

You see, speaking in tongues means speaking in other languages, when those hearing can understand what is spoken, whether it be a special revelation of God or knowledge of God's Word or some prophecy or doctrine. Paul gives then the clear-cut statement, "So likewise ye, except ye utter by the tongue words easy to be understood, how shall it be known what is spoken? for ye shall speak into the air."

In I Corinthians 14:14 Paul says, "For if I pray in an unknown tongue, my spirit prayeth, but my understanding is unfruitful." "Tongues" means simply foreign languages, remember, and the word "unknown" is not in the original Greek. If one prays in a language unknown to those present, he is not understood by those who hear. It is fruitless and senseless to talk in a language when people do not understand.

That is the reason he said, "Else when thou shalt bless with the spirit, how shall he that occupieth the room of the unlearned say Amen at thy giving of thanks, seeing he understandeth not what thou sayest?" (I Cor. 14:16). It can do no one any good to hear one speak in an unknown language which he does not understand. He cannot say amen intelligently at the giving of thanks any more than he can learn by doctrine, teaching or revelation in a foreign language unknown to him.

You see, Paul is clearly teaching that when there is no practical reason for speaking in a foreign language, it should be omitted. And in verse 19 he said, "Yet in the church I had rather speak five words with my understanding, that by my voice I might teach others also, than ten thousand words in an unknown tongue."

We will further explain this fourteenth chapter of I Corinthians a little later. But here let us accept it as a clearly stated fact of the Scripture that speaking in tongues was simply a gift that God gave when it was necessary to let men speak to a foreigner in his own language. The genuine gift of tongues was a miracle, but it was an incidental and secondary miracle. It was the very least of the gifts, was not to be used except when it could do some good. But tongues are natural languages, not necessarily a miracle.

Here I should like to quote the Jamieson, Fausset and Brown commentary which says, "Tongues must therefore mean *languages*, not ecstatic, unintelligible rhapsodies (as NEANDER fancied)...."

Thus we see the meaning of speaking in tongues in the Bible. It was a miraculous gift, on certain limited occasions used as an emergency measure. Only three particular cases are mentioned in the whole Bible that could *possibly* have been a miraculous gift, only one *certainly* miraculous. It was not an ecstasy or a rhapsody, but a simple miraculous use of a foreign language to witness for Christ.

SECTION III
Speaking in Tongues Is Not the Bible Evidence of the Baptism of the Holy Spirit

One good Christian brother of a Pentecostal assembly said to me, "Speaking in tongues as the initial evidence of the baptism of the Holy Spirit is our principal doctrine." I think he did not mean that speaking in tongues was more important than the plan of salvation by the blood of Christ, nor than the inspiration of the Bible, nor Christ's virgin birth, incarnation and bodily resurrection. Surely he would agree that these great foundation doctrines are more important than speaking in tongues. But I think he meant that speaking in tongues was the most *distinctive* doctrine of his denomination, the one that sets his group apart from others more than any other single doctrine.

Notice carefully that our brother did not say that the fullness of the Spirit, as soul-winning power, was the main distinguishing doctrine, but the teaching that speaking in tongues is the initial evidence of this power of the Holy Spirit.

I mention this statement because I believe it represents the attitude of many people. It shows how important in their understanding of Bible truth is their doctrine of speaking in tongues.

Now here is an amazing thing:

Before me is a booklet, *Speaking in Tongues—the Initial Evidence of the Baptism in the Holy Spirit,* by Pastor Donald Gee. It is published by the Full Gospel Publishing House, Toronto, Canada. Donald Gee is a well-known writer of the Pentecostal movement. I have been impressed with his sweet spirit and have been blessed by his written messages. Mr. Gee says:

> Now the doctrine that speaking with other tongues is the initial evidence of the baptism of the Holy Spirit rests upon the accumulated evidence of the recorded cases in the Book of Acts where this experience is received. Any doctrine on this point must necessarily be confined within these limits for its basis, for the New Testament contains no plain, categorical statement anywhere as to what must be regarded as THE sign. Nevertheless, the circumstantial evidence is quite sufficient to clearly reveal God's mind and will in the matter.

Note again this statement, "...*the New Testament contains no plain, categorical statement anywhere as to what must be regarded as THE sign.*"

To this I think every intelligent Bible student will agree. There is not a single statement, either before Pentecost or at Pentecost or after it, in which the Bible speaks of the gift of tongues or speaking in tongues as the evidence, the initial evidence or part of the evidence of being filled with the Spirit or baptized with the Spirit. *This is a doctrine not founded upon a single clear statement in the Word of God!*

Do not misunderstand me. I did not say that the duty to be filled with the Spirit is a doctrine not clearly stated in the Bible. That doctrine *is* clearly stated. I did not say that the gift of tongues is not clearly discussed in the Bible. It is. But I say that the Bible nowhere says that speaking in tongues is the Bible evidence or even the initial evidence of the fullness of the Holy Spirit. That is a doctrine founded on inference alone, or on human reasoning, not on any statement of the Word of God.

I. The Case of Speaking in Tongues at Pentecost Did Not Indicate That It Was the Necessary Evidence of the Baptism in the Spirit or Fullness of the Spirit

In Pentecost we clearly have a model revival. There the disciples for the first time were empowered to carry out the Great Commission and begin the evangelization of the whole world, under the command of Christ. And there, after waiting in the Upper Room, one hundred and twenty were wonderfully filled with the Holy Spirit and spoke with other tongues as the Spirit gave them utterance (Acts 2:4). But is there indication in this account that the speaking in tongues was the necessary evidence or the initial evidence of the fullness of the Holy Spirit? There is not! We have already shown that there is no clear statement anywhere that speaking in tongues is the Bible evidence of the fullness of the Holy Spirit. Now we must plainly draw the inference that if that were an important doctrine of the Bible, it would be stated in connection with Pentecost when speaking with tongues first appeared in the New Testament.

We believe in the virgin birth of Christ because that is clearly stated in Isaiah 7:14, in Luke 1:31–35, in Matthew 1:20–23. We believe in the bodily resurrection of Christ because it is clearly related in each of the Gospels and then referred to repeatedly in the Acts and the Epistles. We are not left to infer this important doctrine.

We believe that salvation is of grace and not of works because the Scripture plainly tells us, "For by grace are ye saved through faith; and that not of yourselves: it is the gift of God" (Eph. 2:8). We do not need to have this doctrine depend on inference or logic.

Christian duties are plainly commanded throughout the Bible. It is wrong to steal, for the Bible plainly says, "Thou shalt not steal," and the New Testament repeats the admonition. So the duties of forgiving our enemies and of praying for those who despitefully use us, of giving to the poor, of winning souls, are repeatedly stated. There is not a single important Christian duty which is left to inference or logic. Every one is clearly stated.

For example, the Scripture plainly commands, "And be not drunk with wine, wherein is excess; but be filled with the Spirit" (Eph. 5:18). It is not left for us to infer that we should be filled with the Spirit. It is plainly commanded.

I insist that it is a duty for us to be filled with the Holy Spirit, because it is stated in the Bible. And if the fullness of the Spirit at Pentecost were proved simply by speaking in tongues, I believe that the Bible would clearly say so. No one has a right to command me to seek what the Bible does not command me to seek, and the Bible nowhere commands that I should seek to speak in tongues. It is never anywhere mentioned as a duty, nor as a necessity, nor even as a privilege! Speaking in tongues is mentioned as the least of the gifts, people are encouraged to seek other gifts instead of this one, and the enthusiasm of the people at Corinth for speaking in tongues was plainly discouraged. The fact that the Bible does not command that we speak in tongues seems to me to be the clearest proof that God does not count that the evidence of the fullness of power.

There are two very strong reasons for us to disbelieve that speaking in tongues was the essential evidence of the fullness of the Spirit at Pentecost.

The first reason, as I have mentioned, is that the Scripture nowhere said speaking in tongues was the essential evidence. But look again at detailed Scriptures where that teaching could have been given and was not.

When Jesus spoke to the disciples in Luke 24:49, He said, "And, behold, I send the promise of my Father upon you: but tarry ye in the city of Jerusalem, until ye be endued with power from on high." Not a word is said about speaking in tongues as the evidence.

Again in Acts 1:4,5 Jesus "commanded them that they should not depart from Jerusalem, but wait for the promise of the Father, which, saith he, ye have heard of me. For John truly baptized with water; but ye shall be baptized with the Holy Ghost not many days hence." Not a word is said about speaking in tongues.

Then at Pentecost itself, in the second chapter of Acts, the account merely records the fact that people of many nationalities heard the Gospel in their own tongues wherein they were born. The inference of the account in the second chapter of Acts is very clear: the preaching of the Gospel and witnessing with power were the important things. It was only an incidental and useful miracle that those who needed to speak in other languages, to people who used those languages, were given the privilege of doing so. The tongues were not important; the message given was important. It was of exactly the same importance whether it was spoken in Latin to the Romans or in Greek to the Greeks or in Aramaic to the native Jews at Jerusalem.

The account of the Pentecostal revival at Jerusalem does not state that speaking in tongues was the Bible sign.

The other strong reason for not believing that speaking in tongues was the Bible evidence of the filling of the Holy Spirit is that another evidence, entirely different, *was* promised. Jesus, questioned about His promise that they should be baptized with the Holy Ghost not many days hence, replied, "But ye shall receive power, after that the Holy Ghost is come upon you: and ye shall be witnesses unto me both in

Jerusalem, and in all Judæa, and in Samaria, and unto the uttermost part of the earth" (Acts 1:8). The power was itself the evidence. I cannot imagine that Peter and James and John and the rest of the hundred and twenty could have any doubt about it.

There was a sound of a great, rushing mighty wind. But that is not what they had been told to expect. It was not the sign, the evidence of the fullness of the Spirit.

There were the cloven tongues like as of fire that rested on the disciples, a wonderful miracle, beautifully symbolical. But that is not what they had been told to expect; it was not the sign, the evidence of the fullness of the Holy Spirit.

They talked in the languages of others who needed to hear the Gospel, and that was a wonderful miracle. But it was not what they had been told to expect; it was not the sign, the evidence.

But when three thousand people turned to God that day under the mighty power of the preaching and testimony of these same Spirit-filled disciples, that was the evidence! "Ye shall receive power, after that the Holy Ghost is come upon you," Jesus said. They received the power, so they knew that the Holy Ghost had come upon them.

Jesus had said, "Tarry ye in the city of Jerusalem, until ye be endued with power from on high." And when the mighty power of God to convict and save sinners was manifested in the salvation of three thousand souls, not a one of those hundred and twenty who had waited for this very same power could doubt the evidence before them. The power to win souls is itself the evidence.

Since God gave another sign, another evidence, of the fullness of the Spirit, it seems to me wrong and foolish for us to believe that speaking in tongues is the evidence, when God says nothing of the kind.

II. In the Second Bible Case of Tongues It Was for Another Purpose, Not as a Required Sign

There are three cases in the Book of Acts where Christians spoke with other tongues when filled with the Holy Ghost. One we have discussed, the account in Acts 2:1–11. The second case is found in Acts 10:44–46. There the Scripture says:

"While Peter yet spake these words, the Holy Ghost fell on all them which heard the word. And they of the circumcision which believed were astonished, as many as came with Peter, because that on the Gentiles also was poured out the gift of the Holy Ghost. For they heard them speak with tongues, and magnify God."

This incident came some eight years after Pentecost. God had dealt specially with Peter to get him to undertake preaching the Gospel to the Gentiles. At last, after being prepared by a vision and the voice of God from Heaven, Peter went with the messengers sent by Cornelius and told Cornelius and his family how to be saved. Immediately they trusted in the Saviour for whom their hearts had hungered, and were filled with the Holy Spirit. Then, in more than one language, they praised God so that Peter and the Jews who came with him understood their praises and decided that these Gentiles were saved.

Notice again that the Scripture does not say that the speaking in tongues was the initial evidence of the fullness of the Holy Spirit. It simply records the fact that these Latin-speaking soldiers, Cornelius and his household, including his servants and his family, we suppose, spoke in languages such as these doubting Jews could hear and understand and be sure that they were saved. Here the incident is not called a gift of tongues. The Bible does not say, even, that it was miraculous.

A little study of the circumstances will show why the speaking in languages (we suppose their own and that of the Jews) was again a very practical matter, as it was at Pentecost. In the following chapter we see Peter called before the apostles and accused by them. They said, "Thou wentest in to men uncircumcised, and didst eat with them" (Acts 11:3). And Peter rehearsed the matter from the beginning to them and told of the miracle of the sheet let down from Heaven and the wild beasts and creeping things and fowls of the air, and the voice from Heaven, saying, "Arise, Peter; slay and eat," and how God made it clear to him that he was not to call anything common or unclean which God had cleansed. He told how the three men came from the house of Cornelius in Caesarea and how the Holy Spirit bade him go with them. As a safety measure so he would not be misunderstood, Peter had taken six brethren with him as witnesses. Peter said then:

"And as I began to speak, the Holy Ghost fell on them, as on us at the beginning. Then remembered I the word of the Lord, how that he said, John indeed baptized with water; but ye shall be baptized with the Holy Ghost. Forasmuch then as God gave them the like gift as he did unto us, who believed on the Lord Jesus Christ; what was I, that I could withstand God?"—Acts 11:15-17.

It was "the gift of the Holy Ghost," Acts 10:45 says. Notice that Peter says that the gift of the Holy Ghost was obvious to him and his six Jewish witnesses and that he thereby decided that God had given to the Gentiles "the like gift as he did unto us, who believed on the Lord Jesus Christ." In other words, Peter, by the praises of these converted Gentiles which he heard and understood, was convinced that the Gentiles were saved.

And those who heard Peter describe the matter came to the same conclusion. The following verse (verse 18) says, "When they heard these things, they held their peace, and glorified God, saying, Then hath God also to the Gentiles granted repentance unto life."

Why did Cornelius and his household speak in tongues, that is, with languages? Why, they spoke certainly in languages that Peter and his six Jewish friends could clearly understand, that by their testimonies these Jews should know they were saved. Acts 10:46 says, "For they heard them speak with tongues, and magnify God." After hearing these people of the Italian band praise God for salvation, which they had long sought—praise Him in Latin, I suppose, and in Aramaic, possibly some of them in Greek, so that all present could understand clearly and no one could doubt that they were saved—Peter was convinced that salvation had been granted to the Gentiles. And the other Jews at Jerusalem agreed, "Then hath God also to the Gentiles granted repentance unto life."

In other words, the doubting Jews with Peter needed to have the evidence that the Gentiles were really saved. The important thing was what these people said. But Peter and his crowd could not understand them well, I suppose, except in their own language.

When Cornelius and his crowd spoke for the purpose mentioned, these doubting Jewish visitors "heard them speak...and magnify God." They evidently heard in their own languages and understood in their own languages what these converts were saying. It is easy for us to see why God thus had Cornelius and his household prove that they were saved. Whether Cornelius and his household already knew these languages, or whether they spoke by a miraculous gift, we are not told. They simply testified in tongues, that is, in languages, and were heard and understood. Their testimonies, given in the power of the Holy Spirit, proved that they were saved.

Remember, this was the first time the Gentiles had had the Gospel preached to them as a group of Gentiles and not as Jewish proselytes. This time the use of tongues was reversed. It was not Peter who spoke in tongues but others who spoke to Peter in tongues for the very practical reason that there was a language barrier that needed to be overcome. It was a practical, reasonable thing. Speaking in tongues was not mentioned as a proof of the fullness of the Spirit or the evidence of the fullness of the Spirit.

III. In Acts 19:1–6 Tongues Are Not Mentioned as a Necessary Sign of the Fullness of the Spirit

The third and last recorded case in the New Testament of Christians filled with the Holy Ghost and speaking in tongues is in Acts 19:1–7 where we read as follows:

"And it came to pass, that, while Apollos was at Corinth, Paul having passed through the upper coasts came to Ephesus: and finding certain disciples, He said unto them, Have ye received the Holy Ghost since ye believed? And they said unto him, We have not so much as heard whether there be any Holy Ghost. And he said unto them, Unto what then were ye baptized? And they said, Unto John's baptism. Then said Paul, John verily baptized with the baptism of repentance, saying unto the people, that they should believe on him which should come after him, that is, on Christ Jesus. When they heard this, they were baptized in the name of the Lord Jesus. And when Paul had laid his hands upon them, the Holy Ghost came on them; and they spake with tongues, and prophesied. And all the men were about twelve."

Ephesus was a great, busy, cosmopolitan city of many languages. In the same nineteenth chapter of Acts we are told that the statue of Diana was worshiped by the Ephesians, and the story is told of a Gentile mob of idolaters who would have killed Paul and his companions, and who specially hated the Jews.

Ephesus would have very strong influences from at least three sources. There were the Roman imperialistic government and officers; there were the strong Grecian cultural influence and, of course, the influence of the Jews also in language and commerce. A number of languages would be spoken in Ephesus. Certainly Latin and Greek and Aramaic would be spoken there regularly. So it is not surprising that these who were filled with the Holy Spirit after Paul laid his hands upon them spoke in languages.

But was this speaking in tongues in Acts, chapter 19, miraculous? I do not know. You do not know. The Bible simply does not say. They spoke with more than one language and prophesied. That is all that the Scripture says in Acts 19:6. It may have been a supernatural gift of tongues, but the Bible does not say so. None of us has a right to say dogmatically what the Bible does not say. It is very possible that these men, "about twelve," represented several different nationalities, and when they were filled with the Holy Ghost and began to witness and prophesy for the Lord, they spoke in their various languages. More than that, we cannot say.

But certainly no Scripture here says that the speaking in tongues is the Bible evidence of the fullness of the Holy Spirit. If God gave them here a gift of tongues for His own reasons, I praise the Lord for it. I do not need even to understand all about it. Whatever God did is all right. But we would be wrong to infer what the Bible does not say, that every person ever filled with the Holy Spirit must speak in tongues. That the Bible does not say, and that we have no right to claim.

You see that in the only three recorded examples of people speaking in tongues, it is never declared to be a sign of the fullness of the Spirit.

We have shown above that there is not a single statement in the Bible declaring that speaking with tongues is the initial evidence of the fullness of the Holy Spirit. Then we particularly discussed the Bible promises preceding Pentecost and the account of the Pentecostal revival and later references to it, and we found that there was no indication that speaking in tongues even at Pentecost was intended as the initial evidence of the baptism of the Holy Ghost. Then a study of the speaking in tongues in the household of Cornelius in Acts, chapter 10, shows that tongues were here not mentioned nor intended as a necessary sign but only a practical use to overcome the language barrier between nationalities. Finally, we studied the third and last example described in the Bible where people actually talked with tongues, that is, Acts 19:1–6. There again we found no statement that speaking in tongues was the initial evidence of the baptism of the Holy Spirit. In fact, there is no particular evidence that the tongues were a miracle at all. It may have been simply natural use of foreign languages.

IV. Bible Examples of People Filled With the Holy Spirit Without Speaking in Tongues Prove Tongues Unnecessary

As the good people of the tongues movement frankly confess, there is no direct scriptural statement that speaking in tongues is the initial evidence of the baptism of the Holy Spirit, the required evidence. Pastor Donald Gee, in his booklet mentioned before, *Speaking in Tongues—the Initial Evidence of the Baptism of the Holy Spirit,* says: "Now the doctrine that speaking with other tongues is the initial evidence of the baptism of the Holy Spirit rests upon the accumulated evidence of the recorded cases in the Book of Acts where this experience is received."

He should have said "in the New Testament" instead of "in the Book of Acts." Or perhaps he should have said "in the Bible." Certainly people were filled with the Holy Spirit as recorded in other books of the Bible besides the Book of Acts. But never mind—the important thing is that *the doctrine of speaking in tongues* as the initial evidence of the baptism of the Holy Spirit or fullness of the Spirit *must stand or fall on the recorded cases in the Bible*.

Of course, if God had wanted to teach that doctrine, He could have taken only one verse anywhere in the Bible to state that speaking in tongues is the Bible evidence of the fullness of the Spirit. He did not do so. It is dangerous and wrong to found any doctrine on implication without a single categorical statement in the Bible. But if there be any Bible proof that speaking in tongues is required as the initial evidence of the fullness of the Spirit, then the recorded cases in the New Testament of people filled with the Holy Spirit would have to show that they spoke in tongues, as a miraculous manifestation, that is, in languages they did not previously know. However, the very obvious truth—the opposite of this—becomes apparent as we read every case in the New Testament where people were filled with the Holy Spirit. In most of such cases not a single word is said about their talking in tongues. In most cases in the Bible where people were filled with the Holy Spirit they definitely did *not* speak with other tongues. The argument for speaking with tongues, as evidence of being filled with the Spirit, falls down.

In fact, there are only three definite cases related in the New Testament where particular people talked with tongues. The first case is described in Acts 2:1–11. The disciples at Pentecost were given the miraculous power to speak in the languages of other people who were present, and these heard the Gospel in their own tongues in which they were born. The second is in Acts 10:46 where we read how Cornelius and his household, of the Italian band, magnified God after believing and gave their testimony in languages. We are not told whether it was a miraculous gift or whether they simply praised God in the Latin and Aramaic, which languages they already knew, so that all present would hear and understand. The third case is in Acts 19:1–6 where about twelve men were filled with the Holy Spirit after Paul laid his hands upon them and prayed and they spake with tongues and prophesied. We are not told what the languages were. We are not told that the languages were the evidence of the fullness of the Spirit. We are not even told that the tongues were a miraculous gift, that the languages were unknown to them before. And remember that these are the only three cases described in the whole Bible where anybody talked with tongues. There is some mention of the tongues question in other places, but no other particular instances are related. These are all the concrete Bible examples that anybody in the world can find for the tongues doctrine.

On the other hand, there are many, many cases related in the Bible of people filled with the Holy Spirit who did *not* speak with tongues. Four of these cases were specially important ones where people were filled with the Holy Spirit for the first time and where speaking in tongues could not have been the initial evidence of the baptism of the Holy Ghost.

FIRST, CONSIDER JOHN THE BAPTIST. We have a Bible account of how he was filled with the Holy Spirit the first time and did not speak with tongues. The angel appeared to Zacharias to promise that he would have a son, John, and said:

"For he shall be great in the sight of the Lord, and shall drink neither wine nor strong drink; and he shall be filled with the Holy Ghost, even from his mother's womb. And many of the children of Israel shall he turn to the Lord their God."— Luke 1:15,16.

Note that John the Baptist had exactly the same enduement that the disciples received at Pentecost. He was "filled with the Holy Ghost." In Acts 2:4 we are told about the disciples at Pentecost, "And they were all filled with the Holy Ghost." It was the same blessing.

Note also that it was for the same soul-winning purpose. The Scripture above says, "And many of the children of Israel shall he turn to the Lord their God."

John the Baptist was filled with the Holy Ghost just as the disciples were later filled at Pentecost; he had the same soul-winning power, but he did not talk in tongues. In the case of John the Baptist, speaking in tongues was not the initial evidence of the baptism of the Holy Ghost.

SECOND, CONSIDER JESUS CHRIST. The Lord Jesus is the pattern and example for Christians, and we are to follow His steps. Jesus as our example was definitely filled with the Holy Spirit. This occurred at His baptism, according to Luke 3:21,22, which says:

"Now when all the people were baptized, it came to pass, that Jesus also being baptized, and praying, the heaven was opened, And the Holy Ghost descended in a bodily shape like a dove upon him, and a voice came from heaven, which said, Thou art my beloved Son; in thee I am well pleased."

Note that this was the first time that Jesus was filled with the Holy Ghost. Up to this time, although the perfect Son of God, He had never preached a sermon, never worked a miracle, never healed the sick, never won a soul. And the language which Luke was inspired to use further on in the same story shows that Jesus had exactly the kind of enduement of power that the apostles and others received at Pentecost.

"And Jesus being full of the Holy Ghost returned from Jordan, and was led by the Spirit into the wilderness."—Luke 4:1.

"And Jesus returned in the power of the Spirit into Galilee...."—Luke 4:14.

Then in the synagogue in Nazareth Jesus quoted from Isaiah 61:1 the Scripture, "The Spirit of the Lord is upon me, because he hath anointed me to preach the gospel" (Luke 4:18). Jesus said then to His hearers, "This day is this scripture fulfilled in your ears" (Luke 4:21).

This special enduement of power which the dear Lord Jesus received at His baptism is described again in Acts 10:38, "How God anointed Jesus of Nazareth with the Holy Ghost and with power: who went about doing good, and healing all that were oppressed of the devil; for God was with him."

You see, then, that the Lord Jesus was "anointed...with the Holy Ghost and with power." We were told that "the Holy Ghost descended...upon him," that He was "full of the Holy Ghost," and that He returned "in the power of the Spirit." Jesus Himself had, as our example, what He commands us to have and what the apostles and others received at Pentecost. But not a word is said about Jesus speaking in other tongues. In His case speaking in tongues was not required and certainly was not the initial evidence of the fullness of the Holy Spirit.

CONSIDER CONVERTS IN SAMARIA. The eighth chapter of Acts tells how Philip went down to Samaria and preached Christ and a great multitude of people were saved. And we are told in detail of how they received the Holy Spirit in power. Acts 8:14–17 says:

"Now when the apostles which were at Jerusalem heard that Samaria had received the word of God, they sent unto them Peter and John: Who, when they were come down, prayed for them, that they might receive the Holy Ghost: (For as yet he was fallen upon none of them: only they were baptized in the name of the Lord Jesus.) Then laid they their hands on them, and they received the Holy Ghost."

The preceding verses have already said that these Samaritans had believed and been baptized. Verse 14 then tells us that they "had received the word of God."

When these converts in Samaria "received the Holy Ghost," we believe that they were simply endued with power from on high, as the apostles and others were at Pentecost. Certainly they had already been saved. And when they were saved, it is equally clear that the Holy

Spirit was the one who had saved them, and they were born of the Spirit and had the Holy Spirit dwelling in them before Peter and John came down from Jerusalem and laid their hands on them that they might receive the Holy Spirit. They received Him in power, in a soul-winning enduement and anointing, just as other Christians in the Book of Acts did.

But note that there is nothing said about speaking in tongues, and certainly speaking in tongues was not necessary to them and was not the initial evidence of the fullness of the Holy Spirit.

CONSIDER THE APOSTLE PAUL. In Acts, chapter 9, we have the story of the salvation of Saul, later called the Apostle Paul. Then after Paul had fasted and prayed three days and nights, Ananias, the disciple, was sent to him. Acts 9:17 says:

"And Ananias went his way, and entered into the house; and putting his hands on him said, Brother Saul, the Lord, even Jesus, that appeared unto thee in the way as thou camest, hath sent me, that thou mightest receive thy sight, and be filled with the Holy Ghost."

After his conversion, after he had already surrendered to Jesus and called Him Lord, after he had already been told that he would be sent far hence to the Gentiles, and after the Christian, Ananias, called him brother, Saul was "filled with the Holy Ghost."

This is the same term used about the disciples at Pentecost. "And they were all filled with the Holy Ghost" (Acts 2:4). So Paul the apostle was here filled with the Holy Spirit, endued with power from on high for the first time, and that within three days after his conversion. But Paul did not speak with other tongues! Speaking in tongues certainly was not necessary in his case and was not the initial evidence of the baptism of the Holy Spirit.

These four cases of John the Baptist, Jesus, the Samaritan Christians and Saul, later called the Apostle Paul, are absolute proof that in Bible times speaking in tongues was not required and was not the initial evidence of the fullness of the Holy Spirit.

Please note very carefully that in every single one of these four cases we have the Bible description of the *first time* they were filled with the Holy Spirit. And they did not speak with tongues.

There are a number of other cases where people were filled with the Holy Spirit, recorded in the Bible, which may have been the first time they were filled with the Spirit. In Luke 1:41 we are told, "...and Elisabeth was filled with the Holy Ghost." In Luke 1:67 we are told,

"And his father Zacharias was filled with the Holy Ghost." Yet neither of these Christians spoke in other languages. Why should they? There was no one else present who could better understand a foreign language than their own! In their cases certainly speaking with tongues was not the evidence required nor given for the fullness of the Holy Spirit.

But why should the first occasion when one is filled with the Holy Spirit require a special sign of speaking with tongues and a second occasion of being filled with the Spirit not require such a sign? There is no such teaching anywhere in the Bible. Pentecostal groups claim tongues are demanded for the first filling, only, not more, because we have so many, many cases in the Bible where people were filled with the Holy Spirit and did not speak with tongues. Consider the following cases where the Scripture is not specially considering the first time people were filled with the Holy Spirit, but where it is plainly said that they were filled with the Holy Spirit. "And when they had prayed, the place was shaken where they were assembled together; and they were all filled with the Holy Ghost, and they spake the word of God with boldness" (Acts 4:31). Note that the same nine words are used as in Acts 2:4, "And they were all filled with the Holy Ghost." Yet no word is said about tongues.

Another case worth study was Stephen. "And the saying pleased the whole multitude: and they chose Stephen, a man full of faith and of the Holy Ghost" (Acts 6:5). The rest of the sixth chapter and all of the seventh chapter of Acts are given to Stephen, the Spirit-filled deacon, and there is not a hint of speaking in tongues.

Barnabas too was filled with the Holy Ghost. Acts 11:24 says: "For he was a good man, and full of the Holy Ghost and of faith: and much people was added unto the Lord." Barnabas is repeatedly mentioned, but no word is said about his speaking in tongues.

It is obvious that speaking in tongues is not the necessary evidence, is not the usual evidence, is not the initial evidence, of being filled with the Holy Spirit, according to the examples given in the Bible. Many people were filled with the Holy Spirit and had the same power that the Christians received at Pentecost. But they did not hear the sound of a rushing mighty wind as people did at Pentecost. There were no visible "tongues like as of fire" resting upon them. They did not need to speak in foreign languages. But they did have the same enduement of power to speak for Jesus Christ.

In Acts 4:31 there was an earthquake, when the disciples were filled again with the Holy Spirit, but no speaking in tongues. It is quite clear that incidental and outward manifestations varied from time to time. But the power of the Holy Spirit was always given to enable Christians to speak for the Lord and to carry His Gospel, as Jesus had plainly promised that it would be given to those who would tarry for this power.

People who believe that speaking in tongues is the necessary initial evidence of the fullness of the Holy Spirit make a great distinction between tongues as an initial evidence of the fullness of the Spirit, and the gift of tongues. They say that every Christian, to be first filled with the Holy Spirit, must talk in tongues. But they say that the gift of tongues whereby people may frequently, or perhaps even at will, talk in tongues, is another gift given only to a few people. But the Scripture has no such teaching, makes no such distinction. Certainly the tongues at Pentecost were "the gift of tongues." The gift of tongues was rare. The gift of tongues was clearly given to those filled with the Holy Spirit at Pentecost in order that they might speak the Gospel to others. There may have been a gift of tongues with Cornelius and his household, but the Scripture does not say so. Perhaps they already knew the languages they used. There may have been a gift of tongues to the twelve men mentioned in Acts 19:1–6, but the Scripture does not say. We know that they praised God in foreign languages. We do not know that it was a miracle. They may have simply used languages they already knew. The Bible does not say. But there was a gift of tongues in Bible times. It was very rarely given. It was certainly not given as the initial evidence of the fullness of the Holy Spirit.

"But wait!" says some dear Christian friend who believes that speaking in tongues is the Bible evidence of the fullness of the Spirit. "We believe that the Samaritan converts mentioned in Acts 8:14–17 *did* talk in tongues. The Scripture does not say so, but we believe they did. We believe that Saul, later called Paul the apostle, *did* speak in tongues when he was filled with the Holy Spirit, though Acts 9:17 and the Scriptures following do not say so."

My answer is that no Christian has a right to read into the Bible what it does not say. If we cannot make a doctrine from what the Bible plainly says, we have no right to found a doctrine on things it does not say. But we have, written down in the divine Word of God, exactly what God wanted us to know about these cases. If God had wanted us to believe that these converts spoke with other tongues or languages when they were filled with the Holy Ghost, He could have said so. He did not say so. It is only fair to believe that God did not want us to believe so. Let me say again, no Christian has a right to read into the

Bible what it does not say, nor to found a doctrine on something that he infers is true, when the Bible never says anything of the kind.

No, those who base their faith upon the Bible must come to the clear conclusion that one need not talk in tongues as the evidence that he is filled with the Holy Spirit. The Bible does not require it. Many Christians in Bible examples did not speak in tongues when they were filled with the Holy Spirit, even the first time. The examples of John the Baptist, Jesus, the Samaritan converts and the Apostle Paul ought to convince every Christian that speaking in tongues is not to be sought and not to be expected or required as the sign of the fullness of the Holy Spirit, not in the initial case or any other case.

V. Great Soul Winners of All the Centuries, Filled With the Holy Spirit, Have Not Talked in Tongues

We have proved from the Bible that speaking in tongues is not required, that it is not the initial evidence of the fullness of the Holy Spirit, and many cases are given in the Bible where people were filled with the Holy Spirit and did not talk in tongues.

Now I want to call your attention to the fact that the greatest soul winners that God has given to His people down through the centuries have been filled with the Holy Spirit without talking in tongues. That ought to be enough to settle for any thinking person the truth that people who are filled with the Holy Spirit need not speak in tongues.

Fortunately we know that it is only through the power of the Holy Spirit that people carry out the Great Commission and win souls. Jesus commanded His disciples "that repentance and remission of sins should be preached in his name among all nations, beginning at Jerusalem," but "tarry ye," said He, "in the city of Jerusalem, until ye be endued with power from on high" (Luke 24:47,49). Jesus Himself plainly said to these disciples, "But ye shall receive power, after that the Holy Ghost is come upon you: and ye shall be witnesses unto me both in Jerusalem, and in all Judæa, and in Samaria, and unto the uttermost part of the earth" (Acts 1:8). We know that the power of the Holy Spirit will make people witnesses, make people anointed, fruitful soul winners. That is what happened to the disciples at Pentecost and others in the New Testament times who were filled with the Holy Spirit, including John the Baptist, Jesus, Deacon Stephen, Barnabas, Paul the apostle, and others.

Now, down through the centuries there have been many men greatly used of God in soul winning. These men, almost without exception or entirely without exception, claimed to have upon them the power of the Holy Spirit, to be endued with power from on high. They were filled with the Holy Ghost. They themselves have said so; their works have proved it. Yet the most useful soul winners through the centuries have not talked with tongues.

Consider D. L. Moody. It is said that he won a million souls to Christ. He was certainly the most influential Christian in the entire world during his century. He himself claimed that he had been definitely filled with the Holy Spirit. He knew when it happened, in Wall Street, New York City. The marvelous ministry God gave him in soul-winning power proved his claim. Yet D. L. Moody never did speak in tongues. Sometimes tongues people have been very careless and quick to claim D. L. Moody as of their persuasion. He *did* have a definite fullness of the Holy Spirit. He definitely *did not* speak in tongues. To this, his own words and the testimony of his family, his co-workers and his biographers all agree. D. L. Moody did not have speaking in tongues, did not need that as a sign that he was filled with the Holy Spirit.

Consider Charles G. Finney, whose marvelous revivals are told about in his autobiography. Finney tells how he had a powerful "baptism with the Spirit." That is what he calls it. He tells of the mighty power of God that came upon him. Immediately this power was manifested in the saving of many souls. Finney was one of the most remarkable characters in modern times, the greatest soul winner in the first half of the nineteenth century, as Moody was in the last half. But Finney did not talk in tongues. Why should he? There was no occasion for it. Finney is an example to prove that people can be filled with the Holy Spirit, just as the Bible commands us to be, without talking in tongues.

Dr. R. A. Torrey was a mighty evangelist, as well as one of the world's best Bible teachers. In his tour around the world, at least a hundred thousand souls turned to Christ. He carried on the mighty work of evangelism, following much in the steps of D. L. Moody. But Torrey himself is on record that though he knew his ministry was empowered by the Holy Spirit in a wonderful way, he never spoke with tongues and was thoroughly convinced that it was not required, was not a sign from God, not the evidence of the fullness of the Holy Spirit. For further information see the comments in his book, *The Holy Spirit: Who He Is, and What He Does*.

John Wesley, George Whitefield, Charles H. Spurgeon, J. Wilbur Chapman, Billy Sunday, Len G. Broughton, George W. Truett, Gipsy Smith—all these mighty soul winners depended upon the power of the Holy Spirit and had that power so that in each case they won many, many tens of thousands, some of them hundreds of thousands of souls, yet none of them talked with tongues!

I am familiar with the leading soul winners on this continent at this time—evangelists, pastors, youth leaders. Name them over: Dr. Bob Jones, Dr. Hyman Appelman, Dr. Charles E. Fuller, Dr. Robert G. Lee, Jack Wyrtzen, Lee Roberson, Torrey Johnson, Jack Hyles and many others. None of these men, remarkably used of God in soul winning, have talked with tongues. All of them know that the souls they have won were won in the power and fullness of the Holy Spirit.

The leading soul winners down through the centuries, endued with the mighty power of God, have not talked in tongues. Surely that helps to prove that speaking with tongues is not the mark, the initial evidence, of the fullness of the Holy Spirit. Speaking in tongues thus is surely not expected nor demanded of Christians who would be filled with the Spirit. It is certainly unscriptural, as well as unkind and somewhat pharisaical, to say that these mighty men of God—like Moody and Torrey and Gipsy Smith, for example—were not filled with the Holy Spirit because they did not speak in tongues, though they won hundreds of thousands, yea, millions of souls altogether.

SECTION IV
A Tongues Heresy in Bible Times

Those who are disturbed by a tongues heresy in modern times should remember that there was a tongues heresy in Bible times also.

According to Paul's Epistles to the Corinthians, the church at Corinth had about all the different kinds of trouble and heresies into which churches today fall. There were divisions and contentions among them (I Cor. 1:11–13). The church members there were carnal, not spiritual (I Cor. 3:1–4). They were not able to bear the strong meat and must be fed on the milk of the gospel (I Cor. 3:2). Some of the Corinthians were puffed up and offended with Paul (I Cor. 4:18). Worse still, there was fornication among them, a man living in sin with his stepmother and the church openly taking his part (I Cor. 5). Church members went to law one with another before unbelievers (I Cor. 6:1–8). Some of the church members ate meats offered to idols, which scandalized others (I Cor.8). There were divisions and heresies at the Lord's Supper, and some came to the Communion drunk (I Cor. 11:17–21).

With these things in mind, it will not be hard to understand that the church members at Corinth were led astray in a tongues heresy, false teaching and false practice on the question of speaking in tongues. And that heresy is discussed and is rebuked in I Corinthians, chapter 14.

We should like to study this chapter with you very carefully. But first note several characteristics and get in mind what God's Word has for us here.

First, I Corinthians 14 does not exhort people to seek to speak in tongues. It does not even encourage them to seek tongues.

Second, it shows the folly of speaking in languages which people present cannot understand.

Third, it shows how much better is the gift of prophecy (speaking by the power of the Holy Spirit and God's revelation) than talking in foreign languages, or unknown tongues.

Fourth, certain definite restrictions are clearly given to help eliminate the abuses and abominations and confusions which had grown up in Corinth and which would grow up in other churches and movements down through the years.

Not a single authentic case of people speaking by a gift of tongues, miraculously speaking foreign languages, is mentioned in this chapter, I Corinthians, chapter 14. It is a chapter of instructions, not on how to speak in tongues but how *not* to speak in tongues. It is encouragement to seek other gifts instead of the gift of tongues. With this in mind, let us study the chapter more carefully.

I. The Languages or Tongues Referred to in I Corinthians 14 Are Natural Foreign Languages, Not Heavenly Languages

It is an amazing matter to find how the Bible commentators down through the years have misunderstood the tongues discussed in I Corinthians, chapter 14! Fanatical fringes of Christians down through the centuries have thought that speaking in tongues meant some ecstatic utterance given from God, which the speaker did not understand and those who heard did not understand—some heavenly language not known by men anywhere. Such is far from the truth. The commentators unfortunately have often gone by such testimonies of men and not by the Word of God in this matter, and those who think in terms of some heavenly, unknowable language get that idea from the heretical extravaganzas, not from the Bible. Speaking in tongues, in the Bible, simply meant talking foreign languages.

That is clear, first of all, from the great example of Pentecost, when the Spirit-filled disciples were given the power to speak in the languages of some sixteen different nationalities of people who were present and heard them speak "in our own tongue, wherein we were born," they said. Quite manifestly the discussion of Pentecost is the central Bible passage on speaking in tongues, and that is the outstanding Bible example, beyond any doubt. But the use of "tongues" there was simply speaking in foreign languages. It was done in Acts, chapter 2, by a miraculous gift of God, but the languages themselves were foreign languages known and used by other people and understood by them when spoken at Pentecost. There is no reason to suppose that the gift of tongues anywhere else in the Bible meant anything else than what it meant at Pentecost. When the Bible speaks of tongues, it means languages, natural languages, foreign languages. It does not mean some heavenly or spiritual or unknown babble of sounds. The pattern of Pentecost must apply to any other Bible cases of the miraculous gift of tongues.

But many verses in I Corinthians, chapter 14, on the tongues heresy in Bible times show that natural languages are meant. For example, verses 10 and 11 say:

"There are, it may be, so many kinds of voices in the world, and none of them is without signification. Therefore if I know not the meaning of the voice, I shall be unto him that speaketh a barbarian, and he that speaketh shall be a barbarian unto me."

There are so many kinds of foreign languages in the world, this Scripture says, and every one of them has definite meaning. Therefore, Paul says by divine inspiration, anyone who hears such a language and does not understand the meaning of it would be a barbarian to the speaker, and the speaker would be a barbarian to the hearer. Clearly he is referring to natural languages.

Again, verses 23 and 24 show that the apostle, writing by inspiration of the Holy Spirit, refers to natural tongues, foreign languages, which the cultured and educated learn and which "unlearned" people might not know. Those two verses say:

"If therefore the whole church be come together into one place, and all speak with tongues, and there come in those that are unlearned, or unbelievers, will they not say that ye are mad? But if all prophesy, and there come in one that believeth not, or one unlearned, he is convinced of all, he is judged of all."

If all in the church should speak foreign languages, and there came in some unlearned people, they would not understand what was said, and they would think that these people were mad, that is, insane. But if all were to prophesy, we are told (that is, speak by divine inspiration but in their own language), then the unbeliever and the *unlearned* who might come in would be convinced and convicted by what they would hear. You see, the Scripture here is clearly speaking of some natural foreign language that educated people in that big cosmopolitan city knew and that "unlearned" or ignorant people did not know. A learned or educated person would not understand a heavenly language any quicker than an ignorant or unlearned person would. So the Word of God is here speaking of natural languages.

Let us remember also that the Greek word *glossa*, here translated "tongues", is used in the New Testament fifty times and never once is it used to teach that there is some heavenly speech that no mortal would understand.

Some would use the second verse in this fourteenth chapter of I Corinthians as evidence that the Holy Spirit is here speaking of some heavenly tongue, not natural foreign languages. In verse 2 Paul said, "For he that speaketh in an unknown tongue speaketh not unto men, but unto God: for no man understandeth him; howbeit in the spirit he speaketh mysteries." But that Scripture simply says what is obvious, when you think about it. If you talk in a foreign language to people who do not understand you, then you talk to yourself and God but not to anybody else, for nobody else understands.

That is the reason that verse 28 says, "But if there be no interpreter, let him keep silence in the church; and let him speak to himself, and to God."

That is, if a man would speak in a foreign language and there is nobody present who understands it and can tell the other people what one says, then since he cannot speak the language of those present, let him keep silence in the church, and he can do his praying and his praising to himself and to God. He would understand and God would understand, but others in the church, not knowing that foreign language, would not understand.

Speaking in tongues, then, means speaking in foreign languages. And that is what it means in this fourteenth chapter of I Corinthians.

II. The Heresy Rebuked in I Corinthians 14 Was Not a Miraculous Gift of Tongues, but Simply Presumptuous Use, Without a Miracle, of Foreign Languages

In the church at Corinth God had distributed many gifts of the

Spirit. Many people suppose that some Corinthians had received the gift of tongues and that they went about promiscuously speaking miraculously in other languages, whenever they chose, whether people present understood them or not! They caused confusion, they neglected prophecy, they left the impression on unsaved people that they were crazy; and yet some would have you believe that all this was done by the miraculous power of God! No, the tongues that were in use at Corinth were not the miraculous gift of tongues. They were simply foreign languages misused by carnal people who wanted to show off and make a big impression in the church. They spoke languages that they knew, but which other people present might not know, and thus they did wrong. This misuse of foreign languages was an *imitation* of the gift of tongues but was *not* the gift of tongues.

Where in the Bible did God ever give a miracle and allow it to be misused, used for an evil purpose? I challenge the reader to find even one such case in the Bible.

God does give us talents, and we sometimes misuse them. But a talent is a gift which we have from birth, which is left to us, and we may use it or not. If I have a talent for music and sing, that is not a miracle. And when I sing with natural talent, it is not God singing. God may bless my singing if I sing for Him. He may despise my singing if I do not sing to please Him. But it is not a miracle, and God is not manifest in a purely natural talent. The Holy Spirit may anoint my singing and may by filling me with the Holy Spirit make it useful. But the voice itself is a natural talent. So one may misuse a talent for making money, a talent for public speech, a talent for art. Those are natural gifts. But a miracle is an entirely different matter. When God allows any man to work a miracle, it is God Himself working, even more than the man.

God miraculously used Moses and his rod. He had Moses stretch out his hand, and the Red Sea opened. Later the Red Sea closed on Pharaoh and his host. God had Moses strike the rock in the wilderness with his rod, and water gushed out to quench the thirst of the starving millions of Israel. When Moses held his hands up, God miraculously gave victory to the Israelites against the Amalekites. There were wonderful miracles done through Moses' rod. But do you suppose that Moses could therefore go about and use that rod in any way he pleased, for his own pleasure, or even in sin? Could Moses use that rod to strike a rock and command it to bring forth silver and gold to make him rich? Could Moses use that rod to threaten people and so compel them to make him king and to do his bidding? The thought is a foolish thought.

God's miraculous power was in the rod only as God chose to put it there. It was God who opened the Red Sea and who closed it, killing Pharaoh's host. It was God who brought water out of the rock. And God would have withdrawn His power any moment the miraculous power was about to be used in sin. God is not a party to sin and wrongdoing.

Peter, in the fifth chapter of Acts, said the word, and Ananias and Sapphira fell dead. That was a wonderful miracle. God Himself struck Ananias and Sapphira dead, though Peter was the one who had the gift of miracles in this case, it seemed. God worked with Peter. But suppose that Peter had said, "Well! Here is a way I can use to make myself rich and famous and have my own way!" Suppose he remembered everybody who had once wronged him and set out to have them struck dead, as were Ananias and Sapphira! Suppose he had turned to the other apostles and demanded that they make him a pope, to be absolute ruler of Christendom, and suppose he had threatened to have them struck dead as he had had Ananias and Sapphira struck dead! Does anybody believe that God would have allowed Peter to retain this miraculous power for misuse? Would God have entered into sin by continuing His miraculous power on a person using this power for sinful purposes? That is unthinkable! God does not sin! God does not put His miraculous power on people for the purpose of sinning.

Just so, God does not give the gifts of the Holy Spirit to people for their own purposes.

Consider the wonderful signs and gifts that are promised to those who have faith for them, in Mark 16:17,18:

"And these signs shall follow them that believe; In my name shall they cast out devils; they shall speak with new tongues; They shall take up serpents; and if they drink any deadly thing, it shall not hurt them; they shall lay hands on the sick, and they shall recover."

Does anybody believe that God would continue His miraculous power to cast out devils on one who did it for his own pleasure and for gain? Do you really believe that God gives people miraculous protection to take up serpents and drink deadly poison just as a show or to set an admission fee and make money out of the miracle? Do you believe that God would allow the miracle-working power of laying hands on the sick, so that they should recover, to one who did that regularly in a manner that would be sinful and hurtful, to make himself rich, while he brought reproach upon Christianity? I do not believe it!

Well, right in this same beautiful cluster of promises is this one: "they shall speak with new tongues." Notice that speaking in tongues is not promised to everybody, just to those who believe for speaking in tongues. That was evidently the case at Pentecost. But if people started to misuse the gift of tongues (remember, that was a miracle at Pentecost)—if they started to speak in other languages for their own pride and sinful self-will, so that Paul needed to write a letter rebuking them and urging them to stop their sinful practices—do you believe that God's Holy Spirit would continue to give them this miraculous gift in that case?

Take the illustration used by the Holy Spirit through the Apostle Paul in this same fourteenth chapter of I Corinthians. Here is a church full of people, with unconverted people and ignorant people present in the audience. The church all begin to speak in foreign languages, and the unconverted people and the ignorant people scoff and laugh and say that they are crazy! And this brings reproach on the cause of Christ. That was the case at Corinth. Certainly that was the condition which Paul was definitely reproving. Now do you believe that God Himself gave His power for that kind of disgraceful affair?

Let's put it in another way. Suppose that these Christians at Corinth had a miraculous gift of tongues and misused it. Suppose we say that they had confusion, they made an unseemly spectacle, they made of themselves barbarians to those who heard (that is the term used in verses 10 and 11), and appeared to be crazy to the unconverted people and unlearned who were present. If that were so, God was in them working this miracle all the time they were misusing the miracle. Then *God* was the author of the confusion there. Then *God* was the author of their ignorance, and *God* was the helper in their sin. And then God put it in the heart of Paul to rebuke the sin which He, God, had helped the people at Corinth to commit? No, that is unthinkable.

In fact, verse 33 plainly says, "For God is not the author of confusion, but of peace, as in all churches of the saints." They had confusion over tongues at Corinth, but God was not in the confusion. It was not a miraculous gift of tongues that caused the confusion. It was a simple but unjustified use of foreign languages in the service by carnal church members.

The same kind of church members who came drunk to the Lord's Supper, who had divisions, who could not be given the strong meat of the Word because they were carnal and so must be fed on milk, the same kind of Christians who went to law with brothers before unsaved men, the same kind of Christians who took up for the man living in adultery—these Corinthians, carnal as they were, though saved, had a tongues heresy. They began to speak in all kinds of foreign languages in the public services, putting on a show and imitating the gift of tongues. And this the fourteenth chapter of I Corinthians clearly rebukes.

Another evidence that it was not a miraculous gift that Paul was discussing through divine inspiration in I Corinthians 14 is what he says in verse 18: "I thank my God, I speak with tongues more than ye all." In the original Greek, "the oldest MSS. has the singular 'in a tongue [foreign],'" says Jamieson, Fausset and Brown. Now if Paul ever had a gift of tongues, the Bible does not mention it. When Paul was filled with the Holy Spirit first, in Acts 9:17, no mention is made of the gift of tongues. Paul wrote fourteen of the twenty-seven books in the New Testament, over half of the whole New Testament (if we include Hebrews, as I believe we must). We know more about Paul from the Bible than about any other Bible character except possibly David. And we have far more of his own words about himself than from any other man mentioned in the whole Word of God. And there is never a mention of Paul's speaking miraculously by a gift of tongues. Without any word in the Bible to the contrary, we believe Paul must refer to the language, *Koine* Greek, in which Paul wrote his epistles and preached, though it was a foreign language, not his native Aramaic.

No, Paul simply meant, "I preach the Gospel in another language more than any of you. I am an educated Jew, a man of Tarsus, a Roman citizen, brought up in Jerusalem at the feet of Gamaliel, a leading Jewish teacher, and now preaching over the whole Roman empire to people of many races. I speak more often in a foreign language than any Christian in the church at Corinth." Paul did not mean that he had the gift of tongues and spoke in some heavenly language, some unknown language that had no meaning to men, simply for his own enjoyment. No, no! We know that Paul preached the Gospel in practically the whole known world of his day. He preached at Jerusalem, at Antioch of Pisidia, at Corinth, at Ephesus, at Athens, at Rome. By divine inspiration he said that he would go to Spain (Rom. 15:24). Paul, one of the best educated, most widely traveled men of his day, spoke more often in a foreign language than any of the poor, carnal church members at Corinth!

And that indicates that the kind of languages of which he was speaking at Corinth were natural languages which people had learned and which they used foolishly, as a show in the public services.

If you will take this position, that the tongues spoken of in I Corinthians, chapter 14, were simply foreign languages and used without the miraculous gift but simply as people had learned these foreign languages, the meaning of the whole chapter will become quite clear in your mind. And that fits the whole chapter and solves the problems that are raised by it.

III. Why the Tongues Heresy Arose in Bible Times and in Many Ages Since

A very serious lesson for Christians today is found in the case of these Corinthian Christians who fell into a tongues heresy. We have called attention to many of the carnal traits and failings of this church at Corinth. But it was a great church. Paul had said to them:

"That in every thing ye are enriched by him, in all utterance, and in all knowledge; Even as the testimony of Christ was confirmed in you: So that ye come behind in no gift; waiting for the coming of our Lord Jesus Christ."—I Cor. 1:5–7.

This great church had as many gifts from God, had manifested as many gifts of the Holy Spirit as any other church in Bible times, we understand. And if Christians in that church were misled on the tongues question, it is not surprising that many others since that time have gone wrong also.

We ought to consider earnestly, then, why they were led wrong in this matter and fell into confusion and bad practices and sin on the tongues matter.

First, there were division and strife among the people—some for Paul, some for Cephas (Peter), some for Apollos. This prideful spirit led them into trouble. They grew to know so much, they thought, that they need not even listen to Paul, the apostle who had founded the church and who won most of them to Christ! Such pride, such a feeling of superiority, leads often to heresies.

There are certain heresies that always appear among some of the best Christians, not only the poorest ones; among some of the better-taught people, not only the most ignorant ones. A pharisaic attitude leads to self-opinionated ideas in doctrine. So these proud and haughty, carnal Christians at Corinth, who fought each other and disregarded Paul's counsel, set out to prove themselves better than others. The least of the gifts they magnified as if it were the greatest and began to imitate it by ordinary, carnal means, speaking in foreign languages. And even today some of the most earnest Christians are led into heresy on this tongues question. Worldly Christians may be misled by Jehovah's Witnesses, by Unity and by Christian Science. But it is the Christians who fast and pray, the Christians who believe the whole Bible, the Christians who are enthusiastic and fervent, who fall into the tongues heresy or who may claim sinless perfection or fall into other errors concerning the work of the Holy Spirit. Heresies and false doctrines about the Holy Spirit are specially attractive to the most earnest Christians, though not the best informed ones.

Then we ought to remember that carnality in itself leads to heresy. The accusation of the Holy Spirit through Paul, that these Christians at Corinth were carnal, not spiritual (that is, that they were worldly-minded, that they understood fleshly things better than spiritual things), shows why they were susceptible to this heresy and wanted to show off by speaking in tongues. Carnal Christians who want to make a show in the flesh, who want to appear especially pious, are more apt to set out to have something other Christians do not have and thus prove that they are better! Let us beware of sinful pride. And spiritual pride is the worst kind of pride. That was back of the big show these carnal Christians at Corinth tried to make by talking in foreign languages.

But the fundamental weakness of these Corinthian Christians, which led them to such an extravagant teaching and practice of the use of foreign languages and the imitation of the spiritual gift of tongues, was that they saw the incidental things instead of the fundamental things. They were more concerned about the outward than the inward. They were more concerned about the temporal than the eternal. They were more occupied with the incidental than with the most important things. In thinking about Pentecost, they thought more about speaking in tongues than they did about getting out the Gospel. In the church, they thought more of their own enjoyment in speaking in foreign languages than the edification of the church.

Paul was referring to their sinful majoring on minors when he said in I Corinthians 14:4, "He that speaketh in an unknown tongue edifieth himself [that is, he enjoys it himself when he speaks in a foreign language in the church]; but he that prophesieth edifieth the church."

Again in verse 5 Paul insists "that the church may receive edifying."

Again in verse 12 Paul said, "Even so ye, forasmuch as ye are zealous of spiritual gifts, seek that ye may excel to the edifying of the church." That is what the carnal Corinthians had forgotten! They were making a public show for their own enjoyment instead of the building up of the church.

These Corinthians had been children in understanding, as Paul tells them in verse 20. But he exhorts them, "...but in understanding be men."

How many Christians today are most concerned about their own feelings, their own emotions! Many people want to be filled with the Holy Ghost, they say, or "receive the baptism," they say, because they want a great ecstasy of feeling! I have read many and many a book by good people of the Pentecostal movement. I have read, I suppose, hundreds of tracts by people of the various tongues groups, and have read many, many testimonies published in denominational papers by them. Again and again they stress what a feeling they had! What wonderful visions they enjoyed! What an ecstasy it was! They have told me personally, and they have often published, particularly of speaking in tongues, that there is such a joy as one could never know otherwise.

O dear reader, whoever you are, get your mind on the main thing! If you are to give a testimony or an exhortation in church, then do it, not for your own enjoyment but for the edifying or building up of the church! Do it that all my profit, not that you may be thought so good and so wise and so spiritual, nor that you may have enjoyment.

In the gift of tongues at Pentecost (and that was clearly a miraculous gift of the use of foreign languages), there was the clear purpose of speaking the Gospel so that people might be saved. The disciples had waited in the Upper Room until Pentecost, waited for power that they might carry out the Great Commission and be witnesses for Christ in Jerusalem and in all Judaea and in Samaria and unto the uttermost part of the earth. So they had in mind the high and holy purpose of preaching the Gospel. They had been commanded to preach the Gospel to every creature and in all nations, beginning at Jerusalem. When the blessed power of God came upon them, they set out to fulfill that command. As a result, there were some three thousands souls saved in Jerusalem and added to them that day. The gift of tongues was intended to be a sign to the unconverted, when they should hear the Gospel in their own language in which they were born.

Paul mentions this fact in his rebuke of the carnal Corinthians. In I Corinthians 14:21,22 he says, by divine inspiration:

"In the law it is written, With men of other tongues and other lips will I speak unto this people; and yet for all that will they not hear me, saith the Lord. Wherefore tongues are for a sign, not to them that believe, but to them that believe not: but prophesying serveth not for them that believe not, but for them which believe."

In verse 21 above the Spirit of God reminds us of the fact that the people at Pentecost heard the Gospel in their own languages—Jews from Rome heard the Gospel from the lips of those who by nature had other tongues and other languages; those from Arabia heard the

Gospel in Arabian, by those who were by nature of another tongue and language. But the sad fact is, we are told, that at Jerusalem and then around the world, wherever the Gospel was preached, a few Jews were saved, and then the rest were blinded and rejected the Saviour, just as they rejected Jesus at Jerusalem and just as they rejected the preaching of Peter and the apostles at Pentecost and thereafter.

Then verse 22 tells us plainly that foreign languages are for a sign, "not to them that believe, but to them that believe not." When God really gave the miraculous gift of tongues, it was in order that the unsaved might hear the Gospel in their own tongue and so understand that God was seeking them and calling them to be saved. But in the church at Corinth they had started out to use foreign languages (not the miraculous gift, of course, but their own natural use of foreign languages in a kind of imitation of the gift of tongues) in the church and among believers for their own enjoyment and to show off before others.

Even today, wherever the tongues movement goes, the tendency is exactly the same as it was in this heresy at Corinth. People set out to speak in tongues, not to the unsaved in their own languages, as people did at Pentecost when they had the real, miraculous gift of tongues, but in their own services and among believers and somewhat for their own pleasure and joy and to prove to others that they are filled with the Spirit and are more spiritual than others!

O dear reader, when you think about the fullness of the Holy Spirit, do not think of something for your own ecstasy. Do not think of and seek for something that will give you a reputation for piety and make everybody think how spiritual you are! Do not expect something to show off before others. If you want spiritual gifts, do not seek tongues but seek to prophesy. At least for us today that would mean we should seek to speak with the power of the Holy Spirit upon us, in the language that people understand, in order to edify the church when we testify among Christians and in order to win souls when we speak to them.

SECTION V
The Proper Attitude for All Toward Speaking in Tongues

What should be the attitude of Bible Christians toward the matter of speaking in tongues? If my readers will be very patient and prayerful, I think we can nearly all agree as to what the Bible teaches is the proper attitude toward speaking in tongues.

I. The Gift of Tongues Might Be Given Today as Well as Other Miraculous Gifts of the Holy Spirit

We take our stand on the plain Word of God on this matter. Two passages in I Corinthians, chapter 12, state the clear position of a Christian on the doctrine of tongues.

"Now there are diversities of gifts, but the same Spirit. And there are differences of administrations, but the same Lord. And there are diversities of operations, but it is the same God which worketh all in all. But the manifestation of the Spirit is given to every man to profit withal. For to one is given by the Spirit the word of wisdom; to another the word of knowledge by the same Spirit; To another faith by the same Spirit; to another the gifts of healing by the same Spirit; To another the working of miracles; to another prophecy; to another discerning of spirits; to another divers kinds of tongues; to another the interpretation of tongues: But all these worketh that one and the selfsame Spirit, dividing to every man severally as he will."— I Cor. 12:4–11.

*"Now ye are the body of Christ, and members in particular. And God hath set some in the church, first apostles, secondarily prophets, thirdly teachers, after that miracles, then gifts of healings, helps, governments, diversities of tongues. Are all apostles? are all prophets? are all teachers? are all workers of miracles? Have all the gifts of healing? do all speak with tongues? do all interpret? But covet earnestly the best gifts: and yet shew I unto you a more excellent way."—*I Cor. 12:27–31.

These Scriptures plainly tells us that the Holy Spirit gives different gifts to different people, not the same gifts. One may have the gift of wisdom; another, the word of knowledge by the same Spirit; another, faith; another, gifts of healing; another, the working of miracles; another, the gift of prophecy; to another may be given the discerning of spirits; to another may be given divers kinds of tongues, or foreign languages; to another, the understanding or interpretation of foreign languages. All these are gifts of the same Holy Spirit. But the Spirit divides "to every man severally as he will."

I believe with verse 7 quoted above that "the manifestation of the Spirit is given to every man to profit withal." That is, I believe that every Christian *may* have some special working of the Holy Spirit to make him useful for the edifying of the church and to help him in getting the Gospel out to sinners, when he is filled with the Holy Spirit. But it is quite clear that God does not give the same gift to all, as inferred by the strong passage in I Corinthians 12:28–30.

And it is equally clear from verse 31, and from the whole thirteenth chapter of I Corinthians, that holy Christian love is more important than any of these particular manifestations. It is certainly held up as much greater than speaking in tongues.

Is there such a thing as the gift of tongues in the world today? I do not deny it. I say with Dr. W. B. Riley and many other saints, that God may see fit to give any of these gifts to His people today.

Let us understand that miracles were never very frequent, not even in the days of the apostles. Peter raised only one from the dead. Paul raised only one. The other apostles raised none at all. There was a miraculous gift of tongues at Pentecost. We do not know certainly when it ever appeared again. The languages used by Cornelius and his household, recorded in Acts 10:46, may have been a miraculous gift of tongues, or they may not have been. The Bible does not say. The gift of tongues may have been given to the twelve brethren at Ephesus, mentioned in Acts 19:1–6, but again we do not know; the Bible does not say it was a miraculous gift of tongues. They may have spoken in foreign languages already known to them. There are no other cases in the New Testament definitely described where people spoke in tongues with a miraculous gift. So not many people had the gift of tongues in Bible times. It is certain that not many people have this miraculous gift in modern times. Some may have it. I do not know of any who have that gift and exercise it as Christians did at Pentecost. But God could do it and may do that again if it pleases Him. I believe that the gifts of the Spirit are to be given at the discretion of the Holy Spirit as He sees fit. And I for one will not rule them out in any generation until Jesus comes.

But remember! We have a right to expect that if anyone has the gift of tongues, it will be used as it was used at Pentecost, the only recorded case of the certainly miraculous gift of tongues in the New Testament. The other cases mentioned in Acts 10:46 and Acts 19:1–6 may have been natural languages, when Christians spoke in tongues. But at Pentecost there was clearly a miraculous gift of tongues, and people understood what they heard in their own languages. So today we have a right to expect that any miraculous gift of tongues would be similar to the use of tongues at Pentecost.

II. Present-Day Use of Tongues Explained

Honest, kindly people everywhere want to know, first, the explanation of the phenomenon of tongues, as used among many godly people today; and second, what the Christian attitude of others ought to be toward those who speak in tongues and those who teach that speaking in tongues is the initial evidence of the fullness of the Holy Spirit or baptism of the Spirit; and third, what restrictions should be put on speaking in tongues by the clear teaching of the Bible.

Surely if we approach the matter with brotherly love and tolerance, we can learn how God wants us to feel and how God wants us to act and how to understand our brethren who differ with us on this matter. As prayerfully and lovingly as I know how, I have tried to find the will of God on this matter, from the Word of God.

At the very beginning let us give honor to whom honor is due. The blessing of God has been wonderfully present on many groups of people in the Pentecostal movement. The Assemblies of God, for example, are a rapidly growing, strong denomination. They have sent missionaries around the world. They have organized strong churches in every civilized country, we suppose. Their Bible institutes and colleges are springing up all over the land. A giant publishing plant is now being built in Springfield, Missouri. In many communities their churches are the strongest single influence for evangelical Christianity. In many cities where the churches of the older denominations have largely gone over into modernism and worldliness and have lost their testimony, the Assemblies of God have larger crowds and win more souls than any other congregations in their cities.

People of the Pentecostal movement are, on the whole, fine Christian people. They are for revival when many other churches have turned away from revivals and evangelism. They are for separation and clean living. They believe all the Bible. They believe in the blood atonement, in the virgin birth and bodily resurrection and miracles of our Lord Jesus Christ. They believe in prayer. Many of them are willing to suffer for Christ. Many are anxious to win souls.

No doubt other Pentecostal groups have been greatly blessed of God too, but we know more about the Assemblies of God. This denomination has joined in with the National Association of Evangelicals. They are brotherly. They want to cooperate in the Lord's business. All over America we have found lovely and devoted Christians among them who are friends to everything good and who show day by day their devotion to Jesus Christ and the Gospel. Honest, godly Christians cannot laugh off the convictions of these good people. They deserve respect and brotherly love and fellowship from God's people.

We ought to say also that Pentecostal people everywhere deserve great credit for laying stress upon the fullness of the Holy Spirit and teaching people to want more than simply to be saved and get to Heaven. God's people ought to want His power, His fullness. God's people ought to be willing to go anywhere He leads, even if it costs reproach and trouble and poverty. Pentecostal groups have done a great service to Christianity in stressing the power of the Holy Spirit. We think they have often confused the issue and have stressed tongues more than they have stressed the need for the power of the Holy Spirit, and if that has been sometimes true, it was a mistake. But they want to be Bible Christians. They want to take the whole Word of God. They want all that God has for them. They are usually willing to pay a serious price to please the Lord and serve Him. So I cannot approach the matter of present-day speaking in tongues without giving the tribute of an honest and loving and admiring heart to these good people. We differ with them on the tongues question, but we love them and respect them. We want fellowship with them. We would not willingly grieve them, and we certainly do not want to misrepresent them. And we speak, not to cause division and strife, but rather to unify God's people by finding what is God's will for us and finding a basis on which Bible-believing Christians who love one another can cooperate even if we do not see eye to eye on every detail.

And before we set out to explain the phenomenon of present-day speaking in tongues, we must say that for people to be sincere does not mean that they are always right in doctrine. Let us grant the sincerity of most people of the tongues movement. Let us grant that most of them are really saved, that they love the Lord Jesus, that they believe the Bible, that they are honestly seeking to have exactly what God wants for them. Let us grant that many such people really believe that they have talked in tongues or believe that they have heard others talk in tongues exactly after the Bible fashion. Let us believe in their sincerity, at least, when they say, "I have the baptism according to Acts 2:4." But that sincerity does not prove that they are right in their understanding of the tongues question.

It would be much better if we could understand that the average group of Christians, even if not absolutely correct in every detail of doctrine, is yet sincere in thinking its position is right. Those who sprinkle for baptism are usually just as honest as those who baptize by immersion, though I personally believe that the Bible teaches baptism by immersion, and of believers only. Quakers, who believe that there is no baptism but the baptism of the Holy Spirit, are often just as honest and sincere as others who baptize. But being sincere does not make them right. They still do not obey the Great Commission which Jesus gave, to go into all the world and teach all nations, baptizing the converts in the name of the Father, Son and the Holy Spirit. Many honest, sincere people believe that they are right in setting dates for the Lord's coming. They are wrong, but they mean to be right. Other earnest, good people, not well taught in the Scriptures, are sincere in believing that we can get the world converted or bring in the kingdom of God on earth through the churches and education and government and benevolence, though the Scripture plainly teaches that evil men and seducers shall wax worse and worse and that the present civilization is headed toward ruin.

Thus we say that the godly sincerity of those who believe in tongues does not prove that their doctrine is correct. Their sincerity makes them worthy of our love and respect and kindness, but it is not a sufficient reason for accepting their teaching. No, the only safe way is to go to the Word of God and find what God's Word says.

Now let us try to understand how it is that many people report that they themselves have talked in tongues after the Bible fashion or declare that they have heard others talk in tongues after the Bible fashion. How can we classify these modern cases of "talking in tongues," as they are called?

1. Some of Those Who Claim to Talk in Tongues Are Clearly Frauds

This much could be said for some of every religious group. One disciple among the twelve Jesus called to be apostles was a traitor. The Bible teaches clearly that many who claim to be saved are not saved. It is a part of the carnal nature that people want to appear good even when they are not good. They want to appear religious even when they are not Christians. They want to make an impression on men whether they are right with God or not. That is true in all religious movements. So it is only fair to believe that some of those who claim to speak in tongues are frauds. Some do not have a divine visitation, and know it, though they pretend to talk in tongues. Some put on a good show and imitate some heavenly speech, or at least imitate others whom they have heard "talk in tongues" and pretend to have a miraculous moving of the Spirit of God upon them.

Perhaps a dozen godly ministers in the Pentecostal movement have told me frankly that they believed many of their people who pretended to talk in tongues had no heavenly moving of the Holy Spirit at all, and that they were not given a supernatural language, as they pretended.

I myself know well, have known for years, a man who was once active in Pentecostal circles. He told me how he had pretended to talk in tongues. He repeated for me the kind of "language" which he had used and said it was like many others who pretended to talk in tongues in order to have what was expected of them in Pentecostal circles. We know that many Pentecostal people are not frauds, are not hypocrites, and do not pretend on this matter. But doubtless many, many of them do pretend.

Godly Pentecostal preachers have often been grieved that someone "talked in tongues" and pretended to be "baptized with the Holy Ghost," and then the next day went on in his carnal and worldly living just the same. Such godly preachers have assumed, and I think rightly, that in many cases these people were pretenders.

2. Many Who "Talk in Tongues" Are Victims of Self-Hypnosis, a Kind of Trance Induced by Earnest Desire and Oft-Repeated Suggestions of Others

Are honest people ever carried into a trance and caused to participate in a physical manifestation over which they have no control, but which manifestation is not necessarily of God? I think that one can prove beyond any doubt that that is true.

Outside the realm of Christianity altogether, it has been proved repeatedly that people can reach a certain state of mind in which they are self-hypnotized or put in a trance where they say and do things without control of the conscious mind. Indians in the snake dances in the Southwest sometimes become so frenzied that they cannot feel pain, that they are not afraid of snakes, and sometimes can be bitten by rattlesnakes without ill effects. In religious ceremonies, Hindu fakirs and African savages and some half-civilized Mohammedans may reach a state where wounds will not bleed, where knives are driven through various parts of the body without any apparent pain, where one can put his hand in the fire without seeming to feel it or can lie on a bed of spikes without apparent pain or injury. A number of heathen cults even "talk in tongues." People can be hypnotized so that they do whatever is suggested to them.

Mind healers often make use of mental suggestion. A suffering one may be taught to say, "I feel no pain. I feel no pain. I am not sick." People can sometimes be taught to say such things and believe such things until the subconscious mind takes control. Such methods have been used in childbirth so that the mother felt no pain at delivery.

And it is a remarkable fact that many times those who "speak with tongues" are beside themselves, do not know what they do, and are as completely carried away from normal consciousness and self-control as one who is hypnotized, as one who goes into a trance in some heathen rites. We are simply saying that there is such a thing as a trance, self-induced, brought on by a combination of intense desire, a steady repetition of certain words, combined with these suggestions of others and steady teaching along one line.

This tendency to fall into a certain pattern which one is led to expect is very common in religious manifestations.

For example, the Society of Friends, a religious denomination, are called "Quakers" because in a great revival movement in which the denomination developed, those who became convicted of their sins fell into an uncontrollable shaking and trembling which went on, ofttimes, for hours.

Another group called the "Shakers" had the same kind of manifestations, and these manifestations followed regularly and almost uniformly with those who became convicted and converted in their meetings. Now we do not say that there was any insincerity in that. We do not say that these people were not truly convicted of sin and were not truly converted. But it certainly is not any law of God that people have to tremble and shake when they are converted. People who believe that that is a necessary part of becoming a Christian may unconsciously follow the pattern which their mind has set as proper in such cases.

A certain man in Dallas, Texas, where we lived, had healing services. Great crowds attended. People who wanted to be healed were taught for a certain number of days, and then they came to the platform to be prayed for. Dramatic preparations were made. Someone stood behind the one for whom prayer was to be made to catch him when he fell, and then the minister would dramatically dip his finger in oil, touch the earnest seeker for healing upon the forehead, and pray for him to be healed in Jesus' name. I think some were healed. Some certainly were not. I am not discussing the sincerity of either the preacher or those who came to the healing service. I know that God can heal the sick in answer to prayer and often does, praise His name. But the remarkable thing is that these who came and expected to "fall under the power," when the preacher touched the oil to their foreheads, regularly fell over backwards! They were not all healed, but nearly all of them "fell under the power" as they were expected to do.

And they were surely not all hypocrites. They were simply prepared to fall, and they fell.

Down South in the most orthodox churches, in some services of great spiritual blessing in my boyhood, it was quite frequent for some-one to shout aloud the praises of God. We do not mean by that that people simply said, "Amen!" We mean an uncontrollable shouting of praises to God in an ecstasy of delight, sometimes with intelligent sen-tences and sometimes with loud cries of emotion without intelligent words. All good Christians like to know that there is a genuine mov-ing of the Spirit of God upon the hearts of Christian people. Yet it is only fair to say that these shouters were usually rather emotional peo-ple, more often women than men, and nearly always those who were not able to give a coherent and frequent testimony for Jesus Christ. It was simply an emotional outburst and was, when genuine, caused by a real moving of spiritual joy, no doubt.

Yet these shoutings followed a regular pattern. Often the shouters used certain regular and expected phrases. Hands held high and clap-ping, without thought of other people present or the continuation of the orderly service, the shouter would praise God. We only use this illustration to show that people can be carried away, may be moved to a kind of religious manifestation that they think is expected, and may have little or no control over themselves in the matter, without it nec-essarily representing a miraculous manifestation.

We like freedom in the services. We like praises of God. Yet in a good many cases such people who were rather professional and regular in their shouting caused commotion, interfered with the sermon, or interfered with giving an earnest invitation for men to accept Christ. People who shouted were honest and good people, perfectly sincere. But in a sense they sometimes fell into a trance and followed a regular pattern which they had been taught was proper. They were carried away by their emotions, did things which the conscious mind did not control. Yet it was clearly not a miraculous gift of God.

Certainly many Christians have been taught that the experience of talking in tongues is desirable. They are taught that the fullness of the Spirit depends entirely on the tongues—that no one has a right to claim to be filled with the Spirit until he talks in tongues. They have been taught that one must seek this experience with all his heart. Therefore, they long to speak in tongues; they pray to speak in tongues. They follow all the suggestions of the godly leaders whom they trust. In scenes of emotionalism and sometimes of frenzy, some people certainly are hysterical, and such people sometimes fall into a trance. In that trance they do what they so long to do. They make sounds such as they have heard other people make. They want to talk in tongues, and as the subconscious mind takes over when the conscious loses control, they make sounds which seem to them to be some beautiful language.

Do such people actually speak in tongues in the Bible sense of a miraculous manifestation from God, a gift of the Holy Ghost? In many cases certainly not. That is made clear because they do not have the fullness of the Spirit. They do not have the evidence given in Acts 1:8 when Jesus promised, "But ye shall receive power, after that the Holy Ghost is come upon you: and ye shall be witnesses unto me both in Jerusalem, and in all Judæa, and in Samaria, and unto the uttermost part of the earth." If people do not witness for Jesus, they are not filled with the Holy Spirit. If they do not have power, they do not have what these Christians had at Pentecost, no matter what outward manifestation they may have. In this matter we must stay with the Bible. So people may fall into a trance, a kind of hypnosis, thinking that they talk in tongues, and be perfectly honest, without really being filled with the Holy Ghost and without having what the Christians had at Pentecost. And this, we feel sure, is the case of multiplied thousands of those who talk in tongues.

At any rate, we may be sure that if one does not follow the Bible pattern given at Pentecost (when people, filled with the Spirit, spoke to others in their own language in which they were born and gave them the Gospel), then he is not filled with the Holy Spirit after the Bible pattern and is not talking with tongues after the Bible pattern.

3. Some Christians Are Between the Two Classes Mentioned Above, and Are Only Half Deceived, Copying Willingly What They See and Hear Others Do

They do not have well-developed consciences on this matter. They feel that a certain kind of manifestation is expected of them. They do not see any fraud in trying to talk in tongues as others do. Such people are not always hypnotized, are not always carried away in a trance; but perhaps without intending to deceive and certainly without an understanding of what it is all about, they make the same kind of sound that others do. I believe that those who have been present in services where there was much "talking in tongues" have seen some, especially younger and immature Christians, who seemed to copy a kind of "talking in tongues" which others did.

4. Some Seem to Speak in Tongues by Demon Possession

In Chicago in 1932 a man came to me in deepest distress. He asked my prayer that he would be delivered from some wicked tendencies that came upon him from time to time. He felt that he was often possessed with demons. This demon possession seemed to come about in connection with his earnest seeking to talk in tongues. He had been taught to give up all control of his mind, to leave his mind open, to let his tongue be loose, so that the Holy Spirit, as he supposed, could take possession of his mind and of his tongue. He had given up the normal control and inhibitions which a Christian observes. He did speak with tongues, he said. But he found that he seemed to be saying shameful and wicked things, and after that experience he had especially vile temptations. He found himself more and more led toward certain temptations. It seemed that evil spirits wanted continually to get control of his mind. In his case he felt sure that the speaking in tongues was the work of demons. It had not helped him. He did not love the Lord any better; he fell into more grievous sins than before; his sweet assurance as a Christian had been greatly disturbed. I do not know, of course, what percentage of speaking in tongues is dominated by evil spirits. But sometimes we may be sure that evil spirits take advantage of people who give up consciousness, who leave their minds and tongues open to be controlled by any spirit who comes along.

Recently word has come from India of evidence of demon possession leading to something like speaking in tongues. Such words have come from several heathen sources. A national magazine recently told of fanatical Mohammedans who worked themselves into a frenzy and talked in tongues.

At least it is significant that those who seek to hypnotize a person and the Spiritist mediums ask for the same state of mind and surrender of the will and self-control as do the teachers who try to induce Christians to speak in tongues. Sometimes, no doubt, when a man abdicates his control of his mind and voice, evil spirits may take control.

The Bible clearly teaches that one serves God best when in the full possession of his faculties. First Corinthians 14:32, speaking of this very matter of tongues, says, "And the spirits of the prophets are subject to the prophets." One who is really endued with the Holy Spirit is in control of himself, knows what he is saying, and is at his highest and best for God as he has himself under the strictest control.

And the following verse says, "For God is not the author of confusion, but of peace, as in all churches of the saints." I can see how evil spirits may sometimes take possession of people who do not follow this Bible injunction that the spirits of the prophets are to be kept in control of the prophets.

5. To Some People God May Give Tongues in Answer to Prayer Even Though It Is Not After the Bible Pattern

God is wonderfully good. He loves His children. And earnest people sometimes, by prayer, get things that do them no good. Israel got a king because they prayed for one, though the king did them no good. One woman told me how, when her daughter died, she prayed long and earnestly that she might see a vision of her daughter and thus she would know that the daughter was safe in Heaven. After days and weeks of agonizing prayer, one night she saw a vision of her daughter, happy and well. And thereby she was convinced that her daughter was happy in Heaven. Perhaps that vision grew partly out of her own longing. Or perhaps God in His mercy gave the vision to comfort a troubled heart. I think the woman would have done much better to have gone to the Bible and to have believed the Scriptures which said that her daughter who had trusted Christ was safe with the Lord. But God is very merciful and long-suffering, and God answers the prayer of faith. So He sometimes gives people things simply because they earnestly pray for them. And so, no doubt, God does give people something that satisfies their hearts. He allows them to have an emotional ecstasy and allows them to chatter, though they say nothing that edifies anybody else and though they do not give any evidence of the fullness of the Holy Spirit in soul-winning power. We do not believe that is a miracle. We do not believe it is the gift of tongues such as the disciples had at Pentecost. But I do believe that some perfectly honest and sincere Christians are allowed by the mercy of a loving Heavenly Father to have the joy that they seek, even though it is a rather selfish joy and does not bring any particular result for God.

6. Doubtless Some Do Have the Bible Gift of Tongues as a Sign to the Unsaved, Speaking the Gospel to Them in Their Own Language

We believe that the Holy Spirit still gives different gifts to different people, dividing severally as He will. We believe that the gifts of the Spirit may be used in this age but that the Holy Spirit Himself must decide when the gifts are needed.

So in these days it may well be that some people have the Bible gift of tongues. In that case they will follow the Bible pattern.

At Pentecost Christians, filled with the Holy Spirit, spoke to others in their own languages the wonderful works of God. Today God may give an American the power to speak the Gospel to some Chinese, or Hindu, in his own language, the same way and for the same purpose. I do not deny it. It is certainly within the realm of what God is able to do. I simply insist that if people speak in tongues after the Bible fashion, they will speak in the language of people who are present and who understand them and that this speaking in tongues will be a sign to the unsaved. As a result, people will be converted as they were at Pentecost. That is the result we should expect today when people really speak with tongues after the Bible fashion—that is, as a miraculous gift of God.

Our friends of the tongues movement say that the gift of tongues and tongues as the "initial evidence of the baptism of the Holy Spirit" are two different things entirely. But they there speak without the Word of God. Not a single statement can be found in Scripture that speaking in tongues is the initial evidence of the baptism or fullness of the Spirit, nor that the use of tongues at Pentecost was not the gift of tongues. And we are compelled by honesty to say that speaking in tongues as it is usually practiced today does not follow the pattern of the example at Pentecost, whether as "the initial evidence" or the gift of tongues. If the manifestation of speaking in tongues is genuinely from God in the Bible fashion, then it must be a miraculously given power to talk in the language of people present who hear the Gospel in their own tongue in which they were born as at Pentecost. We frankly say there may be such speaking in tongues or any other gift of the Holy Spirit mentioned in the Bible and if it follows the pattern of Pentecost, Christians can recognize it as such.

Since only God can see the heart, I do not attempt to judge how many people fool others by pretending to speak in tongues, how many are brought into a trance and half-hypnotized into speaking as they hear others speak, or as they are taught to expect to speak, some words or syllables that have no particular meaning. I have no way to know how many simply follow the pattern of others before them, without intentional deceit, and talk as they hear others talk. I have no way to know how many are demon possessed. Certainly I do not pretend to know to how many God gives certain ecstasies for their own joy, in answer to prayer, though not after the Bible fashion and not a miraculous gift. And I do not know how many really do have the Bible gift of talking in other languages to the unsaved. It is sufficient for me to know that honest and good people who want to do right have often been deceived on this matter. I know that speaking in tongues is not the Bible evidence of the fullness of the Holy Spirit. Yet I know that God has given the gift of tongues in the past and may give such a gift in the future as it pleases Him.

III. The Problems of Fellowship Between Pentecostal Groups and Other Christians

1949

Probably Bible believers everywhere should seek to have happy Christian fellowship with Christians of the Pentecostal movement or those sometimes called tongues people. Let us thank God that they believe in the fundamentals of the Faith. Let us be grateful that God has blessed their work in evangelism and that their churches have multiplied rapidly. Let us thank God for their emphasis that God answers prayer, their tendency to take the Bible literally, their willingness to go to any extreme measures to serve the Lord. Let us particularly be grateful to God for their emphasis on the fact that every Christian needs the power of the Holy Spirit upon him, a special enduement to enable him to win souls.

It is a matter of real joy to me that several Pentecostal groups, including the largest one, the Assemblies of God, cooperate in union revival campaigns. I have found that Assemblies of God usually are glad to participate, that they are modest and sincere in their cooperation and do not seek to dominate the situation more than others. They are happy to hear plain Bible preaching against sin, clear teaching on consecration and separation and prayer. They are glad to join in prayer. They have a genuine contribution to make to any fellowship of Christians.

On the part of Pentecostal groups there is also an essential duty, if they are to have pleasant and genuine Christian fellowship with other devoted Christians. Some Pentecostal groups have a tendency to set themselves up as better than other devoted Christians. Some are very frank to say that no matter how many souls one wins, how holy and blameless his life, how powerful his testimony for Jesus Christ, he is not filled with the Spirit or baptized with the Spirit unless he talks in tongues after the fashion of their own denomination. When one sets out to say that all the great soul winners were not good Christians, not filled with God's Spirit, he naturally causes offense. Here is some Christian who, simply because he talks in tongues but never won a single soul to Christ, thinks he has something better than D. L. Moody ever had or R. A. Torrey or J. Wilbur Chapman or Charles G. Finney, because they did not talk in tongues! Our Pentecostal friends will forgive us if we say frankly that this appears to be sinful pride. Many, many times we have been accosted by people who did not know a fraction as much Scripture as we know, who did not weep over sinners as we do, who do not have the fruit in soul-winning results which God in mercy has given us, who have not suffered for the Lord as we have, but who told us that they were filled with the Spirit and we were not, that they were better Christians than we were because they spoke in tongues and we did not! Such a "holier-than-thou" attitude, of course, disrupts Christian fellowship.

Here is a difficult problem for those who honestly believe that speaking in tongues is the Bible evidence of the fullness of the Holy Spirit. They must face it. But as they face it they must remember that God expects good Christians to prove their spiritual maturity by loving other Christians and having fellowship with other Christians. To be filled with the Holy Spirit is tremendously important. But to boast about it is not important, certainly. If one believes that he is filled with the Holy Spirit but never wins as many souls as someone else and shows no evidence that he loves the Lord and the Bible as much as someone else, then surely Christian modesty should prevent him from making an issue of his alleged superiority. There cannot be the happy fellowship and cooperation between those of the tongues movement and other fundamental Christians that there ought to be unless each group is prepared to give honor to those who are holy in life and fervent in spirit, serving the Lord and fruitful, with the power of God upon them. It is not too much to ask of any Christian that he should remember the scriptural command, "In honour preferring one another" (Rom. 12:10). And another command is, "Let each esteem other better than themselves" (Phil. 2:3). No one proves that he is filled with the Holy Spirit by boasting about how much better he is than someone else who loves the Lord as much, labors as hard, suffers as much, lives as sacrificially and wins as many souls as he.

I say that there are genuine problems for each side to face in close Christian fellowship between those who believe in speaking in tongues as the Bible evidence of the fullness of the Spirit and other Christians. And yet that fellowship is clearly commanded and taught in the Word of God.

The psalmist says in Psalm 119:63, "I am a companion of all them that fear thee, and of them that keep thy precepts." And if we are to have the wonderful power of God come upon His people to bring great revivals, such as we need, then we must come back to the same kind of brotherly love and fellowship which prevailed before Pentecost (Acts 1:14), at Pentecost (Acts 2:1), and after Pentecost (Acts 2:46; Acts 4:24). They were "with one accord" as they prayed before Pentecost. "They were all with one accord in one place" when the power of God came mightily upon them at Pentecost. They continued daily "with one accord in the temple, and breaking bread from house to house, did eat their meat with gladness and singleness of heart." They were even united when they prayed—"they lifted up their voice to God with one accord." So fellowship of all God's people who believe His Word, who are saved by His blood, who are concerned about carrying out His Great Commission, who long to be filled with His power, is of desperate importance. Those who want God's fullness of power and His outpouring in great revivals must get together in fellowship in mind and heart.

IV. Clear Bible Restrictions on Speaking With Tongues

The Bible does have some clear instructions, some restrictions, some rules about talking in tongues. We do well to find what restrictions and controls God's Word requires should be exercised about speaking in tongues as given in I Corinthians, chapter 14. We will do well to remember that there was a tongues heresy at Corinth which Paul plainly rebuked, and it seems evident that the misuse of "tongues" which he rebuked was not the miraculous gift of tongues but an imitation which was not of God and which caused confusion. However, those same instructions, so carefully given by the Holy Spirit through Paul, are God's divinely given restrictions on the tongues matter, and Christians who are not willful will surely want to be controlled by these divinely given restrictions on speaking in tongues.

1. One Is to Seek Other Gifts, Not Tongues

Every Christian is commanded to be filled with the Spirit. Ephesians 5:18 says, "And be not drunk with wine, wherein is excess; but be filled with the Spirit." Speaking of the gifts of the Holy Ghost, which he and others had received that day, Peter said at Pentecost, "For the promise is unto you, and to your children, and to all that are afar off, even as many as the Lord our God shall call" (Acts 2:39). So it is quite clear that the gift of the Holy Spirit Himself, that is, His fullness for soul-winning power, is to be sought by every Christian.

Christians are commanded to be filled with the Holy Spirit. They have the promise of the Father that they may be so filled.

But the gifts which the Spirit gives are another matter. We are plainly told that not every Christian is promised all of the gifts of the Spirit. First Corinthians 12:4–11 lists the various gifts of the Spirit as follows:

"Now there are diversities of gifts, but the same Spirit. And there are differences of administrations, but the same Lord. And there are diversities of operations, but it is the same God which worketh all in all. But the manifestation of the Spirit is given to every man to profit withal. For to one is given by the Spirit the word of wisdom; to another the word of knowledge by the same Spirit; To another faith by the same Spirit; to another the gifts of healing by the same Spirit; To another the working of miracles; to another prophecy; to another discerning of spirits; to another divers kinds of tongues; to another the interpretation of tongues: But all these worketh that one and the selfsame Spirit, dividing to every man severally as he will."

Now note that "divers kinds of tongues" and "the interpretation of tongues" (that is, the translation of languages) are the least and last of the gifts which the Spirit may give to people.

In the same chapter, I Corinthians 12:28–31, we have another listing of these gifts:

"And God hath set some in the church, first apostles, secondarily prophets, thirdly teachers, after that miracles, then gifts of healings, helps, governments, diversities of tongues. Are all apostles? are all prophets? are all teachers? are all workers of miracles? Have all the gifts of healing? do all speak with tongues? do all interpret? But covet earnestly the best gifts: and yet shew I unto you a more excellent way."

Here again speaking in tongues and interpretation of tongues are the last of the gifts and the least in importance. It is clear that the work of the apostles, named first, is of the most importance. The work of prophets—that is, speaking out by divine inspiration—is second in importance; and teaching the Word of God is third in importance. After that in decreasing order are miracles, gifts of healing, helps, governments, diversities of tongues.

Now see this strange command in I Corinthians 12:31: "But covet earnestly the best gifts." Covet not *all* the gifts of the Spirit, but the best gifts. Speaking with tongues, the tail end and the last of the gifts of the Spirit, is not to be coveted. But if one is to covet gifts, he should covet the best gifts.

Then God follows the discussion on tongues with the wonderful thirteenth chapter of I Corinthians on Christian love or charity. That is more important than the talking in tongues. That is the "more excellent way" that God says He will show these people who want gifts of the Spirit (I Cor. 12:31).

After this marvelous love chapter (I Corinthians 13), the Lord begins again on gifts and particularly on the last and least, the gift of speaking in foreign languages. In the first verse He says plainly, "Follow after charity, and desire spiritual gifts, but rather that ye may prophesy."

Go back to the list of gifts in the last of the twelfth chapter of I Corinthians; there we notice that after the gifts given to an apostle, the next gift was the gift of prophecy. Now God does not need any more apostles. We have the Bible all written, the pattern all set for New Testament Christianity. God does not, these days, appoint any apostles. But in Corinth there was need for people to speak by divine inspiration from God, in exhortation and revelation. In other words, there was a need for Spirit-filled people to witness for Christ. There is the same need today. *And that is what God says we ought to covet!* We are to desire spiritual gifts, but the main thing to desire is not even to work miracles, not even the gift of healings, and certainly not the last and least of the gifts, speaking in tongues. No, rather let us covet to be filled with the Spirit of God and speak and witness for God in His power and by His revelation. No Christian, then, is to covet nor specially seek a gift of tongues. Nor should he seek to speak foreign languages which he has learned, in the church. The reason is plainly given in the next verse: "For he that speaketh in an unknown tongue speaketh not unto men, but unto God: for no man understandeth him; howbeit in the spirit he speaketh mysteries." If one speaks in a foreign language when people present do not understand, then he does not edify them, does not convert them, does not help them. For that reason alone, speaking in tongues is the least of the gifts. Except when foreign language groups are present, it does not do people any good. Just talking in tongues alone is a useless end. The miraculous gift of tongues was never given except for the purpose of witnessing where it was needed, in a language not otherwise known, to people who could understand the Gospel in their own tongues. Where that need does not arise, it is specially foolish for anybody to seek the gift of tongues.

Note clearly the contrast between I Corinthians 14:1 and verse 5 in the same chapter. Why the difference? The first verse says, "...desire spiritual gifts, but rather that ye may prophesy." And in verse 5 Paul says, "I would that ye all spake with tongues, but rather that ye prophesied." First Corinthians 12:31 had already commanded them, "But covet earnestly *the best gifts*," inferring that they were not to covet the gifts that were not best, the lesser gifts. The same inference is rightly drawn from the first verse in I Corinthians 14. Why then would Paul say in verse 5, "I would that ye all spake with tongues"?

I think the difference is that in the first verse the Holy Spirit through Paul speaks of spiritual gifts, that is, miraculous work of the Holy Spirit, and in verse 5 he simply speaks about talking in foreign languages. Paul is saying, in effect, "I wish that you all spoke foreign languages, so that you could preach the Gospel to the dozen nationalities of people who live in the vast city of Corinth. It would be fine if you were equipped to carry the Gospel to everybody you see, no matter what his nationality. But even so, I would 'rather that ye prophesied: for greater is he that prophesieth than he that speaketh with tongues, except he interpret, that the church may receive edifying.'" It would have been nice if *all* these Corinthians knew foreign languages, as some of them did. But he would not want them speaking in foreign languages in the church unless people present could all understand, and particularly he was much more concerned about their being filled with the Spirit and speaking with God's power in witnessing than in talking in other languages. But these Corinthians are plainly told, about spiritual gifts, to seek earnestly the *best* gifts, not tongues.

So it is only fair to say that we have not a single encouragement to seek the miraculous gift of tongues. If there is ever a time when we need to speak in a foreign language to get the Gospel to sinners, and if God in His mercy works a miracle to enable us to preach the Gospel to them so that they will hear and be saved, well and good. But otherwise, for ordinary Christians, with people all around them who understand only English, to seek a miraculous gift of talking in some other languages simply for their own pleasure is a mistake not encouraged in the Bible. We are to covet the best gifts. We are not to covet speaking in tongues. Such is the teaching of the Word of God. Men have put an emphasis here contrary to the Bible emphasis. And our friends who say so much about tongues would please God much more if they talked about the fullness of the Spirit and prophesying or speaking in God's power and witnessing, than to speak about tongues. We are to covet the best gifts, not the lesser ones.

2. No Tongues or Foreign Languages Are to Be Used in the Church Except When People Present Understand What Is Said

Paul, by divine inspiration, gave certain plain restrictions on speaking in languages or tongues in the church. In I Corinthians 14:27, 28 we read:

"If any man speak in an unknown tongue, let it be by two, or at the most by three, and that by course; and let one interpret. But if there be no interpreter, let him keep silence in the church; and let him speak to himself, and to God."

First, in the above Scripture is this clear teaching: there is to be no kind of speech used in the service of God which people do not understand. If a man speaks in a foreign language that people present do not understand, he must have an interpreter (that is, a translator) to tell what is said. If there is nobody to translate the message, then it must not be given in the church.

That is the sense of the whole chapter. In the first three verses of the chapter, Paul shows how prophecy—that is, being filled with the Spirit and speaking what God gives in His power—is so much more important than any kind of foreign language for the simple reason that people do not understand an unknown language and it does them no good. God may understand and the speaker may enjoy it, but it does not edify nor build up the church. Then Paul reminds them in verse 6, "Now, brethren, if I come unto you speaking with tongues, what shall I profit you, except I shall speak to you either by revelation, or by knowledge, or by prophesying, or by doctrine?" What is the sense of speaking unless there is a clear message given? Paul says. And then he reminds them that music on a pipe (flute) or a harp is not music unless there is a clear distinction in the sounds—in other words, unless there is a distinct melody. The sound of a trumpet is no good unless it plays a certain call, with a definite meaning like reveille or retreat. Then verse 9 gives the general rule that it is absolutely necessary that anyone speaking for the Lord should "utter by the tongue words easy to be understood."

In verses 10 and 11 we are reminded that there are many kinds of languages in the world, and every one of them has definite meaning, and to use a language that is not understood is a kind of barbarism that has no blessing from God and no edifying to the church. Verse 12 says frankly that one reason people should not seek to speak in tongues is that it does not edify the church.

Then Paul emphasizes even further the need for everybody who hears to understand what is spoken, when he says, "Yet in the church I had rather speak five words with my understanding, that by my voice I might teach others also, than ten thousand words in an unknown tongue." Let it be a general rule, then, that no one is ever to use a foreign language in speaking for God to others unless someone present can interpret the language to them, explain and translate what is said.

I was in a tent revival campaign at the little town of Kaw, Oklahoma, in the center of what was once the reservation for Kaw Indians in the Indian territory. A great many Indians were in the town and the surrounding country, and many attended our tent campaign. A good many of then had been saved; some were converted in our revival services.

One Kaw Indian man attended the services and had his friend speak to me. He wanted to testify for Christ, but he could not speak English except a few broken words. Would it be all right for him to give his testimony in the Kaw Indian language? I assured him that it would be all right for him to do so, provided there was a friend present who could tell us what he said. If one did not tell us what he said, then his testimony would be useless. He might understand it, and God would understand it, but it would not edify the church.

That is the rule that Paul gives here, by divine inspiration. Remember that a miraculous gift will not have to be controlled. God Himself is not going to do wrong on this matter. And let everybody make sure that he does not overstep this divinely given rule. No foreign language is to be used except such as are understood by those present or unless there is an interpreter to translate what is said.

Of course, in ordinary cases when everybody in the congregation speaks the same language, there is no need to speak in a foreign language at all. But to safeguard the churches and weaker Christians, let everyone who feels that he must speak in tongues follow this plain rule: let him never talk to people unless someone can tell what is said.

3. There Should Never Be More Than Two or Three in Any Service Speaking in Other Languages or Tongues

In the divine rule for controlling the tongues heresy at Corinth and elsewhere, Paul said, "If any man speak in an unknown tongue, let it be by two, or at the most by three, and that by course." The idea of having the kind of service where every Christian seeks to say something in some unknown tongue is certainly forbidden here. Not more than two or at the very most, three, in any one service—that is God's clear restriction to control the tongues heresy. And they must speak one at a time, under careful control and in order. It must be an intelligent message; it must be clearly understood by those present; and it must be in an orderly way—not more than two or, at the most, three in any one service, and those, one at a time. For two people to talk at

once is forbidden. For one to seize the service and take it out of control is plainly wrong. Only two or three in a service, and that one at a
time, in careful order, are ever to be allowed.

Remember that Paul would not have to order such restrictions if the
Spirit of God were really working the miracles of the gift of tongues.
The church at Corinth would not have to control God. But they did
need to control the fanatical disturbance of people who wanted to talk
foreign languages in the church and imitate the gift of tongues and so
make a display and get a good name for themselves.

4. Any Religious Service Where Speaking in Tongues Causes Confusion Is Clearly Not of God

God had already given the rules: no speaking without having those
present clearly understand it, no two people speaking at the same time,
not over two or three speaking in any different languages in a single
service. And then He says:

*"Let the prophets speak two or three, and let the other judge. If any thing be
revealed to another that sitteth by, let the first hold his peace. For ye may all prophesy one by one, that all may learn, and all may be comforted. And the spirits of the
prophets are subject to the prophets. For God is not the author of confusion, but of
peace, as in all churches of the saints."*—I Cor. 14:29–33.

Confusion? God is not the author of it! People who think that they
"speak with tongues" after the Bible fashion and who lose control of
themselves, who do not know what they say, who are not subject to
orderly rules, interrupt others and are carried out of normal self-control
are not speaking for God; and God is not the author of what they do.
Confusion in the services is not of God! That is what the Scripture
clearly says. "And the spirits of the prophets are subject to the
prophets." When one cannot control himself, then the spirit that
presses is not the Spirit of God. It may be his own spirit or an evil spirit. But the Spirit within a prophet of God is subject to the prophet.

Oh, the burning in my heart sometimes when the Spirit of God
gives me a message to preach to an audience or an individual! I know
what Jeremiah meant when he said, "But his word was in mine heart as
a burning fire shut up in my bones, and I was weary with forbearing,
and I could not stay" (Jer. 20:9). I say, I know what it is to have a holy
burden, a message from God that must be delivered. Oh, the joy of
being able to deliver it in the power of the Holy Spirit! But is my mind
vacant when I so speak for God? Does reason leave the throne, and is
my speech simply something that I know nothing of? No! Rather, I find

in such a case, my mind is keener than before. The Holy Spirit brings to mind Scriptures that I had not planned to use. Compelling reasons burn on my tongue. My own mind is stirred to the highest pitch of understanding, and my heart is melted with the holy burden of the message I give. I believe that no man was ever so at his mental best as when he speaks for God, filled with the Holy Spirit. And the kind of speech which occurs when people want to speak for God but do not know what they are saying and do not speak coherently and reasonably and in orderly fashion—that confusion is not of God.

Let us speak kindly while we speak plainly on this matter. I have been in some services where people "spoke in tongues" or where they sought to "speak in tongues" when it was a bedlam of sound. We do not wonder that Paul was inspired to warn the Corinthians that if they all spoke with tongues like that, unbelievers would say that they were mad, or insane. I have been in some such services when I felt compelled to arise and leave, not as a mark of criticism of my brethren, but because I felt that the Spirit of God was grieved at practices that were clearly forbidden in the Bible, and the mad scene of confusion was so unlike what God's Spirit would have us have in the services.

We like a reasonable and reverent informality in services. We like the freedom of the Holy Spirit. We want people to be willing to do what God's Spirit leads them to do. But always when it is the Spirit of God who leads, He will lead one person to be quiet when another speaks. He will lead the services to be orderly and sensible. The service of a Spirit-filled Christian is the service of a man with his wits about him, who reverently and understandingly gives the message God has given him to give. A wild hubbub and talk in a language which others do not understand and several people speaking at once—that is confusion, and it is not of God. So says the Word. All who acknowledge the authority of the Word of God will surely feel constrained to try to follow these clear instructions of God's Word. The spirits of true prophets are subject to the prophets, for God is not the author of confusion.

5. Let Women Keep Silent in Such Services Where Foreign Languages Are Spoken

We have just quoted above I Corinthians 14:29–33. And the next two verses say:

"Let your women keep silence in the churches: for it is not permitted unto them to speak; but they are commanded to be under obedience, as also saith the law. And

if they will learn any thing, let them ask their husbands at home: for it is a shame for women to speak in the church."

Now we believe that this is a good general rule for all the services. Women are not to take places of leadership over men in the services. Women are not to take the pulpit as official spokesmen for God, in expounding of the Word of God. We believe that God intended every Christian to be able to give a testimony in a service under control of the leaders of the church. We believe that God wants all together sometimes to join in prayer, and each may pray in turn, not seizing control of the services. But God certainly teaches here that a woman is not allowed to speak before the whole church, speaking officially and with authority. A woman is to be under obedience in the church, as in the home.

First Timothy 2:11,12 says, "Let the woman learn in silence with all subjection. But I suffer not a woman to teach, nor to usurp authority over the man, but to be in silence." That Scripture is clear. A woman is not to teach officially in the church. She may teach a Sunday school class of children or a class of women, but she certainly should not teach the whole church nor a class of men nor, as we see it, a mixed class of men and women. A woman is to learn in silence with all subjection. God has a place for men that He does not have for women. That is true in the home. That is true in the church. That is a general teaching for all the churches which we do not care to go into further, for its own sake, just here.

In the Bible there were no women pastors of churches, no women apostles, no women evangelists. Women prophesied—that is, they were filled with the Spirit like other Christians and witnessed for Christ and won souls, but they did not preach in the accepted sense of taking a place of leadership in the church, of preaching in the pulpit.

Strangely enough, right in the midst of this chapter which puts certain restrictions on tongues and languages, for the control of the tongues heresy at Corinth and elsewhere, Paul puts this statement: "Let your women keep silence in the churches: for it is not permitted unto them to speak." Look at the chapter again carefully, and you will see that Paul is not done with the discussion of the tongues question. He is still summing the matter up in verse 37 below, when he says: "If any man think himself to be a prophet, or spiritual, let him acknowledge that the things that I write unto you are the commandments of the Lord." And in verse 39 he says, "Wherefore, brethren, covet to prophesy, and forbid not to speak with tongues." Then the last verse in the chapter is still summing up the command and repeating the order that they must not have confusion in the churches by talking in tongues. "Let all things be done decently and in order."

So verses 34 and 35 are set here in the midst of the discussion on tongues for a very particular reason. Those who are familiar with the modern tongues movement can see why God inspired the statement at this very point.

1949

It is women who do most of the modern speaking in tongues! It is services which women control where the greatest confusion abounds! It seems clear that at Corinth it was women who made more trouble by wanting to show off their different languages, and therefore the special restriction is put here in the midst of this discussion on tongues. Paul says that the church must carefully control this outbreak of public display of languages that did nobody any good. First, he said that no one should talk in the service unless it were understood or translated. Second, not more than two, or at most three, should be allowed to speak in any foreign language in a single service. Third, he said it must all be done in order, without any confusion, one must speak at a time and then sit still and hold his peace while another spoke and the message was translated if necessary. Then as further control on this tongues heresy, he said that they must remember that the women are to have no part in public official speaking to the whole church. Women are not to be preachers in the language of those present or some foreign language. Women are not to seize attention or take charge of the services. Let the women keep silence, and if they want to learn anything, they may ask their husbands at home. Paul infers that this will help to stop the heresy of tongues in Corinth.

Let us thank God for Christian women. God has a place for every one of them, a place of usefulness and happiness, both in the church and in the home. But that place is not the place of leadership over men. And where women usurp a place not intended for them, the result is some false cult, some heresy, some gross confusion. Women have greatly contributed to the confusion and false emphasis in Christian Science so-called, in Unity, in Spiritism and in speaking in tongues. I do not mean that good Pentecostal people are to be compared with false cults that deny the inspiration of the Bible, the deity of Christ and salvation by the blood. I only mean that anywhere women step out of their place and go against the command of God, the result is false teaching and harm to the cause of Christ. And that is certainly true in the tongues movement. So those who would control the heresy of tongues in their churches should follow the command of the

Bible and insist that women take no public part in such matters. Let them be silent and learn from their husbands at home what they do not learn in the church.

6. "Forbid Not to Speak With Tongues"

Paul gives a parting word by the Spirit of God in the last two verses of I Corinthians, chapter 14: "Wherefore, brethren, covet to prophesy, and forbid not to speak with tongues. Let all things be done decently and in order."

This sums up the matter briefly. Christians are to long to be filled with the Spirit and to witness for Christ, yet they are not to forbid others to speak with tongues. All things are to be done decently and in order so that fellowship with good Christians will not be broken, the church will not appear a scandal to unbelievers, and the cause of Christ may prosper.

"Forbid not to speak with tongues," the Scripture says. Remember that "tongues" means languages. And there are two ways, certainly, that we should not forbid people to speak with languages.

First of all, we should not forbid anybody to speak with the miraculous gift of tongues, a gift which the Holy Spirit Himself puts on some individuals in some special times of need, as we are told in several Scriptures. That gift that the Holy Ghost gave some Christians at Pentecost, to give the Gospel to others in their own language—no one must forbid that. We must not forbid it even in these modern times. Let the Holy Spirit of God give what He will. The miraculous speaking with new tongues, as promised in Mark 16:17, to certain people of great faith for such matters, let us not forbid. For my part, I do not agree with those who do not accept the authenticity of the last twelve verses of the Gospel of Mark. And if a miracle-working God sees fit to give any of the miracles there promised, let no Christian be unbelieving, let no Christian forbid. If any Christian is given the wonderful gift to speak the Gospel to someone in another language, his own language, and so win him to Christ, rather let every Christian rejoice and thank God.

Second, let us not forbid the speaking in other languages which are spoken without a miraculous gift, but rather by natural knowledge and use. On my desk just now I have a letter from a pastor in Germany, a minister with a doctor's degree. He wrote me in the German language, and I had to have the letter translated, but it is heart-moving. I had a letter in the last week from a Swedish lady whose writing I could hardly decipher. Some of the words were more Swedish than English, and the accent was as decided in the writing as if the dear lady were in my presence and speaking. But her letter was a blessing to my heart. Let us be kind and Christian toward those who talk other languages, and let us make sure that differences in language do not become a barrier between Christians.

At Spearman, Texas years ago I won a French war bride to Christ. She had come home with her soldier husband soon after World War I. A beautiful and talented lady, she learned a little English with great difficulty. She could understand what I said though she spoke very little English herself. When she was ready to trust Christ and claim Him as her own Saviour, we knelt to pray, and she confided in me, "I have never prayed in English. I do not know how. I never prayed except in French." But I told her that God could understand French as well as English, and so she made her confession to Christ in French.

Most of us live in communities where everybody speaks English and understands it. The command to "forbid not to speak with tongues" will have little meaning for most of us in ordinary church services. But let us remember to have a tender heart toward all the dear souls Christ has, other sheep which are not of the same fold, though they have the same Shepherd.

In conclusion, I would say that if dear people are sometimes misguided, or at least if they do not see the tongues question as we do, let us insist with brotherly kindness that they follow the restrictions in the Scriptures, and beyond that let us not go! If people follow the rules laid down in the Word of God, they are welcome in our services, and they will, like other Christians, sing and pray and listen and help win souls without disturbing the service and without causing confusion or bringing reproach on the name and cause of Christ.

Now let me say an earnest closing word on this question of speaking in tongues. What does it matter if you speak with the tongues of men and angels and do not carry out the Great Commission which Jesus gave? Of what use is it if you could talk in a dozen languages, whether by human wisdom or by a miracle, if you do not have the power of God upon you to win souls? I have sought to show what the Bible teaches on the tongues question, but out of my heart I say that my intention is simply to get Christians to seek and find the power of the Holy Spirit. If false teaching and confusion on the tongues question keeps people from seeking and having the mighty fullness of God, the power of the Holy Spirit, then it is important to get the tongues

question out of the way so people will see that God does command us
to be filled with His Spirit for soul-winning power. If you speak in
tongues and have raptures but do not win as many souls as another
Christian, then you do not please Christ as well as he. I have written
as simply and as plainly as possible, with brotherly love and earnest
entreaty and prayer, trying to get the minds of Christian people off of
incidental and selfish, personal experiences so they may give their
attention to the plain command of God, that each should be filled with
the Holy Spirit for soul-winning power, tongues or no tongues, orthodox or heretic.

Dear reader, if you do not have upon you the breath of Heaven to
make you a soul winner, then, whatever else you may have, you are out
of the will of God and failing of your heritage!

Chapter 9

The Power of Pentecost for Every Christian

"...And ye shall receive the gift of the Holy Ghost. For the promise is unto you, and to your children, and to all that are afar off, even as many as the Lord our God shall call."—Acts 2:38,39.

The fullness of power is the heritage of every Christian! It may be an unclaimed heritage, but the power of God which enables a Christian to witness for Christ and win souls is the right of every Christian. Not to be filled with the Holy Spirit, not to be endued with power from on high, is to miss the highest good and fail to claim the highest blessing offered to every child of God. Every Christian may have the fullness of the Holy Spirit, a definite experience besides regeneration, "a definite experience of which one may and ought to know whether he has received it or not," as Dr. R. A. Torrey says in *What the Bible Teaches*. And this fullness of the Holy Spirit is connected with and primarily for the purpose of service to God, soul-winning witnessing.

In another chapter we have talked about the usual work of the Holy Spirit, the work which He does for every Christian. The Holy Spirit has regenerated everyone who is a child of God, dwells in the body of every Christian; and to some degree He comforts and instructs and helps the Christian to pray and to grow in Christian graces. Since all of this is done in some measure for every child of God, we speak of it as the usual and ordinary work of the Holy Spirit.

But that does not mean that the fullness of the Holy Spirit, the extraordinary and miraculous work of the Spirit in empowering a Christian for witnessing, is not also possible for every Christian. Not every Christian does win souls, but every Christian could. Not every Christian *does* have the fullness of the Holy Spirit, but every Christian *should* have the fullness of the Holy Spirit. Not every Christian does have the manifestation of the Holy Spirit in his life, but I Corinthians 12:7 says, "But the manifestation of the Spirit is given to every man to profit withal."

May the Spirit of God move on the heart of everyone who reads this until he shall see that to go on day by day without the fullness of the Spirit of God is a tragedy unspeakable, an unnecessary tragedy, even disobedience and sin, because God intends every Christian to be filled with the Holy Spirit.

That the power of Pentecost is for every Christian is made clear: first, by the promises which are to all alike; second, by the New Testament examples; third, because the indwelling of the Holy Spirit in every Christian makes the enduement for service logical for every Christian; fourth, by the fact that the soul-winning task demands supernatural power; and, fifth, because the Word of God clearly commands Christians to be filled with the Holy Spirit.

I. The Bible Plainly Promises the Fullness of the Holy Spirit to Every Christian

We are not left to doubt or to wonder whether every Christian may have the fullness of the Holy Spirit or not. Several Scriptures expressly declare that the blessing of Pentecost, the enduement of power from on high, is for every Christian.

1. In Luke 11:13 Jesus Says That the Heavenly Father Gives the Holy Spirit to Them That Ask Him

Listen to this remarkable promise: "If ye then, being evil, know how to give good gifts unto your children: how much more shall your heavenly Father give the Holy Spirit to them that ask him?" (Luke 11:13).

This promise is introduced by the parable of the man who came to his friend's door at midnight, saying, "Friend, lend me three loaves; For a friend of mine in his journey is come to me, and I have nothing to set before him." The neighbor stands and knocks and knocks at the door, pleading for bread for a friend. And that pictures a Christian longing for power to win souls, longing for power to witness effectively to those dear to him. Here Jesus promises that the Father gives the Holy Spirit in soul-winning power to them that ask Him. "Them" is an indefinite, third-person, plural pronoun which certainly means anybody. Anybody who beseeches God, who keeps on pleading with the heavenly Father, is certainly promised the fullness of the Holy Spirit.

2. The Holy Spirit in Power Is Promised to Them That Obey God

Peter, preaching at Jerusalem soon after Pentecost, said to his hearers, "And we are his witnesses of these things; and so is also the Holy Ghost, whom God hath given to them that obey him" (Acts 5:32).

Peter was glad to stand there and witness before Jewish rulers. The

Holy Spirit gave him power. And the same Holy Spirit spoke to the hearts of the wicked men who had crucified the Saviour. The Holy Spirit, to give people power so they can witness for Him and win souls, is given by the Father to everyone who obeys Him. It refers here to obedience in soul winning particularly, as we will discuss elsewhere. But the phrase "them that obey him" certainly refers to any Christian who sets out to follow perfectly the will of God for his life and to do his part to win souls. Every Christian who obeys God can have the fullness of the Holy Spirit!

3. Acts 2:38, 39 Plainly Says That the Promise of the Fullness of the Holy Spirit Is for Everyone Who Will Ever Be Saved

A wonderful promise is given us in Acts 2:38, 39:

"Then Peter said unto them, Repent, and be baptized every one of you in the name of Jesus Christ for the remission of sins, and ye shall receive the gift of the Holy Ghost. For the promise is unto you, and to your children, and to all that are afar off, even as many as the Lord our God shall call."

These convicted men of Israel had said to Peter and the rest of the apostles, "Men and brethren, what shall we do?" Mark that they had not asked simply what to do in order to be saved. They wanted to be saved, truly; but they wanted more than that. They wanted to do everything that they ought to do. Doubtless they wanted the kind of Christianity—the power and joy and fruitful testimony—which the hundred and twenty who were filled with the Spirit that day had manifested before them. They wanted to be saved and to be filled with the Holy Spirit. So Peter told them what to do to be saved and then what to do to have the fullness of the Holy Spirit too.

We will discuss this Scripture at another place and show that the repentance was for salvation and that the baptism symbolized the obedience of heart which one needs to have to be filled with the Holy Spirit. But just now note the last of verse 38 and all of verse 39: "...and ye shall receive the gift of the Holy Ghost. For the promise is unto you, and to your children, and to all that are afar off, even as many as the Lord our God shall call."

We know that the term, "the gift of the Holy Ghost," refers to the fullness of the Spirit, the enduement with power from on high, which the one hundred and twenty, after waiting in the Upper Room, received at Pentecost. In Acts 10:44–47 the same term is used about the coming of the Holy Spirit in power upon Cornelius and his household: "...on the Gentiles also was poured out the gift of the Holy

Ghost" (Acts 10:45). Then Peter says that these Gentiles "have received the Holy Ghost as well as we" (Acts 10:47). Then in Acts 11:15–17 Peter plainly says that he was referring to the baptism of the Holy Ghost, says that God gave Cornelius and his household "the like gift as he did unto us" (Acts 11:17). So "the gift of the Holy Ghost" refers to the same fullness of the Holy Spirit as came upon the waiting disciples at Pentecost.

"For the promise" of the gift of the Holy Ghost, Peter said, "is unto you, and to your children, and to all that are afar off, even as many as the Lord our God shall call." Peter said that this promise meant that every man who was ever convicted of his sins and ever called of God to be saved, could be saved, and also was promised that he could have the fullness of the Spirit, or the gift of the Holy Ghost! The gift of the Holy Ghost, in soul-winning power, was for those Jews who heard Peter preach. It was for their children. It is also for all that were afar off, even as many as God shall ever call to be saved!

II. Examples in the New Testament Show That the Fullness of the Holy Spirit Is Intended for Every Christian

Let us look at the crowd who were filled with the Holy Spirit at Pentecost. It is a very enlightening study. Here were the eleven apostles. Judas had killed himself. But Matthias had been elected with the eleven and was doubtless here waiting in the Upper Room before Pentecost. But Acts 1:13 names the eleven original apostles. Then the following verse says: "These all continued with one accord in prayer and supplication, with the women, and Mary the mother of Jesus, and with his brethren." That is the crowd that began the prayer meeting which ended in the fullness of the Holy Spirit at Pentecost. There were about a hundred and twenty, the next verse tells us. In this hundred and twenty there were preachers and laymen, men and women, Christian leaders and unlettered people whose names are never told! And that indicates that preachers and laymen alike need the fullness of the Holy Spirit. And that indicates that men and women alike need the fullness of God, the enduement of power for testimony.

It is important to notice too that it was a voluntary company. The command of the Lord Jesus to tarry in Jerusalem until they should be endued with power from on high seems to have been given primarily to the apostles. Acts 1:1–5 tells us that it was "unto the apostles whom he had chosen" that He gave certain commandments; and it was these same apostles, no doubt, who received the special injunction that they should wait at Jerusalem to be endued with power from on high. But it is quite clear that both the promise and the command were intended for all the Christians, for a hundred and twenty altogether gathered and waited at Jerusalem, and all of these were filled with the Holy Spirit.

"When the day of Pentecost was fully come, they were ALL with one accord in one place." Who were the "all" at Pentecost? Again in Acts 2:4 we are told, "And they were ALL filled with the Holy Ghost." And the "all" included the witnessing too in the sixteen different nationalities—Spirit-filled witnessing by every Christian who was willing to tarry at Jerusalem and wait on God until he was filled with the Holy Spirit! It was a voluntary matter. Those Christians who were willing to be filled with the Spirit and willing to meet God's requirements waited and pleaded with God in prayer and supplication and received the same blessing, the same fullness, the same power as the apostles received!

In Acts 4:23–35 we find that the whole company of believers at Jerusalem were filled with the Holy Spirit again. There were multitudes of them. In fact, verse 32 says, "And the multitude of them that believed were of one heart and of one soul." Everybody who desired had a part in that prayer meeting. Everybody who stayed in that prayer meeting was filled with the Holy Spirit. And that seems to have included the whole "multitude of them that believed."

The implication of the New Testament example is that whole churches ought to be filled with the Holy Spirit, that every Christian ought to be filled with the Holy Spirit, and that everyone who cares enough to seek God's face and meet God's conditions may have the fullness of the Spirit as they did.

What a list is given of those who were filled with the Holy Spirit in the Bible! Apostles, elders, deacons, "servants and...handmaidens," Zacharias and Elisabeth and John the Baptist, Jesus and the twelve apostles, the whole company at Pentecost, Barnabas and Mary the mother of Jesus and the women, and Christ's blood half brothers—all these were filled with the Holy Spirit.

Acts 13:52 tells of the church at Antioch of Pisidia where Paul and Barnabas preached the Gospel and won many souls. "And the disciples were filled with joy, and with the Holy Ghost." How many were filled with the Holy Ghost? The answer is, "the disciples." We can only infer that the whole body of Christians, these new converts at Antioch of Pisidia, were "filled with joy, and with the Holy Ghost."

The New Testament example everywhere indicates that it is the privilege and duty of every Christian to be filled with the Holy Spirit.

III. The Indwelling of the Holy Spirit in Every Christian Makes It Logical and Proper That He Should Fill Every Christian and Endue Every Christian With Soul-Winning Power

The Holy Spirit abides in the body of every Christian. First Corinthians 6:19, 20 says,

"What? know ye not that your body is the temple of the Holy Ghost which is in you, which ye have of God, and ye are not your own? For ye are bought with a price: therefore glorify God in your body, and in your spirit, which are God's."

The Holy Spirit makes His home in the body of every Christian. It is the Holy Spirit who has regenerated every penitent sinner. And then He remains always in Christians' bodies, making them His temple, His home.

But if every Christian has the Holy Spirit, why not let Him fill us and master us and control us? It is unreasonable for any Christian not to make way perfectly and completely for the blessed Holy Spirit who dwells within him.

I have heard people pray, "O Holy Spirit, come and dwell within us!" But that prayer is out of place, for the Holy Spirit already dwells in the body of every Christian.

Thank God, we are not orphans! Thank God, we are not left in this world without anyone to whom we may turn for power and wisdom and everything else that we need! The Holy Spirit lives in my body. He loves me! He is at hand to be a Comforter and a Teacher. He is to help me understand the Word of God, to help me remember and bring to my mind the words that Jesus said. He is to pray with me and for me with groanings that cannot be uttered, we are told. He is to grow in me the Christian graces. Oh, then why should He not also give me the power to witness for Christ? If He lives within me, and if my body is His house, then why should He not fill His own house and take perfect control of His own body?

Thus it turns out that the Scriptures which speak of the indwelling of the Holy Spirit imply, necessarily, that He wants to fill the body where He dwells and take complete possession of the body that belongs to Him.

Consider John 7:37–39:

"In the last day, that great day of the feast, Jesus stood and cried, saying, If any man thirst, let him come unto me, and drink. He that believeth on me, as the scripture hath said, out of his belly shall flow rivers of living water. (But this spake he of the Spirit, which they that believe on him should receive: for the Holy Ghost was not yet given; because that Jesus was not yet glorified.)"

I think it is quite clear that the Lord Jesus here is promising the indwelling of the Holy Spirit in every believer. The Holy Spirit will make His headquarters in the body of a Christian. "He that believeth on me, as the scripture hath said, out of his belly shall flow rivers of living water." And we are plainly told that He is speaking of the Holy Ghost. But the Holy Ghost was not yet given in the sense of His indwelling, because that was not to happen until Jesus should rise from the dead and be glorified. Then the Holy Spirit would be given to dwell in people's bodies. We know, of course, that before this the Holy Spirit did come in power on many apostles and prophets, on Jesus and John the Baptist and Mary and Elisabeth and Zacharias and many others. The enduement of power had been experienced by many Christians before this time. But the *indwelling* of the Holy Spirit was never experienced by any Christian until Christ rose from the dead. So this Scripture speaks of the time when the Holy Spirit would be given to dwell in the bodies of Christians and make human bodies His headquarters.

But it is equally clear that the fullness of the Holy Spirit in soulwinning testimony is offered also. Every Christian is to be a living spring of water! And out of the Christian's innermost being should flow a river of blessing and power and testimony to all who are about him!

It would be impossible, surely, for any intelligent reader to deny that this Scripture quoted above means that every Christian who has the Holy Spirit living in his body should be a living spring of water and that out from him should flow the power of God. And every Scripture that clearly speaks of the indwelling of the Holy Spirit necessarily implies the fact that one who has the Spirit dwelling in his body *may* have Him in His fullness!

Consider another Scripture. In John 20:19–22 we have an account of the fulfillment of the promise Jesus had made the disciples in John 7:37–39. The same day Jesus rose from the dead He came to His disciples and breathed on them, and they received the Holy Spirit. The indwelling of the Holy Spirit surely began that day, the day Jesus rose from the dead, when He was glorified and His promise was fulfilled. He commanded the disciples, "Receive ye the Holy Ghost," and they received the Holy Spirit to live in their bodies. But notice two verses particularly: *"Then said Jesus to them again, Peace be unto you: as my Father hath sent me, even so send I you. And when he had said this, he breathed on them, and saith unto them, Receive ye the Holy Ghost."*—John 20:21,22.

Again let me say that it seems clear that Jesus is speaking about the indwelling of the Holy Spirit. The disciples here received the Holy Spirit. And yet Jesus commanded them later that they were still to tarry in Jerusalem to be endued with power from on high. We are not to infer that here, the day Jesus rose from the dead, the disciples received the fullness of power. Why should they wait and tarry to be endued with power from on high if already they had been endued with that power that they sought? No, it was not the power they received, but they did receive the Holy Spirit to live in their bodies. It is the indwelling of the Holy Spirit which the disciples here received.

But that Scripture certainly implies that they should receive the fullness of the Holy Spirit in power. Jesus said to them, "As my Father hath sent me, even so send I you." In that simple promise and command Jesus surely refers to the power for witnessing, the power for soul winning. As Jesus was sent by the Father from Heaven, so these disciples were sent forth by Jesus. As Jesus was to do all His ministry in the power of the Holy Spirit, so these disciples could do the work assigned to them only by the miracle-working power of the Holy Spirit. Jesus was commissioning them to do wonders which could be done only with supernatural power!

So when Jesus said, "Receive ye the Holy Ghost," He certainly meant that they then and there received the Holy Spirit to live in their bodies. But He also certainly commanded them to wait on God in the future until they should receive Him in *fullness* and mighty power for witnessing.

You see, wherever the Bible teaches that a Christian has the Holy Spirit abiding in his body, that Scripture necessarily implies that one who has the Holy Spirit should be filled with the Spirit. One who has the Spirit of God dwelling in him should also have the manifestation, the anointing and enduement and the fruit bearing which are the ministry of this same blessed Holy Spirit.

Christian, don't you see that it is wicked and unseemly and illogical that the Spirit of God should dwell in your body and not have His perfect way? Don't you see that it is an unreasonable situation that the blessed Spirit of God, who is so willing to do everything necessary for you, is not earnestly sought in His fullness to endue you with power from on high? The very fact that the Spirit of God dwells in every Christian's body indicates that it is logical and proper for every Christian to be filled with the Holy Spirit.

Jesus said, "I am come that they might have life, and that they might have it more abundantly" (John 10:10). The Christian who has life should also have it *more abundantly*. One who has salvation should also have power.

When Jesus died, a soldier thrust a spear into His side, and there came out blood and water. The blood pictured the atonement which Christ made for every one of us. But the water, mingled with it, pictured the fullness of the Holy Spirit which every Christian can have. Calvary paid for salvation. But Calvary also paid for the abundant life, the power-filled life, the gloriously effective soul-winning life! The presence of the Holy Spirit in the Christian's life means that He ought to be manifested in mighty power, and He *will* be manifested in power in the life of every Christian who meets God's requirements.

IV. The Soul-Winning Task, Commanded for Every Christian, Makes the Power of the Holy Spirit Imperative

Let me remind you again that every Christian is commanded to win souls. The Great Commission, given by the Saviour in Matthew 28:18–20, shows us this.

"And Jesus came and spake unto them, saying, All power is given unto me in heaven and in earth. Go ye therefore, and teach all nations, baptizing them in the name of the Father, and of the Son, and of the Holy Ghost: Teaching them to observe all things whatsoever I have commanded you: and, lo, I am with you alway, even unto the end of the world."

It is important to notice that this commission is given not simply nor only to the twelve apostles. "All power [authority] is given unto me in heaven and in earth." Is not the authority of Jesus over every Christian as absolute as His authority over the twelve apostles?

And the command is given to "teach all nations," or make disciples in all nations. The twelve apostles could not cover the whole world.

And Jesus promised, "Lo, I am with you alway, even unto the end of the world." The end of the world, the consummation of this age, has not come even yet, after more than nineteen hundred years. Not a one of the original apostles was left alive after the first century. So the promise of the Lord Jesus would be incomprehensible and meaningless if He did not include the rest of us in the Great Commission. Now, if you read carefully what the disciples were to do, you will see that the Great Commission was for every Christian.

1. The apostles were to make disciples in all nations. That means they were to get people saved.

2. The apostles and others, then, were to baptize these new converts as a mark of their utter surrender to the will of God, counting the old life dead and buried and announcing a new life in Christ, according to His will. Every new convert was to be baptized.

3. Then the apostles and others were to teach the new converts "to observe all things whatsoever" Jesus had commanded the apostles! That is, every new convert was to be given the Great Commission afresh! Every new convert was as much obligated to carry the Gospel to all the world, to get people saved, to get people baptized and to teach the new converts to win souls as the original apostles themselves. You see, the Great Commission clearly teaches that everybody who is ever converted should be baptized and then taught to win souls and carry on all the commands of Jesus to the apostles.

Many, many Scriptures make it clear that God intends for every Christian to win souls. In Matthew 4:19 Jesus said, "Follow me, and I will make you fishers of men." Those who do not become fishers of men, soul winners, are simply not following Jesus as they should!

In John 15:5 Jesus said, "I am the vine, ye are the branches: He that abideth in me, and I in him, the same bringeth forth much fruit: for without me ye can do nothing." Every Christian who really abides in Christ will bear much fruit. That means that he will get many people saved. The fruit of a Christian is another Christian. There is no such thing as being a good Christian, abiding in Christ and having His fullness and power, without winning souls.

 Proverbs 11:30 says, "The fruit of the righteous is a tree of life; and he that winneth souls is wise." In the Bible, to be wise means to be spiritually wise, and one who does not win souls is not spiritually wise, but a fool.

In Daniel 12:3 we are told, "They that be wise shall shine as the brightness of the firmament; and they that turn many to righteousness as the stars for ever and ever." So that means that the rewards of Heaven will be given to soul winners!

Can anyone doubt what is dearest to the heart of God? After God gave His Son to die for sinners, has anyone a right to suppose that anything else in the universe is as important as getting people saved, as important as keeping sinners out of Hell? You remember that Paul knew so well this blessed truth. He said, "This is a faithful saying, and worthy of all acceptation, that Christ Jesus came into the world TO SAVE SINNERS; of whom I am chief" (I Tim. 1:15). And Jesus Himself said, "Joy shall be in heaven over one sinner that repenteth, more than over ninety and nine just persons, which need no repentance" (Luke 15:7). Any Christian who would make Heaven happy must win souls. Any Christian who would shine in Heaven must win souls. Any Christian who follows Jesus will be a fisher of men. Any Christian who really abides in Christ will bring forth much fruit—that is, will win many precious souls. Any Christian who obeys the Great Commission will set out to get people saved.

But to win souls—how shall we do it? Sometimes people say to me, "It is so hard to win souls these days!" These days? It always was hard to win souls. These alibis, that the days are getting too hard for God, that this generation is harder to reach than other generations, are really very foolish. It is not only hard to win souls; it is impossible—unless one has the mighty power of God! It takes just one thing to be a soul winner, and that is the special enduement of power from God, the power John the Baptist had, the power Peter and other disciples had at Pentecost, the power that Barnabas had, who was "a good man, and full of the Holy Ghost and of faith: and much people was added unto the Lord" (Acts 11:24). It takes just what D. L. Moody had, a special enduement of power from God. Charles G. Finney had the same power, and R. A. Torrey and Billy Sunday. Oh, friends, to win souls without help from Heaven is impossible!

Can you imagine how Simon Peter and the other disciples faced that crowd at Pentecost? Remember, they faced the murderers of the Lord Jesus! Remember, all these hearers had heard Jesus Christ Himself and had hated Him and rejected Him! And to a Gospel-hardened generation of wicked, self-righteous, hypocritical people, murderers of the Lord Jesus, Peter preached in boldness; and they were cut to the heart. Disciples went and witnessed in mighty power, and some three thousand turned to the Lord that day. There is no possible explanation for the revival at Pentecost except that people had power that was supernatural, power on their witnessing that turned men to God.

John Wesley had this breath of Heaven upon him, and marvels were done that turned the whole of England from the abyss of immorality and destruction. We are told that France had her French Revolution but England had John Wesley and the Wesleyan revival! There is no logical and adequate explanation of the civilization and freedom which England and America possess today except as it is based on an understanding of what the evangelical movement in England and the Wesleyan revival did.

The great evangelists have passed off the scene in America. I knew Billy Sunday, but Billy Sunday is dead! I knew and loved Gipsy Smith, but the Gipsy with his sweet voice and his eyes which so easily gave way to tears as he talked about "the beauty of Jesus"—dear Gipsy is dead! Moody and Torrey and J. Wilbur Chapman are all gone to Heaven. A generation ago there were some five hundred evangelists holding large union revival campaigns in America. With few exceptions, they are gone from our land. There has been an alarming wane in revivals in America. The schools of America have turned against God. Atheism is rampant. Communism is infiltrating labor unions and farm circles and stalks on many a university campus. The sanctity of the home is broken down. Morality is laughed at by both men and women. The movies have molded the morals of a generation. No one thinks anything of women filling the taprooms and taverns. Drunkenness is on the increase and greater now than before the prohibition amendment and the interlude of outlawed liquor. Sin everywhere abounds.

But wait! I am still commanded to get the Gospel to every creature. And so are you. Every Christian is still commanded to win souls. We are to win people who are hardened, people who are self-satisfied. We are to win people who have no fear of God. We are to win people who are enslaved by passions and sin. We are to win people who despise goodness, who have no confidence in the church and preachers. We are to win people who believe that the Bible is a myth and a legend. We are to win people who have been taught in the schools that the Bible is out of date and that Christianity is only a part of the evolutionary process. We are to win people to trust in Jesus as Saviour when they think of Him only as the illegitimate son of a Jewish woman, a Nazarene peasant, a great teacher, a martyr even, but only a man! God in Heaven help us, how can we win souls if we do not have a supernatural enduement from Heaven!

If God helped Peter at Pentecost, then every preacher who ever stands up to preach has a right to call on God for the same kind of supernatural enduement and help. If God helped those disciples— Mary and the women and the half brothers of Jesus and the other nondescript crowd who waited in the Upper Room and were filled with the

Holy Spirit at Pentecost—then every wife who has an unsaved husband, every mother who would win her children, every worker who would talk to the man at the next bench or his crony with whom he plays golf about his soul, has a right to the same enduement from Heaven as these New Testament Christians had!

D. L. Moody used to say that "it is wicked and foolish to try to do God's work without God's power." Oh, may we learn the lesson! Soul winning is not done with human equipment. All the learning in the world does not make a soul winner. All the personal magnetism does not make a soul winner. All the fluency of words, all the polished phrases and rounded periods of an orator do not make a soul winner. Oh, only the moving of the Spirit of God upon men's hearts can convict them and save them from sin and make them into children of God. I cannot make a drunkard sober. I cannot make a harlot pure. I cannot make an infidel into a believer. Only the Spirit of God can do that. It would be unreasonable, it would be mockery, it would be a heartbreaking tragedy without any amelioration, if God should command me to win souls and then not show me some way to have the power of God to do what He asks me to do!

The task of soul winning requires and demands the power of the Holy Spirit. If people are to win souls, then they are to be filled with the Holy Spirit. And that shows that God intends every Christian to be filled with the Spirit so he can do the thing God has commanded every Christian to do—that is, to win souls.

V. The Word of God Clearly Commands Christians to Be Filled With the Spirit

I have already shown that the Bible promises the fullness of the Spirit to all. I have shown that the New Testament example indicates God intended whole churches, Christians of every kind—preachers, deacons, laymen, men, women all alike—to be filled with the Holy Spirit. I have shown that the indwelling of the Holy Spirit necessarily makes it logical that one who has the Holy Spirit should have His fullness. And I have shown that the soul-winning task is commanded for every Christian and that it is impossible without an enduement of power from Heaven. Now I am ready to give the plain command of God that each Christian is to be filled with the Holy Spirit.

Ephesians 5:18 gives this plain command of God: "Be not drunk with wine, wherein is excess; but be filled with the Spirit."

"BE FILLED WITH THE SPIRIT," God's Word commands us.

The Book of Ephesians was addressed to the saints in the city of Ephesus, but it is also to us. The first verse in the book says, "Paul, an apostle of Jesus Christ by the will of God, to the saints which are at Ephesus, and to the faithful in Christ Jesus." To all the faithful in Christ Jesus the Book of Ephesians is written. And to all who would be faithful in Christ Jesus is the plain command given, "Be not drunk with wine, wherein is excess; but be filled with the Spirit."

It is a sin for a Christian to get drunk. Some Christians have. Some Christians, with the old habit still pulling, have weakened and fallen into the temptation of Satan and have gotten drunk. I have known of such cases, and they always brought disgrace on the cause of Christ. They always broke people's hearts.

I remember being called across Dallas to a little home where lived a streetcar conductor, a member of the church of which I was pastor. He sat with his head in his hands and sobbed. His wife berated him indignantly, accused him that he did not love her and his two sons, berated him that he surely was never a Christian or he would not have committed such a sin. It was a tragic scene. The man gave evidence that he really loved God, that he wanted to do right, and that he had succumbed to a very common temptation. He had taken a glass of beer to celebrate the success of a friend and was led to drink more and more until his pay for the week was gone. He should never have taken the first glass of beer, of course. I am just showing that for a Christian to get drunk brings heartache and trouble. It is a terrible sin.

How strange that the Lord should put in the same verse these two commands: "Be not drunk with wine" and "be filled with the Spirit."

Now who has a right to say that one who violates the first command is a terrible sinner and that one who violates the second command does not sin equally as much? It is a sin to get drunk. It is a sin not to be filled with the Holy Spirit. God's Word puts the two sins in the same verse!

Christian, God commands you, "Be filled with the Spirit." It is a command, and not only to preachers. It is a command to "the faithful in Christ Jesus." It is a command for all Christians everywhere who want to please God.

Let every Christian, then, solemnly face this truth: if you are not filled with the Spirit, you do not have all that God has for you. If you are not filled with the Spirit, you have not obeyed all the commands that God has given. If you are not filled with the Spirit, then you have missed your great inheritance. Oh, in Jesus' name, I beg you first to acknowledge that it is your privilege and duty and right to be filled with the Spirit and then to set out, by God's grace, to meet all His requirements and be mightily filled with the Holy Spirit, endued with power from on high.

Chapter 10

How to Be Filled With the Holy Spirit: Wholehearted Obedience to Christ's Soul-Winning Command

"And we are his witnesses of these things; and so is also the Holy Ghost, whom God hath given to them that obey him."—Acts 5:32.

Every Christian is commanded, "Be filled with the Spirit" (Eph. 5:18). Obviously, then, one would expect the Scripture to tell us how to be filled with the Spirit. God has definite requirements which He asks us to meet and promises us then that we will be filled with the Holy Spirit, endued with power from on high. It would be as unreasonable for God to command people to be saved and not tell them how to be saved as to command Christians to be filled with the Holy Spirit and not tell them how to be filled with the Holy Spirit. All that God commands us to do, He makes it possible for us to do. Those who long with all their hearts to do God's will in the matter can certainly find how to be filled with the Holy Spirit.

I think of four Scriptures which name definite requirements for the fullness of the Holy Spirit. They are as follows:

"And we are his witnesses of these things; and so is also the Holy Ghost, whom God hath given to them that obey him."—Acts 5:32.

"If ye then, being evil, know how to give good gifts unto your children: how much more shall your heavenly Father give the Holy Spirit to them that ask him?"—Luke 11:13.

"For I will pour water upon him that is thirsty, and floods upon the dry ground: I will pour my spirit upon thy seed, and my blessing upon thine offspring."—Isa. 44:3.

"Then Peter said unto them, Repent, and be baptized every one of you in the name of Jesus Christ for the remission of sins, and ye shall receive the gift of the Holy Ghost."—Acts 2:38.

At first it may seem that here are four different requirements for the fullness of the Holy Spirit. And other requirements are implied.

Dr. R. A. Torrey in that fine book, *The Holy Spirit, Who He Is, and*

What He Does, published the year before he died, gives seven requirements for the fullness of the Holy Spirit, as follows:

1. Accept Jesus as Saviour.

2. Repent; that is, renounce all sin.

3. An open confession before the world of our renunciation of sin and of our acceptance of Jesus Christ, as implied in baptism.

4. Obedience, doing everything God commands; that is, the unconditional surrender of the will to God.

5. Thirst, or holy desire for the Spirit's power.

6. Asking, definite prayer for this definite blessing.

7. Believe the promise and confidently expect God to do what He has definitely promised to do.

The above are the seven steps needed to be filled with the Holy Spirit, as Dr. Torrey explained them.

Now I believe that every person who meets those seven requirements will be filled with the Spirit, or baptized with the Spirit, endued with power for service; and I believe that those conditions are required in the Word of God. But I believe it will be simpler to divide those requirements into two main heads, based upon two definite Scriptures.

First, in Acts 5:32 Peter clearly says, "...the Holy Ghost, whom God hath given to them that obey him." Wholehearted obedience to Jesus Christ is certainly one requirement of the fullness of the Holy Spirit. The other requirement is asking. Jesus said, "...how much more shall your heavenly Father give the Holy Spirit to them that ask him?" So in this chapter we discuss the first requirement for the fullness of the Holy Spirit—that is, wholehearted obedience to Christ's soul-winning command. The next chapters will discuss prevailing prayer as a condition of the fullness of the Holy Spirit.

Before we begin a detailed discussion of the conditions required for being filled with the Holy Spirit, let me say positively that certainly regeneration comes before being filled with the Spirit of God. In Acts 2:38 Peter plainly told inquirers that they were first to repent before being baptized and then receiving the gift of the Holy Ghost. If you have not put your faith in Christ as your own personal Saviour and depended upon Him for salvation on the merits of His blood shed on Calvary, then certainly you are not ready even to discuss the matter of being filled with the Holy Spirit.

John the Baptist was "filled with the Holy Ghost, even from his mother's womb." In answer to the fervent, earnest prayers of his parents

Zacharias and Elisabeth, John the Baptist, the forerunner of the Lord Jesus, was filled with the Holy Ghost in babyhood. But we know that one could not be consciously a rebel against God, rejecting Christ as Saviour, and be filled with the Holy Spirit. So we judge that John the Baptist was filled with the Holy Ghost in his babyhood and early childhood; then the very moment that he came to know himself a sinner, we believe, he put his trust in the coming Saviour and was forgiven and born again. Then he continued, filled with the Holy Spirit. It is unthinkable that anyone could be old enough to be an accountable sinner, and unsaved, and be filled with the Holy Spirit. And it is certain that the Holy Spirit cannot fill one if He does not already dwell in the body in regeneration. If one is not born again by personal faith in the Saviour, that is the first question to settle. It will be foolish to talk about being filled with the Spirit until one trusts Christ and lets the Spirit of God make him a new creature. Salvation is one question; the fullness of the Spirit, another. Be saved first!

But after one is a child of God, there are certain definite conditions to be met in order that one may be filled with the Holy Spirit. And the first general condition, which we discuss in this chapter, is that one must be obedient—that is, fully surrendered to the will of God.

I. This Obedience Would Involve, First, Commitment to God's Soul-Winning Plan

When Peter said, "And we are his witnesses of these things; and so is also the Holy Ghost, whom God hath given to them that obey him," it is obvious that he referred to the power of the Holy Spirit for witnessing, personal testimony, soul-winning effort. How can any Christian be an obedient Christian who does not win souls?

1. Soul Winning Is the Plain Duty of Every Christian

This is made plain in the Great Commission as given by the Saviour in Matthew 28:19,20. There Jesus told the disciples to go make disciples in all nations, to baptize these converts in the name of the Father, Son and Holy Spirit, and then to teach the new converts "to observe all things whatsoever I have commanded *you*." Every new convert was to carry out the very command *given to the apostles!* In other words, any Christian today is as much commanded by the Lord Jesus Christ to win souls as was Peter or James or John or any of the other twelve apostles to whom He gave the Great Commission. Every one of us is commanded "to observe all things whatsoever" Jesus commanded the apostles!

And it was in connection with this Great Commission (though as recorded by Luke) that Jesus gave the apostles commandment to "tarry ye in the city of Jerusalem, until ye be endued with power from on high." Read Luke 24:46–49, and you will see that Jesus plainly commanded "that repentance and remission of sins should be preached in his name among all nations, beginning at Jerusalem." You will see also that Jesus there told these apostles that they were the witnesses of these things but that they must tarry first in Jerusalem for power before carrying the Gospel to the unsaved world. The fullness of the Holy Spirit was simply an enduement of power for the soul-winning work Jesus commanded in the Great Commission.

Forgive me for repetition, but please remember again the promise of Jesus in Acts 1:8: "But ye shall receive power, after that the Holy Ghost is come upon you: and ye shall be witnesses unto me both in Jerusalem, and in all Judæa, and in Samaria, and unto the uttermost part of the earth." Power for witnessing is the very object of the enduement of power from on high. And unless one is thoroughly committed to do this one main thing that Jesus has commanded, it would be foolish rebellion for him to seek the power of the Holy Spirit. God would not give the equipment to do the job when one did not intend to use the equipment for the purpose for which it was given.

Some people have foolishly thought that the fullness of the Holy Spirit is given to some people for soul winning and to other people for other purposes. But there is no promise or teaching in the Word of God for such a claim. The enduement of power from on high which Jesus gave at Pentecost and for which the disciples tarried and prayed, was for the one purpose of being His witnesses.

And let us be reminded here that the one purpose for which Jesus came into the world was "to save sinners." This is the one thing dearest to the heart of God, the one thing for which Jesus died, the one thing that causes rejoicing in the presence of the angels of God in Heaven. This is the one thing for which preachers are called to preach. This is the one excuse for the existence of churches! Preachers who do not win souls may have been *called* to preach, but they have never *answered* the call to preach! Every gift among the ministry gifts mentioned in I Corinthians 12 was to be used for the purpose of carrying on the soul-winning work of the Lord Jesus Christ. Even speaking in tongues, a gift that so many people covet, was given plainly and only for this purpose, as was manifest at Pentecost.

Churches are to be built up simply to win souls. First Corinthians

14:3,4 says, "But he that prophesieth speaketh unto men to edification, and exhortation, and comfort. He that speaketh in an unknown tongue edifieth himself; but he that prophesieth edifieth the church." But it must be remembered that to edify (build up) the church is itself for the purpose of making the church a more powerful soul-winning organism. Christians are to be edified, or built up, for exactly the same reason that every godly and spiritual evangelist seeks to build up the church— that is, to make Christians into soul winners and to help them to do the thing the Lord Jesus put the church in the world to do. A good example is in that same fourteenth chapter of I Corinthians. Verses 24 and 25 say:

"But if all prophesy, and there come in one that believeth not, or one unlearned, he is convinced of all, he is judged of all: And thus are the secrets of his heart made manifest; and so falling down on his face he will worship God, and report that God is in you of a truth."

Prophecy does bless the church, but best of all, these Spirit-filled ones speaking for God would be enabled so to convict the unbeliever who would come into the services that the secrets of his heart would be made manifest, he would feel his guilt before God and fall down on his face to worship God with a penitent heart. You see that prophecy, one of the ministry gifts of the Holy Spirit, is primarily for the purpose of winning souls and enabling Christians to win souls.

In I Corinthians 12:28 we are told that these ministry gifts, wrought in Christians by the fullness of the Holy Spirit, are "first apostles, secondarily prophets, thirdly teachers, after that miracles, then gifts of healings, helps, governments, diversities of tongues." It is the fullness of the Holy Spirit that makes an apostle (that is, that made apostles when apostles were needed) or prophets, or that gives any other miraculous manifestations in the church. Ephesians 4:11–16 discusses the fruit of these heavenly gifts in the church. Again, apostles, prophets, evangelists, pastors and teachers are mentioned, as gifts God gives a church, with the equipment of the fullness of the Holy Spirit. And here we are told that all these—apostles, prophets, evangelists, pastors and teachers—are "for the perfecting of the saints, for the work of the ministry, for the edifying of the body of Christ." Evangelists are to build up the church, the same as pastors are. You can see that if a pastor is to preach to the church, evangelists are to preach to the church too. And if an evangelist needs the enduement of the Holy Spirit, then the pastor who builds up the same body of Christ, perfecting the saints for the work of the ministry, needs the same fullness of the Spirit.

But *that is not all!* In the same passage verse 16 tells us that the object of the building up of the church is to make "increase of the body"—that is, we are to make increase of the body of Christ by getting others saved! A healthy church is a growing church. A spiritually healthy Christian is a soul-winning Christian. A spiritually prospered pastor is a soul-winning pastor. In the nature of the case, one simply could not be filled with the Spirit and not have in mind the first main duty and purpose of soul winning.

The Apostle Paul would pass very well for a Bible teacher, but he was filled with the Holy Ghost! And with him, it was for soul winning. Apollos was "mighty in the scriptures," we are told, but he was filled with the Holy Spirit—as the Scripture puts it, "...fervent in the spirit" (that is, in the Holy Spirit)— and got many saved. It is noteworthy that at Antioch "certain prophets and teachers" ministered to the Lord and fasted when the Holy Spirit came upon them and commanded that Barnabas and Saul should be separated to the soul-winning work for which God had chosen them, and these were "sent forth by the Holy Ghost." No one can teach the Bible acceptable to God except as he is filled with the Holy Spirit for soul-winning power. We may be sure that this fullness of the Holy Spirit is intended primarily as an enduement of power from on high for witnessing and soul winning.

I love to teach the Word of God. If I may be pardoned for the statement, I feel that I have more natural gifts for teaching than for the strenuous and fearfully important work of an evangelist. I have to turn down many Bible teaching engagements. But I am certain that all Bible teaching ought to be, on the one hand, addressed to making soul winners out of Christians and, on the other hand, addressed to bringing sinners to repent of their sins. It is noteworthy that the Great Commission says, "...teach all nations," when it is referring to evangelism (Matt. 28:19).

One of the abominations that must grieve the heart of God in this generation is that many so-called Bible teachers never have a soul saved. They are content to "feed the sheep" and ignore the plain command of Jesus Christ in the Great Commission. How could such men be filled with the Holy Spirit! And it is small wonder that such people, who themselves have no burden, no passion, no tears, no sacrifice for soul winning, minimize the power of the Holy Spirit and teach people not to wait on God for this enduement of power from on high!

I am saying that one who is not obedient in this main matter of soul winning could not be filled with the Holy Spirit. In fact, one is not an obedient Christian at all who does not put soul winning first.

2. The Obedient Christian Must Not Only Try to Win Souls but Must Also Make Everything Else in the World Second to That Main Command of Jesus Christ

[handwritten: Die to yourself]

I think we may truly say that every child of God likes to see other sinners saved. I have found that there is something in the heart of a saved person which is warmed and blessed, nearly always, to hear of someone's finding the Saviour. But the sad truth is that many who want to see souls saved are not willing to pay the price to get souls saved. Many preachers would love to see many souls saved in their own ministry, but they are not willing to strike out boldly against sin. They are not willing to warn and chasten Christians to make them willing to do the work God has commanded Christians to do in soul winning. Many people would like to be soul winners, but they do not wish that badly enough to be thought fanatics on the question. They are not concerned enough about soul winning to give up worldly amusements or money-making or the esteem of friends and loved ones.

[handwritten: This is take up your cross + follow Christ]

You see, then, that if one would like to be a soul winner but is not willing to put that first in his life, he is not really and fully obedient to Jesus Christ. "A double minded man is unstable in all his ways" (Jas. 1:8). People want the power of the Holy Spirit, but they do not want to give themselves wholly to soul winning. People want the power of the Holy Spirit but are not willing to pay God's price for His power.

[handwritten: Die]

Don't you see that for one really to be obedient to Christ he would need not only to want to win souls but to want that more than anything else in the world? I have no doubt that the Lord Jesus wanted souls saved more than He wanted anything else when He came to the earth. And the dear heavenly Father who gave His Son felt the same way. And I cannot imagine that Jesus would have left Heaven to found schools or hospitals or orphan's homes. I cannot imagine that the Lord Jesus would have left Heaven to build nice church buildings with Gothic windows and lovely pipe organs and carpeted aisles and oak pews and reverent congregations, with robed choirs and scholarly ministers. I say, the secondary and incidental byproducts of Christianity were not what Jesus primarily had in mind when He came to this world. He came to die for sinners! Oh, how dear to His heart are the poor lost souls for whom He died! And He feels today, I know, just as He did when He was here. He wants souls saved! He wanted that more than He wanted the joys of Heaven and the praises of the angels or ease or comfort or anything else. And you are not truly obedient to Christ as a Christian until you come to have a consuming passion to win souls.

I can understand how God would put His blessed Holy Spirit in power on Paul who said:

"I say the truth in Christ, I lie not, my conscience also bearing me witness in the Holy Ghost, That I have great heaviness and continual sorrow in my heart. For I could wish that myself were accursed from Christ for my brethren, my kinsmen according to the flesh."—Rom. 9:1-3.

All the joy Paul sought on earth and all the reward to which he looked forward in Heaven were wrapped up in the winning of souls. And so will we be when we become wholly obedient in heart to the Lord Jesus who has called us with a heavenly calling and breathed upon us and said, "As my Father hath sent me, even so send I you" (John 20:21).

Obedience is a big word, and God gave Peter the inspired words that God gives the Holy Spirit "to them that obey him." Obedience means that soul winning becomes the greatest desire and purpose of the heart and that one at any cost wants to set out to do what Jesus has commanded us to do on this matter.

II. Baptism Is Often Mentioned as the Symbol of Full Obedience

Is it necessary to be baptized in water in order to be filled with the Holy Spirit? No, it is not always so. We may be sure that what God requires is not an outward ordinance or ceremony but an inward attitude of heart. But one should be baptized, and if one were intentionally disobedient in this, he could not be Spirit-filled. Baptism perfectly pictures the attitude of heart which God requires in those who would be filled with the Spirit. It is remarkable how many times baptism is mentioned in connection with the fullness of the Spirit, or baptism with the Spirit.

1. Four Times John the Baptist Is Quoted as Connecting Baptism in Water and Baptism With the Holy Ghost

In Matthew 3:11 is the record of this saying by John the Baptist:

"I indeed baptize you with water unto repentance: but he that cometh after me is mightier than I, whose shoes I am not worthy to bear: he shall baptize you with the Holy Ghost, and with fire."

In Mark 1:8 John the Baptist is quoted again as saying:

"I indeed have baptized you with water: but he shall baptize you with the Holy Ghost."

Again, the third time John the Baptist is quoted as connecting baptism in water and the baptism of the Holy Spirit which Christ would give at Pentecost, in Luke 3:16:

"John answered, saying unto them all, I indeed baptize you with water; but one mightier than I cometh, the latchet of whose shoes I am not worthy to unloose: he shall baptize you with the Holy Ghost and with fire."

A slightly different saying of John the Baptist is recorded by the Spirit of God in John 1:33:

"And I knew him not: but he that sent me to baptize with water, the same said unto me, Upon whom thou shalt see the Spirit descending, and remaining on him, the same is he which baptizeth with the Holy Ghost."

Every one of these statements is slightly different. I believe that every one is verbally inspired. I believe that John the Baptist mentioned this matter again and again. He was sent as a forerunner of Jesus. I think that in every sermon that he preached he talked about the coming Saviour. And I think that to every congregation he faced, perhaps, John promised that though he, the baptizer, baptized people in water, the Messiah Himself would baptize believers with the Holy Ghost! How important, then, is baptism, as making clear the condition God required for the fullness of the Holy Spirit.

2. Jesus Himself Connected Baptism in Water and Baptism With the Holy Ghost

Jesus took up the same teaching of John in many cases. In Acts 1:5 He seems to have deliberately reminded the disciples of the promise they had heard John the Baptist make many times. Jesus said, "For John truly baptized with water; but ye shall be baptized with the Holy Ghost not many days hence."

You see, Jesus intended everybody to keep in his mind that there are some things about the baptism in water which are connected with the baptism with the Holy Ghost.

3. Jesus Was Filled With the Holy Ghost at His Own Baptism in Water!

From the account given of the baptism of the Lord Jesus, it appears that immediately following His baptism He was baptized with the Holy Ghost, or filled with the Holy Spirit. Luke 3:21,22 says:

Die to self

"Now when all the people were baptized, it came to pass, that Jesus also being baptized, and praying, the heaven was opened, And the Holy Ghost descended in a bodily shape like a dove upon him, and a voice came from heaven, which said, Thou art my beloved Son; in thee I am well pleased."

In fact, Mark 1:10 says, "And straightway coming up out of the water, he saw the heavens opened, and the Spirit like a dove descending upon him."

It is obvious that God intended us to think of baptism in connection with the fullness of the Holy Spirit. And the Lord Jesus, our example, was filled with the Holy Spirit immediately after His baptism as a sign that even so we, when we have been baptized, ought immediately to be filled with the Holy Spirit. Baptism is the first duty commanded a new convert. One who is baptized, then, should so meet God's requirements as to be filled with the Holy Spirit immediately for service.

4. At Pentecost Peter Gave Baptism in Water as a Condition of "the Gift of the Holy Ghost"

Any Christian who is baptized and to whom baptism means what it ought to mean would have fulfilled the requirements for the fullness of the Holy Spirit. For Peter in Acts 2:38 said to those inquiring, "Repent, and be baptized every one of you in the name of Jesus Christ for the remission of sins, and ye shall receive the gift of the Holy Ghost."

And the next verse says that the promise is for their children and all that are afar off, even as many as the Lord our God shall call. In other words, baptism is as important for us as for them, and we are promised the fullness of the Holy Spirit on the same condition on which this blessing was promised to those at Pentecost.

In this verses, two conditions are given. Repentance is given as a condition of salvation. Repentance, a heart-turning from sin to trust in Christ, is always required in salvation. Faith and repentance are inseparable; and though the Bible sometimes mentions only one, in the very nature of the case, both are implied. One cannot trust in Christ without a change of mind about Christ and about sin. And that change of mind, or heart-turning from sin and from the rejection of Christ, necessarily involves faith in Christ as Saviour. So, the first requirement Peter made of these hearers at Pentecost is that they repent. Repenting, they would be saved.

The second requirement is that they should "be baptized every one of you in the name of Jesus Christ for the remission of sins." Not baptized *in order* to get their sins remitted, but baptized "for", or referring

to, or pointing to, the remission of sins which one gets when he
repents. This verse does not teach baptismal regeneration. Baptism is
not a condition of salvation. But in this verse baptism is given as a condition of the fullness of the Holy Spirit.

5. It Is Clearly Inferred in Acts 19:1—6 That Those Who Are Properly Baptized in Water Should Have Been Filled With the Holy Spirit

In Acts 19:1–6 is a Scripture which makes it clear that Paul expected people who had been baptized to be filled with the Holy Spirit. He
came to Ephesus and found some converts there. They are plainly
called "certain disciples." And Paul was surprised to find that they had
not received the Holy Ghost since they had believed. They did not
even know about the Holy Spirit's power. They had been taught, it
seems, by Apollos, a man mighty in the Scriptures and fervent in the
Spirit, mightily used in soul winning, but a man of Alexandria in Egypt
who had not been present, we suppose, at Pentecost and had not
learned to teach the new converts how to have what he himself had—
the fullness of the Holy Spirit. So these dozen men were disciples; they
had believed, they had been baptized, but they had not received the
enduement of power of the Holy Spirit. And Paul immediately took up
the matter of baptism. Verses 3–6 tell us:

"*And he said unto them, Unto what then were ye baptized? And they said, Unto
John's baptism. Then said Paul, John verily baptized with the baptism of repentance,
saying unto the people, that they should believe on him which should come after him,
that is, on Christ Jesus. When they heard this, they were baptized in the name of the
Lord Jesus. And when Paul had laid his hands upon them, the Holy Ghost came on
them; and they spake with tongues, and prophesied.*"

Some people very foolishly infer that there was something wrong
with the baptism of John. Not so! Not one verse in the Bible anywhere
teaches that there was anything wrong with the baptism administered
by John the Baptist. It was the only baptism that Jesus Himself had. It
was the only baptism received by the twelve apostles. In fact, one of
the conditions required of every apostle was that he must have com-
panied with the disciples "all the time that the Lord Jesus went in and
out among us, Beginning from the baptism of John" (Acts 1:21,22).
John the Baptist baptized people with exactly the same purpose as we,
in the Great Commission, are commanded to have when we baptize
converts. Baptism is the public profession of men's faith in Christ. So
here Paul went into some detail of the meaning of baptism. When they

understood the full meaning of baptism and when it to them represented the wholehearted surrender to God's perfect will, the dying out to
self and being raised up to a new life in the power of the Spirit of God,
they were baptized; and immediately the Holy Ghost came upon them.

6. But the Bible Clearly Gives Exceptions: Men Filled With the Holy Spirit Who Were Not Baptized

That there might be no mistake, and lest thoughtless people might
believe that the physical rite and ceremony of baptism in water is the
thing that secures the fullness of the Holy Spirit for a Christian, the
Bible clearly gives us several cases that are exceptions, cases of people
filled with the Holy Spirit without being baptized.

In the first case, all those who were filled with the Holy Spirit in
Old Testament times were filled without baptism in water. Baptism in
water is a New Testament ordinance and ceremony. It has a New
Testament meaning. But as we have seen before, Old Testament
prophets and saints were frequently filled with the Holy Spirit, for the
Spirit of the Lord came upon them, and they were endued with power
from on high for service, prophecy and witnessing.

John the Baptist is another example. In Luke 1:15 we are told that
he was "filled with the Holy Ghost, even from his mother's womb."
That obviously means that he was filled with the Holy Spirit before his
baptism. In fact, John the Baptist himself was never baptized, as far as
we know. He himself was the first baptizer. But he was filled with the
Holy Spirit.

Saul of Tarsus, who became Paul the apostle, was saved first and
then filled with the Holy Spirit and later baptized. In Acts 9:17, 18 we
are told:

*"Ananias went his way, and entered into the house; and putting his hands on
him said, Brother Saul, the Lord, even Jesus, that appeared unto thee in the way as
thou camest, hath sent me, that thou mightest receive thy sight, and be filled with the
Holy Ghost. And immediately there fell from his eyes as it had been scales: and he
received sight forthwith, and arose, and was baptized."*

Here we see that Saul (after fasting and praying three days and
nights) was filled with the Holy Spirit and then "he received sight
forthwith, and arose, and was baptized." He was filled with the Holy
Spirit *before* he was baptized in water.

So we must conclude, as the Scriptures obviously intend to teach,
that baptism in water is not itself a condition of the fullness of the Holy
Spirit. But the meaning of baptism and the attitude of heart which it

represents is obviously required of those who would be filled with the Holy Spirit. *FAITH + Repentance*

I do not know that D. L. Moody was ever scripturally baptized. But I believe that in every detail of his heart he meant exactly what people mean who are thoroughly instructed in the Scriptures and who follow Christ in baptism, and would have been baptized had he known what was right. You see, it is not baptism itself which fits one to be filled with the Holy Spirit, but it is the heart attitude which baptism is supposed to picture, which meets God's requirements. *CHANGe*

7. The Heart Attitude Pictured by Baptism Is Absolute Committal to Christ and Death to Self

When John the Baptist was baptizing multitudes in the river Jordan and it became very popular to be baptized, then Pharisees and Sadducees came too, to be baptized. But John the Baptist said to them, "O generation of vipers, who hath warned you to flee from the wrath to come? Bring forth therefore fruits meet for repentance" (Matt. 3:7,8). Obviously, one who does not heartily turn from his sins is not fit to be baptized in water.

The meaning of baptism is very clearly given in Romans 6:1–5:

> *"What shall we say then? Shall we continue in sin, that grace may abound? God forbid. How shall we, that are dead to sin, live any longer therein? Know ye not, that so many of us as were baptized into Jesus Christ were baptized into his death? Therefore we are buried with him by baptism into death: that like as Christ was raised up from the dead by the glory of the Father, even so we also should walk in newness of life. For if we have been planted together in the likeness of his death, we shall be also in the likeness of his resurrection."*

You see, the thought here is that when one has turned to Christ and trusted Him, he should reckon himself to be dead to sin. I should say to myself, "This old sinner is dead. The old life is gone. We will bury the old sinner and try to keep him buried away. The man who will live now will be the new man, in the power of Christ and living for Christ. If Christ died in my place, then I will count myself dead. And I will count the life that I live to be Christ's own life." So one who is baptized goes down into a watery grave to bury himself there. There he proclaims to the world that the old sinner that he has been has no right to live, that the old life has no right to continue. As the Lord Jesus was buried and rose again, so the Christian buries the old life and then is raised "in the likeness of his resurrection."

If any man believes, after he is baptized, that he has a right to live his own life, that he has a right to choose where he lives or the means of his livelihood or whom he shall marry or what he shall spend upon himself, then he has wholly misunderstood the meaning of baptism. Anyone who has been baptized and did not mean to count the old life dead and buried, did not mean to live a new life in the power of God, did not mean really to count himself simply alive to God and dead to the old life and the old world, lied to God and lied to every man who saw him baptized!

You see, baptism is a beautiful and perfect picture of self-renunciation and surrender to the will of God and the plan of God. Baptism means the same thing as Romans 12:1: "I beseech you therefore, brethren, by the mercies of God, that ye present your bodies a living sacrifice, holy, acceptable unto God, which is your reasonable service."

Do you wonder, then, that Jesus was filled with the Holy Ghost when He was baptized? The Lord Jesus, being baptized, offered Himself to die for sinners. He offered Himself not to follow His own will but the will of the Father. He was perfectly given over to the matter of saving poor lost sinners, at any cost to Himself. To Jesus, the watery grave pictured that He would be crucified and would be buried in Joseph's new tomb and then would rise again. And so it ought to mean to every Christian. So every Christian who understands truly the meaning of baptism and gives himself unreservedly to God in baptism should have the fullness of the Holy Spirit. For hence he lives for God's purposes, not his own. And of course we must remember that God's purpose is primarily to save souls.

Every Christian, that is, every person who trusts Christ as his Saviour, should then as soon as possible be taught perfect surrender to the will and plan of God and should be baptized as a picture of his dying to the old world and to self and of his being alive to God and to God's plan and work. And then the Christian should be filled with the Holy Spirit in order to carry out the work he has surrendered to do and should be empowered to obey the command of the Saviour to which he has now committed himself.

You see, Saul—blinded and fasting and praying for three days for the fullness of the Holy Spirit—was filled with the Holy Spirit before he was baptized in water. But he had already been baptized in his own mind, in his own full surrender. He had already given himself to Jesus Christ for a ministry far from that place, as he would be sent to the Gentiles. So he was filled with the Holy Spirit because he had met the heart requirement that is involved in proper scriptural baptism. Then he was baptized immediately thereafter.

III. This Obedience Is More Than Righteous Living or "Surrender" or Consecration, More Than Separation

I hesitated to mention obedience as a condition of the fullness of the Holy Spirit for the simple reason that people have such diluted ideas of obedience. The obedience that fits a Christian to be filled with the Holy Spirit is not mere godly living, is not giving up worldly amusements, is not simply "the deeper life" nor consecration, as these terms are ordinarily understood.

1. Morality Is Not Complete Obedience to Christ

I believe in holy living. Surely those who want to win souls and those who would be filled with the Holy Spirit should set themselves to please God in their daily walk and talk, yea, in their heart's attitude. But we need to remember that the righteousness of the scribes and Pharisees was never enough to get them into Heaven, and certainly it was not enough to fit them for the fullness of the Spirit of God! Suppose since you have been saved you gave up drink. You no longer gamble. You do not curse and take God's name in vain. You go to church perhaps twice on Sunday, and possibly you attend the Sunday school service and the midweek prayer meeting. You live a moral and godly life. But that does not mean that you are fitted to be filled with the Holy Spirit. Obedience to Christ is not merely the letter of the law as observed by Pharisees and scribes.

Nothing could make this plainer than the fact that the perfect and holy Jesus Himself, without a sin or a stain, without one breath or thought that displeased the Father, was yet not filled with the Holy Spirit until He came to be baptized and so publicly proclaim Himself headed for the cross and publicly given over to the Father's will. We are not to suppose that Jesus was less willing before. But the Father had planned for Him to announce His ministry publicly and thus foretell His own death and resurrection by baptism. And if the godliness of the perfect God-man, Jesus Christ, before His baptism did not cause Him to be filled with the Holy Spirit, you may be sure that the moral righteousness of any human being is insufficient for that purpose.

So it turns out that there are many "separated Christians" who are not filled with the Holy Spirit. How many Christians I have known who would not attend a picture show, would never smoke a cigarette, who did not have a pack of playing cards in the house, who would not wear extremes in dress nor do anything else that smacked of worldliness, and yet who never won a soul to Christ! Many, many Christians think it is more important not to wear lipstick or rouge than to win souls! How far they are from knowing the mind and heart of God! How far they are from true heart obedience! I am anxious for Christians to avoid the appearance of evil and to come out and be separate, to touch not the unclean thing. I thank God that I have diligently taught Christians to avoid the dance and the theater and cigarettes and other worldly and hurtful things that would grieve the Spirit of God and would hurt their testimony. But we ought to know that that kind of separation is only an outward separation. It is not enough! One ought to be separated to the business of getting sinners saved, to the business of living Christ over again before men with a holy passion and with miraculous power, if he expects to be filled with the Holy Spirit.

2. Even the Study of the Word of God Does Not Meet the Conditions for the Fullness of the Holy Spirit

The Word of God should be the very breath of a Christian. It should be our meditation day and night. It is the Word of God that is able to sanctify us and build us up. The Holy Spirit Himself is to bring to our remembrance the things that Jesus said and to help us understand God's Word. I would not minimize the importance of the Word of God in the life of every Christian. It is our meat and drink, our breath, our joy and the rejoicings of our heart. Oh, Christian, love the Word of God, read the Word of God, learn the Word of God and live it! But we should remember that to know and read and love the Word of God is not in itself obedience.

I know Christians who go from one Bible conference to another, who carry Bibles and mark special verses and get the autographs of all the Bible teachers. I know Christians who diligently make charts to show the order of events in Christ's coming, who try to trace out the bounds of the Roman Empire so they will know the extent of the kingdom of the Antichrist! I know Christians who enter into excited speculation as to whether or not world events recorded in the newspapers are the signs that prove the Saviour will return very, very soon! And I am sad to tell you that multitudes of these Christians never win a soul. They are not endued with power from on high. They are not filled with the Holy Ghost. And the reason is this: they are not truly obedient to Jesus Christ. They have not wholeheartedly surrendered themselves, body and soul, to the business for which He died—that is, getting the

Gospel to sinners and getting them saved. Such Christians love to "gather around the Word," which means that their attention is on the Word itself instead of taking the Word of God as a sword and setting out to fight the battles of the Lord, or instead of taking the Word of God as the bread of life and carrying it to dying, starving, famishing sinners everywhere! "The letter killeth," the Scripture says. And to take the bare letter of the Word of God and learn it and love it and try to follow it, without a holy passion, without a dying out to self in order to win souls, is in some sense a perversion, an abomination, a hypocritical Christianity. Oh, how will "Bible teachers" meet the Lord Jesus at the judgment seat of Christ, when they have simply taught people the Word of God and taught them to love the Word and to know facts about the Word, but have not taught people to obey the Word in winning souls?

3. Various Deeper-Life Movements Miss the Point of Wholehearted Obedience to Christ's Command

Months ago I was in a great citywide revival campaign. Thirty or forty churches and their pastors had united and had invited me to come and lead them in a campaign in a great city auditorium. Thousands of people came. Hundreds of souls found Christ as Saviour.

At the same time a little group in that city carried on regular "Bible classes" and "prayer meetings." They prayed for "the deeper life." They told of how earnestly they searched their own hearts. They criticized very severely others who were not of their movement and did not meet in their prayer meetings. They talked of "the crucified life" and "the deeper life." But I was astonished when one of their number told me that they were entirely too busy in seeking the deeper life and learning the mysteries of God's Word to attend the revival services. So they carried on their little group meetings, they scorned the other Christians who did not live "crucified lives" and did not understand "the deeper life," but they never lifted a finger to get sinners saved! I wonder, oh, I wonder how their prayers sounded to God who gave His Son to save sinners!

Do you suppose I am speaking of some strange and fanatical talk, some false religion? Oh, no! These of whom I speak were members of the churches which were united in this great revival and soul-winning effort. They were orthodox in the principal doctrines of salvation by the blood, the deity of Christ, the inspiration of the Scriptures, and Heaven and Hell. But I sadly fear that all their talk about a deeper life was an abomination to God and that there was a secret and hateful rebellion in their hearts, since they did not give themselves to the one main command that Jesus had left them. They did not win souls! They were not burdened about sinners being saved.

Everywhere I go I find people who boast that they are sanctified, or they rejoice in public testimony that they have "received the baptism." But with all the solemnity of my soul, I press upon your heart this solemn truth: any kind of "sanctification" or "baptism" or "separation" or "con-secration" or "deeper life" that does not make soul winners is essentially still rebellion against Jesus Christ! What an abomination to God are all our finespun doctrines and our boastful claims if we do not seek with all of our hearts to do the one main thing He has left for us to do!

You see, surely, that many of the consecration movements and deeper-life movements have failed utterly to understand the mind of God and the will of God for His people. Until one is wholly given up to soul winning as the main business in life, he is not an obedient Christian. And such an one, not obeying from the heart the Lord Jesus and giving himself wholly to this soul-winning business, certainly can-not be filled with the Holy Spirit while that obedience is lacking.

IV. What Obedience Means

What does it mean to obey Christ so that you may be filled with the Holy Spirit? I will briefly summarize what I believe is involved in the obedience.

1. First, the Christian Should Make a Definite, Once-for-All Surrender of Himself to Christ

Promise the Saviour that you here and now resolve to follow His will at any cost the rest of your life. Resolve that in every particular, large and small, as soon as you know the will of Christ, you will try to do it. Nothing less than that could satisfy Jesus Christ. Oh, I cannot say that I have lived up to that vow; but with all my heart I made it! And then I have made it again and again and again! I want to do the will of Jesus Christ. Oh, if He but give me grace, I will—I will do what He wishes me to do, when He shows me His will.

Some people have more light than others. Every Christian will gain more light daily as he follows on to know the will of Christ and to do it. Light will come from the study of the Word of God. Light will come from the clear leading of the Holy Spirit. But every Christian, to be wholly obedient to Jesus Christ, must resolve that as fast as he can learn the will of Christ, he will do it at any cost, in every particular. I do not say that in his living any Christian can perfectly fulfill all the will of Christ. At least, I do not claim that for myself, and I do not believe that any other Christian that I know has a right to claim that he has, in every particular, pleased the Lord Jesus. But I know that I *want* to please Him. I know that it is the deepest passion of my soul to do the will of Jesus Christ. May He give me more grace to fulfill what my heart offers and longs to do.

2. Second, the Christian Should Give Up Every Known Sin, Renounce It Completely

I do not say that I live above sin. But I certainly say that I have had my fill of sin and do not want to sin. I hate sin and avoid it. Thank God for the victory He gives me! I ought to have more perfect victory. But certainly I must say, if I claim to be obedient to Christ, that I will not willingly continue in anything in the world that grieves my Saviour. When I come to know that something in my heart or in my life or attitude or thoughts is displeasing to God, I must confess it and forsake it, or I must cease all pretense of being obedient in heart. Oh, what searching and what carefulness and watching and what confession and what holy zeal will come to the Christian who really tries to please Jesus Christ by avoiding and hating and confessing and forsaking utterly every known sin! And it might be just an outward righteousness if one were trying, like the Pharisees, to seek some outward standing, some praise from men. But if this purity of heart and this holy longing are based upon a desire to win souls and to have the fullness of the Holy Spirit, then how proper it is. And how deeply careful and sensitive of the heart and life and motives will this soul-winning aim make us! Oh, Christian, if you would be filled with the Holy Spirit, then set out to "slay utterly" any of the things in your life that offend the dear Lord Jesus and would grieve Him and hinder His power.

3. Obedience Means Definite Soul-Winning Effort

We are so poorly equipped by nature to win souls. It takes a supernatural enduement of God's power to win souls. And yet I would say that every Christian ought to set out to win souls at any cost. Should one wait and never try to win a soul until he has been marvelously filled with the Holy Ghost? Well, there is a sense in which one should put waiting on God in prayer and heart-searching before everything else until he has an enduement of power. And yet with most Christians, God's blessing comes first in sprinkles before it comes in downpours. With most Christians there is a little blessing before the fullness of blessing comes. In my own heart I know that I won some precious souls (with what crying of soul, with what tears, with what blundering but struggling efforts!) before I received the greater anointing of the Spirit. I know that it was in some measure the fullness of the Spirit upon me that helped me to win souls. No one can win a soul without the supernatural power of God. But at least I was committed to soul winning and gave my heart and effort to it.

D. L. Moody was committed to soul winning and was trying to win souls before he was filled with the Holy Spirit. Christmas Evans, who led in the Welsh revival, cried to God for thirteen years for his baptism of the Holy Spirit and struggled to win souls before the revival in its fullness came and the power of God in its magnitude was poured upon him.

The dear Lord Jesus did not win a soul before He was filled with the Holy Spirit. In His case, the perfect case, the Holy Spirit came without any measure the first time He asked for the fullness of power upon Himself. We are not so single-hearted as Jesus. We are not so worthy. We need longer to cry and pray and search our hearts and forsake our sins, perhaps. But at any rate, Jesus was thoroughly committed to soul winning and to dying for sinners from the moment He came into the world until He was filled with the Holy Ghost at His baptism.

So I would say to anyone who seeks to be filled with the Holy Spirit, set out to win souls! And as you cry to God with deep longings of soul for His fullness, let your tears be shed too for sinners and earnestly try to win them. Remember this, that the fullness of the Holy Spirit is never given except for soul-winning testimony and service, and one of the best ways you could prove your obedience is to trim all your sails for this destination and commit yourself in obedience to the soul-winning business.

4. And This Obedience Involves Heartbroken, Prevailing Prayer

There is a sense in which you cannot separate the two conditions—wholehearted obedience and prevailing prayer—for if one obeys the Lord Jesus, how can he avoid pleading for this power of God? So, I would set out to surrender to the perfect will of God in every detail of my life. I would forsake every known sin and commit myself to the death of every ambition and thought and dream that were not in the will of God. I would prepare myself and school myself in soul winning. But then one who will obey Christ must wait on Him with longing of soul until the fullness be poured out and until the breath of Heaven gives the supernatural enduement for soul winning.

Chapter 11

Prayer—a Condition of Holy Spirit Fullness

"If ye then, being evil, know how to give good gifts unto your children: how much more shall your heavenly Father give the Holy Spirit to them that ask him?"— Luke 11:13.

"I don't believe in praying for the Holy Spirit," says some reader. But you are mistaken, my friend. If you believe in prayer at all and if you are a Bible Christian, however mistaught in your theology, you do believe in praying for the fullness of the Holy Spirit, and I can prove that you do.

Did you ever pray for a revival? I hope you have. How can anybody draw near to God without pleading for the poor sinning, dying world about us! How can any earnest Christian fail to pray for a revival in the church and a reviving upon all the hearts of God's people, on the one hand, and on the other, for a turning of poor lost sinners to Christ as a result of this revival in the church? But who brings revival? It is the Holy Spirit. Only the Holy Spirit can bring revival among the saints and regeneration to the lost. So if you prayed for a revival, you prayed for the enduement of power from on high, the coming of the Holy Spirit in fullness upon Christians.

Did you ever pray for God to bless a preacher, to give him boldness, wisdom and power, and to open the hearts of sinners who heard the preacher? Then, whether you knew it or not, you were praying for that preacher to be endued with power from on high, praying for him to be filled with the Holy Spirit or for the Holy Spirit to come upon him.

Did you ever ask the dear Lord to help you in dealing with some soul, in showing some sinner the way of salvation? Did you ever pray for God to convict this sinner and cause him to repent? Then you were praying for the Holy Spirit of God to be with you in power to fill you and make you able to win souls. It is only the Holy Spirit who convicts sinners. And He does it particularly through the preached Word and the testimony of Christians when they are filled with the Holy Spirit.

You see that Christians who follow the Bible command and example to pray for revival are really praying for the fullness of the Spirit to come upon God's people. Second Chronicles 7:14 teaches people to pray for revival. Habakkuk prayed, "O LORD, revive thy work in the midst of the years" (Hab. 3:2). The psalmist cried out, "Wilt thou not revive us again: that thy people may rejoice in thee?" (Ps. 85:6). The only way God can answer prayer for revival is to fill His people with the Holy Spirit. Thus He enables preachers to preach, enables parents, teachers and friends to do effective soul winning. Only by the fullness of the Holy Spirit can any Christian do the soul-saving work that is done in a revival. And all who long for the salvation of sinners are longing for something that can come only as God's people are filled with the Spirit and thus are enabled and empowered to carry the Gospel and witness effectively.

The blessed Holy Spirit Himself seems to teach people this lesson. The ultradispensationalists, the followers of Darby and others, have builded a theology that discourages prayer for the fullness of the Holy Spirit, that discourages a hope for a repetition of such anointings and baptisms of the Spirit as occurred in Bible times. Yet new converts come along and, led of the Spirit, ignorant of man-made theology, pray to be filled with the Holy Spirit! Our seminaries pour out men who are taught to play down the enduement of power from on high and to minimize any teaching of waiting upon God for the fullness of the Spirit. Yet the songwriters, led of the Spirit, keep on writing great songs which are prayers for the coming of the Spirit. Among famous hymns I think of these: "Come, Holy Spirit, Heavenly Dove"; "Spirit of God, Descend Upon My Heart"; "Holy Ghost, With Light Divine"; "Holy Spirit, Faithful Guide"; "Holy Spirit, From on High." These are not all prayer songs for Holy Spirit power in witnessing, but they are all prayers to the Holy Spirit. And there are many, many songs written by Spirit-filled men which do plead for the Holy Spirit's power in soul winning. "Pentecostal Power" by Gabriel has been blessed to thousands. Bathurst and Towner wrote "The Old-Time Fire" which pleads,

> Oh, for that flame of living fire
> Which shone so bright in saints of old.

It pleads for the power of Elijah:

> And while to Thee our hearts we raise,
> On us Thy Holy Spirit pour!

Another song, "Fill Me Now," by E. H. Stokes and John R. Sweney:

> Hover o'er me, Holy Spirit,
>   Bathe my trembling heart and brow;
> Fill me with Thy hallowed presence,
>   Come, O come, and fill me now.

And again,

> ...*Eternal Spirit,*
> *Fill with pow'r, and fill me now.*

Paul Rader's famous hymn, "Old-Time Power," teaches people to sing the prayer,

> *Spirit, now melt and move*
> *All of our hearts with love;*
> *Breathe on us from above*
> *With old-time power.*

Is it any accident that Spirit-filled songwriters like Fanny Crosby, Peter Billhorn, B. B. McKinney, Paul Rader, A. B. Simpson, Oswald J. Smith and others like them have felt moved of God to write songs which are inspired prayers pleading for the power of the Holy Spirit?

I live in a region where it is the popular fad these recent decades to teach that any prayer for the fullness of the Spirit is fanaticism, that Pentecost can never be repeated, that every Christian has all of the Holy Spirit there is for him, and that Christians are simply to believe that they are filled with the Spirit, and they are. But in this same area, among these good Christians with the ultradispensational tinge and bent to their theology, there ever recurs again and again this theme in songs and choruses which move the hearts of people to pray for Holy Spirit power. The chorus which was arranged and popularized in America by my friend, Rev. Daniel Iverson, "Spirit of the living God, fall fresh on me," has been used all over this country with great blessing to Christians as they prayed for the fullness of the Holy Spirit, despite their ultradispensational theology! The old song, "O Lord, Send the Power Just Now"; Harry D. Clarke's chorus, "Breathe on Me!" and many others have been most helpful.

The simple truth is that spiritually minded Christians are moved and taught by the Holy Spirit to pray for His fullness and power and to wait on Him for His pouring out upon them as a miraculous enduement of power for witnessing! Indeed, Bible Christians do believe in praying for the Holy Spirit.

In the former chapter we said that wholehearted obedience to the soul-winning program of Christ is a condition of being filled with the Holy Spirit. But this chapter is to show that those who are to be filled with the Spirit must also seek God's face with prevailing prayer. Obedience and prayer are the two great conditions that cover all the requirements for those who would be filled with the Holy Spirit.

Now I should like to show you, first, that the fullness of the Spirit is plainly promised in answer to prayer; second, that there are many Bible examples of Christians who were filled with the Spirit as a result of their own prayers; and third, that there are Bible examples of people filled with the Holy Spirit because others prayed.

I. The Fullness of the Spirit Plainly Promised in Answer to Prayer

1. Jesus Said in Luke 11:13, "How Much More Shall Your Heavenly Father Give the Holy Spirit to Them That Ask Him?"

Here is a plain statement that God gives the Holy Spirit to them that ask Him.

It is always a sad thing when anybody's theology leads him to discount or practically throw away any of the promises in the Bible. Unfortunately, with many people that is what has happened to this blessed verse in Luke 11:13. A certain group, of ultra-dispensational tendencies, have influenced some to believe that Luke 11:13 is out of date, that that promise no longer holds good for Christians. And the notes in the Scofield Bible, unfortunately, have been influenced by this ultradispensational tendency taught by Darby and others. The Scofield Reference Bible is the best reference Bible in the world. I use it constantly. It has blessed thousands. But on this matter its notes are wrong.

In a note on this verse, this great reference Bible says:

> It is evident that none of the disciples, with the possible exception of Mary of Bethany, asked for the Spirit in the faith of this promise. It was a new and staggering thing to a Jew that, in advance of the fulfillment of Joel 2:28,29, all might receive the Spirit. Mary alone of the disciples understood Christ's repeated declaration concerning His own death and resurrection (John 12:3-7). Save Mary, not one of the disciples but Peter, and he only in the great confession (Matt. 16:16), manifested a spark of spiritual intelligence till after the resurrection of Christ and the impartation of the Spirit (John 20:22; Acts 2:1-4). To go back to the promise of Luke 11:13, is to forget Pentecost, and to ignore the truth that now every believer has the indwelling Spirit (Rom. 8:9,15; I Cor. 6:19; Gal. 4:6; I John 2:20,27).

Note the following mistakes in the above footnote from the Scofield Bible: (a) The Scripture does not say a word about Mary of Bethany being filled with the Spirit. The note here is mistaken. (b) Dr. Scofield forgot or ignored entirely the fact that John the Baptist was "filled with the Holy Ghost," that Elisabeth and Zacharias were "filled with the Holy Ghost," and that the Spirit came upon David, came mightily upon Samson, and that Bezaleel was "filled with the Spirit of God." Blinded by his ultradispensational conception, acquired late in life, that Pentecost was an entirely new thing never heard of before, the origin of the church, and that Pentecost simply marked the beginning of a new dispensation, Dr. Scofield entirely missed the point that Jesus made in Luke 11:13. (c) Dr. Scofield says, "To go back to the promise of Luke 11:13, is to forget Pentecost, and to ignore the truth that now every believer has the indwelling Spirit...." Here Dr. Scofield shows that he thinks Jesus in Luke 11:13 was speaking about the *indwelling* of the Holy Spirit, which is certainly not what Jesus had in mind. It is certain that no one was ever taught, in the Bible, to pray for the indwelling of the Holy Spirit. That happens automatically for Christians now when they are saved. It did not happen at all in Old Testament times. But in Luke 11:13 Jesus was promising the fullness of the Spirit, soul-winning power, to those who would ask the Father.

Let us study the context of Luke 11:13 very carefully. It will pay you to read very carefully again and study the first thirteen verses of that chapter, and so I give them here.

"And it came to pass, that, as he was praying in a certain place, when he ceased, one of his disciples said unto him, Lord, teach us to pray, as John also taught his disciples. And he said unto them, When ye pray, say, Our Father which art in heaven, Hallowed be thy name. Thy kingdom come. Thy will be done, as in heaven, so in earth. Give us day by day our daily bread. And forgive us our sins; for we also forgive every one that is indebted to us. And lead us not into temptation; but deliver us from evil. And he said unto them, Which of you shall have a friend, and shall go unto him at midnight, and say unto him, Friend, lend me three loaves; For a friend of mine in his journey is come to me, and I have nothing to set before him? And he from within shall answer and say, Trouble me not: the door is now shut, and my children are with me in bed; I cannot rise and give thee. I say unto you, Though he will not rise and give him, because he is his friend, yet because of his importunity he will rise and give him as many as he needeth. And I say unto you, Ask, and it shall be given you; seek, and ye shall find; knock, and it shall be opened unto you. For every one that asketh receiveth; and he that seeketh findeth; and to him that knocketh it shall be opened. If a son shall ask bread of any of you that is a father, will he give him a stone? or if he ask a fish, will he for a fish give him a serpent? Or if he shall ask an egg, will he offer him a scorpion? If ye then, being evil, know how to give good gifts unto your children: how much more shall your heavenly Father give the Holy Spirit to them that ask him?"—Luke 11:1–13.

Now notice the following clear truths about the teaching of Jesus in the above passage:

(a) It is all one lesson on prayer, given at one time by the Saviour. Jesus was simply answering the request, "Lord, teach us to pray."

(b) That means that if any part of this passage is out of date, all of it is out of date. For this reason many ultradispensationalists have argued that the Lord's Prayer does not belong to this "dispensation" at all! But I maintain, and certainly nineteen out of twenty of all the great Bible commentators will agree, that this model prayer is for all Christians who can honestly say, "Our Father which art in heaven." And every Christian has a right to pray that God's name will be hallowed, that the kingdom will come and His will be done in earth as it is now done in Heaven. Every Christian has a right to pray for daily bread, for forgiveness and cleansing of sins; that God will lead us away from temptation and deliver us from the evil one. But if the model prayer is for Christians, then the rest of the same passage, given from the lips of the Saviour at the same time, must be for us today also.

(c) It is important to note that from verse 5 to verse 13 the Lord is speaking about intercessory prayer, about getting the bread of life for sinners. Jesus, in this lesson on prayer, tells of one friend who goes to another's house at midnight, saying, "Friend, lend me three loaves; For a friend of mine in his journey is come to me, and I have nothing to set before him." The only adequate interpretation of this parable is that it represents a Christian coming to God, the great Friend who has all power, and pleading that He will give the Christian the bread of life for sinners for whom we are responsible, whom we could not win in our own strength and power. It is plainly a prayer that God will enable us to carry the bread of life to sinners.

(d) In verse 13, then, the Saviour plainly says that this power to carry the saving bread of life to others is simply the fullness of the Holy Spirit, and we are to ask our heavenly Father to give us the Holy Spirit, in His power. We already have the Holy Spirit dwelling in our bodies, but many Christians do not have His fullness, His anointing, His enduement, His supernatural manifestation in soul-winning power. And Christians should pray for the Holy Spirit in this sense, according to the clear command of Jesus Christ in Luke 11:13.

In the Fifty-first Psalm, David promised that if God would "take not thy holy spirit from me," then he would teach transgressors God's way and sinners would be converted. And here, with the same meaning, Jesus teaches us to pray for this fullness of the Holy Spirit—that is, for the Holy Spirit to come upon us in power so we may carry the bread of life to sinners. And that kind of prayer would have been perfectly proper in the Old Testament times, or during the ministry of Jesus Christ, or after Pentecost, or in this twentieth century. There always has been but one way for sinners to be saved, and that way is by faith in the Saviour. But the only way God has of winning men in Old Testament times or New Testament times is for God's Spirit-filled people to be witnesses. Psalm 126:5,6, urging Christians to go and weep and carry the precious seed of the Word of God, speaks of the same duty and power and result as Jesus referred to in the Great Commission!

"To go back to this promise of Luke 11:13, is to forget Pentecost...," says Dr. Scofield. Others push away lightly this tremendous promise, saying, "Oh, but that was before Pentecost!" But let me show you how foolish it is to ignore this great promise of God because it was given before Pentecost.

First, the promise given here by the Lord Jesus is exactly the same promise which He gave to the same disciples again just before Pentecost. In Luke 24:49 He said, "...but tarry ye in the city of Jerusalem, until ye be endued with power from on high." And in Acts 1:4 we are told that Jesus commanded the disciples "that they should not depart from Jerusalem, but wait for the promise of the Father, which, saith he, ye have heard of me." And this same promise of Luke 11:13 surely is what Jesus had in mind when He commanded the disciples, "Receive ye the Holy Ghost" and told them that as the Father had sent Him, He would send the disciples. To regard the promise of Luke 11:13, "...how much more shall your heavenly Father give the Holy Spirit to them that ask him?" as an isolated instance, a promise never repeated, a promise now out of date, is foolish in view of other like promises.

Second, the idea that praying for the Holy Spirit is out of date because the promise of Jesus in Luke 11:13 was given before Pentecost, is made ridiculous by a simple fact. That fact is that *this promise was not even written down till long after Pentecost!* The Scofield Bible, for example, says, "The date of Luke falls between A.D. 63 and 68." About the Book of Acts, written by the same divinely inspired man, the Scofield Bible says, "The Acts concludes with the account of Paul's earliest ministry in Rome, A.D. 65, and appears to have been written at or near that time." So our best authorities agree that the Book of Luke was written at least thirty years after Pentecost! In fact, it was written about the same time as the Book of Acts. How silly it is to suppose that the Holy Spirit of God put down this wonderful promise, "...how much more shall your heavenly Father give the Holy Spirit to them that ask him?" when the promise had been out of date thirty years when the

Holy Spirit had it written down! I do not believe it! It offends a spiritual mind; it is inconsistent with the plan of God in writing the Scripture. Any simplehearted Christian who, upon reading the blessed promise of Jesus in Luke, chapter 11, should plead with the Father for bread for sinners, should earnestly wait on God to be endued with power from on high because he found the promise here in the Bible, would have a right to feel that God was trifling with him, if God should take the side of the ultradispensationalists and laugh at him and say that the promises were good long ago, but that they were only written down thirty years too late to do anybody any good! I do not believe it. The rest of the Bible does not bear it out. There is not one statement in the Bible anywhere to indicate that this blessed promise is out of date. And we would be wrong to follow those who chop up the Bible and throw most of the pieces away and make most of the promises out of date.

Third, I can prove, and will prove a little further on, that the promise that the Father will give the Holy Spirit to them that ask Him is not out of date because *after Pentecost* a number of times we have clear examples of Christians doing exactly what this promise encourages them to do—that is, praying for the Holy Spirit and receiving His fullness and power. So we must count Luke 11:13 as a promise for today that God will give the fullness of the Spirit to those that ask Him.

2. In Luke 24:49 and in Acts 1:4 Jesus Commanded the Disciples to Pray for the Holy Spirit in His Fullness

Before Jesus went away He commanded the disciples to tarry at Jerusalem for the power of the Holy Spirit. Here are His words:

"...*but tarry ye in the city of Jerusalem, until ye be endued with power from on high.*"—Luke 24:49.

"*And, being assembled together with them, commanded them that they should not depart from Jerusalem, but wait for the promise of the Father, which, saith he, ye have heard of me. For John truly baptized with water; but ye shall be baptized with the Holy Ghost not many days hence.*"—Acts 1:4,5.

One of the Scriptures quoted above commanded the disciples to "tarry" in the city of Jerusalem for the Holy Spirit's power. The other verse commanded them to "wait" for the promised baptism of the Holy Ghost. But I maintain that these two words, "tarry" and "wait," in this case mean that they were to pray for the fullness of the Holy Spirit. The reason I know that is what Jesus meant is that that is exactly what the disciples who heard Him understood Him to mean. Turn to Acts

1:14 where we are told of the apostles, "These all continued with one accord in prayer and supplication, with the women, and Mary the mother of Jesus, and with his brethren."

How did the disciples fulfill the command to "tarry," to "wait," for the coming of the Holy Spirit's power upon them? They obeyed by continuing steadfastly in prayer and supplication. They understood that Jesus meant for them to pray, and pray they did, even with supplications.

You see, it was not hard for them to understand what Jesus wanted them to do. He had already given them the promise that the heavenly Father would give the Holy Spirit to them that ask Him. In fact, Jesus had plainly told them that when He, the Bridegroom, was taken away, then the disciples would not only pray, but fast (Mark 2:20). So when Jesus commanded them to wait in Jerusalem and tarry until they were endued with power from on high, the disciples knew that He meant them to continue in prayer and supplication and even with fasting. And that is exactly what they did. No Christian has a right to say that he knows better what Jesus meant by His command than these disciples who heard Him and waited in the Upper Room until they were endued with power from on high.

"But," someone says, "Pentecost would have come, and with it the birth of the church and the pouring out of the Holy Spirit, even if the disciples had not prayed."

In answer to that we may say three things: First, we cannot be very sure that the feasts in Leviticus 23:9–32 picture the resurrection of Christ and the coming of the Holy Spirit at Pentecost. We know that Pentecost itself was the holiday fifty days after the offering of the wave sheaf. But if the wave sheaf pictured the resurrection of Christ because the term "firstfruits" is mentioned, as in I Corinthians 15:23, then the Feast of Pentecost may well mean the same thing because the same term, "firstfruits," is also used of the wave loaves which were offered at that time. (Compare Lev. 23:10 with Lev. 23:20). It is quite certain that the Bible itself never mentions that Pentecost is the time of the founding of the church; or that Pentecost (the Feast of Weeks or of the wave loaves) pictured the coming of the Holy Spirit to form the church. That teaching of Plymouth Brethren is not borne out by many of the best commentaries. For example, *Jamieson, Fausset and Brown* and *Matthew Henry* do not teach it, nor do many others of the best commentaries. So it is foolish to found a doctrine on our understanding of a type where there is no clear statement of the Word of God. There is no Bible teaching that the church began at Pentecost, and we cannot be sure that the Holy Spirit would have come in power at Pentecost if the disciples had not prayed. It is certain that Jesus, talking to the disciples, did not tell them when the Holy Spirit would come. He did not say, "Tarry until Pentecost." He said simply, "Tarry ye in...Jerusalem until ye be endued with power from on high."

Second, even if God had planned to give the Holy Spirit at Pentecost, as I think He did, it would not be because He must have the fullness of the Spirit come upon the waiting disciples on the Jewish feast day. I think, as many of the best commentators do, that at Pentecost the city would be crowded with people who ought to hear the Gospel, and then would be the proper time for the Christians to be filled with the Spirit and sent out to witness as Jesus had commanded them to do. When "there were...Jews, devout men, out of every nation under heaven" temporarily dwelling at Jerusalem for the feast of Pentecost, it was a good time for Christians to have their great revival and their beginning of the fulfillment of the Great Commission in carrying the Gospel to every creature.

But we know that the principal thing in the mind of the Lord Jesus was that His disciples should have power to witness for Him and should carry the Gospel to sinners. The Bible leaves no possibility of doubt on that score. He said nothing about Pentecost being a type that must be fulfilled. So often the Lord Jesus did speak of the fulfilling of Scriptures that it is remarkable that He did not say so here if that was what He had in mind. We do well not to set other reasons when the Lord Jesus has plainly given us the reasons why the disciples were to wait and pray. They were to tarry to be filled with power.

Third, even if the Lord Jesus had planned to fill His disciples at Pentecost, that would not mean that they should not pray for this power and wait before God. Cannot God move the hearts of His people to be prepared for the blessing He intends to bestow? If God is to bring a great revival on your city at a certain time, you may be sure that He intends before that to lay on the hearts of many to pray and seek His face. When God gives the blessing which He plans, He will have fitted all the elements together so that He will reward those who seek Him and that those who do not seek His blessing will not find it. It is always wrong to put God's sovereign grace over against human will and obedience. For example, it is wrong to suppose that men can, of themselves, be saved without God's election and God's choosing. It is equally wrong to suppose that God will save people who do not seek Him and who do not repent. Just so, you may be sure that when the great revival at Pentecost came, it came because God's people worked with God's plan and paid God's price for the blessing that He intended to give. If God had planned ahead of time to give His power only on the precise date of Pentecost (which is nowhere declared in the Bible), then you may be sure that He laid a burden on these waiting disciples and made them willing to wait upon Him and call upon Him. The blessing came, therefore, of God's choice on the one hand, and because men pleaded and waited for it on the other. God never makes people have a revival who do not want one. God does not make a soul winner out of one who is not willing to be a soul winner. God does not fill with the Spirit those who do not seek to be filled with the Spirit.

II. Many Bible Christians Were Filled With the Spirit Because They Prayed

Fortunately, honest, seeking hearts do not have to quarrel about whether or not the promise that God will give the Holy Spirit to them that ask Him is for all ages. We have Bible examples, many of them, of people who prayed and, as a result of their prayers, were filled with the Holy Spirit. These examples range from Old Testament to the life of Christ and to Pentecost and then following Pentecost. They prove that the promise is for all ages. Those who want to be filled with the Spirit of God may do so if they earnestly prevail in prayer for this power.

1. Elisha Filled With the Spirit in Answer to Prayer

The second chapter of II Kings tells of the translation of Elijah and of how Elisha, the servant of the elder prophet, prayed and waited until he himself should have this same power of the Holy Spirit which rested upon Elijah. Any Christian may read it and meditate upon it with great blessing.

But first it is well to remember that Elijah was filled with the Holy Spirit in the New Testament fashion. This is clearly taught in Luke 1:15–17. There Zacharias was told that John the Baptist should "be filled with the Holy Ghost" and turn many of the children of Israel to the Lord their God. The term, "filled with the Holy Ghost," is the same term, exactly, as that used in Acts 2:4 about Pentecost. It is the same term as that used in Acts 4:31 about the disciples, and in Acts 9:17 about the Apostle Paul. It is almost exactly the same words as the command to us in Ephesians 5:18, "Be filled with the Spirit." But what John the Baptist had when he was "filled with the Holy Ghost" was exactly what Elijah had! For Luke 1:17, following, says, "And he shall go before him in the spirit and power of Elias...." John the Baptist, as the forerunner of Jesus, had upon him the Spirit and the power of Elijah. John, who turned many of the children of Israel to the Lord his God, as we are told, had this same Spirit and power that Elijah had! Elijah was filled with the Holy Spirit in the New Testament manner. He had the same power the disciples received at Pentecost. The same Bible term is used about it. With that in mind, let us study how Elisha too was filled with the power of God as Elijah was. Elisha in the Old Testament and John the Baptist in the New Testament were both filled with the Spirit after the pattern of Elijah.

Now read II Kings 2:1–15:

"And it came to pass, when the LORD would take up Elijah into heaven by a whirlwind, that Elijah went with Elisha from Gilgal. And Elijah said unto Elisha, Tarry here, I pray thee; for the LORD hath sent me to Beth-el. And Elisha said unto him, As the LORD liveth, and as thy soul liveth, I will not leave thee. So they went down to Beth-el. And the sons of the prophets that were at Beth-el came forth to Elisha, and said unto him, Knowest thou that the LORD will take away thy master from thy head to day? And he said, Yea, I know it; hold ye your peace. And Elijah said unto him, Elisha, tarry here, I pray thee; for the LORD hath sent me to Jericho. And he said, As the LORD liveth, and as thy soul liveth, I will not leave thee. So they came to Jericho. And the sons of the prophets that were at Jericho came to Elisha, and said unto him, Knowest thou that the LORD will take away thy master from thy head to day? And he answered, Yea, I know it; hold ye your peace. And Elijah said unto him, Tarry, I pray thee, here; for the LORD hath sent me to Jordan. And he said, As the LORD liveth, and as thy soul liveth, I will not leave thee. And they two went on. And fifty men of the sons of the prophets went, and stood to view afar off: and they two stood by Jordan. And Elijah took his mantle, and wrapped it together, and smote the waters, and they were divided hither and thither, so that they two went over on dry ground. And it came to pass, when they were gone over, that Elijah said unto Elisha, Ask what I shall do for thee, before I be taken away from thee. And Elisha said, I pray thee, let a double portion of thy spirit be upon me. And he said, Thou hast asked a hard thing; nevertheless, if thou see me when I am taken from thee, it shall be so unto thee; but if not, it shall not be so. And it came to pass, as they still went on, and talked, that, behold, there appeared a chariot of fire, and horses of fire, and parted them both asunder; and Elijah went up by a whirlwind into heaven. And Elisha saw it, and he cried, My father, my father, the chariot of Israel, and the horsemen thereof. And he saw him no more: and he took hold of his own clothes, and rent them in two pieces. He took up also the mantle of Elijah that fell from him, and went back, and stood by the bank of Jordan; And he took the mantle of Elijah that fell from him, and smote the waters, and said, Where is the LORD God of Elijah? and when he also had smitten the waters, they parted hither and thither: and Elisha went over. And when the sons of the prophets which were to view at Jericho saw him, they said, The spirit of Elijah doth rest on Elisha. And they came to meet him, and bowed themselves to the ground before him."

In this remarkable story note that:

(a) Elisha made his request in these words, "I pray thee, let a double portion of thy spirit be upon me." This prayer, though uttered to Elijah, was certainly a prayer to God. And God heard and answered.

(b) The persistence of Elisha in replying again and again, "As the LORD liveth, and as thy soul liveth, I will not leave thee," shows that he was determined and that he waited on God continually for this blessing—a double portion of the Spirit of God which rested on Elijah.

(c) Elisha got the blessing he requested. The mantle of Elijah was only a symbol of the mighty power of God which was upon him.

The miracle-working manifestation of the Holy Spirit came upon Elisha as it had been upon Elijah. Remember that the ministry gifts are simply the manifestation of the fullness of the Holy Spirit. And even the sons of the prophets said, "The spirit of Elijah doth rest on Elisha" (vs. 15). It is very, very significant that Elisha asked for "a double portion" of the Spirit that rested on Elijah, and that while we have eight recorded major miracles by Elijah, there are sixteen recorded major miracles by Elisha! The list is given in full in my book *Prayer—Asking and Receiving*.

Here we have a remarkable instance of the fullness of the Holy Spirit which came in answer to a man's prayer.

2. The Power of Pentecost Came in Answer to Prayer

Let us remind you again of Acts 1:14 which tells what brought the blessing of Pentecost: "These all continued with one accord in prayer and supplication, with the women, and Mary the mother of Jesus, and with his brethren."

3. After Pentecost This Same Group Prayed and Again "Were All Filled With the Holy Ghost"

Many people believe that up until Pentecost it was all right for Christians to pray for the fullness of the Spirit, but that after Pentecost, since all Christians have the Holy Spirit, it would be needless and out of order to pray for the Holy Spirit. However, the same group of disciples, and perhaps many of the new converts, prayed again after Pentecost, and again were filled with the Holy Spirit. This is recorded in Acts 4:31 as follows: "And when they had prayed, the place was shaken where they were assembled together; and they were all filled with the Holy Ghost, and they spake the word of God with boldness." It is important to notice that in Acts 2:4, speaking of the power which came at Pentecost, and in Acts 4:31, speaking of the blessing which came later to the same group, the same nine words are used. Check these nine words in the two verses: *"And they were all filled with the Holy Ghost."* Before Pentecost they prayed and were all filled with the Holy Ghost. After Pentecost they prayed again and were all filled with the Holy Ghost! So, beyond any peradventure of a doubt, after Pentecost was over and gone, it was still proper for people to pray and to be filled with the Holy Spirit as a result of prayer.

If you will study the prayer which brought the fullness of the Holy Spirit in Acts 4:31 you will see that Christians prayed, "And now, Lord...grant unto thy servants, that with all boldness they may speak thy word, By stretching forth thine hand to heal; and that signs and wonders may be done by the name of thy holy child Jesus" (vss. 29,30). The boldness they sought, the miracles and signs and wonders which they begged for, could come only as the ministry gifts, the manifestations of the fullness of the Holy Spirit. You may be sure that they knew for what they prayed. They prayed to be filled with the Holy Ghost, and they were filled with the Holy Ghost. They prayed for the same blessing that they had prayed for before Pentecost and received on that day. They prayed again and they received the same blessing. And so it is proper for Christians to pray for the power of the Holy Spirit since Pentecost.

4. Saul, Later Called Paul the Apostle, Was Filled With the Holy Spirit After Three Days of Fasting and Prayer

In the ninth chapter of Acts is the marvelous story of the conversion of Saul. He was on his road down to Damascus breathing out threatenings and slaughter, intending to seize Christians and to bring them bound, both men and women, to Jerusalem for trial and perhaps for stoning. But a light from Heaven shone round about him, and he fell to the earth and heard the voice of the Lord Jesus saying, "Saul, Saul, why persecutest thou me?" Then we are told, "And he said, Who art thou, Lord? And the Lord said, I am Jesus whom thou persecutest: it is hard for thee to kick against the pricks. And he trembling and astonished said, Lord, what wilt thou have me to do? And the Lord said unto him, Arise, and go into the city, and it shall be told thee what thou must do" (Acts 9:5,6).

Please consider carefully that Saul was here immediately converted. In fact, there are no conversions in the Bible which were gradual. There were no cases of people saved little by little, or saved any other way but instantly. In every case in the Bible inquirers were taught to put their trust in Christ and be saved. Saul had heard Stephen preach with great power, and we may be sure he had heard the Gospel plainly. Here Saul, with a penitent heart, down on his face, called Jesus "Lord," surrendered to Him and offered to do anything Jesus wanted him to do. He said, "Lord, what wilt thou have me to do?" This penitent man, who accepted Jesus as Saviour and Lord and surrendered his will to Him, here became a Christian. And it was here on the Damascus road that Paul was born again, "as of one born out of due time" (I Cor. 15:8). So Paul himself declared that he was born again when he saw Jesus. And now Paul the believer, the new convert, blinded, is led by the hand to Damascus.

But strangely enough, Paul "was three days without sight, and did neither eat nor drink." And when the Lord went to Ananias and told him to come to see Paul, he said, "Behold, he prayeth" (Acts 9:11). But Paul was fasting and praying for three days and nights after he found Christ! For what, do you suppose, did Paul pray? He was not praying for salvation—he already had that. He was not praying for the forgiveness of his sins. They were already forgiven. And when Ananias came to him, he said, "Brother Saul, the Lord, even Jesus, that appeared unto thee in the way as thou camest, hath sent me, that thou mightest receive thy sight, and be filled with the Holy Ghost" (Acts 9:17). Note that Ananias called Saul "Brother Saul." Paul was a brother Christian now. And note that Ananias did not say that the Lord had sent him "that thou mightest be saved." No, no, Paul was already saved. Ananias was sent to this Christian brother that Paul might receive his sight "and be filled with the Holy Ghost."

I know that Paul was praying to be filled with the Holy Spirit because that is what he got. Let me illustrate it by the following simple story.

Once in Dallas, Texas, I sat in my study on the second floor of the Galilean Baptist Church. Across the street men were painting a house. Under the hackberry trees that grew outside my window I could see the lawn and the first story of the house. The upper story was hidden by the leafy branches. But I saw a man come around from the back of the house and stand by the front porch and lift his face and his hands as if he were in prayer. He looked up, though I could not see that which he saw. He spoke, but I could not hear his words. Suddenly from above I saw a ladder descend. He seized it with his hands, laid it on his shoulders and, turning, walked around the house and out of sight. The man asked an unseen person for something; I could not hear him, but I know what he said. To the man on top of the front porch he said, "Hand me down the ladder, Bill!" I know that is what he said because he took the ladder and went on his way satisfied. He got that which he requested.

Just so, I am sure that Paul, during those three days and nights when he fasted and prayed, was pleading for the power of the Holy Spirit. He had been convicted under the mighty preaching of Spirit-filled Stephen. He had seen Stephen stoned to death, but with a face like an angel's, and Stephen's message had pricked his heart ever since. Paul wanted to be like Stephen—filled with the Holy Ghost! And he waited on God until he got the blessing he sought. Then straightway he arose and was baptized and began to preach Christ!

Paul, then, is another example of one this side of Pentecost who prayed to be filled with the Holy Spirit and was filled, in answer to prayer. In answer to earnest prevailing prayer, Paul was endued with power from on high, baptized with the Holy Ghost.

5. Paul and Barnabas Filled With the Holy Ghost for Missionary Journeys in Answer to Prayer

It is interesting that the people who were filled with the Holy Spirit at Pentecost were filled again with the Holy Spirit the same way, when they prayed again, as recorded in Acts 4:31. Just so, we are pleased to find that Paul himself was filled with the Holy Spirit afresh on another occasion, in answer to prayer. The story is told in Acts 13:1–4, as follows:

"Now there were in the church that was at Antioch certain prophets and teachers; as Barnabas, and Simeon that was called Niger, and Lucius of Cyrene, and Manaen, which had been brought up with Herod the tetrarch, and Saul. As they ministered to the Lord, and fasted, the Holy Ghost said, Separate me Barnabas and Saul for the work whereunto I have called them. And when they had fasted and prayed, and laid their hands on them, they sent them away. So they, being sent forth by the Holy Ghost, departed unto Seleucia; and from thence they sailed to Cyprus."

An earnest prayer meeting was going on in the church at Antioch. Barnabas, Simeon called Niger, Lucius of Cyrene, Manaen, and the young preacher Paul were present. They "ministered to the Lord, and fasted." The Holy Spirit had His blessed freedom and spoke to them, saying, "Separate me Barnabas and Saul for the work whereunto I have called them." Is it strange that Barnabas and Saul did not immediately set out on their missionary journeys? If they had done so, they would not have been following the example of the first eleven disciples, when they were given the Great Commission. Those eleven were commanded to tarry at Jerusalem until they were endued with power from on high. So Paul and Barnabas, called to the great missionary journeys, yet stayed and fasted and prayed. "And when they had fasted and prayed, and laid their hands on them, they sent them away." We do not know how long the prayer meeting continued after they had instructions from God, but it was long enough to involve fasting, the missing of meals and perhaps the missing of sleep. Then they sent them away.

Or rather, the Holy Spirit sent them away. "So they, being sent forth by the Holy Ghost, departed unto Seleucia." The Holy Spirit had filled Paul and Barnabas afresh. For this is the same kind of language as was used about the Lord Jesus after He was filled with the Holy Spirit. Luke 4:1 says, "And Jesus being full of the Holy Ghost returned from Jordan, and was led by the Spirit into the wilderness." The same Holy Spirit, now filling Paul and Barnabas afresh, led them out or thrust them out on the missionary journey.

As they went on their journey we find that they came to Paphos and found a false prophet, and Acts 13:9 tells us, "Then Saul, (who also is called Paul,) filled with the Holy Ghost, set his eyes on him, And said,…"

Now surely Bible-believing Christians must be impressed with the fact that this fullness of the Spirit came upon Paul and Barnabas because they ministered to the Lord and fasted, and again when they had instructions from God still they fasted and prayed.

It is clear, then, that this side of Pentecost, just as on the other side of Pentecost, people have a right to ask for the fullness of the Spirit and that He comes in the power of Pentecost in answer to prevailing prayer.

6. Cornelius and His Household Were Filled With the Holy Spirit in Answer to Prayer

A remarkable case is that of Cornelius, the Roman centurion of the Italian band, who was filled with the Holy Spirit as soon as he was saved. Why, do you suppose, was he filled with the Holy Spirit without a season of waiting on God in prayer, after he was saved?

The answer is quite clear, I think, if one reads carefully the whole story of Cornelius. In Acts 10:2 we are told that he was "a devout man, and one that feared God with all his house, which gave much alms to the people, *and prayed to God alway*." Even before he was saved, Cornelius prayed all the time. His heart was crying out to God.

Although God had not revealed to Cornelius the way to be saved, but chose to use His own blessed plan of having the Gospel proclaimed by redeemed sinners instead of by angels, yet Cornelius continued to fast and pray. Cornelius told Peter, as recorded in Acts 10:30,31, "Four days ago I was fasting until this hour; and at the ninth hour I prayed in my house, and, behold, a man stood before me in bright clothing, And said, Cornelius, thy prayer is heard, and thine alms are had in remembrance in the sight of God."

Cornelius said, "I was fasting until this hour; and at the ninth hour I prayed in my house." Cornelius had been fasting and praying all day, till three o'clock in the afternoon, having had neither breakfast nor lunch. How earnestly this Gentile man sought God! How his heart turned from his sins and longed to know how to be saved! Surely he considered his own waywardness and folly and whether or not he was willing to surrender his will to God and do the will of God. The whole matter of righteousness and pleasing God and complete surrender was gone over in his mind, no doubt. And the angel said then to Cornelius, 'Thy prayer is heard!'

You and I know that it does not take days of prayer for one to be saved. Throughout the Bible the promise is everywhere the same. The one who comes to Christ even the first time is never cast out. One who believes in Christ has instantly everlasting life. There is nothing in the Bible to encourage anybody to go one full minute without settling with Christ once and forever the matter of salvation. One who receives Christ then *has* everlasting life. So say the Scriptures again and again. But God had planned it that at the name of Jesus men shall bow. He had planned it that only by personal faith in Christ are people to be saved; not by good resolves, not by surrender of the will, not by righteous deeds and giving alms. All these things Cornelius did, and did them with all of his heart—not as a Pharisee, but with a heart that longed to know God and please God. Therefore, of course the moment that he heard the plan of salvation he trusted Christ and was saved. As soon as Peter had said that "whosoever believeth in him shall receive remission of sins" (Acts 10:43), Cornelius trusted the Lord and was saved. But now that Cornelius is saved, he has also met the necessary conditions for the fullness of the Holy Spirit. He has already been seeking God. He has already had his heart searched. He is already glad to do the perfect will of the Father and so is filled with the Holy Spirit. I think that we may properly say that all the heart-searching and prayer and pleading that had gone before had fitted him now to make a complete decision and to trust the Lord for the fullness of the Holy Spirit. We must say that the fullness of the Holy Spirit in this case was given in answer to prayer. It is an unusual case in that the fullness of the

Spirit came immediately at his regeneration. But we must say that the power of the Holy Spirit came in answer to the cry of his earnest, pleading heart.

Some people today do not know how to trust simply in Christ because they have not been enlightened by the Bible. I have known such people to spend days and nights in earnest, heart-searching prayer, pleading with the Lord for salvation. I have known them during this period of mourning and conviction and praying to give up every known sin, to try to find and do the will of God about every detail of their lives. You and I know that these good thoughts and good words and good deeds and good resolutions do not save a soul. But the prayers and tears and repentings that go in such a time certainly do fit one to do the will of God. I have known a good many such cases when such people who finally learned God's simple plan of salvation by penitent faith were wonderfully filled with the Holy Spirit at the same time as their conversion. I have known such people to become instantly active and powerful soul winners.

In fact, Charles G. Finney's conversion and his baptism of the Holy Spirit (for that is what he called it) came at about the same time. Almost immediately when he was assured of salvation, he was filled with the Holy Spirit, in mighty soul-winning power. But no reader of Finney's autobiography can avoid the conclusion that the fullness of the Holy Spirit came after most earnest and brokenhearted prayer.

Cornelius and his household are simply another example of people, long after Pentecost, being filled with the Holy Spirit as a result of prayer.

Surely you must be impressed with the case of Christians in Acts 4:31; of Paul in Acts, chapter 9; of Paul and Barnabas again in Acts, chapter 13; and of Cornelius in Acts, chapter 10, all of whom were filled with the Holy Spirit in answer to their prayers, all after Pentecost.

III. The Bible Gives Us Clear Examples of Some Filled With the Holy Spirit Because of the Prayers of Others

It is not surprising that some people are filled with the Holy Spirit largely as a result of the prayers of others. When we pray for a revival and the revival comes, we may be sure that some are blessed, not only because of their own prayers, but largely because of the prayers of others. My mother gave me to God when I was born. She prayed for God to make me a preacher and called me her "preacher boy." She died before I was six years old. Yet I am certain in my heart that much of the blessing of God on my ministry could be traced back to the prayers of my mother that I would be a Spirit-filled, soul-winning preacher.

1. Consider the Case at Pentecost When "They Were All Filled With the Holy Ghost..."

Do you suppose that every one of the Christians who were filled with the Holy Spirit at Pentecost just accidentally happened to get the thing prayed through and settled at the same time? No, we must be impressed with the fact that they were all with one accord in one place and that they were all filled with the Holy Spirit at one time, because God heard their *united* prayers. The united prayers of these Christians, that *all* of them might be filled with the Holy Spirit, were answered. Each one, then, could properly believe that he was filled with the Holy Spirit partly as a result of the prayers of others. Oh, how the churches today ought to learn united praying for the coming of the Holy Spirit upon the pastor and all of the members!

It was such a prayer meeting, I think, at Herrnhut, in Austria, on August 13, 1727, when the Holy Spirit was poured out in great power upon Count Zinzendorf and the Moravian congregation, so that, fifty years before the beginning of modern foreign missions by William Carey, the Moravian church led the way in mission work in pagan countries. As a result of united prayer, God often sends the fullness of the Spirit upon many, some of whom are filled partly because of the prayers of others.

2. New Converts in Samaria Were Filled With the Holy Ghost When Peter and John Prayed for Them

When persecution arose in the thriving church at Jerusalem, after Pentecost, Deacon Philip went down to the city of Samaria and preached Christ to them. Great numbers were saved. God's mighty power was manifest in Philip, "and there was great joy in that city" (Acts 8:3–8). Again an interesting passage tells us how the apostles heard of this revival and sent Peter and John to pray for the new converts that they might be filled with the Holy Spirit.

"Now when the apostles which were at Jerusalem heard that Samaria had received the word of God, they sent unto them Peter and John: Who, when they were come down, prayed for them, that they might receive the Holy Ghost: (For as yet he was fallen upon none of them: only they were baptized in the name of the Lord Jesus.) Then laid they their hands on them, and they received the Holy Ghost."— Acts 8:14–17.

Some have foolishly made a rule here where God makes none. I think that God wanted the people to look up to the apostles and listen to their guiding counsel until the New Testament should be written. So He gave Peter and John the privilege of coming down and setting the apostolic seal somewhat on the revival efforts of Philip the deacon and of seeing these new converts filled with the Holy Spirit. These converts had already believed, and they were already baptized in the name of the Lord Jesus. Peter and John, "when they were come down, prayed for them, that they might receive the Holy Ghost." The apostles laid their hands on these new converts even as one might lay his hand on a sick person in praying for his recovery, or on the head of a sinner while praying for his salvation, or as we who are on ordaining councils and presbyteries lay our hands on the heads of young ministers when they are ordained to the ministry, while we pray God to fill them with the Holy Spirit. And these converts, when Peter and John had prayed for them, received the Holy Ghost—that is, the Holy Ghost fell on them, even as He was poured out at Pentecost upon the disciples in Jerusalem. They were filled with the Holy Spirit, endued with power from on high. And this was an answer to the prayer of others.

I do not suppose that these new converts did not pray for themselves. We take it for granted that they longed to be filled with the Spirit and that their own prayers were mingled with those of the apostles, Peter and John. God answered the united praying and filled them with the Spirit.

It is important to notice that this was since Pentecost and was certainly clearly in the present dispensation and a proper model today for Christians. We should pray and be filled with the Spirit, and we should pray for others that they may be filled with the Spirit.

3. John the Baptist Seems to Have Been Filled With the Holy Spirit in Answer to the Prayers of His Father and Mother

It was said of John the Baptist, "and he shall be filled with the Holy Ghost, even from his mother's womb." Later in life, after John had come to see himself a sinner and trusted Christ, we may be sure that he joined his own prayers to those of his father and mother. But in his babyhood he was filled with the Holy Spirit. He was filled with the Holy Spirit before he had prayed, but his parents had prayed earnestly and long. Doubtless in answer to their prayers, John was filled with the Holy Spirit.

In Luke 1:13 we are told how the angel came to announce to

Zacharias the coming birth of his son: "But the angel said unto him, Fear not, Zacharias: for thy prayer is heard; and thy wife Elisabeth shall bear thee a son, and thou shalt call his name John." Then the angel continued to tell the great joy and gladness that would come, because John would be great in the sight of the Lord and should drink neither wine nor strong drink and should be filled with the Holy Spirit, even from his mother's womb, and would turn many to God (Luke 1:13–17). The angel evidently was going over the very things for which Zacharias and Elisabeth had prayed. They had prayed for a son. They had prayed for many years, for verse 7 tells us that "they both were now well stricken in years." They had prayed for a son who would bring great joy to them because he would be great in the sight of the Lord. They had prayed for a son who would never drink, a son who would be filled with the Holy Ghost, a son who would be a soul winner, a son who would go before the Lord Jesus in the spirit and power of Elijah! The angel recounted each point to Zacharias as a part of the message, "Thy prayer is heard"! That prayer was not just for a son but for the kind of son that John the Baptist turned out to be, a son filled with the Spirit of God, a forerunner of the Saviour, a great soul winner.

We must surely believe that John was the kind of preacher that he was, a Spirit-filled, soul-winning preacher, because of the prayers of Zacharias and Elisabeth.

I am quite certain that John, when he saw himself a sinner and repented and then consciously put his trust in the coming Messiah and set out to live for God, earnestly prayed to be filled with the Holy Spirit. Yet Zacharias and Elisabeth had prayed before John prayed, and their prayer was already partly answered before John himself ever learned to pray. Mothers and fathers should pray for their children. They should pray that God would give them boys to be preachers, girls to be soul winners. They should pray that God would fill their children with the Holy Spirit and mighty power. Such prayers are heard, thank God! Samuel was the mighty Spirit-filled prophet of God which he was largely because of the prayers of Hannah. Many a preacher, greatly used of God, has learned that his mother gave him to God in babyhood and for long years besought God to use him in the ministry.

4. Paul the Apostle Earnestly Prayed for Others to Be Filled With the Holy Spirit

You do not believe in praying for the fullness of the Spirit, you say? How different you are, then, from the Apostle Paul! For in his letter to the church at Ephesus, Paul reminded them that he was praying for them to be filled with the Spirit.

The first mention of this constant prayer of Paul is in Ephesians 1:15–19, as follows:

"Wherefore I also, after I heard of your faith in the Lord Jesus, and love unto all the saints, Cease not to give thanks for you, making mention of you in my prayers; That the God of our Lord Jesus Christ, the Father of glory, may give unto you the spirit of wisdom and revelation in the knowledge of him: The eyes of your understanding being enlightened; that ye may know what is the hope of his calling, and what the riches of the glory of his inheritance in the saints, And what is the exceeding greatness of his power to us-ward who believe, according to the working of his mighty power."

Paul continually gave thanks for the Ephesians, making mention of them in his prayers, that God would give unto them "the spirit of wisdom and revelation in the knowledge of him" and that they might know "what is the exceeding greatness of his power to us-ward who believe, according to the working of his mighty power." He was praying for them to know the fullness of God's power and to have the spirit of wisdom and revelation. The word "spirit" in verse 17 is spelled with a small letter by the translators, but it evidently refers to the Holy Spirit. Verses 19 and 20 make it clear that this mighty power of God is the power of the Holy Spirit "which he wrought in Christ, when he raised him from the dead." Paul prayed for the people at Ephesus to be filled with the Holy Spirit.

Again this earnest and continual prayer of Paul for the Ephesians to be filled with the Spirit is mentioned in the third chapter. In verse 14 Paul tells them that he bows his knees unto the Father in prayer, and verses 16 to 19 tell us the things for which Paul pleaded for them:

"That he would grant you, according to the riches of his glory, to be strengthened with might by his Spirit in the inner man; That Christ may dwell in your hearts by faith; that ye, being rooted and grounded in love, May be able to comprehend with all saints what is the breadth, and length, and depth, and height; And to know the love of Christ, which passeth knowledge, that ye might be filled with all the fulness of God."—Eph. 3:16–19.

Paul prayed that they might "be strengthened with might [or power] by his Spirit in the inner man." He prayed "that ye might be filled with all the fulness of God." The fullness of God is the fullness of the Holy Spirit. He prayed that they might have the power of the Holy Spirit in the inner man and be filled with all the fullness of God.

Paul plainly told these Ephesians twice in the same letter that it was his constant prayer for them that they should have the might of the

Holy Spirit and be filled with His fullness. Oh, how we preachers ought to pray for our people that they might be filled with the Holy Spirit!

You can see, then, that it is right and proper for all Christians to pray to be filled with the Spirit and to pray for others that they too might be filled with all the fullness of God, the enduement of power from on high. It is right that we should pray to have the power of Pentecost for ourselves and that others may have the same mighty power.

There is more to be said on this subject. But before we close this chapter, let me plead with you to have it forever settled that you have a right to beg God for His power and that you may pray to be filled with the Holy Spirit, or, if you prefer the term, that you may be baptized (overwhelmed, surrounded and covered) with the Spirit of God, so you may be a soul winner, that you may witness with power. So the promise that the heavenly Father will give the Holy Spirit to them that ask Him is for this dispensation as well as others. The many, many examples in the Bible prove that Christians have a right to pray to be filled with the Holy Spirit.

IV. Many, Many Promises of Answers to Prayer Surely Cover the Matter of Praying for the Holy Spirit's Fullness

Jesus did promise the Holy Spirit to them who asked the Father. Jesus did plainly command the disciples to tarry in Jerusalem until they should be endued with power from on high. The disciples surely did understand that the command with a promise involved prayer, for they continued steadfastly in prayer and supplication until the power of Pentecost came upon them. We certainly do have many, many clear Bible instances of people who prayed and were filled with the Holy Spirit long after Pentecost. But if there were not a single verse in the Bible that specifically promised the power of the Holy Spirit in answer to prayer, I would still be compelled to believe that God must give His power to those who seek it and plead for it with all of their hearts; for many, many Scriptures clearly promise anything that is asked for in Jesus' name, or in faith, or according to God's will. And such promises clearly cover the matter of Holy Spirit power.

This is true in Mark 11:24 where Jesus said, "What things soever ye desire, when ye pray, believe that ye receive them, and ye shall have them." Here is a promise that anything people pray for in faith they may have. To be sure, God gives faith only for right and proper things. But it is certainly right and proper for Christians who want to do God's will to have God's power. And if there were no other promises in the Bible, Mark 11:24 promises me that I may have the fullness of the Holy Spirit when I ask, if I believe and do not doubt.

Consider John 14:13,14: "Whatsoever ye shall ask in my name, that will I do, that the Father may be glorified in the Son. If ye shall ask any thing in my name, I will do it."

Here is a promise that is for "whatsoever," just so we ask it in Jesus' name. I once put the name of a lost, rebellious young woman in place of the word "whatsoever" in verse 13, and instead of the words "any-thing" in verse 14; I claimed the promise, and God answered. "Any thing" means "anything." "Whatsoever" means "whatsoever." I have a right to read John 14:14 as follows: 'If ye shall ask the fullness of the Spirit in My name, I will do it.' If I realize that soul winning can be done only in the power of God; if I realize that poor doomed souls will burn forever in Hell unless somebody rescues them, and that the only way I can win them is to have the power of God; if I earnestly claim this promise and do it in Jesus' name, I certainly may have the power of the Holy Spirit upon me. You see, if there were no other promises in the Bible on this question, all these promises that we may have what-ever we desire when it is in Jesus' name, or when we pray in faith, or when we pray according to His will, are enough to justify our praying for the power of the Holy Spirit.

Consider another Scripture. First John 3:21,22 says: "Beloved, if our heart condemn us not, then have we confidence toward God. And whatsoever we ask, we receive of him, because we keep his command-ments, and do those things that are pleasing in his sight." If my heart, when lifted up to God in prayer, does not find any of His displeasure upon me, and I know that I am praying in His will and keeping His Word in this matter, then, says the Scripture, whatsoever I ask I receive of Him. I believe that this might mean daily bread. It has meant that to me many a time. I believe it might mean money for God's cause. Many and many a time this promise and like promises have meant help for the Lord's work when I prayed. But certainly it could mean and does mean that I may ask for supernatural enduement of power—the anointing, or baptism, or the fullness, or pouring out of the Holy Spirit upon me, to do the work He has commanded me to do. I have a right to pray for that. Many, many Scriptures authorize me to pray for what-ever God gives me faith for, or whatever is according to His will, or whatever I can ask in His name.

There is a general doctrine throughout the Bible that a Christian has a right to pray for anything which will honor God, anything that he needs for Christ's service, anything that God reveals to him is in the will of God. Such promises authorize a Christian to pray for the fullness of the Holy Spirit, even if there were not a single promise in the Bible which particularly offered us the power of the Holy Spirit in answer to prayer.

But certain particular promises *necessarily* involve the power of the Holy Spirit. In II Chronicles 7:14 God makes this sweet offer:

"If my people, which are called by my name, shall humble themselves, and pray, and seek my face, and turn from their wicked ways; then will I hear from heaven, and will forgive their sin, and will heal their land."

Down through the ages God's saints have regarded this as a promise of revival, of a moving of God's Spirit upon His people, for the convicting and saving of sinners and the healing of the spiritual ills of the land, as well as the material ills. If this is a promise for revival, then it is a promise of the fullness of the Holy Spirit, for God can send revival only through the work of His blessed Spirit. God can convict and save sinners only through the work of His blessed Spirit. When God invites us to pray for revival, therefore, He invites us to pray for the fullness of the Holy Spirit.

I would be gentle here. I would not willingly cause a moment of grief to any Christian brother who differs with me. And yet I feel that some good men have robbed God's people of their heritage, have unwittingly aided apostasy, have unwittingly hindered revival by teaching people that they are not to pray for that for which Jesus encouraged us to pray. And we ought to be careful in instructing people to give them scriptural instruction. Certainly we ought to avoid as far as possible fanaticism and confusion. But wildfire is better than no fire. The loud cries, the inconvenience and some disorder brought by a new baby in the house are better than barren wombs and empty arms and cold hearts. Oh, may God give us a revival and conviction and souls saved and the blessing and power of God upon His people, at whatever cost! Oh, how dearly some of us must pay if we discourage God's people from seeking the power of the Holy Ghost to do the will of God!

Chapter 12

Why Prevailing, Persistent Praying Is Necessary for Holy Spirit Power

"...*But tarry ye in the city of Jerusalem, until ye be endued with power from on high.*"—Luke 24:49.

"*These all continued with one accord in prayer and supplication, with the women, and Mary the mother of Jesus, and with his brethren.*"—Acts 1:14.

The Saviour commanded the disciples to "tarry...in the city of Jerusalem" until they should be endued with power from on high. Following that plain command the disciples, along with Mary the mother of Jesus, His half brothers and some others, "continued with one accord in prayer and supplication" in the Upper Room. To be filled with the Holy Spirit, in the case of these disciples, required long waiting on God, ten days of tarrying, which included prayer and probably included fasting.

Many questions come to our minds as we think about the command of Jesus and the earnest waiting and pleading in prayer which the disciples found necessary before they received the power of Pentecost, being filled with the Holy Spirit. Why did it take so long? Is it necessary now for Christians to wait on God and continue for long seasons in prayer before they are filled with the Holy Spirit in soul-winning power? Why would so much time be necessary? Is not God ready to fill anyone who honestly wants to be filled with the Spirit? In this chapter we will seek to answer such questions plainly from the Word of God.

We will show by the Word of God that long, continued prayer is often necessary to get other things from God, not only the fullness of the Spirit. We will show why the time element in persistent prayer is often necessary. We will show that Bible Christians often waited long before God to be filled with the Holy Spirit.

In a preceding chapter it was made clear that prayer is a condition of Holy Spirit power. Jesus in Luke 11:13 expressly said, "...how much more shall your heavenly Father give the Holy Spirit to them that ask him?" And the context clearly shows that Jesus was talking about power to take the bread of life to sinners, soul-winning power. Jesus prayed, standing in the baptismal waters, and was filled with the Holy

Spirit. We showed that Elisha continued in persistent prayer to have upon him a double portion of the Holy Spirit which was upon Elijah (II Kings 2:1–15). We showed that the one hundred and twenty waited in the Upper Room for ten days with prayer and supplication to be endued with power from on high (Acts 1:14). In Acts 4:31 the disciples prayed again and were filled with the Spirit again. Saul, later called Paul the apostle, was filled with the Holy Spirit after three days of prayer, and Paul and Barnabas were filled anew with the Holy Spirit for their missionary journeys after fasting and prayer (Acts 9:1–17; Acts 13:1–4). Cornelius and the Christians at Samaria were filled with the Holy Spirit as recorded in the eighth and tenth chapters of Acts.

It is obvious that prayer is a condition of the fullness of the Holy Spirit. But now we consider why persistent prayer, prevailing prayer, including long periods of waiting on God and pleading, is sometimes necessary to meet God's requirements for the fullness of the Holy Spirit.

I. Persistent Supplication Often Necessary in Successful Prayer for Anything

"Tarrying meetings" have fallen into disrepute in many quarters because often they are associated with doctrinal heresies like speaking in tongues or claims of sinless perfection or other fanaticism. So good Christians, anxious to avoid fanaticism, often frown on any teaching that people ought to wait on God and continue in prayer for the fullness of the Holy Spirit.

However, this objection is instantly answered when one calls to mind the clear teaching throughout the Bible that continued seasons of prayer and long waiting on God in prayer are often necessary when praying for anything else.

1. Five Commands to Pray Constantly

I call to mind five plain commands of the Scripture that Christians are to pray all the time. They are:

"And he spake a parable unto them to this end, that men ought always to pray, and not to faint."—Luke 18:1.

"Pray without ceasing."—I Thess. 5:17.

"Continuing instant in prayer."—Rom. 12:12.

"Continue in prayer, and watch in the same with thanksgiving."—Col. 4:2.

"Praying always with all prayer and supplication in the Spirit, and watching *thereunto with all perseverance and supplication for all saints."*—Eph. 6:18.

It is obvious that in the very nature of the case God intends for Christians to pray again and again, literally to pray all the time. Why should anyone feel, then, that it would be out of place to pray persistently, continually, for soul-winning power, pray with earnest burden and heart searching and pleading and tears, until one should be filled with the Holy Spirit and be enabled to follow the plain command of Christ in soul winning?

2. Terms Used About Prayer Necessarily Involve Continued Pleading

"Supplication" is a term often used in the Scripture for continued, importunate prayer. That is the word used in Acts 1:14 about the disciples who with one accord continued "in prayer and supplication." Christians are commanded to be "praying always with all prayer and supplication." We are commanded, "Be careful for nothing; but in every thing by prayer and supplication with thanksgiving let your requests be made known unto God" (Phil. 4:6). The very word "supplication" involves continued prayer. Don't you see that it is proper and normal for Christians to have long seasons of earnest prayer about anything they need from God?"

Many other terms are used about prayer to show that we should continue in prayer for any burden that is on our hearts, for any serious need yet unfulfilled. For example, in II Chronicles 7:14 is the blessed promise: "If my people, which are called by my name, shall humble themselves, and pray, and *seek my face,* and turn from their wicked ways; then will I hear from heaven, and will forgive their sin, and will heal their land." The words "seek my face" here evidently mean continued prayer, waiting on God, earnestly seeking God's face. It necessarily involves the time element. So anyone who prays for revival should wait on God and continue in prayer and pleading.

In fact, the very word "prayer" itself as used in our Bible often means continued asking. An example is given in Matthew 7:7,8 where Jesus said: "Ask, and it shall be given you; seek, and ye shall find; knock, and it shall be opened unto you: For every one that asketh receiveth; and he that seeketh findeth; and to him that knocketh it shall be opened."

Now is it true that "every one that asketh receiveth"? Well, if you make the word *ask* here mean to ask only one time, then it would not be true. Millions of people can testify that they asked one time for something and never did receive it. That statement of Jesus, "Ask, and it shall be given you," would not be true. The statement, "For every one that asketh receiveth," would not be true if Jesus meant simply to pray one time.

But is that what Jesus meant? If He had meant that everyone who asks one time receives, then He would have used the *aorist* tense in Greek which means simply that. But He did not! Jesus used the *present* tense. The words *ask, seek* and *knock* in verse 7 are present imperative. The verbs *asketh* and *seeketh* and *knocketh* in verse 8 are present. In each case they mean continued action. One who keeps on asking receives. One who keeps on seeking finds. One who keeps on knocking has the door opened to him!

The same lesson is clear in James 4:2 where we are told, "Ye have not, because ye ask not." In these verses prayer means continued asking, persistent praying.

3. Jesus Pleaded With His Disciples to Continue Always in Persistent Prayer and Not to Faint!

How clear is the teaching of the dear Lord Jesus on this matter. Note that precious parable that Jesus spake "to this end, that men ought always to pray, and not to faint":

"Saying, There was in a city a judge, which feared not God, neither regarded man: And there was a widow in that city; and she came unto him, saying, Avenge me of mine adversary. And he would not for a while: but afterward he said within himself, Though I fear not God, nor regard man; Yet because this widow troubleth me, I will avenge her, lest by her continual coming she weary me. And the Lord said, Hear what the unjust judge saith. And shall not God avenge his own elect, which cry day and night unto him, though he bear long with them? I tell you that he will avenge them speedily. Nevertheless when the Son of man cometh, shall he find faith on the earth?"—Luke 18:2–8.

Here is the clear teaching of Jesus Christ. People ought to keep on praying, pray without ceasing, on any matter of earnest burden, and never give up! They ought to "cry day and night unto him, though he bear long with them." If God seems not to answer, then a Christian should still plead with God and wait on Him like that poor widow who so wore out the unjust judge that he, in despair for his peace of mind, heard her cry and gave her justice!

And then in the closing word of application in Luke 18:8 Jesus speaks rather sadly, saying, "Nevertheless when the Son of man cometh, shall he find faith on the earth?" He evidently means, Will the

Son of Man find *that kind* of faith, the kind of faith that cries day and night to God and will not give up! Oh, how we sin not to keep on praying!

In Luke 11:8 Jesus was teaching particularly the matter of praying for the Holy Spirit, as you see from verse 13 just below. But here Jesus states a principle of successful prayer. The friend within who had plenty of loaves did not instantly rise and give bread to the one who knocked at his door. Jesus said: "I say unto you, Though he will not rise and give him, because he is his friend, yet because of his *importunity* he will rise and give him as many as he needeth." Here we see that *importunity*—pleading, begging, persistent, prevailing prayer—pleases God very much and is the very greatest essential to effectual prayer!

In view of all these teachings, how normal it is, how sensible it obviously is for those who want the fullness of God, want the abundant power of the Holy Spirit, want the enduement of power from on high for soul winning, to wait on God until they have that fullness, that anointing, that enduement of power from on high!

4. Bible Examples of Persistent, Prevailing Prayer

Consider the examples of prevailing prayer, people who waited on God, who begged, who would not give up; there are such examples throughout the Bible.

There was Jacob who met the angel of God and wrestled all the night long and said, "I will not let thee go, except thou bless me"! (Gen. 32:26).

There was Nehemiah who prayed to God "day and night" for the restoration of Jerusalem (Neh. 1:6).

There was Elijah, who after the great victory on Mount Carmel went and "cast himself down upon the earth, and put his face between his knees" and prayed and prayed and sent his servant seven different times to look toward the sea and seek the rain clouds. And at last a cloud the size of a man's hand arose, and Elijah knew his prayer was answered. And a great rain came from Heaven on the ground which had known no rain or dew for three and a half years! (I Kings 18:42–45).

There was Samuel who "cried unto the LORD all night" (I Sam. 15:11).

There was Daniel who set his face unto the Lord God "to seek by prayer and supplications, with fasting, and sackcloth, and ashes" (Dan. 9:3).

And time would fail to tell of Ezra, or Esther and Mordecai, and of all in Bible times who waited on God with heartbroken, persistent praying, until the answer came.

We must not forget that the dear Lord Jesus Himself, our perfect example, "went out into a mountain to pray, and continued all night in prayer to God" (Luke 6:12).

And how joyfully the Saviour praised the Syrophenician woman, the woman of Canaan who kept following Him when she was rebuked, still pleading for her daughter, grievously vexed with a devil. When Jesus apparently insulted her, she kept on praying. When the disciples would have sent her away, she kept pleading. She argued with the Master! "Then Jesus answered and said unto her, O woman, great is thy faith: be it unto thee even as thou wilt" (Matt. 15:28). And her daughter, that very hour, was made well! You see, continued prayer is here given as a synonym and sign of faith, and it pleases the Lord very greatly.

Anything we have a right to pray about, we have a right to *keep on praying about* until we either learn that the prayer is against the will of God or until we receive our request. Anything we have a right to pray about we have a right to keep on praying about.

Do not think that one needs to be earnest and persistent in prayer only for the fullness of the Spirit. One ought to be persistent and earnest in prayer for wisdom, for revival, for conversion of sinners, for daily supplies, for anything we need. And in view of the clear teaching of the Word of God about the need for persistent prayer—believing, long-continued waiting on God and seeking God's face—it is easy to see that God would often require the same kind of praying for the fullness of the Spirit.

II. Why the Time Element in Persistent Prayer Is Often Necessary

We have seen that persistence in prayer is one of the most important elements in prevailing prayer. In other words, it is obviously clear that God often demands a considerable time spent in prayer before the answer is given. Now can we find the reason why God so often requires us to keep on praying before the answer comes? I think we can.

1. First, Pleasing God Always Costs Heavily. So Successful Prayer Must Often Take Time

Time is, in some sense, the most valuable thing in the world. A man may be a multimillionaire, but he still has only twenty-four hours a day.

All the money, all the skill, all the learning and wisdom in the world, all the political influence cannot add one second to the time allotted to a certain man. Time, like diamonds, is precious because of its scarcity. A man may give away money without affecting his life a particle. Some men can give away a million dollars and have just as much to eat, just as many fine clothes, just as nice a car. But no one can give time without giving of his very life and altering his plans. Everyone who gives times gives up other things he would do in that time. So God demands that people take time to serve Him. "Take time to be holy," the old hymn pleads; and you may be sure that nobody can ever be holy who does not take time to seek God, take time to meditate on God's Word, take time to abide in Christ and find His will and feel His presence. How many people would like to feel, when they pay the preacher or give to missions, that they then owe God none of their time! I have sometimes heard preachers foolishly say about soul winning, "If you cannot go, you can give." I solemnly warn every reader that giving is no substitute for going. There is no way to please God without giving Him of your time—that is, of your very life itself.

Do you remember how King David answered when Araunah offered to give him freely the threshing floor for the building of an altar, the oxen for sacrifices and the threshing instruments for wood, that the plague on Israel might be stayed? In II Samuel 24:24 is David's reply:

"And the king said unto Araunah, Nay; but I will surely buy it of thee at a price: neither will I offer burnt-offerings unto the LORD my God of that which doth cost me nothing. So David bought the threshingfloor and the oxen for fifty shekels of silver."

Oh, if every Christian would only make the vow that David made: "Neither will I offer...unto the LORD my God of that which doth cost me nothing"!

A high school student wrote to me and said:

"Dear Brother Rice: I read the SWORD OF THE LORD and am greatly helped by your sermons and your counsel to young people. Please write and tell me how to be the best Christian possible, the best soul winner. I want to do everything for Jesus that I can. But please tell me how to do it without being thought queer or losing any friends. I have many friends in high school, and I do not want them to think me fanatical."

I wrote the dear young woman and told her that she could not have her cake and eat it too, that she could not please God and please the world. And no one can serve God acceptably who does not expect it to cost and cost and cost!

Someone wants to be a wonderful soul winner without paying any price! You would like to be a wonderful soul winner without any self-examination, without any waiting on God, without any tears of penitence! You would want to have the mighty fullness of God's power without any persecution, without making any restitution for past wrongs, without judging yourself. You would win multitudes without leaving bad habits or companions. Oh, many would like to be filled with the Holy Spirit and have the power of God to win many, just so it did not take tears and heartache and long pleading on your face before God! Well, dear friend, you will never have God's power the easy way!

It cost the dear Lord Jesus thirty-three or thirty-four long, lonely years, homesick for Heaven, in the direst poverty, despised of men, in the form of a servant on earth. It cost Him the bloody sweat of Gethsemane, the traitor's kiss upon His cheek. It cost Him the accusations that He cast out devils by the power of Beelzebub, the intimation that He was born of fornication. It cost Him the Roman cat-o'-nine-tails on His back, the vinegar and gall on His parched lips, the weight of the cross on His back until He fainted, and then the spikes through His hands and feet, a crown of thorns on His head and the agony of the cross when God the Father turned His face away from His dear Son who hung there with the sins of the world upon Him! It cost the dear Lord Jesus all of that just to save sinners; and you want to have a part in this work without taking any time, without waiting on God, without any tears, without any heart searchings You want the power of God without any pleadings! Shame! Shame!

It cost Stephen the stoning that crushed his skull and battered his poor body into a bloody mass in the dirt. It cost Paul the apostle beatings with rods, shipwreck, fighting with wild beasts at Ephesus, a lonely life without wife or child—yea, the loss of all things! Many another saint of God was burned at the stake or sawn asunder or wandered in sheepskins or dwelt in caves, to have the favor of God upon him and His power for soul winning. If you think you may have the power of God cheaply when others paid such a price, then you have shamefully misjudged the Lord Jesus and the kind of heart service He requires!

If you would have the power of God, it takes time. It takes time for heart searching. It takes time for confession of sin. It takes time for holy resolves. It takes time to hear the accusing voice of a Spirit-enlightened conscience. It takes time to fast, sometimes. It takes time to attain a certain singleness of mind and heart, a certain carelessness about other matters, that we may be careful about the one main thing. It takes time to be filled with the Spirit because it takes time to be emptied of other things. In the nature of the case, the heavy cost that one must pay to please God means that it will take time to seek His face aright and have His best blessing and the fullness of His power for His greatest work, soul winning.

2. Persistence in Prayer Is the Mark and Accompaniment of Faith

Remember that Jesus said to the Syrophenician woman who pleaded and argued and would not give up her begging, "O woman, great is thy faith"! (Matt. 15:28).

Remember that after that wonderful parable, "to this end, that men ought always to pray, and not to faint" (the parable of the widow and the unjust judge), Jesus said, "Nevertheless when the Son of man cometh, shall he find faith on the earth?" (Luke 18:8). In other words, persistence in prayer is a synonym for faith. And if Jesus comes and finds no one willing to wait on Him in prayer, then that means that a certain kind of faith or a certain degree of faith is lacking.

Jacob's faith was indicated by the night he wrestled with the angel and said, "I will not let thee go, except thou bless me."

So the faith of the apostles and others of the one hundred and twenty was manifested as they continued with one accord in prayer and supplication in that Upper Room at Jerusalem until the mighty enduement of power came after ten days, on the day of Pentecost.

Some of you long to have more faith in God. You may think that faith is a certain feeling, a certain assurance that may come whether or no, without any special connection with your actions. But that is not true. Faith without works is dead. And the remarkable instances of faith in the Bible prove that faith is essentially the determination to hold onto God until the answer comes. Pleading, begging, seeking God's face, persevering in one's request, is itself the sign and the substance of faith.

Some will say, "Why wait on God and plead for the power of the Holy Spirit? Just take the blessing by faith!" But every Spirit-taught Christian must surely know that those who take things by faith, like the Syrophenician woman, like the widow before the unjust judge, are usually those who keep on pleading and waiting before God! It is certainly true that God gives anything under Heaven to those who trust Him truly for the blessing they seek. But all of us ought to remember that often faith itself takes time and faith itself is proved in persistent waiting on God. Dear brother, if you believe God's promises, believe that the fullness of the Holy Spirit is needed in your soul-winning work, believe that God wants you to have this fullness, then I urge you to show your faith by your works and wait on God and not take "no" for an answer until the breath of Heaven comes upon you for soul winning. Oh, faith itself requires persistent prayer.

3. Persistent Prayer Prepares the Christian to Receive God's Power

It is not difficult for me to see some of the reasons why the Lord Jesus would require the apostles to wait on God ten days before they were filled with the Holy Spirit. For example, only forty-three days before, Simon Peter had denied the Saviour and shamefully cursed and sworn. It is true that he had confessed that sin and turned his heart away from it and had been forgiven. But no doubt he desperately needed to face the conditions and the lack in his own life which had allowed him to fall into such grievous sin. I know that one who is forgiven of his sin does not always instantly have all the understanding of his fault, does not see all the shameful result of it. In my own life I have sometimes grieved and penitently waited before God over failures and sins committed years before and long since confessed and forgiven. I can imagine that during those ten days Peter dwelt upon his own pride and prayerlessness and boastfulness and again and again confessed his failure and faced his faults, until he was somewhat prepared never to fall into the same kind of sin again.

I suppose that during those ten days "doubting Thomas" thought over again and again his unbelief, his requirement of a sign, and the black despair that had laid hold on him when he thought Jesus was dead forever and His body sealed and rotting in Joseph's grave! Thomas had put his fingers in the nail prints and had brokenly confessed that Christ was "My Lord and my God!" But I solemnly warn every Christian now that your unbelief and the prayerlessness and self-will and the inattention toward the Scriptures which made that unbelief possible need a far more solemn facing and judging than is possible in an instant of time. I feel sure that Thomas in those ten days weighed his sins and failures and pleaded with God for an entire revamping of his life habits and purposes and motives so that he could live in the power of the Spirit and be fit to receive the fullness of that power.

James and John had ignored the compassion of Jesus for the multitudes about Him and had not caught His burden for the unsaved multitudes that followed them. Rather, they had argued which should be first in the kingdom. They had enlisted their own mother to plead with Jesus privately, that one should sit on His right hand and the other on His left hand in the coming kingdom. I am sure they had confessed their sin. There is no evidence that when they saw the resurrected Jesus and were glad in His resurrection, they kept any known sin in their hearts without forgiveness. But to confess a thing and have it forgiven is one thing; to meditate over the ruin one's sin has caused and face the consequences of it to Christ's work and thus to come to see things as God sees them, often takes more time than a moment's confession.

I believe that every one of these twelve apostles in the transcendent ministry that followed Pentecost gave good evidence that he was not at all the same man. They had supernatural power, it is true; and that was important. But more than that, they had waited on their faces with fastings and prayer for ten days, emptying themselves of the past and preparing for the future. They had judged themselves. They had faced their failures. They had earnestly pleaded with God until the fullness of the Spirit and the Great Commission to win souls assumed a greater importance than everything else in the world. They waited on God until they were ready for persecution. They waited on God until they were willing to die, as many of them did die, for the Gospel. They had given up secondary things. You see, persistence in prayer helps to prepare the Christian to receive the answer he seeks and to be a fit vessel for the fullness of the Spirit.

Many people are not filled because they are not first emptied. Many people would like to be filled with the Holy Spirit, but that is not their first desire. That desire, that prayer, that aim, has not reached the overwhelming proportions that it ought to have. Who can pray a right for the fullness of the Holy Spirit until he practices prayer? Who can become single-hearted on this matter until he deliberately takes time to conquer other desires and lay aside other business for this one main thing? O, dear Christian, you are not fit to be filled with the Spirit until you are willing to wait on God and let Him do what He will with you to prepare you for His fullness, His soul-saving power.

I think we may say that God was ready, before Pentecost, to put His power upon the disciples. But they themselves were not ready. Just as Jacob was not fit to meet Esau in peace until he waited on God all night and wrestled with the Angel, and just as the Syrophenician woman's heart was not prepared for the glorious answer to her prayers until she had proved her faith, so we should know that we are not prepared to receive God's blessings until we are willing to wait on God, however long He may see that we need to wait before we receive the fullness of His power.

Dr. Hyman Appelman tells how he came home from an evangelistic campaign to see his new baby boy. The little one was so tiny that he did not recognize his own father, could not focus his eyes upon him, had not yet even learned to smile. And Dr. Appelman said, "I wish he were two years old!"

His mother-in-law said, "But they don't come that way, son!"

Indeed, they do not. Even before the years of motherly care, feeding, washing, training the helpless infant, there are the long days of waiting during gestation. Then there is the time of travail and pain when the little one comes into the world.

But it is not hard for any of us to see that babies are worth their trouble. They are worth the trouble of the nine uncomfortable months for the mother; worth the travail and suffering of childbirth; worth all the soiled diapers, the nights of disturbed rest and the expense in money they cost. And how foolish we would be not to see that the infinite power of God coming upon poor Christians to make them soul winners is worth all the waiting on God, all the heart searching, all the pleadings and importunities and supplications which it may require! Oh, it costs something to have the fullness of the Spirit, but that is the way God gives His most precious gifts. It is true that we have salvation freely because of the sufferings of Christ for us. But if we are to enter into His sufferings and into His power and into His soul-winning business, then we must be willing to wait on God and be prepared in heart to be filled with the Holy Spirit.

Does any reader suppose that this book on the Holy Spirit was lightly and easily and quickly prepared? Then let me tell you that I have been writing it for more than sixteen years! More than sixteen years ago I completed a book-size manuscript on this subject. But it was not ripe. It was not quite ready. I was conscious that God had a richer understanding of the Word and a richer experience of His power in soul winning for me. So for those sixteen long years I have studied and prayed, have written articles and taught congregations about the power of the Holy Spirit, and all the time my heart was crying to God on this matter. Only God knows the toil and heart searching and study and counsel which have gone into the making of this book. Since I began preparation for this book, I have written some forty other books and pamphlets, and some of them have been most widely used. But this book required the kind of preparation both of mind and heart that took long years. And if it costs me so much of time and earnest waiting on God and study to prepare this book, why should it not cost the Christian something of time and tears and pleading to have the mighty power about which I am writing? Oh, I assure you that waiting on God prepares a Christian to receive the answer for which he waits—the power of the Holy Spirit to win souls.

III. Bible Christians Often Waited Long Before God to Be Filled With the Holy Spirit

Many Bible Christians had long periods of waiting on God before they were filled with the Holy Spirit. At first it may seem strange that the Lord Jesus seems simply to have asked the Father and to have been instantly filled with the Holy Spirit. In Luke 3:21,22 is this account of how the Saviour was filled with the Holy Spirit:

"Now when all the people were baptized, it came to pass, that Jesus also being baptized, and praying, the heaven was opened, And the Holy Ghost descended in a bodily shape like a dove upon him, and a voice came from heaven, which said, Thou art my beloved Son; in thee I am well pleased."

Why is it that Jesus, being baptized, simply prayed and the heavens were opened and the Holy Ghost descended upon Him? Why did Jesus not need to wait and plead and search His motives and confess His failures and lack?

I think the answer is very simple: Jesus did not need to confess His sins, for He had no sins. He did not need to wait on the Father to analyze His own desires, to give up anything between Him and God that would hinder. He did not need to face the Great Commission and examine His own heart as to whether or not He really wanted to win souls. In all these matters Jesus was already prepared for the fullness of the Holy Spirit. There was no wavering in His purpose. There was no lack in His understanding. There was no self-will, no false motive to be judged and put aside before He could be filled with the Holy Spirit. The Saviour was perfectly ready to be filled when He prayed, and so there was no need for delay.

The very reasons we give to show that Jesus would not need to wait and examine His heart and plead with God before He was filled with the Spirit are the reasons that the rest of us do need to wait on God. We have faults that He never had. We have divided aims and unholy purposes which never moved His heart and which He never needed to confess nor even to examine.

In truth, we may well say that the dear Saviour had prepared His heart for the fullness of power before He ever came into the world! He had loved sinners with an everlasting love before He left the courts of Heaven, laying aside the glory that He had with the Father and taking on Himself the form of a servant. He had prepared Himself to be filled with the Holy Spirit when He came into the world saying, "Lo, I come to do thy will, O God" (Heb. 10:7,9). As Jesus could be baptized and not shrink from it (knowing that the baptism pictured His own death and burial and resurrection, paying the price of man's sins), so He could with an open, confident heart ask the Father for the fullness of the Spirit and receive the power to which He had a perfect right, now that the time was come for Him to enter into His public ministry.

When the Saviour was a twelve-year-old boy in the temple astounding the doctors with His knowledge of the Scriptures, He was preparing His heart and mind for the fullness of the Spirit. When He went home and was subject to Mary and Joseph and "increased in wisdom and stature, and in favour with God and man," there was not one thought nor word nor deed of which the Saviour would ever be ashamed or which He would ever need to forget or renounce. It is not difficult to see why the dear Saviour, the perfect, sinless Lamb of God, did not need to wait long before God to plead for the fullness of the Spirit while His own heart should be prepared. No, He was ready for the fullness of the Spirit, and when the proper time was come, He asked the Father and immediately received the Holy Spirit in His mighty power.

But we are not so. If we are to have the same fullness of the Holy Spirit which Jesus had, then it is only proper and fitting that we should wait before God for the purifying of our motives, for the centering of our aims and hopes and to let patience have her perfect work in our lives. As we Christians need to wait on God in prayer for many other things, we need to wait on God for the power of the Holy Spirit.

And this was often true of those who, in Bible times, pleaded for God's power.

1. Let Us Consider Again the Tarrying Before Pentecost

Jesus had commanded the disciples, "Tarry ye in the city of Jerusalem, until ye be endued with power from on high" (Luke 24:49). And they did tarry, and their time was spent, we are told, "in prayer and supplication" (Acts 1:14).

Not only did the disciples continue steadfastly in prayer and supplication as they waited ten days before they were filled with the Holy Spirit at Pentecost, but the Scripture seems to teach clearly that they also fasted and prayed. That must be the meaning of the Scripture in Matthew 9:14,15:

> *"Then came to him the disciples of John, saying, Why do we and the Pharisees fast oft, but thy disciples fast not? And Jesus said unto them, Can the children of the bridechamber mourn, as long as the bridegroom is with them? but the days will come, when the bridegroom shall be taken from them, and then shall they fast."*

The disciples did not fast much while Jesus, the Bridegroom, was with them. But when He ascended to Heaven leaving them on the Mount of Olivet, then we may be sure that the disciples fasted. "When the bridegroom shall be taken from them...then shall they fast," says the Scripture. So in the holy sincerity and fervor of their hearts, these men and women, to whom the Saviour had given His Great Commission to go into all the world and preach the Gospel to every creature, waited on God with strong crying and pleading, and even with fasting. How earnest, how persistent were the pleadings of these who waited on God before Pentecost!

And I must remind you again that Pentecost is the great example of people filled with the Holy Spirit. It was "a specimen day." And the story is given in quite a bit of detail, to the intent that we might understand how people were then filled with the Holy Spirit. Surely waiting on God and pleading and laying aside ordinary matters that we may receive this greatest need of a Christian is right and important, as judged by the example of the apostles.

It is interesting that the same group later prayed again and again were filled with the Holy Spirit, as recorded in Acts 4:31: "And when they had prayed, the place was shaken where they were assembled together; and they were all filled with the Holy Ghost, and they spake the word of God with boldness." But here the same group seemed not to need the same heart searching, the same waiting on God. So they were filled again with the Holy Spirit without waiting ten days. And from this I think we are encouraged to believe that a Christian who stays on the altar and is filled with the Spirit of God should then be able day by day to be filled anew for every need and circumstance. One who is to be continually busy about soul winning should be continually filled with the Holy Spirit. And in some sense one who is in constant waiting on God ought to be able to be filled anew with the Holy Spirit whenever he needs power for a new soul-winning opportunity and task.

2. Paul's Three Days and Nights of Prayer and Fasting

The ninth chapter of Acts tells how Paul was converted. And after he had met the Saviour and been born again, "he was three days without sight, and neither did eat nor drink" (vs. 9). Then the Lord told Ananias to inquire for Saul, for said the Lord, "Behold, he prayeth." Saul of Tarsus fasted and prayed three days and nights before he was filled with the Holy Spirit. Then Ananias came to him and told him, "Brother Saul, the Lord, even Jesus, that appeared unto thee in the way as thou camest, hath sent me, that thou mightest receive thy sight, AND BE FILLED WITH THE HOLY GHOST" (vs. 17).

Paul, *after he was saved*, fasted and prayed three days and nights, until he was filled with the Holy Spirit! And if such earnest waiting on God was necessary for Saul of Tarsus to be filled with the Spirit, then we may well expect that many of us will need to wait on God with the same earnestness to have God's mighty power.

3. Paul and Barnabas Before Their Great Missionary Journeys Spent Much Time in Fasting and Prayer for the Power of the Holy Spirit

In the church at Antioch, Barnabas and Simeon, who was called Niger, and Lucius and Manaen waited and prayed. God had laid a great burden on their hearts, we suppose. Then Acts 13:2,3 tells us:

"As they ministered to the Lord, and fasted, the Holy Ghost said, Separate me Barnabas and Saul for the work whereunto I have called them. And when they had fasted and prayed, and laid their hands on them, they sent them away."

As these men "ministered to the Lord," or waited on the Lord with fasting, the Holy Spirit commanded that Paul and Barnabas be set aside for this blessed missionary work. Then they fasted more and prayed before putting their hands on Barnabas and Saul to send them away on the great missionary journeys that would take them through most of the Roman Empire.

And were they praying for the fullness of the Holy Spirit? And did they receive this fullness, this soul-winning power? I think that is obvious, for the next verse says, "So they, being sent forth by the Holy Ghost, departed unto Seleucia." They were sent forth by the Holy Ghost. Then the Scripture continues the story of how, at Paphos, they preached the Gospel to Sergius Paulus and how they were withstood by Elymas the sorcerer. "Then Saul, (who also is called Paul,) filled with the Holy Ghost, set his eyes on him..." and in the mighty power of God pronounced judgment upon Elymas and won Sergius Paulus to

Christ! (Acts 13:9–12). Paul and Barnabas were sent forth by the Holy Ghost and filled with the Holy Ghost for their missionary journeys. But for this mighty anointing, this power from on high, Paul and Barnabas with other friends who were burdened about the matter "ministered to the Lord, and fasted." Then again they "fasted and prayed."

What a shameful thing it is that many missionaries go out across the ocean without ever being filled with the Holy Spirit!

A friend gave a missionary embarking for India a note which he read after he got on board. It simply said, "Are you filled with the Holy Spirit?" And that question, so urgently put, led the missionary to wait on God until he was really filled with the Holy Spirit, and he became widely known as "Praying Hyde." And multiplied thousands were saved under his ministry.

Jonathan Goforth also learned this secret, that a missionary needs to be filled with the Holy Spirit, and the wonderful revivals which God gave him in Korea and Manchuria, to the winning of many thousands of heathens to Christ, show that God's requirement for a missionary is still that he be filled with the Holy Spirit, and show too that this blessed anointing and power of Pentecost comes only to those who are willing to wait on God earnestly enough for His fullness.

4. Elisha Persistently Waited on God for the Fullness of the Holy Spirit

Elijah the prophet was so filled with the Holy Spirit that it is said that John the Baptist, "filled with the Holy Ghost, even from his mother's womb," was to go forth "in the spirit and power of Elias" (Luke 1:15–17). The Spirit-filled Elijah had as his helper and understudy Elisha. And when God was about to take Elijah to Heaven, Elisha determined not to be left without the same power of God, the power of the Holy Spirit, which Elijah exercised. The story is told in II Kings 2:1–15. There Elijah urged Elisha to remain while he, Elijah, went on to Bethel. But the younger prophet refused. He said, "As the LORD liveth, and as thy soul liveth, I will not leave thee." Then the sons of the prophets wanted to chat with Elisha, and he brusquely turned them aside, ordering them, "Hold ye your peace." Elijah then said, "Elisha, tarry here, I pray thee; for the LORD hath sent me to Jericho." Again Elisha vowed that he would never leave Elijah, and they came to Jericho. There again Elisha brushed aside the sons of the prophets who wanted to chat about the Home-going of Elijah. Then Elijah asked the younger prophet to tarry at Jericho while he would go on to the river

Jordan. But again Elisha refused, and they crossed over the Jordan. Then Elijah turned to the younger prophet and said to him, "Ask what I shall do for thee, before I be taken away from thee. And Elisha said, I pray thee, let a double portion of thy spirit be upon me."

What a hard thing to ask! And how presumptuous it may have seemed. But the young prophet had made his earnest plea and would not give up his hope, his heart-cry. If he were to be the prophet of God in Israel in the room of Elijah, then he must have the same power, even a double portion of the same power, of the Spirit that was upon Elijah! And God rewarded his pleading, his waiting, his importunity. And even the sons of the prophets could well see that the "spirit of Elijah doth rest on Elisha."

Here we have again a simple example of one who would not be denied, who continued steadfastly in prayer and supplication for the power of the Holy Spirit.

Let us sum up the matter briefly thus: In many matters Christians need to continue steadfastly in prayer until the answer comes. Long, continued prayer is a sign of faith and is very pleasing to God. And persistent prayer is often necessary because prayer ought to cost something. A Christian ought to be willing to spend himself and his time and energy to please God. And other things ought to be secondary. That is a good reason for prevailing, persistent prayer. Persistent waiting on God prepares the Christian to receive the power of God.

And it is clear that in Bible times men often needed to wait long on God before they were endued with power from on high. After one is filled with the Holy Spirit and is regularly in the soul-winning work, he may not need to wait so long to be filled afresh with the power of God. But the most precious thing God has to give to His children is the power of the Holy Spirit, and if we are to enter into His work in saving souls we must be willing to pay any price that He requires.

Have you hesitated to wait on God in this matter? Have you soon given up your cry and in discouragement resigned yourself to a powerless ministry or a powerless testimony? Oh, beloved, do not give up! Keep on praying and waiting on God until He breathes upon you from Heaven in mighty power!

Chapter 13

Do You Really Want to Be Spirit-Filled?

"For I will pour water upon him that is thirsty, and floods upon the dry ground: I will pour my spirit upon thy seed, and my blessing upon thine offspring."— Isa. 44:3.

Do you want to be filled with the Holy Spirit? Do you really WANT to be filled with the Holy Spirit? Then you may be! A sincere, deep-seated desire is itself a condition of the fullness of the Holy Spirit. There are two other conditions to the fullness of the Holy Spirit: one is wholehearted obedience to Christ's soul-winning command (Acts 5:32), and the other is prevailing, importunate prayer (Luke 11:8,13). But before you set out to meet any other conditions you had better earnestly examine your own heart to see if you really want to be filled with the Holy Spirit!

"I will pour water upon him that is thirsty, and floods upon the dry ground," says the Lord. And He speaks of the fullness of the Holy Spirit, for the Scripture continues, "I will pour my spirit upon thy seed, and my blessing upon thine offspring." God will pour out the Holy Spirit on those who are really thirsty!

On anyone who is thirsty? May anyone whose soul cries out for the fullness of God's blessing, for the power of Pentecost, supernatural enduement of soul-winning power—may anyone whose soul thirsts and longs for the power of God—have it? Yes, thank God! The preceding two verses are addressed to Israel, to Jacob. It is clearly intended that God had Isaiah promise the Old Testament saints that they, when they earnestly desired it, might have poured upon them the Holy Spirit. But the verse stands on its own merit. God did not simply say He would pour the Holy Spirit on Jews. No, no, only upon thirsting Jews! And not only upon thirsting Jews, but on anyone who thirsts will the Holy Spirit be poured, for the plain Word of God is, "I will pour water upon him that is thirsty." "Him that is thirsty" applies today exactly as it did before Christ came. And God never said more than He meant. He intended every believer of the Word of God to take this promise for himself. If your heart hungers and thirsts and cries out to God for His fullness and power, then you may have it. Wonderful promise! This is a promise to "whosoever," just like John 3:16.

What a flood tide of blessing is here promised! "Floods upon the dry ground" is the promise.

I have known the drought in West Texas when the grass dried up in midsummer, when the crops withered in the field, when the dust made a reddish haze in the atmosphere, and when the pitiless sun beat down on an earth that was cracked and dry, and when cattle died around the water holes. I have smelled the stench from the bodies of starved, bony cattle. I have seen the time when the water holes went dry and the water had to be shipped by train that people might drink. But such a drought is not so terrible as the spiritual drought that is on the land. Fathers and mothers, powerless, see their children plunge into sin. On every hand drunkenness, divorce, adultery, lawlessness spring forth. Pastors preach to pitiful handfuls; and the power of God is not present to change lives, to convict sinners, to revive the saints. O God, send the rain! May God send the rain of the Holy Spirit on His people. May God send "floods upon the dry ground."

Is that not what we need today? Or, dear reader, may I be more personal and say, is that not what *you* need in your own heart, in your own home, in your own daily efforts to serve God and win souls? Is the ground of your life barren and drought-stricken? Then I pray that God will give you a holy thirst that can be satisfied only by the "floods upon the dry ground" of the pouring out of the Holy Spirit!

God says, "I will pour my spirit upon thy seed, and my blessing upon thine offspring." Here is a blessing not only for the saints of God, but for their families, their loved ones, their associates. The fullness of the Spirit was never given primarily for the *enjoyment* of the saints. It is given to make the saints streams of living water, fountains of life to the unsaved! Jesus said in John 7:37,38, "If any man thirst, let him come unto me, and drink. He that believeth on me, as the scripture hath said, out of his belly shall flow rivers of living water." The Saviour promises that when we really thirst and are filled with the Holy Spirit, then rivers of living water will flow out from our innermost beings to those all about us. So every Christian needs the fullness of the Spirit to be poured upon him so God's blessing may come also upon his offspring.

Christians should be able to win their families. Joshua said, "As for me and my house, we will serve the LORD" (Josh. 24:15). The old jailer at Philippi, converted, was able to see his whole household saved and baptized the same hour of the night! Oh, you fathers and mothers who are saved and cannot win your children, you are missing the fullness of Bible Christianity! You should be ashamed before God and man that you do not have the life-giving stream for those round about you. When God pours the water of the Holy Spirit on them that are thirsty, floods on the dry ground, then your seed, your offspring, will receive the blessing of God too! Such is the promise of God's blessed Word here. Oh that He may send it upon the readers of these words!

The promise of Isaiah 44:3, about which we have been speaking, is similar to that in Joel 2:28,29:

"And it shall come to pass afterward, that I will pour out my spirit upon all flesh; and your sons and your daughters shall prophesy, your old men shall dream dreams, your young men shall see visions: And also upon the servants and upon the hand-maids in those days will I pour out my spirit."

Here, then, is the teaching that when the Holy Spirit is poured out, His power it will come upon "all flesh," that is, on all kinds of people. And then the Scripture makes it clear that "your sons and your daughters" shall be filled with the Spirit too, and even servants and hand-maids! Not only is the Holy Spirit to be poured out upon Christians, but upon all kinds of people. But when He is poured out upon Christians, then their sons and their daughters will be won to Christ, will be interested in Christian service and will rejoice in the blessing of God, like their fathers and mothers. The servants and workmen associated with those filled with the Holy Spirit will know the power and blessing of God too. Joel 2:32, just following and still talking about the great outpouring of the Holy Spirit, says, "And it shall come to pass, that whosoever shall call on the name of the LORD shall be deliv-ered." And the New Testament translation as given by Peter in Acts 2:21 says, "Whosoever shall call on the name of the Lord shall be saved." Salvation comes to sinners when the power of God comes to the saints! There is no such thing as the outpouring of the Spirit of God upon Christians that does not result in salvation of sinners.

Dear Christian, this mighty revival blessing, this heavenly rain, these "floods upon the dry ground," this coming of the Holy Spirit on seed and offspring, is promised to those who are really thirsty. Do you really want to be filled with the Spirit of God?

I. A Single-Hearted Desire Is Essential to the Power of Pentecost

It is not surprising that the Saviour had the apostles and others waiting in the Upper Room some ten days before the mighty power of the Holy Spirit fell upon them at Pentecost. In the waiting and pleading and supplication, the desire burning in their hearts was inten-sified, purified and clarified. If they began to pray with mixed motives, they ended up praying with pure motives. If they began to pray with divided attention and garbled intentions, they ended up by praying with all their souls and with single-hearted attention to one thought. Oh, they must be filled with the Spirit of God in order to carry the Gospel to every creature! And we may be sure that one reason the time element is required in waiting on God for His power is that by self-examination while we pray, by judging our sins while we pray, by giving up secondary desires while we pray, then we may come to the pure desire, that holy thirst for the power of God which may make us fit to have the power He has promised. Fervent, single-hearted desire is essential to the fullness of God's power.

1. Consider What a Sin of Hypocrisy It Is to Ask for What We Do Not Truly Want, Prayer Without Sincere Desire!

When, oh, when will we learn that God is not pleased by the out-ward trappings of religion! When will we learn that God is not moved by burnt offerings and pipe organ music, stained-glass windows and the chanting of the Doxology or the Gloria? When will we learn that for-mal speeches and memorized prayers and worship centers mean noth-ing at all to God? The man who gives money, who attends services, who says his prayers would indeed appear righteous unto men. But to God who knows the heart, he may be a Pharisee like a whited sepul-chre, stinking with dead men's bones! I am persuaded that we lay alto-gether too much stress on unctuous words and beautiful phrases and theological accuracy in the terms of our prayers. The one great essen-tial of prayer in God's sight is sincerity. And what hypocrites we are when we say the words of a prayer which is not the cry of our hearts!

Thus, many people pray for the fullness of the Holy Spirit—that is, their words ask for the fullness of the Spirit.

A Buddhist goes down the road with a prayer wheel on his stick so that the wheel turns with the movement of the stick and the written prayer, fas-tened to the wheel, goes around! The heathen man does not know that God cares about the desires of the heart and does not care about how many times the prayer wheel goes around! Some fervent but misguided Catholic thinks to gain merit by saying so many Ave Marias or so many Pater Nosters, forgetting that God does not hear us for our much speaking. I believe that many Christians lightly pray God to fill them with the Holy Spirit when there is no genuine, single-hearted desire, no thirst of soul for the fullness of God! Some are not filled with the Holy Spirit because they do not mean what they say when they ask to be filled with the Spirit.

In Shakespeare's *Hamlet*, wicked King Claudius, after murdering his brother, the king of Denmark, has ascended to his brother's throne and married his brother's wife. Conscience-stricken, he tries to pray. But how can he repent of his sins and yet retain the stolen throne and the stolen wife? After an agonized period of trying to pray, the wicked man cries out:

> My words fly up, my thoughts remain below:
> Words without thoughts never to Heaven go.

His words confessed his sins, begged for forgiveness and mercy; but his wicked heart did not repent, did not forsake his sin, did not long for God's blessing more than he wanted a stolen throne and his illicit love! Oh, dear friend, when you come to pray for the fullness of the Spirit, I beseech you to make sure that your heart goes up as well as your words, else God will not hear.

2. Many Scriptures Teach Us That the Prayer That Reaches God Must Be the Expression of an Honest Heart's Desire

One who prays to be filled with the Spirit must be thirsty for the Spirit, must have earnest desire in his heart. But is not that what God requires in every prayer, whatever the request may be? Consider Mark 11:24:

"Therefore I say unto you, What things soever ye desire, when ye pray, believe that ye receive them, and ye shall have them."

We are encouraged to pray for anything, just so it is the honest outpouring of a hungry heart! "What things soever ye desire, when ye pray," the Scripture says. Desire is an essential of honest prayer. Desire is back of trust, back of every other condition of answered prayer.

Consider Jeremiah 29:12, 13:

"Then shall ye call upon me, and ye shall go and pray unto me, and I will hearken unto you. And ye shall seek me, and find me, when ye shall search for me with all your heart."

How many people pray for the fullness of the Spirit but do not find what they seek because they do not thirst for His fullness with all their hearts! Surely we cannot overemphasize the need for hearts to be honest when they come to talk to God! Do not, I beg you, expect to be filled with the Holy Spirit unless you long to be filled with the Holy Spirit.

3. Do You Want to Be Filled With the Spirit More Than You Want Other Things?

What relative place does the desire to be filled with the Holy Spirit have in your heart? Is this the first desire of your heart or the third or the fourth or tenth? Do you so long to have the power of God so that you may win souls and do the one thing dearest to God's heart, that nothing in the world is so important as this? Or, this matter that is first with God, is it last with you? What an offense it is to God to give first things any place but first. But God will not have second place. How would any honorable man feel if his wife should say to him, "I love you very much; I want to please you; I want to make you happy; I like to be near you. In fact, there are only three men I love more than you. After them, you are the next one that I want to please and make happy"? To any sensible husband such a love would be an abomination.

Now consider that Jesus died to save sinners. His Great Commission commands us to go and take the Gospel to every creature. But, Jesus warns us, we cannot win souls until we are endued with power from on high. The main business for the Christian is to have the power of God so he can do the work of God. Now when you pray for the fullness of the Holy Spirit, is this really the first desire of your heart? We had as well face it frankly: we cannot be filled with the Holy Spirit and filled with everything else too. We cannot have God's best and all of the pleasures of the world at the same time. We have to choose between the fullness of the Spirit and other things. In the very nature of the case, we must learn to want first the things that God wants first if we are to have God's fullness of power upon us.

"I will pour water upon him that is thirsty, and floods upon the dry ground," says the Lord in Isaiah 44:3. Surely if you realized the barren desert that your life is, you would long to be filled with the Holy Spirit—want that more than anything else in the world.

Do you want the fullness of the Spirit more than you want the praise of men? Do you want God's mighty power more than you want your friends and their companionship and love? Do you want the fullness of the Holy Spirit more than you want your night's sleep and your pleasant meal? If we are to put first things first we must learn that nothing in all the world can compare in importance with the power and blessing of God. In winning souls, in doing any service for God, education is secondary and incidental; peculiar aptitudes and talents are incidental; influence with people is of relatively minor importance; propitious circumstances and adequate equipment are secondary and incidental. Oh, when will we learn that to do the work of God, the one absolute necessity is the breath of Heaven upon us, the enduement of power from on high! And it is a kind of insincere hypocrisy for a

Christian to ask to be filled with the Holy Spirit who does not put this blessing above all other things for which his heart may crave. God pours water on the thirsty. Are you really thirsty? Do you really want to be filled with the Holy Spirit?

4. Is Your Desire for God's Power to Win Souls Sincere Enough to Keep You Praying Until the Answer Comes?

I do not believe that God sets any certain number of hours, days, weeks or months which a Christian must spend in prayer before he is filled with the Holy Spirit. But certain it is that of the apostles we are told, "These all continued with one accord in prayer and supplication" before Pentecost (Acts 1:14). Certain it is that the man knocking at the door of his friend, begging for bread for another, could not receive what he asked because the man was his friend, but only because of his "importunity" (Luke 11:8). How often we are taught in the Bible that one's heart's desire may be had only by continuing to wait on God. Second Chronicles 7:14 tells us that if we are to have revival, we must not only pray, but God commands us, "...and seek my face." So I think we may properly say that those who want to be filled with the Holy Spirit should want that badly enough that they are willing to wait on God and keep on praying until the answer comes.

II. Is It the Spirit's Fullness You Really Want or Something Else?

What do you really want? You are thirsty, you say, but are you thirsty for the fullness of the Spirit or something else? Thousands of people who say they want to be filled with the Holy Spirit do not have a deep burden for soul winning and do not tarry to be endued with power from on high so they may be acceptable witnesses for Christ. If you do not have in mind what God has in mind, then you cannot claim His promise.

1. The Fullness of the Spirit Is Not Sanctification

There is a Bible kind of sanctification, but it is not the fullness of the Holy Spirit.

What Christian has not longed to be free from sin, free from the temptations of sin, free from the trouble of heart that sin brings? Oh, how many, many times I have longed to be done with sin! If only God would not wait until Jesus comes, but change this vile body now! If only God would burn out the carnal nature and make me forever and entirely, perfectly holy, sinless, pure! Yet if it is this eradication of the carnal nature which you seek, you are, however good your intentions, seeking something different from the fullness of the Spirit which God has promised to him that is thirsty. Is it really the fullness of the Spirit, power from on high to make you fruitful as a soul-winning witness, which you want, or is it that you long to be free from temptation and long to be free from the shame and reproach of sin? These two are not the same goals. If you mean eradication, do not ask for the fullness of the Spirit. To be tired of sin and to be thirsty for the fullness of the Spirit are two entirely different things.

I kindly urge that you go back and study again what Jesus promised to His disciples who waited in the Upper Room before Pentecost. Read the story in Luke 24:45–49, and read it again in the first chapter of Acts. You will not find anywhere that Jesus promised them that when the Spirit came He would cleanse them and make them perfect; that He would take out the sinful, carnal nature. Read again that account of the marvelous blessing that came at Pentecost, as recorded in the second chapter of Acts. You will see that the disciples waited for power and that power came! You will see that they were commanded to be witnesses and that the power of God came upon them to enable them wonderfully, miraculously, to win three thousand souls in a day. But you will not see a word about their having the carnal nature eradicated. You will not find a word in the Scriptures about Pentecost to indicate that the disciples expected or that they received "Christian perfection"!

Those who have taken for granted that when the Holy Spirit comes in power He will burn out all the sinful taint which the Christian has inherited by his human nature should read again Matthew 3:10–12 where John the Baptist speaks of this matter.

"And now also the axe is laid unto the root of the trees: therefore every tree which bringeth not forth good fruit is hewn down, and cast into the fire. I indeed baptize you with water unto repentance: but he that cometh after me is mightier than I, whose shoes I am not worthy to bear: he shall baptize you with the Holy Ghost, and with fire: Whose fan is in his hand, and he will throughly purge his floor, and gather his wheat into the garner; but he will burn up the chaff with unquenchable fire."

It is clear from the above that John the Baptist is preaching to both the unconverted and the converted, to the saved and the unsaved. The axe of judgment was laid to the root of the tree; and the trees which did not bring forth fruit—the fruit of repentance toward God and faith toward Christ—such trees were to be hewn down and cast into the fire. That is the fire with which Christ will baptize some people, and verse 12 makes it clear that two classes of people are considered. Christ will gather the wheat into His garner, but "he will burn up the chaff with unquenchable fire." It is the same Christ who offers to baptize Christians in the Holy Spirit and threatens to baptize Christ-rejecting, unrepentant sinners in the fires of torment. But to be baptized with the Holy Spirit here does not mean at all that a Christian will have all the sin burned out.

Let me ask you again earnestly: Is it the fullness of the Spirit you want, or is it sinless perfection?

But even if the word *sanctification* to you does not mean sinless perfection, still sanctification is not the meaning of Pentecost. To be filled with the Spirit does not necessarily mean victory over particular habits. I grant you that Christ has victory for us day by day—glorious, continual victory—if one will take it. But that victory is one thing, and the fullness of the Spirit, which means an enduement of power from on high for soul winning, is an entirely different thing. Those who are troubled about some habit, those who are ashamed of a wicked temper, some worldly amusement, some ungodly association or some lust of the flesh, do well to take it to God in prayer and claim His help. But to want victory is not the same as wanting to be filled with the Holy Spirit to win souls.

So I ask you again: is it the fullness of the Spirit that you really want or something else?

2. To Want to Speak in Tongues Is Not a Thirst for the Holy Spirit

Any Christian who wants to be filled with the Holy Spirit, who longs to have the power of God upon him that he may win souls as Christ commands us to do, should be willing for God to send upon him any sign or evidence that pleases God.

I know that before I began the work of an evangelist, when I sought the power of God upon me with tears and prayers and holy earnestness and fasting and waiting on God day and night, I was willing for God to give any sign that He desired, just so I might have His power to do His work. Good, earnest Christian people of the tongues movement said that if I were filled with the Holy Spirit I would speak in tongues. I told God not once, but many times, that if He wanted me to speak in tongues, well and good, just so I could be filled with His Spirit and power! I said again and again that if rolling on the floor and being thought a nut and a fool would glorify God in any wise, and if it were necessary in order that I might be filled with the Holy Spirit, I would gladly have it so. I wanted the power of God, and I wanted it on God's own terms, no matter what those terms were!

But I remind you that what I wanted was to be filled with the Holy Spirit. I was not seeking tongues; neither should anyone else seek tongues. Praise the dear Lord, He did breathe upon me in power! To His glory let me say that God has lifted up His mighty arm and has shown me great wonders. Tens of thousands of souls have turned to Christ under the anointed preaching of this unworthy preacher, so weak, so frail. If God had wanted to give me tongues, He would have done so, and I would have been willing for Him to do so. But I was not thirsty for a jabber in tongues. I was thirsting for "floods upon the dry ground." I was thirsty for the pouring out of the Holy Spirit in mighty power in order that we might see souls saved.

Perhaps some people tell you that you cannot be filled with the Holy Spirit without talking in tongues, but do you seek to please God or men? Do you seek the approval of your friends, or do you seek power to win souls? Remember those are two entirely different ends. Is it the fullness of the Spirit you want or something else?

3. To Long for Ecstasy and Joy Is Not a Thirst for the Holy Spirit

I am sure that the disciples were happy at Pentecost when three thousand souls were saved. The salvation of souls makes any good Christian rejoice. It even brings rejoicing in the presence of the angels in Heaven, Jesus said. But the same disciples were glad *before* Pentecost. When Jesus appeared to them on the day of the resurrection and showed them His wounded hands and feet and proved that He was really risen from the dead, the Scripture tells us, "Then were the disciples glad, when they saw the Lord" (John 20:20). No Christian should wait for the fullness of the Spirit to be happy. And no Christian should pray to be filled with the Spirit simply for reasons of happiness.

Dr. Bob Jones, Sr., has well said, "Happiness is not something that is found by seeking it; it is something one stumbles over on the road of duty." The ecstasy and joy that come when we see loved ones saved are blessed, but they are incidental by-products of the fullness of the Holy Spirit.

"I want to be so happy I will shout God's praises like my mother did," said a woman to me.

Do you think that was a holy thirst for the fullness of the Holy Spirit of God? No, it was a selfish request, the kind that is very rarely granted. I have known a good many people who "tarried for the baptism," as they said, and they revealed to me that they longed to have the wonderful ecstasy which others reported they had when they talked in tongues! Many, many tracts on the tongues question say that one will never know the purest happiness on earth until God takes hold of his tongue and speaks through him wonderful mysteries in a language which he does not understand. And thousands of people are eager to have this oft-reported ecstasy, though they have no burden for souls and do not agonize before God over lost and ruined sinners who will, unless rescued, spend eternity in Hell. But to want a selfish joy is not the same thing as being thirsty for the fullness of the Spirit.

In a restaurant recently I saw these words on the menu, "No substitutions, please." With pork chops one would have apple-sauce, cole slaw, mashed potatoes and coffee. With roast veal one would have sage dressing, green peas and combination salad, with coffee. If one ordered a certain entree, he took what came with it, with no substitutions. And about this matter of the fullness of the Holy Spirit, God says, "No substitutions, please!" You say that you want to be filled with the Spirit. All right, God says that the fullness of the Spirit brings an enduement of power from on high so that you will be a witness, a soul-winning witness. Do not ask for substitutions! Do not ask God for the fullness of the Spirit and expect sanctification or tongues or a selfish enjoyment of an "experience."

4. Even to Long for Success in Christian Work Is Not Necessarily the Same as a Holy Thirst for the Spirit's Power

Jesus said, "Ye shall receive power, after that the Holy Ghost is come upon you: and ye shall be witnesses unto me..." (Acts 1:8). But sometimes one who really wants the power of the Holy Spirit does not want it for honest reasons. A pastor of a church may long to have success, larger crowds, increased offerings, more honor among men. He may long to give a better annual report to his denomination. He may long to have the approval or the envy of fellow ministers. He wants the success, the blessings that go with the fullness of the Holy Spirit. But it is not necessarily true that his heart honestly thirsts for the pouring out of the Holy Spirit like "floods upon the dry ground," as God has promised. Spiritual pride is the worst of all pride. Spiritual ambition may be a very unholy thing.

I believe that Simon the sorcerer of Acts 8:9–24 was genuinely converted. He besought Peter and John that he might have the power to lay his hands on people and that they might receive the Holy Ghost. Here is a man who not only wanted to have the power of the Holy

Spirit for himself but who also wanted to be able to impart it to others. He offered to buy this gift with money! But his desire was an unholy desire. It is obvious that he had no real conception of what was involved in his request. He had not yet broken away from the old and worldly conceptions of power and fame and popularity. Let this remind us that prayers for holy things may be unholy prayers because our motives are not pure motives.

A woman asked me to pray for her unsaved husband. "If he were converted it would be so much happier a home," she said. "He would be kinder to me. He would take us to church. He would give me more money to spend. Oh, pray for my husband!" She was not praying primarily for her husband to be saved in order that he might love the Lord Jesus Christ and that his poor soul might be kept out of Hell. She wanted to have him saved for the selfish reason that it would be easier on her in the home if her husband were saved!

How often we make prayers that seem to be holy prayers, but underneath, in the heart of them, God sees the abomination of a selfish motive, of a worldly ambition that is entirely at variance with the wording of our prayers. Do you want to be filled with the Holy Spirit, or is it something else you really want? May God help us to search our hearts when we pray. God pours water on those who are thirsty, but only those who really thirst for the power of God to do the will of God.

III. Are You Thirsty Enough to Pay the Price for Fullness of Power?

It is remarkable that the Lord Jesus, before He ever began His public ministry, went to John the Baptist, preaching in the wilderness of Judaea, and there offered Himself to be baptized. There Jesus was baptized in the likeness of His own death and burial and was raised up out of the watery grave in the likeness of His own coming resurrection from the dead. Then being baptized and praying, Jesus saw the Holy Spirit come in form like a dove and rest upon Him. The Holy Spirit came upon Him in mighty power for His ministry after He publicly offered Himself for His death. Even Jesus was not filled with the Holy Spirit until He publicly and officially faced the matter of giving Himself up to die, offering Himself for crucifixion. When Jesus publicly took on Himself the ceremony which proclaimed that He was willing to suffer all the torments of the damned in order to keep sinners out of Hell, and so to do the will of the heavenly Father, He was filled with the Holy Spirit!

It is remarkable that Peter commanded those who came to him at

Pentecost, "Repent, and be baptized every one of you in the name of Jesus Christ...and ye shall receive the gift of the Holy Ghost" (Acts 2:38). Every Christian who longs to be filled with the Holy Spirit to win souls must, like Jesus, face a self-crucifixion. He must face the inevitable persecution that comes to the Spirit-filled Christian.

Reader, are you thirsty enough for the fullness of the Spirit, for the mighty power of Pentecost, that you would be willing to pay God's price for His fullness? Are you willing to pay the price necessary to be filled with the Spirit of God?

The late Dr. R. A. Torrey said, "I fear that many pray, 'O Lord, fill me with the Holy Spirit,' who, if they really knew what it would cost them, would pray, 'O Lord, please do not fill me with the Holy Spirit.'" I believe that many who are really saved and would like to have soul-winning power never are abundantly filled with the Holy Spirit because they do not have a genuine thirst for God's fullness, the kind of honest, single-hearted desire that is willing to pay any necessary price to have God's power and do God's work in soul winning.

1. Are You Thirsty Enough for the Spirit's Power to Live a Life of Daily Crucifixion?

It ought to be obvious to any spiritually minded Christian that to follow self is not to follow God, and that if a Christian has his own way, God cannot have His way. So, to be filled with the Spirit—baptized, covered, overwhelmed, mastered by the Spirit—necessarily means a renunciation of self. That is what it meant for Jesus Himself! He said, "For I came down from heaven, not to do mine own will, but the will of him that sent me" (John 6:38).

Galatians 5:17 says: "For the flesh lusteth against the Spirit, and the Spirit against the flesh: and these are contrary the one to the other: so that ye cannot do the things that ye would."

"Ye cannot do the things that ye would," says this remarkable Scripture! That is, if the Holy Spirit has His way and if you really submit to the Spirit, you must take sides against the flesh. You must turn your back on your own will. You cannot have your own way and be filled with the Spirit.

To be filled with the Holy Spirit requires really that the Christian set out to have himself crucified daily. Paul said, "I die daily" (I Cor. 15:31).

You see, one can be a child of God, born of the Spirit, without being filled with the Holy Spirit. But to be a real *disciple* of Jesus, a genuine learner and follower, having His power and doing His work, involves more than just being saved. And Jesus said in Luke 9:22–24:

"The Son of man must suffer many things, and be rejected of the elders and chief priests and scribes, and be slain, and be raised the third day. And he said to them all, If any man will come after me, let him deny himself, and take up his cross daily, and follow me. For whosoever will save his life shall lose it: but whosoever will lose his life for my sake, the same shall save it."

Jesus gave Himself up to die, and that was in His heart when He was baptized, picturing His own death and resurrection. Jesus was filled with the Holy Spirit completely, unchangeably and without measure because He was always perfectly surrendered to the will of the Father, headed toward the cross, giving the last measure of devotion for the saving of souls. And Jesus says that we too, if we are to come after Him and really follow His footsteps, really do His work, are to deny ourselves or condemn ourselves to die and daily take up our cross and follow Him. We may have the full-fruited, Spirit-filled, soul-winning life by losing our own will, our own way. Only by losing our lives for Christ's sake can we save our lives.

I am not talking about saving ourselves from getting killed or offering ourselves to get killed physically. That is a part of it, of course. Every Christian who is wholly surrendered to Christ ought to be able to say, like Paul, "...by life, or by death" (Phil. 1:20). But though I may not be expected to die on a wooden cross or be burned to death on a pile of fagots or to be sawn asunder or have my head chopped off as other martyrs may, yet I must give myself daily, repeatedly, again and again to be Christ's at any cost in the world. And that means I turn my back on my own wishes. That means I crucify my own desires. Oh, to have God's fullness I must empty myself first!

In Luke 14:26,27 Jesus spoke of this matter again. He said:

"If any man come to me, and hate not his father, and mother, and wife, and children, and brethren, and sisters, yea, and his own life also, he cannot be my disciple. And whosoever doth not bear his cross, and come after me, cannot be my disciple."

You see, it is not only bad things we must turn away from, but good things, if we would be wholly sold out for Christ and have His fullness, His power, and really be His disciples. Remember that being a disciple is more than just being saved. To be a disciple means to be a real follower, to be what Christ wants us to be, doing the work He does.

Must a man hate his father or his mother or his wife and children or his brothers and sisters? At least his love for Christ must be so all-consuming, so preeminent, that it hardly matters about other people at all. The best Christians make the best sons and daughters, the best wives and husbands, the best brothers and sisters. And yet there is a sense in which every man who puts Christ absolutely first turns his back on everybody else in the world. Oh, it is a lonely business to please Christ and be filled with His power!

But then it was lonely for the Lord Jesus too. How He must have missed Heaven! There is something strangely plaintive in the words of the Saviour, "Foxes have holes, and birds of the air have nests; but the Son of man hath not where to lay his head" (Luke 9:58). Jesus literally gave up everything in the world to do the will of the Father. And those who would be filled with the Spirit must in the same way make a choice, for the Scripture says that the flesh and the Spirit lust against each other. One who is to have the fullness of the Spirit cannot have his own way. For the perfect will of God, missionaries leave fathers and mothers behind, and sometimes wives and children. To be evangelists, men must leave homes and families and have the heartbreak and loneliness in strange cities. How many wives have said to evangelists, "Don't you love me enough to stay with me and the children? We need you so badly!" And many an evangelist has had to reply, "But God's work comes first, and even wife and children must be secondary to the saving of souls."

I heard Dr. L. R. Scarborough, long president of the Southwestern Baptist Theological Seminary, tell how he received word that one of his sons was near death and a telegram urgently insisted that he leave a revival campaign and come home. What a struggle went on in his breast! But finally, triumphantly, he turned to the soul-winning work and left his boy with God. God raised the boy up. But sometimes God does not raise up the boy. Sometimes breaches are never completely healed. Sometimes losses can never be completely repaid on earth. Nevertheless, the soul winner who is to have the fullness of God's power must say goodbye to everybody and everything in the world, "yea, and his own life also"!

Some years ago I was the speaker at an evangelistic conference at Cedar Lake, Indiana, sponsored by the Christian Business Men's Committee of Chicago. After a busy, busy day Mr. Frank Sheriff and I sat on a bench on the hotel lawn at midnight. I felt so wrung out from the burdens of the day. I had wept over sinners. I had pleaded with Christians to lay all on the altar. I had expounded the Word of God. Meantime, I carried also the burdens of publishing the SWORD OF

THE LORD, answering a heavy mail and getting out Christian litera-
ture. Mr. Sheriff and I at midnight talked over our burdens, and then
Mr. Sheriff said, "Oh, the main price is this constant purging, purging,
purging! This constant renunciation of self, this laying self on the altar
again every day, this saying goodbye to everything precious in the
world!"

The cost of the fullness of the Spirit is tremendous. There is a constant fight between the flesh and the Spirit. If you will help the Holy
Spirit to win in this fight, if there be a constant purging of self, a constant self-renunciation, a constant dying, then perhaps you really are
thirsty to be filled with the Holy Spirit!

Some men think they do much for God when they quit drinking. I
know Christians who are proud and self-righteous Pharisees because
they do not go to picture shows, do not smoke cigarettes and do not
belong to secret orders. I know Christian women whose total claim to
holiness is that they do not paint their faces. Well, I certainly believe
that a Christian ought to give up anything that defiles the body, like
tobacco or drink. I certainly believe that a Christian ought not to
attend and put his influence back of the worldliness and license and
wickedness that is in the theater. But, oh, dear friends, one may quit a
habit or give up some little bit of worldliness without really paying the
price for the fullness of the Spirit.

I am not just asking that you give up tobacco or the movies. I am not
just asking that you give up cocktails. I am asking, and God is asking,
that you give up mother, father, wife, children, brethren, sisters, houses,
lands, yes, and your own life, your own will, your own comfort, your own
joy also! If Jesus paid such a price for the fullness of the Holy Spirit that
He might be our perfect example, we too should expect to offer ourselves
as fully and as willingly. Are you willing to die, and die every day? If you
are willing to pay that kind of price, perhaps you are thirsty for the fullness of the Holy Spirit. And God said, "I will pour water upon him that
is thirsty." Oh, how seriously concerned we ought to be, and with what
holy watchfulness we ought to regard this matter of pleasing Christ and
putting soul winning first and the power of God first!

A brilliant young minister, a graduate of Princeton and pastor of a
great and honored church, heard me preach one weekday afternoon.
He came to me later to say that he had made a holy vow. He was a really remarkable golfer. He said to me, "I know there is no harm in golf. I
do not say I will never play again. But I told the dear Lord today that
the love of it in my heart was too much and that I would tear that love

out of my heart to make sure that He was always first."

I talked to a wonderful soul winner, a man of passion and mighty power. He had been in his college days an all-conference football fullback. He played with zeal and delight. But now he tells me that he never goes to a football game. He does not think there is anything necessarily wrong in football. But he said, "I love it too well—too well for a man who is in the business of saving souls. It is all right for a Christian to enjoy football, but no Christian ought to love it as much as I have loved it." I say he never attends. And when I was preparing one of his messages for publication in the SWORD OF THE LORD, I found that he had carefully marked out a football story which told of his own last exploits on the gridiron. He simply meant that football had to die, as everything else but soul winning and the power of Christ had to die in his life.

D. L. Moody, after two years of pleading and heartbroken waiting, met God on Wall Street, New York, one day, in the fullness of the Holy Spirit. It was such a time of blessing and enduement as he had never had, the outstanding experience in all his life after he became a Christian. He himself tells that where before there had been fives and tens saved, now there were hundreds. And when later someone wanted to write the story of Moody's life, he said in effect, "Since God put His power upon me I have determined to walk very softly. I do not want the story of my life published lest I should someway grieve God. I would rather have the power of the Holy Spirit than anything else in the world."

Later D. L. Moody's life story was written, and it has been a tremendous blessing to multiplied thousands, as it has been to me. In fact, it would have been a most grievous mistake for the story not to have been written. But I am only illustrating the fact that D. L. Moody knew that self must die and the praises of men must be literally trampled underfoot in order that the Holy Spirit might have His full way in D. L. Moody's life.

You see, I am not talking about giving up football or golf, and I am not suggesting that it is wrong to have your life story written. I am saying that just to give up *things* is not enough or to give up *amusements* is not enough. I am saying that you must give up yourself, even your life and plans and your own will, emptying self of other things that you may be filled with the fullness of God. That is what is meant, I think, by being thirsty for the fullness of the Holy Spirit.

God will pour water on him that is thirsty and floods upon the dry ground, He promises. But, oh, dear friend, are you really, really thirsty? Are you thirsty enough to pay the price of self-crucifixion day by day?

2. Are You Willing to Pay the Price in Persecution That Inevitably Follows the Fullness of the Holy Spirit?

"For the flesh lusteth against the Spirit, and the Spirit against the flesh: and these are contrary the one to the other," says Galatians 5:17. Anyone who is filled with the Spirit has a fight on his hands. The flesh does not like the fullness of the Spirit.

The Scripture given above in Galatians 5:17 is simply the divine application of an allegory plainly stated in the preceding chapter. Paul says that Ishmael, the son of the bondwoman, represents the flesh, and Isaac, the son according to promise, represents those who are born of the Spirit and follow the Spirit. Then Paul says by divine inspiration in Galatians 4:29, "But as then he that was born after the flesh perse-cuted him *that was born* after the Spirit, even so it is now."

There are three words in that verse in italics. The three words, "that was born," are not in the original. So we might read the verse, "But as then he that was born after the flesh persecuted him after the Spirit, even so it is now." The work of the Holy Spirit is particularly offensive to the flesh. So persecution inevitably follows those who are filled with the Holy Spirit.

Do I say that the fullness of the Holy Spirit inevitably leads to per-secution? Yes indeed! And the life of the Lord Jesus Himself quickly proves that fact.

Jesus grew to be about thirty years old before He began His public ministry. Yet He lived a perfect, sinless, holy life. He attended the syna-gogue in Galilee, as His custom was, and there He read the Scriptures. He knew more about divine things even when He was twelve years old than the doctors of the law in Jerusalem did. Yet He was greatly respect-ed in Galilee and everywhere He went, and there was never a breath of persecution against Him by those who knew Him, as far as we know, until He was thirty. Herod had tried to kill Him to save his throne, and we know that Satan hated Him. But people did not personally hate Jesus nor persecute Him until He was filled with the Holy Spirit.

Luke 3:21,22 tells us how Jesus came to the Jordan River and was baptized of John; there He prayed, and the Holy Spirit descended in a bodily shape upon Him. And from that moment Jesus was filled with the Spirit, the Scriptures tell us. Acts 10:38, referring to that time "after the baptism which John preached," says, "How God anointed

Jesus of Nazareth with the Holy Ghost and with power: who went about doing good, and healing all that were oppressed of the devil; for God was with him."

Now if you follow the life story of Jesus in the same Gospel of Luke which tells us how He was filled with the Spirit, you will find that He met His great temptation in the wilderness (Luke, chapter 4), "being full of the Holy Ghost," and then "returned in the power of the Spirit into Galilee." Then He came to Nazareth where He was brought up, went into the synagogue on the Sabbath day "as his custom was" and stood up to read. And there He found Isaiah 61:1 and read to the people these words:

"The Spirit of the Lord is upon me, because he hath anointed me to preach the gospel to the poor; he hath sent me to heal the brokenhearted, to preach deliverance to the captives, and recovering of sight to the blind, to set at liberty them that are bruised, To preach the acceptable year of the Lord."—Luke 4:18,19.

He quoted the Scripture, prophesying that the Spirit of the Lord would be upon Him and that He would be anointed to preach, and then He said, "This day is this scripture fulfilled in your ears."

And these neighbors of the Lord Jesus who had known Him nearly thirty years, how did they then receive Him? These neighbors who had met with Him in the synagogue and asked Him to read the Scriptures, how did they feel about Him after He was filled with the Holy Spirit? Wonder of wonders, that very same day "all they in the synagogue, when they heard these things, were filled with wrath, And rose up, and thrust him out of the city, and led him unto the brow of the hill whereon their city was built, that they might cast him down headlong" (Luke 4:28,29). Within an hour, we suppose, after Jesus appeared in His home synagogue, filled with the Holy Ghost, His neighbors tried to kill Him! This persecution of Jesus Christ began when He was filled with the Holy Spirit!

The flesh and the Spirit are against each other.

The world does not mind a man getting saved and holding a better job. The world does not mind a man getting saved when he quits getting drunk and quits beating his wife and makes a better citizen. But if that man gets on fire for God and neglects his job for soul winning and embarrasses his friends by pleading with them to get saved and tries to win multitudes in the power of the Holy Spirit, then he is certain to be hated. Persecution inevitably follows the fullness of the Holy Spirit!

There was no persecution of the apostles those ten days they wait-

ed in the Upper Room or about Jerusalem. But the second chapter of
Acts tells of the pouring out of the Holy Spirit and of many being
saved, and after that persecution began. As soon as Peter and the others were filled with the Holy Spirit, the ungodly began to mock, saying,
"These men are full of new wine." The persecution began when the
power came. Peter healed a lame man at the temple, and immediately
he and John were arrested and put in jail, and great persecution began.
Stephen was filled with the Holy Spirit, and those wicked men who
"were not able to resist the wisdom and the spirit by which he spake"
then suborned men, hired blasphemers and slanderers, to get Stephen
arrested. The seventh chapter of Acts is an address by the Spirit-filled
Stephen and tells of his martyrdom because "they were cut to the heart,
and they gnashed on him with their teeth." They hated the Spirit-
filled Stephen, as they hated the Spirit-filled Son of God. If we are
filled with the Holy Spirit many will hate us too.

Consider for a moment that many, many godly Christian men are
college presidents. But are college presidents slandered as evangelists
are slandered? There are godly Bible teachers in abundance, but are
Bible teachers persecuted and despised as evangelists are? You know
the answer. They are not. One who is filled with the power of God to
win souls should expect opposition and persecution more than others.

The Spirit-filled Saviour was said to have "cast out devils...by
Beelzebub the prince of the devils" (Matt. 12:24). To the Spirit-filled
Paul, trying to win souls, it was said, "Thou art beside thyself; much
learning doth make thee mad" (Acts 26:24).

D. L. Moody was known for years in Chicago as "Crazy Moody."
And Spirit-filled Christians everywhere are called "fanatics" and
"extremists."

Christian, are you willing to suffer persecution for Jesus Christ?
Persecution naturally follows being filled with the Holy Spirit. For
when one is filled with the Holy Spirit he is really attacking Satan's
stronghold, plucking sinners out of the hands of the evil one. Soul winning is the one business that Satan hates the most! Soul winning got
Paul and Silas in jail, as recorded in the sixteenth chapter of Acts. Soul
winning had led people to say of them, "These men, being Jews, do
exceedingly trouble our city, And teach customs, which are not lawful
for us to receive, neither to observe, being Romans" (Acts 16:20,21).
And Spirit-filled Christians today will be hated and slandered and
sometimes attacked bodily.

Are you really thirsty? Do you want the power of God enough to pay the price in persecution that will necessarily come if one be filled with the Holy Spirit?

Our Pentecostal friends who believe that speaking in tongues is the Bible evidence of the fullness of the Holy Spirit say that speaking in tongues is unpopular and that they suffer persecution because they speak in tongues. It is true that many think that speaking in a tongue which no one can understand and which does not advance the cause of Christ and does not fit into the pattern of the power of the Holy Spirit poured out at Pentecost is foolish. First Corinthians 14:23 says: "If therefore the whole church be come together into one place, and all speak with tongues, and there come in those that are unlearned, or unbelievers, will they not say that ye are mad?" The Bible, of course, is right. To speak in languages which people cannot understand will bring scoffing. And the Bible warns us not to have that but rather that all speak in the power of the Holy Spirit so every unlearned one and unbeliever will be convinced of all, judged of all, and will be convicted and converted.

But speaking in tongues is not the great reproach. The reproach is on the fullness of the Spirit Himself. The flesh and the Spirit are contrary the one to the other. The son of the bond-woman persecuted the son of the freewoman, and so it is today.

Not until people are so concerned about soul-winning power that they are willing to suffer persecution are they thirsty enough to receive the promised blessing. "I will pour water upon him that is thirsty, and floods upon the dry ground," the Lord said. "I will pour my spirit upon thy seed, and my blessing upon thine offspring."

3. Are You Thirsty Enough to Wait Before God as Long as Necessary for the Fullness of the Holy Spirit?

When Jesus rose from the grave, taught His disciples forty days, and ascended to Heaven, there were many thousands of converts on earth. John the Baptist had baptized thousands of truly penitent believers in the Lamb of God. And we are told that "Jesus made and baptized more disciples than John" (John 4:1). Many were truly converted who did not follow Jesus very closely. Many had learned to trust in Christ as their own personal Saviour, though they were not in the Upper Room prayer meeting for ten days and they were not among the hundred and twenty upon whom the power of the Holy Spirit fell so wonderfully at Pentecost.

Jesus, after He was risen from the dead, "was seen of above five hundred brethren at once" (I Cor. 15:6). The hundred and twenty who were present in that pre-pentecostal prayer meeting were only a small part of the Christians even in Jerusalem. Yet the hundred and twenty alone, at first, were filled with the Holy Spirit!

It becomes clear after a little prayerful thought that only those who waited steadfastly in prayer were filled with the Holy Spirit. There are some people who thoughtlessly say, "Well, Pentecost would have come just the same whether the disciples prayed or not." Yes, the Jewish feast day on the calendar would have come, but the Holy Spirit in His power did not come upon others. How did He happen to come to the hundred and twenty who "all continued with one accord in prayer and supplication, with the women, and Mary the mother of Jesus, and with his brethren"? (See Acts 1:14.) The fullness of Holy Spirit power came upon Christians who were waiting in continual prayer. His power did not come upon other Christians in Jerusalem and scattered all over Palestine who were not waiting on God in prayer.

Surely of those five hundred brethren who saw Jesus at one time after His resurrection, every one longed to be filled with the Holy Spirit and to be a soul-winning witness for Christ. I cannot believe that Jesus did not give them the Great Commission too. I must believe that Jesus gave them the commands and promises in Luke 24:46–49 which He gave to the others who waited in constant supplication and prayer for the fullness of power. How, then, does it happen that only a hundred and twenty received the great anointing, the pouring out of the Holy Spirit at Pentecost, and won three thousand souls? Where were the other three hundred eighty of the Christians who saw Jesus all at one time after His resurrection? Where were many others who loved Him and wanted to please Him?

It is my solemn conviction that some started to wait and pray but gave up and went about their business. Praying is hard work. Some prayed awhile, perhaps, and then said, "I will pray at home, when I can. I cannot leave my business so long." I have been in many an all-night prayer meeting. Every one of them started with the larger crowd and ended with a smaller crowd. Some people do not stay even all night. We can well understand how some did not stay to pray ten days. But if some went away without continuing in earnest prayer, if some failed to keep on pleading expectantly, then they missed the great blessing of the pouring out of the Holy Spirit. They did not receive the same power from Heaven that others received. Waiting on God is an essential to the fullness of His power.

I wonder, dear reader, if you are thirsty enough for God's power to keep on waiting until He fills you.

In 1941 a young couple were deeply in love. The young man was called to the army, but the young woman who loved him promised to wait for him. He was soon sent overseas. The war raged on and on. The weeks became weary months; the months became dragging years! Her letters became cooler, less frequent. Then she wrote him that "it was all a mistake." She sent him back the ring. She was not willing to wait longer and had fallen in love with another man. When the soldier returned, the girl he loved, the girl who had promised to wait, was another man's wife!

Are you willing to wait on God until He fills you with the Holy Spirit?

Many a young man wants to be a physician, though he knows it will involve college, medical school and then internship in a hospital before he is ready to begin practice. But an element of time is absolutely essential to a medical education. A source of abomination to the medical practice in the last century was the short-term medical college, giving a poorly earned degree to inadequately trained men who would hold the lives of others in their unskilled fingers.

As a former educator, I well know that just reading a certain number of books, answering a certain number of questions, memorizing a certain number of facts—that these do not really constitute an education. We have now learned that it is not wise to graduate people from college at too young an age. Part of the educational process involves time. Strong colleges require that part of the work for a degree must be done in residence, not all of it by correspondence courses. The time element is an absolute essential in good education.

Young preachers take from three to eight years of special training after high school to finish Bible school or college and seminary, perhaps. But every spiritually instructed Christian knows that the principal equipment for a soul-winning ministry is not a college degree nor a seminary diploma. The power of the Holy Spirit, an anointing from Heaven, is more essential to a godly ministry than all the training the schools can give. Why, oh why, then, should people think it strange that God requires us to wait on Him with all our hearts to be filled with the Holy Spirit? If a man is willing to spend years in training, why not spend however long a time may be necessary in waiting upon God to be filled with the Holy Spirit?

It took D. L. Moody some two years of heartbroken waiting on God before he was filled with the Holy Spirit in mighty power. He was really thirsty, so he kept on pleading with God until he was wonderfully anointed from Heaven.

Are you thirsty enough for the fullness of power that you are willing to keep on praying, keeping this burden always before God, until you may have all of His power you need for doing His bidding and carrying His Gospel? Then if you are thirsty, remember that God says, "I will pour water upon him that is thirsty, and floods upon the dry ground: I will pour my spirit upon thy seed, and my blessing upon thine offspring."

Oh, in Jesus' name let us set out to become so single-minded in our devotion to soul winning, so given over to the one task and business committed to us that we will long at any cost to be filled with the Holy Spirit! Oh, the flood tides of blessing will come upon God's people when they are thirsty!

Are you really thirsty? Do you really long to be filled with the Holy Spirit?

Chapter 14

How Great Soul Winners Were Filled With the Holy Spirit

"But ye shall receive power, after that the Holy Ghost is come upon you: and ye shall be witnesses unto me both in Jerusalem, and in all Judæa, and in Samaria, and unto the uttermost part of the earth."—Acts 1:8.

"...In the mouth of two or three witnesses shall every word be established."—II Cor. 13:1.

Someone has said that one example is worth a thousand arguments. We do not believe that one human illustration is worth more than any statement of Scripture, and yet illustrations help us to understand the statements of Scripture, and often one illustration does more to show what the Bible really means by what it says than much human logical explanation.

It is not wise to base a doctrine upon human experiences. For example, thousands of people have been converted to God, really saved, at mourner's benches. But that is not any reason for anybody to say that a mourner's bench is essential to salvation. Some people delight in their "experience," remembering that they felt a great ecstasy and shouted the praises of God when they were born again. But it would be foolish for us thereby to conclude that one cannot be saved without shouting the praises of God. It is never wise to make a doctrine out of our human experiences. Nevertheless, when the Bible clearly teaches a truth, it is refreshing and helpful to have human experiences testify ✗ to the truth of the Bible doctrine.

So in this chapter, I want to tell the story of how great soul winners were filled with the Holy Spirit. And we will find that the experiences of the greatest soul winners verify the clear statements of Jesus Christ in Acts 1:8, given above. When great men of God were filled with the Holy Spirit, they received power for soul-winning witness and testimony. The best soul winners did not talk in tongues, they did not claim to have the carnal nature eradicated, but they did receive power from God for soul-winning work.

In that great book *The Holy Spirit: Who He Is, and What He Does*, Dr. R. A. Torrey in chapter five gives three defining statements as to what the baptism of the Holy Spirit is. So, before we consider the experiences of great soul winners and how they were filled with the Spirit, let us consider Dr. Torrey's definition. Dr. Torrey says the following:

> 1. In the first place, the Baptism of the Holy Spirit is a definite experience of which one may know whether he has received it or not....

> 2. In the second place, the Baptism with the Holy Spirit is a work of the Holy Spirit distinct from and additional to His regenerating work....

> 3. In the third place, the Baptism with the Holy Spirit is a work of the Holy Spirit always connected with and primarily for the purpose of testimony and service.

While we do not insist on the term "the Baptism with the Holy Spirit," we believe Dr. Torrey has given a good definition of this special enduement of power from on high. With this in mind, we will do well to consider the testimonies of great men who were filled with the Holy Spirit and see that the fullness of the Holy Spirit is indeed a special enduement of power fitting Christians to win souls, and we will see how other Christians received this enduement of power.

D. L. Moody's Enduement

In *The Life of D. L. Moody*, written by his son, is a very simple but striking account of the secret of D. L. Moody's power. Here is the story of Mr. Moody's enduement of power, as given on pages 146, 147 and 149:

> The year 1871 was a critical one in Mr. Moody's career. He realized more and more how little he was fitted by personal acquirements for his work. An intense hunger and thirst for spiritual power were aroused in him by two women who used to attend the meetings and sit on the front seat. He could see by the expression on their faces that they were praying. At the close of services they would say to him:
>
> "We have been praying for you."
>
> "Why don't you pray for the people?" Mr. Moody would ask.
>
> "Because you need the power of the Spirit," they would say.
>
> "I need the power! Why," said Mr. Moody, in relating the incident years after, "I thought I had power. I had the largest congregations in Chicago, and there were many conversions. I was in a sense satisfied. But right along, those two godly women kept praying for me, and their earnest talk about anointing for special service set me to thinking. I asked them to come and talk with me, and they poured out their hearts in prayer that I might receive the filling of the Holy Spirit. There came

a great hunger into my soul. I did not know what it was. I began to cry out as I never did before. I really felt that I did not want to live if I could not have this power for service."

Then the book tells of the great Chicago fire, of D. L. Moody's relief work, the building of the North Side Tabernacle, and of his visiting in the East to secure funds for his work. Then the narrative continues:

During this Eastern visit the hunger for more spiritual power was still upon Mr. Moody.

"My heart was not in the work of begging," he said. "I could not appeal. I was crying all the time that God would fill me with His Spirit. Well, one day, in the city of New York—oh, what a day!—I cannot describe it, I seldom refer to it; it is almost too sacred an experience to name. Paul had an experience of which he never spoke for fourteen years. I can only say that God revealed Himself to me, and I had such an experience of His love that I had to ask Him to stay His hand. I went to preaching again. The sermons were not different; I did not present any new truths, and yet hundreds were converted. I would not now be placed back where I was before that blessed experience if you should give me all the world—it would be as the small dust of the balance."

Notice in the above account, in the words of D. L. Moody himself, that while he had great joy in the coming of the Holy Spirit upon him in power, yet the principal result was: "The sermons were not different; I did not present any new truths, and yet hundreds were converted."

D. L. Moody himself made much of this doctrine that Christians should be filled with the Holy Spirit, or baptized with the Holy Spirit, as he himself often put it.

In the book, *Moody, His Words, Work, and Workers,* edited by Rev. W. H. Daniels, are given representative doctrinal messages by D. L. Moody. I want to quote here from one message, beginning on page 396 of that book, to show Moody's clear doctrine on this matter of an enduement of power from on high.

D. L. Moody's Article on
THE BAPTISM OF THE HOLY SPIRIT FOR SERVICE

In some sense, and to some extent, the Holy Spirit dwells with every believer; but there is another gift, which may be called the gift of the Holy Spirit for service. This gift, it strikes me, is entirely distinct and separate from conversion and assurance. God has a great many children that have no power, and the reason is, they have not the gift of the Holy Ghost for service. God doesn't seem to work with them, and I believe it is because they have not sought this gift.

In the opening of the eleventh chapter of Luke we find the disciples asking Christ to teach them how to pray. After doing so He goes on to explain it, and in the ninth, tenth, and thirteenth verses says: "And I say unto you, Ask, and it shall be given you; seek, and ye shall find; knock, and it shall be opened unto you. For every one that asketh receiveth....If ye then, being evil, know how to give good gifts unto your children: how much more shall your heavenly Father give the Holy Spirit to them that ask him?"

Now the lesson to be learned from this is, that we must pray for the Holy Spirit for service; pray that we may be anointed and qualified to do the work that God has for us to do. I believe that Elisha was a child of God before Elijah met him; but he was not qualified for the work of a prophet until the spirit of Elijah came upon him. We have to ask for this blessing, to knock for it, to seek for it, and find out why it does not come. If we regard iniquity in our hearts, if we have some hidden sin, God is not going to give us the baptism of power. We are not as "an empty vessel"; we are not ready to receive the blessing, and so it doesn't come.

In the third chapter of Luke we find that Christ was baptized by the Holy Ghost before He entered upon His ministry. This should teach us to get anointed before starting out to do the Lord's work. Christ was the Son of God just as much before His baptism as afterward, but even He needed this power; and if the Son of God, who never had sinned, needed it, how much more do we need it, and how hopeless it will be if we attempt to work before we get it.

Again you will notice Mr. Moody's teaching that the coming of the Holy Spirit upon Christians, what Moody and Torrey and most other great soul winners have called "the baptism of the Holy Spirit," is simply an enduement of power for soul-winning service; that Christians should pray for this enduement of power from on high.

That Moody's work was done in the mighty power of the Holy Spirit, that he really had upon him the power of Pentecost, was obvious to all who knew him well. At Moody's funeral C. I. Scofield, then about 56 years old, spoke. And though later—when there was such a hue and cry raised by the followers of Darby against the terminology of Moody and Torrey and other great soul winners on this matter of the baptism of the Holy Spirit, or the fullness of the Spirit—Scofield avoided it, yet on this occasion he used the terminology of Moody and of Torrey and of Finney. Here are Dr. Scofield's words over the body of the great soul winner, Moody:

The secrets of Dwight L. Moody's power were: First, in a definite experience of Christ's saving grace. He had passed out of death into life, and he knew it. Secondly, he believed in the divine authority of the Scriptures. The Bible was to him the voice of God, and he made it resound as such in the consciences of men. *Thirdly, he was baptized with the Holy Spirit, and he knew it.* [Italics supplied] It was to him as definite an experience as his conversion (*The Life of D. L. Moody* by his son, page 561).

Oh, how earnest was Moody in his burden to keep the power of the Spirit of God upon him! He said once, in his sermon on "Hindered Power" in the book *Secret Power*, "I have lived long enough to know that if I cannot have the power of the Spirit of God on me to help me to work for Him, I would rather die, than to live just for the sake of living."

In Dr. R. A. Torrey's great message on *Why God Used D. L. Moody*, he named seven qualities that made Moody the wonderfully used man that he was. And the seventh, last and most important was that Moody was "definitely endued with power from on high." Listen to what R. A. Torrey said (pages 51–55) about Mr. Moody:

The seventh thing that was the secret of why God used D. L. Moody was that, *he had a very definite enduement with power from on high*, a very clear and definite *baptism with the Holy Ghost*. Mr. Moody knew he had the "baptism with the Holy Ghost"; he had no doubt about it. In his early days he was a great hustler, he had a tremendous desire to do something, but he had no real power. He worked very largely in the energy of the flesh. But there were two humble Free Methodist women who used to come over to his meetings in the Y.M.C.A. One was "Auntie Cook" and the other Mrs. Snow. (I think her name was not Snow at that time.) These two women would come to Mr. Moody at the close of his meetings and say: "We are praying for you." Finally, Mr. Moody became somewhat nettled and said to them one night: "Why are you praying for me? Why don't you pray for the unsaved?" They replied: "We are praying that you may get the power." Mr. Moody did not know what that meant, but he got to thinking about it, and then went to these women and said: "I wish you would tell me what you mean," and they told him about the definite baptism with the Holy Ghost. Then he asked that he might pray with them and not they merely pray for him.

Auntie Cook once told me of the intense fervour with which Mr. Moody prayed on that occasion. She told me in words that I scarcely dare repeat, though I have never forgotten them. And he not only prayed with them, but he also prayed alone. Not long after, one day on his way to England, he was walking up Wall Street in New York (Mr. Moody very seldom told this and I almost hesitate to tell it), and in the midst of the bustle and hurry of that city his prayer was answered; the power of God fell upon him as he walked up the street, and he had to hurry off to the house of a friend and ask that he might have a room by himself, and in that room he stayed alone for hours; and the Holy Ghost came upon him filling his soul with such joy that at last he had to ask God to withhold His hand, lest he die on the spot from very joy. He went out from that place with the power of the Holy Ghost upon him, and when he got to London (partly through the prayers of a bedridden saint in Mr. Lessey's church), the power of God wrought through him mightily in North London, and hundreds were added to the churches, and that was what led to his being invited over to the wonderful campaign that followed in later years.

Time and again Mr. Moody would come to me and say: "Torrey, I want you to preach on baptism with the Holy Ghost." I do not know how many times he asked me to speak on that subject. Once, when I had been invited to preach in the Fifth Avenue Presbyterian Church, New York (invited at Mr. Moody's suggestion; had it not been for his suggestion the invitation would never have been extended to me), just before I started for New York, Mr. Moody drove up to my house and said: "Torrey, they want you to preach at the Fifth Avenue Presbyterian Church in New York. It is a great, big church, cost a million dollars to build it." Then he continued: "Torrey, I just want to ask one thing of you. I want to tell you what to preach about. You will preach that sermon of yours on 'Ten Reasons Why I Believe the Bible to Be the Word of God' and your sermon on 'The Baptism with the Holy Ghost.'" Time and again, when a call came to me to go off to some church, he would come up to me and say: "Now, Torrey, be sure and preach on the baptism with the Holy Ghost."

Oh, if we had more men filled with the Holy Spirit, endued with power from on high as Moody was, we would have more men showing Moody's results!

R. A. Torrey Was Definitely Filled With the Holy Ghost for Soul-Winning Power

Already you know, by what Dr. Torrey said about D. L. Moody, that he believed, as Moody did, that one to win souls for Christ must have the power of God, a special enduement of power; that is, must be filled with the Spirit of God. Torrey was in some sense the successor of D. L. Moody. He was certainly Moody's most trusted helper. In one world-wide tour, R. A. Torrey's campaigns resulted in a hundred thousand souls saved. So says George T. B. Davis in his book, *Twice Around the World With Alexander*. Mr. Davis says that Torrey and Alexander were the "successors of Moody and Sankey." Telling of Torrey's and Alexander's campaigns in England, Davis said, "In Birmingham during a single month's campaign 7,700 confessed Christ; while in London, in a five months' Mission, held in Royal Albert Hall, England's finest auditorium, and in two specially erected iron buildings, about 17,000 made public profession. In all, during the three years' work in the British Isles, about 80,000 converts were recorded...." Thousands of others were saved in Australia; and, of course, many, many thousands in campaigns in America. So the scholarly Torrey walked in the steps of the uneducated Moody. Both of them alike were filled with the Holy Spirit. And let us read what Dr. Torrey says about himself.

In his book *The Holy Spirit: Who He Is, and What He Does,* in the chapter "The Baptism With the Holy Spirit," pages 107, 108, Dr. Torrey says:

> The address of this afternoon, and the addresses of the days immediately to follow, are the outcome of an experience, and that experience was the outcome of a study of the Word of God. After I had been a Christian for some years, and after I had been in the ministry for some years, my attention was strongly attracted to certain phrases found in the Gospels and in the Acts of the Apostles, and in the Epistles, such as "baptized with the Holy Spirit," "filled with the Spirit," "the Holy Spirit fell upon them," "the gift of the Holy Spirit," "endued with power from on high," and other closely allied phrases. As I studied these various phrases in their context, it became clear to me that they all stood for essentially the same experience; and it also became clear to me that God has provided for each child of His in this present dispensation that they should be thus "baptized with the Spirit," or, "filled with the Spirit."
>
> As I studied the subject still further, I became convinced that they described an experience which I did not myself possess, and I went to work to secure for myself the experience thus described. I sought earnestly that I might "be baptized with the Holy Spirit." I went at it very ignorantly. I have often wondered if anyone ever went at it any more ignorantly than I did. But while I was ignorant, I was thoroughly sincere and in earnest, and God met me, as He always meets the sincere and earnest soul, no matter how ignorant he may be; and God gave me what I sought. I was "baptized with the Holy Spirit." And the result was a transformed Christian life and a transformed ministry.

Torrey too was filled with the Holy Spirit. He did not talk in tongues; he never claimed to have the carnal nature eradicated, but he did receive a mighty enduement of power from on high. It came after he was saved and made him a mighty soul winner.

In the book *Holiness and Power,* pages 337, 338, Rev. A. M. Hills tells of a letter from Dr. Torrey in the following words:

> I wrote a letter to Brother Torrey of Chicago, a month ago, asking
> him to tell me how he came to seek the baptism of the Holy Spirit, and
> what the blessing had done for him. He replied as follows: "I was led to
> seek the baptism with the Holy Spirit because I became convinced
> from the study of the Acts of the Apostles that no one had a right to
> preach the Gospel until he had been baptized with the Holy Spirit. At
> last I was led to the place where I said that I would never enter the pul-
> pit again until I had been baptized with the Holy Ghost and knew it,
> or until God in some way told me to go. I obtained the blessing in less
> than a week. If I had understood the Bible as I do now there need not
> have passed any days.

> "As to what the blessing has done for me, I could not begin to tell.
> It has brought a joy into my soul that I never dreamed of before; a lib-
> erty in preaching that makes preaching an unspeakable delight where
> before it was a matter of dread; it has opened to me a door of useful-
> ness, so that now, instead of preaching to a very little church, I have
> calls every year to proclaim the truth to very many thousands, being
> invited to conventions in every part of the land to address vast audi-
> ences; and I have a church today, in addition to my work in the
> Institute, that has a membership of upwards of thirteen hundred, with
> an evening audience that sometimes overflows the auditorium of the
> church, into which we can pack twenty-five hundred people, into the
> lecture-room below."

This letter by Dr. Torrey was written before he made his worldwide
tour and before he was in a life of evangelistic campaigns. Yet he knew
that he had been definitely endued with power from on high. He had
had a definite time of seeking the power of God and knew that he had
found that which he sought. God gave him power in preaching the
Word and teaching, and it resulted in multitudes saved.

Dr. J. Wilbur Chapman Filled With the Holy Spirit

Rev. A. M. Hills was state evangelist in Michigan for the
Congregational church. His book, *Holiness and Power*, is a good book,
though we do not vouch for Brother Hills' position on holiness. But
Hills tells in the following words, page 336, of a time when Dr. J.
Wilbur Chapman went before God and sought His power and found it:

> Dr. Wilbur Chapman tells us how he went before God and conse-
> crated himself, and then said in faith, "My Father, I now claim from
> Thee the infilling of the Holy Ghost," and he says: "From that moment
> to this He has been a living reality. I never knew what it was to love
> my family before. I never knew what it was to study the Bible before.

And why should I, for had I not just then found the key? I never knew what it was to preach before. 'Old things have passed away' in my experience. 'Behold, all things have become new.'"

Even more revealing of Dr. Chapman's teaching and practice and experience in the power of the Holy Spirit is the following passage by Dr. Chapman:

"I had," said Dr. Chapman, "an ignorant man in my church in Philadelphia, by the name of S., who utterly murdered the king's English. When he first stood up to talk, and you heard him for the first time, you would be amazed, and would hope that he would not speak long. But soon you would begin to wonder at the marvelous power of his words. I will tell you the secret of it. I once called thirty of the workers of my church together to pray for the baptism of power for a special work. He rose and left the room. I afterward found him alone in a little room of the church pleading in prayer: 'O Lord, take all sin from me. Teach me what it is that hinders Thy coming. I will give up everything. Come, O Holy Spirit, come and take possession of me, and help me to win men.' He arose from his knees and met me face to face, and said: 'Pastor, I have received the Holy Ghost.' To my certain knowledge, since that time (about three years) that ignorant man has led more than a hundred men to Jesus" (Holiness and Power, pages 329, 330).

The marvelous ministry of J. Wilbur Chapman can be explained only by the fact that he, like Moody and Torrey, was filled with the Holy Spirit, definitely endued with the Holy Spirit, or filled with the Holy Spirit, or baptized with the Holy Spirit, whichever term you care to use. Chapman was associated with Moody, was selected by Moody to be vice-president of Moody Bible Institute and was the author of the book, The Life and Work of D. L. Moody. In fact, Dr. Chapman tells us that it was Moody himself who led Chapman to the first full assurance of salvation.

In the biography of J. Wilbur Chapman by Ottman is this striking statement: "He had witnessed such marvelous manifestations of the Spirit of God in so many of his meetings that he felt a keen disappointment when the tide failed to reach the full flood." He was a mighty, heart-moving preacher, filled with the Holy Ghost. Chapman himself had prayed for the fullness of the Spirit. He taught others to pray for "the baptism of power for a special work."

Billy Sunday, Who Won Over a Million Souls to Christ, Was Definitely Filled With the Holy Spirit

Mr. Homer Rodeheaver, Billy Sunday's song leader for the most powerful years of his ministry, has the following to say about Mr. Sunday:

Mr. Sunday was criticized as few men. He could stand criticism. Put the spotlight on Mr. Sunday from any point of view. The result is to expose the pitiable smallness of his critics. He did things that were epic. Under his ministry more lives were changed than by any man who has preached the Gospel. More than a million men and women "hit the sawdust trail." He was responsible for multitudes of ministers, missionaries, revived churches, Bible schools, and Christian activities that reach to the four corners of the earth (*Twenty Years With Billy Sunday*, p. 24).

It seems probable that in a harder day and with greater competition, Billy Sunday won more souls than did D. L. Moody, or any other single man who ever lived, as Mr. Rodeheaver says. Again Mr. Rodeheaver says, "No doubt he spoke directly to more people in the course of his career than any other man in the world. He did this without amplifiers or mechanical devices to carry his voice" (*Twenty Years With Billy Sunday*, p. 18).

Now, was Billy Sunday himself filled with the Holy Spirit? Did he have a special anointing of God, an enduement of power from on high such as made possible the ministry of Moody and of Torrey and of Chapman and of other great soul winners? Beyond any shadow of doubt, Billy Sunday did have such an enduement of power, such a definite filling of the Spirit!

When I first considered this matter I was disappointed that we did not have from Billy Sunday's lips the naming of a certain date and the description of a certain experience, when the Spirit of the Lord came upon him in a special enduement of soul-winning power. I rather wanted it down in black and white in Billy Sunday's own words, some account of a wonderful period of emotion and crisis and glory to which we could point. I do not know of any such statement by Billy Sunday or of any published record of a time when Billy Sunday was definitely endued with power.

And the more I think about it, and pray about it the more clearly God has seemed to speak to my heart in this matter and to show me His infinite wisdom in not allowing us to have a definite description of the time when Sunday was first filled with the Holy Spirit. I cannot describe the first time I myself was filled with the Holy Spirit. For one thing, I began winning souls when I was fifteen years old. For another thing, I had the mighty power of God upon me in soul winning before I understood the doctrine of the Holy Spirit. I prayed for power before I knew the Bible terminology for the power I needed and wanted. I made the surrender to the will of God and gave myself wholly to soul-winning work before I knew that these were the requirements which God made for the fullness of the Holy Spirit. So I cannot describe a certain climax and a crisis of emotion and glorious assurance to mark the first time I was filled with the Holy Spirit. And the same thing seems to have been true about Billy Sunday and of thousands of other remarkable soul winners. No doubt God in His mercy wanted us to see that the evidence that He Himself describes in Acts 1:8 is enough: "Ye shall receive power, after that the Holy Ghost is come upon you" Soul-winning power *is* enough.

But was Billy Sunday conscious of being filled with the Holy Spirit? Did he meet the requirements for a special enduement of power as other soul winners have, the same conditions? Was he conscious of a supernatural enabling that turned the hearts of sinners to Christ when he preached? Assuredly, beyond any shadow of doubt, he not only had met God's requirements, the same requirements that other men met, and had the same supernatural enabling, the same enduement of power; but he was definitely conscious of that fullness of the Spirit and relied upon the Holy Spirit to do His wondrous pentecostal work through him, Mr. Sunday, in saving souls.

We would not need further evidence on this matter than the million souls, and more who turned to God under Mr. Sunday's preaching. Souls are saved by the power of the Holy Spirit. No one ever wins souls through any other power. Not human zeal, not human personality, not scholarship nor even the preaching of the Word of God in human wisdom can save souls. Even of the Word of God itself we are told, "the letter killeth..." (II Cor. 3:6). So if I never had a word from Billy Sunday, never had any indication of his doctrinal position on this matter, I would know that Mr. Sunday was mightily filled with the Spirit of God for winning souls.

But the evidence is overwhelming that Billy Sunday knew what God's conditions were, that he consciously met those conditions, and that he knew he was supremely filled with the Spirit of God.

Remember, first, that Billy Sunday was a disciple of J. Wilbur Chapman. He worked with the famous evangelist three years when Mr. Chapman was having great union revival campaigns. Then when Billy Sunday started his own work as an evangelist, it was sermons by Dr. Chapman which he preached. "Seven sermons given him by Dr. Chapman, plus his own testimony, made the eight with which he started his evangelistic career" (*Twenty Years With Billy Sunday*, p. 21). His three years under J. Wilbur Chapman molded his doctrine on the power of the Holy Spirit just as Moody's influence molded Dr. Chapman's. Billy Sunday always gave more credit to Dr. J. Wilbur Chapman for his preaching than to anybody else. Hence, Billy Sunday believed in and preached a definite fullness of the Holy Spirit as Dr. Chapman believed and preached it.

Billy Sunday's position on this matter is made clear all the more by his own preaching. I have, for example, his printed sermons preached in the Omaha, Nebraska, campaign in 1915. He preached one time on "Have ye received the Holy Ghost since ye believed?" (Acts 19:2); once on "But tarry ye in the city of Jerusalem, until ye be endued with power from on high" (Luke 24:49); once on "But ye shall receive power, after that the Holy Ghost is come upon you: and ye shall be witnesses unto me both in Jerusalem, and in all Judæa, and in Samaria, and unto the uttermost part of the earth" (Acts 1:8); and once on "The Revival at Pentecost." Those sermons upon those texts and subjects indicate the importance Billy Sunday himself placed upon a definite enduement of power from on high for soul winning.

But there is an even more remarkable evidence that Billy Sunday felt he was endued with power from on high and that he preached in a wonderful anointing from Heaven. Every time Billy Sunday preached, he opened his Bible to one text of Scripture that declares, "The Spirit of the Lord GOD is upon me; because the LORD hath anointed me to preach...", laid his sermon notes upon that Scripture and preached with the fire and power of God! On this matter Mr. Rodeheaver, his assistant for twenty years, says:

> "Invariably he opened the Bible and placed his sermon notes upon the passage in Isaiah, first verse of the sixty-first chapter, which reads: 'The Spirit of the Lord GOD is upon me; because the LORD hath anointed me to preach good tidings unto the meek; he hath sent me to bind up the brokenhearted, to proclaim liberty to the captives, and the opening of the prison to them that are bound.'

> "Many people wanted to possess the Bible Mr. Sunday had used during a campaign. When he granted the request it would be found that these pages in the Book of Isaiah were almost worn out" (*Twenty Years With Billy Sunday*, by Homer Rodeheaver, p. 10).

What experience with God did Billy Sunday have that made him always open the Bible to that one verse of Scripture? What holy vow, what compact with God, moved this mighty soul winner that *always* when he preached the Gospel his Bible lay open on the pulpit with these words, "The Spirit of the Lord GOD is upon me; because the Lord hath anointed me to preach..."? Surely Mr. Sunday *knew* beyond a shadow of doubt that the Spirit of the Lord was upon him. And he surely knew that he was anointed to preach. I have no doubt he treasured, beyond any other knowledge, the knowledge that his power was the power of God and that he dare not trifle with it. Knowing that he had a holy anointing, he pleased God instead of men; he preached without any compromise, preached in a way that offended, that cut, that burned and that assaulted and captured the castles of men's hearts for Christ. If Billy Sunday had told me with his own voice, looking me in the face, that he knew he had a definite enduement of power from God for soul winning and that it was a holy trust with which he dared not trifle but must keep its conditions always in mind, it would not be more certain in my mind than it is.

When Mr. Sunday and I were on a radio program together, sat on the same platform, and were once guests at the same table, he did not tell me of such a definite secret experience. But he was filled with the Holy Ghost and knew it, and claimed this as his treasure above all treasure, his one indispensable equipment for soul winning. That we certainly know by his own emphasis on the power of the Holy Spirit in his preaching and by the fact that he always opened his Bible to this one text in Isaiah 61:1 before preaching the Gospel.

Other people may not have known where Billy Sunday got his power; but he knew, he knew! And he reminded himself of the one source from which he could have blessing and power every time he ever preached! And we are justified in supposing that every time Billy Sunday opened his Bible to Isaiah 61:1 and laid it on the pulpit before him before beginning his sermon, he made a fresh covenant with God, relying upon the power of the Holy Spirit for that sermon and humbly beseeching God for His blessing. A definite enduement of power from on high is the only possible explanation of Billy Sunday's ministry.

Charles G. Finney, Mighty Soul Winner, Baptized With the Holy Ghost!

The *Autobiography of Charles G. Finney* is one of the most helpful books in print. It was one of four books that have had the greatest influence on my Christian life and ministry. The others were *George Müller of Bristol* by A. T. Pierson, *How to Pray* by R. A. Torrey and *In His Steps* or *What Would Jesus Do?* by Charles M. Sheldon. But for a pungent and powerful revelation of how God works in soul winning and revival, few if any books ever written can exceed the *Autobiography of Charles G. Finney*. Finney won multiplied thousands of souls.

Although he preached in a smaller area, and though he was handicapped by some errors in theology, Finney probably had as powerful a manifestation of the power of God upon his ministry as did D. L. Moody or any other preacher since the days of Paul, and in the smaller area which he covered in his revival work a larger proportion of the population was saved than has been true, we suppose, in the ministry of any other great evangelist. How he was filled with the Holy Spirit is told on pages 19–23 of the autobiography. Elsewhere Charles G. Finney writes, as quoted by Dr. Oswald J. Smith, in *The Revival We Need*:

I was powerfully converted on the morning of the 10th of October, 1821. In the evening of the same day I received overwhelming baptisms of the Holy Ghost, that went through me, as it seemed to me, body and soul. I immediately found myself endued with such power from on high that a few words dropped here and there to individuals were the means of their immediate conversion. My words seemed to fasten like barbed arrows in the souls of men. They cut like a sword. They broke the heart like a hammer. Multitudes can attest to this. Oftentimes a word dropped without my remembering it would fasten conviction, and often result in almost immediate conversion. Sometimes I would find myself, in a great measure, empty of this power. I would go and visit, and find that I made no saving impression. I would exhort and pray, with the same result. I would then set apart a day for private fasting and prayer, fearing that this power had departed from me, and would inquire anxiously after the reason of this apparent emptiness. After humbling myself, and crying out for help, the power would return upon me with all its freshness. This has been the experience of my life.

This power is a great marvel. I have many times seen people unable to endure the Word. The most simple and ordinary statements would cut men off their seats like a sword, would take away their strength, and render them almost helpless as dead men. Several times it has been true in my experience that I could not raise my voice, or say anything in prayer or exhortation, except in the mildest manner, without overcoming them. This power seems sometimes to pervade the atmosphere of the one who is highly charged with it. Many times great numbers of persons in a community will be clothed with this power when the very atmosphere of the whole place seems to be charged with the life of God. Strangers coming into it and passing through the place will be instantly smitten with conviction of sin and in many instances converted to Christ. When Christians humble themselves and consecrate their all afresh to Christ, and ask for this power, they will often receive such a baptism that they will be instrumental in converting more souls in one day than in all their lifetime before. While Christians remain humble enough to retain this power, the work of conversion will go on, till whole communities and regions of country are converted to Christ. The same is true of the ministry.

It is important to notice that Charles G. Finney uses the term "baptisms of the Holy Ghost." We do not insist upon the term, but sensible people ought not to scoff at the term, a scriptural term, as understood and used by Finney, Moody, Torrey and Chapman. Note also that this fullness of the Spirit comes, says Finney, in answer to prayer. He says that when he found himself losing power, "I would then set apart a day for private fasting and prayer...." Then he says, "After humbling myself, and crying out for help, the power would return upon me with all its freshness. This has been the experience of my life."

Note again that Charles G. Finney is not talking about the eradication of the carnal nature. He did not talk in tongues. He was not seeking some special feeling, though he did have a wonderful sense of God's presence upon him. He sought and found an enduement of power from on high that made him a mighty soul winner!

Charles H. Spurgeon, Spirit-Filled Soul Winner

Charles H. Spurgeon, pastor of the Metropolitan Tabernacle in London, had as profound an effect on his age as D. L. Moody. In England he was even more eminent, we suppose, than Moody was in America. It is doubtful if any man who ever lived would be a serious competitor to Spurgeon for the title of the greatest preacher since Paul. W. Robertson Nicoll says, "...His was a ministry unparalleled in the whole history of the Christian church. No one but Mr. Spurgeon has steadily preached for forty years and three times a week to such audiences as he commanded.

"There were hundreds of thousands who owed him their own souls."

I do not find from Mr. Spurgeon's pen a description of a certain time and crisis when he was obviously and consciously filled for the first time with the Holy Spirit. But perhaps that is well. We should do wrong to expect every man to have the same kind of experience as far as outward manifestation and feeling are concerned. More than that, we should do wrong to believe that any such conscious period of joy or perfect understanding of the fullness of God should necessarily come at once like a glory light shining from Heaven. I am as certain as I can be that the breath of God, the power of the Holy Spirit, has, in God's great mercy, been breathed upon me. Yet I cannot name the day nor describe the experience. So Spurgeon, like Billy Sunday, has left no record of the particular time when he was first mightily filled with the power of God for soul winning. Yet the mighty anointing of the Spirit was on Spurgeon. That, we know, is the only explanation for the hundreds of thousands saved under his ministry. He himself knew that too; and many quotations from his sermons give witness to his consciousness of the Spirit's mighty power.

In the book *Twelve Sermons on the Holy Spirit* and in the sermon "The Outpouring of the Holy Spirit" (p. 50), Spurgeon says:

> Jesus Christ said, 'Greater works than these shall ye do because I go to My Father, in order to send the Holy Spirit'; and recollect that those few who were converted under Christ's ministry were not converted by Him, but by the Holy Spirit that rested upon Him at that time. Jesus of Nazareth was anointed of the Holy Spirit. Now then, if Jesus Christ, the great founder of our religion, needed to be anointed of the Holy Spirit, how much more our ministers?

Again in the same sermon, on page 51, Spurgeon says:

> Let the preacher always confess before he preaches that he relies upon the Holy Spirit. Let him burn his manuscript and depend upon the Holy Spirit. If the Spirit does not come to help him, let him be still and let the people go home and pray that the Spirit will help him next Sunday.
>
> And best of all, if you would have the Holy Spirit, let us meet together earnestly to pray for Him. Remember, the Holy Spirit will not come to us as a church, unless we seek Him. 'For this thing will I be enquired of by the house of Israel to do it for them.' 'Prove me now herewith, saith the Lord of hosts, and see if I do not pour you out a blessing so that there shall not be room enough to receive it.' Let us meet and pray, and if God doth not hear us, it will be the first time He has broken His promise.

In the same book, in the sermon on "The Indwelling and Outflowing of the Holy Spirit" (pp. 113,114), Spurgeon says:

> But there is another thing to be done as well, and that is *to pray*; and here I want to remind you of those blessed words of the Master, "Every one that asketh receiveth; and he that seeketh findeth; and to him that knocketh it shall be opened. If a son shall ask bread of any of you that is a father, will he give him a stone? or if he ask a fish, will he for a fish give him a serpent? Or if he shall ask an egg, will he offer him a scorpion? If ye then, being evil, know how to give good gifts unto your children: how much more shall your heavenly Father give the Holy Spirit to them that ask him?" You see, there is a distinct promise to the children of God, that their heavenly Father will give them the Holy Spirit if they ask for His power; and that promise is made to be

exceedingly strong by the instances joined to it. But He says, "*How much more* shall your heavenly Father give the Holy Spirit to them that ask him?" He makes it a stronger case than that of an ordinary parent. The Lord must give us the Spirit when we ask Him, for He has herein bound Himself by no ordinary pledge. He has used a simile which would bring dishonour on His own name, and that of the very grossest kind, if He did not give the Holy Spirit to them that ask Him.

Oh, then, let us ask Him at once, with all of our hearts. Am I not so happy as to have in this audience some who will immediately ask? I pray that some who have never received the Holy Spirit at all may now be led, while I am speaking, to pray, "Blessed Spirit, visit me; lead me to Jesus." But especially those of you that are the children of God, to you is this promise especially made. Ask God to make you all that the Spirit of God can make you, not only a satisfied believer who has drunk for himself, but a useful believer, who overflows the neighborhood with blessing. I see here a number of friends from the country who have come to spend their holiday in London. What a blessing it would be if they went back to their respective churches overflowing; for there are numbers of churches that need flooding; they are dry as a barn-floor, and little dew ever falls on them. Oh that they might be flooded!

I was delighted to find what I did not know before, that Spurgeon understood how Jesus our Saviour was filled with the Holy Spirit as our example, and how all Christ's marvelous ministry on earth was done in the power of the Holy Spirit, not in His own power. And Spurgeon, I find, understood what I had found from the Scriptures, that the parable of the importunate friend in Luke, chapter 11, begging for bread for a friend who had journeyed to the pleader's house, pictured a Christian waiting on God for the power of the Holy Spirit to carry bread for sinners!

Let us say, then, that Spurgeon was conscious of the fullness of the Holy Spirit upon himself and that he knew whence his power came. We see also that this mighty power of God came on Spurgeon in answer to pleading prayer; yea, in answer to prayer this power came again and again upon the mighty "prince of preachers."

Evan Roberts, Welsh Evangelist, Filled With the Holy Ghost

Dr. Oswald J. Smith, in his book, *The Revival We Need*, pages 42, 43, has the following quotation from Evan Roberts, Welsh evangelist:

"For thirteen years," writes Evan Roberts, "I had prayed for the Spirit; and this is the way I was led to pray. William Davies, the deacon, said one night in the society: 'Remember to be faithful. What if the Spirit descended and you were absent? Remember Thomas! What a loss he had!'

"I said to myself: 'I will have the Spirit,' and through every kind of weather and in spite of all difficulties, I went to the meetings. Many times, on seeing other boys with the boats on the tide, I was tempted to turn back and join them. But, no. I said to myself: 'Remember your resolve,' and on I went. I went faithfully to the meetings for prayer throughout the ten or eleven years I prayed for a revival. It was the Spirit that moved me thus to think."

At a certain morning meeting which Evan Roberts attended, the evangelist in one of his petitions besought that the Lord would "bend us." The Spirit seemed to say to Roberts: "That's what you need, to be bent." And thus he describes his experience: "I felt a living force coming into my bosom. This grew and grew, and I was almost bursting. My bosom was boiling. What boiled in me was that verse: 'God commending His love.' I fell on my knees with my arms over the seat in front of me; the tears and perspiration flowed freely. I thought blood was gushing forth." Certain friends approached to wipe his face. Meanwhile he was crying out, "O Lord, bend me! Bend me!" Then suddenly the glory broke.

Mr. Roberts adds: "After I was bent, a wave of peace came over me, and the audience sang, 'I hear Thy welcome voice.' And as they sang, I thought about the bending at the Judgment Day, and I was filled with compassion for those that would have to bend on that day, and I wept.

"Henceforth, the salvation of souls became the burden of my heart. From that time I was on fire with a desire to go through all Wales; and if it were possible, I was willing to pay God for the privilege of going."

Note that Evan Roberts prayed for thirteen years before the mighty revival for which he prayed came, and that the fullness of the Spirit made him the great soul winner that he became.

Many Other Mighty Soul Winners Claimed to Be Definitely Filled With the Holy Spirit

We do not have space here to give accounts of all the great men of God of whom we have a record who definitely claimed that they had a mighty enduement of power from on high, which came to them aside from their conversion to Christ. Let us mention briefly some of them.

Rev. A. B. Earle, D.D., was a Baptist evangelist who began preaching in 1830. He wrote a book, *The Rest of Faith*, telling of some of his experiences. In the introduction to one of his books, Evangelist Earle said that God had enabled him to lead 157,000 souls to Christ, and Hills in his book, *Holiness and Power*, says, "A book lies before me which says that 'he had no special power as a preacher before the Holy Ghost fell upon him.'" Dr. Earle came before D. L. Moody but was a union evangelist wonderfully blessed of God. And he attributed his power to a definite enduement from Heaven, the fullness of the Holy Spirit for soul winning.

Mr. Hills says of A. T. Pierson, "Dr. A. T. Pierson preached eighteen years trusting to literary power and oratory and culture. He then sought and obtained 'holiness and power' by the baptism of the Holy Spirit! He afterward testified to a body of ministers: 'Brethren, I have seen more conversions and accomplished more in the eighteen months since I received that blessing than in the eighteen years previous'" (*Holiness and Power*, p. 336). And those who know the writings of Dr. Pierson will understand that he did not mean that he had had the carnal nature eradicated, nor that he had talked in tongues, but that he received power from on high for winning souls.

How many more greatly-used men of God, anointed soul winners, have testified that they had a definite time, in response to earnest prayer for the power of God in soul winning, when they were filled with the Holy Spirit. There was Christmas Evans, the one-eyed Welsh evangelist wonderfully filled with the Spirit after three hours of pleading with God. There was Len G. Broughton, Southern Baptist pastor whose ministry was transformed one night as he knelt at an altar and pleaded with God for the fullness of the Spirit and claimed that power and went back to baptize three hundred converts within the year and began a marvelously increased ministry of soul winning. There was "Praying Hyde," the missionary to India. As he sailed from America, a friend handed him a sealed note which he later found said, "Are you filled with the Holy Spirit?" He was first angry, then troubled, and then sought God with all of his heart until he was wonderfully filled. Great revivals with the winning of thousands of souls in India resulted. There was Dr. L. R. Scarborough, president of the Southwestern Baptist Theological Seminary, who had won twenty thousand souls for Christ and taught in our class on evangelism the need for a definite enduement of power from on high, a fullness of the Holy Spirit, which he himself had definitely received.

Mighty Lessons From the Testimony of These Spirit-Filled Giants

Every reader who is familiar with the history of great revival movements in modern times must be impressed with the fact that we have in this chapter given the position and testimony of all the mightiest soul winners—Moody, Torrey, Chapman, Sunday, Finney, Spurgeon. Who else was of their stature in revivals and soul winning? Other mighty men organized much, built great denominations, founded great schools; but the men we have named in this chapter won more souls and preached with more power than any men who have lived since the Apostle Paul, as far as we know. And it seems wonderful, to me, that these spiritual giants, manifestly filled with the power of God, were all united on the essential facts regarding the fullness of the Holy Spirit, or baptism of the Spirit, the mighty anointing of God, the power of Pentecost.

Some of the men named were better theologians than others. Some had better education than others. But all of them were mightily filled with the power of God and knew how they were filled. And all of them were agreed on the essentials of this power of Pentecost. Notice, then, some lessons from the testimony of these mighty men:

1. All of them believed that the fullness of the Holy Spirit as experienced by Christians in the Book of Acts is for us today! In fact, each claimed for himself and offered for his hearers the power of the Holy Spirit.

2. All of them, without exception, believed that the fullness of the Holy Spirit was given for soul-winning power.

3. Every one of these mighty men believed that the power of Pentecost, the fullness of the Holy Spirit, came in answer to prevailing prayer.

4. How many of these soul winners, the greatest of these twenty centuries, believed that speaking in tongues was the necessary sign of the baptism of the Holy Spirit? Not a one of them! None of them "spoke in tongues," and none of them preached that speaking in tongues was necessary or desirable as a sign of the fullness of the Holy Spirit!

5. None of the greatest soul winners of the centuries claimed the eradication of the carnal nature nor that the baptism of the Holy Spirit brought sinlessness! Charles G. Finney later taught a doctrine of sanctification but never did claim that his own mighty baptism with the Spirit (that is what he called it) made him sinless or eradicated the carnal nature at the time. (See his autobiography.) Even John Wesley, whose testimony is not given here, did not develop his idea of Christian perfection until long after he himself had his wonderful Aldersgate experience with the Holy Spirit.

I believe that the experience and the testimony of the mighty men of God whose words we have given in this chapter are overwhelming in their unity. Let no one think that the doctrine of this book is new or strange. Essentially it is the same as the teaching of Spurgeon, Moody, Torrey, Chapman, Sunday, Finney, Christmas Evans, A. T. Pierson, Len G. Broughton, "Praying Hyde," A. B. Earle and L. R. Scarborough.

Those who have gone away from the doctrine of the fullness of the Spirit, the power of Pentecost, as a special enduement of power for soul winning possible for every Christian and to be sought with prevailing prayer, have departed from the position of the great soul winners. This falling away in doctrine came with the falling away from revival! Men do not believe in the power of Pentecost simply because they do not themselves have the power of Pentecost.

I leave this chapter feeling that every reader will be held accountable to God for what he does about the overwhelming testimony of the great soul-winning giants of the centuries who say that they themselves were mightily filled with the Holy Spirit for soul winning, and in answer to prayer, and that this mighty enduement of power did not cause them to speak in tongues, did not eradicate the carnal nature. May God speak to every humble heart who reads and make him willing to receive the testimony of those upon whom God has breathed in His mighty power.

Chapter 15

Claim Your Blessing

"...And ye shall receive the gift of the Holy Ghost. For the promise is unto you...."—Acts 2:38,39.

"...Concerning the work of my hands command ye me."—Isa. 45:11.

"And this is the confidence that we have in him, that, if we ask any thing according to his will, he heareth us: And if we know that he hear us, whatsoever we ask, we know that we have the petitions that we desired of him."—I John 5:14,15.

Perhaps we have now had about enough of theology in this book; it is time for practical experience! Any honest reader who has prayerfully studied the preceding chapters on this matter of the Holy Spirit will understand the gist of it. You will not understand all about the power of Pentecost and the fullness of the Holy Spirit, but surely earnest readers now know that there is an enduement of power from on high which may be given to people who are already saved to enable them to win souls. This power is given to those who wait upon God and give themselves wholly to His will, particularly in soul winning. But, alas, many a reader has grown wiser in his head, and his heart may still be cold! Perhaps many a reader has now more clearly-formed opinions but has no more power for soul winning, no more holy moving of the mighty Spirit of God in his witnessing than he had before! Now it is time for every honest reader to claim his blessing! It is time to set out definitely to be filled with the Holy Spirit, endued with power from on high.

Never mind about some difference in terminology. Never mind about some point with which you disagree. Oh, the burden of my heart as I write these words is not that people shall agree with me about doctrine but that people shall obtain the power of God! Do not argue about this blessing—take it! Never mind the name for it, whether you would call it the baptism of the Spirit, or the fullness of the Spirit, or the gift of the Holy Ghost, or perhaps some other name favored by some other group. What does it matter whether it is the deeper life, or sanctification, or perfect love, if you do not have it? I say, never mind about the terminology; in Jesus' name claim the power of the Holy Spirit and, endued with that breath from Heaven, that anointing of God, go out to win souls today!

Ask

I have waited seventeen years to publish the book of which this is a chapter. Seventeen years ago, after months and months of study, I wrote out a manuscript on the fullness of the Holy Spirit. But it was a matter of such importance that I dared not publish the book. I have taken years to study, to wait upon God, to prove His power upon my life before I published a book on this subject. My heavenly Father knows with what earnest pleading, with what long waiting upon God, with what diligent searching of the Scriptures, with what holy desire to bless and help the people of God and to hurt no one I have prepared these messages on the fullness of the Spirit and the power of Pentecost. It was a matter of awful importance that the doctrine be scriptural and be plainly stated, with holy simplicity.

But while I delayed to go in print on the doctrine, thank God, I took God up on His promises and have had His blessed power. Multiplied thousands of souls have come to Christ under the ministry of this unworthy author while I waited to perfect the manuscript of this book. I needed to wait, perhaps, to get the doctrine clear, to answer every question possible. But I did not need to wait for the power of God.

As a fifteen-year-old boy I won my first soul. By God's mercy I won hundreds of souls before I set out to preach from the pulpit. It is infinitely more important to be doing the will of God and be right in the heart than to know a doctrine.

How many Pharisees curse the church today! How many know to 'tithe mint and anise and cummin' and do not have the power of God upon them to keep a soul out of Hell! Oh, dear reader, in Christ's name, make this fullness of the Holy Spirit your own experience and joy and power! Get out of the realm of technical theology and into the realm of New Testament Christian experience. Let your heart go beyond the bare framework of doctrine and enter into the living power of Christ for soul winning!

I. This Blessing Is for You!

I urge you to claim the fullness of the Holy Spirit, to be endued with power from on high, because this power is *for you*. God intended the fullness of the Spirit for everyone who has trusted in Christ for salvation.

This is made clear by the inspired words of Peter at Pentecost, recorded in Acts 2:38,39:

"Then Peter said unto them, Repent, and be baptized every one of you in the name of Jesus Christ for the remission of sins, and ye shall receive the gift of the Holy Ghost. For the promise is unto you, and to your children, and to all that are afar off, even as many as the Lord our God shall call."

Repentance—that is, the sincere turning of the heart away from sin and turning to Christ in faith—is the way of salvation; and all who genuinely repent are saved. Then to those who go on honestly to be baptized in the name of Jesus Christ, publicly declaring that remission of sins which they have already received, is promised, "Ye shall receive the gift of the Holy Ghost." When these verses are compared with Acts 11:15–17, "the gift," one finds, is this special enduement of power such as the disciples received at Pentecost and Cornelius received when he was converted.

So "the promise is unto you." The promise of the fullness of the Holy Spirit was to those who heard Peter at Pentecost. The promise was to their children. The promise was to "all that are afar off, even as many as the Lord our God shall call." Thus, everyone who is ever called to be saved has the promise of the fullness of the Spirit.

It is instructive and helpful to follow this term, "the promise," about the fullness of the Spirit. John the Baptist looked for Jesus before He was manifested publicly as "he which baptizeth with the Holy Ghost" (John 1:33). Then the disciples were told by the Saviour in Luke 24:49, "And, behold, I send THE PROMISE of my Father upon you: but tarry ye in the city of Jerusalem, until ye be endued with power from on high." In Acts 1:4,5 Jesus again reminded the disciples of the same promise: "And, being assembled together with them, commanded them that they should not depart from Jerusalem, but wait for THE PROMISE of the Father, which, saith he, ye have heard of me. For John truly baptized with water; but ye shall be baptized with the Holy Ghost not many days hence." So when Peter, standing before the convicted multitude assembled at Pentecost, says, "THE PROMISE is unto you…," he means (and the Holy Spirit means) the same promise! And the same promise is to you too, dear reader, whoever you are, whom God has called to come and be saved. And lest we should ever forget that the fullness of the Holy Spirit is promised to all of us, Ephesians 1:13 names the Holy Spirit, "that holy Spirit OF PROMISE."

How boldly, then, we ought to come to God when claiming the promise He has made so often! How clearly it is intended that every Christian should have the fullness of the Holy Spirit!

Our boldness in coming to God and pleading with Him and waiting upon Him for His enduement of power for soul winning ought to be increased when we remember that He has given us a task that absolutely requires His power. We are commanded to take the Gospel to every creature. Jesus in Matthew 28:18–20 plainly says that all authority in Heaven and in earth is given to Him and that every one of us, when we are saved and baptized, should then set out to observe everything that Christ commanded the apostles in the Great Commission! The Great Commission to preach the Gospel to all the world belongs to every person ever saved. Then we surely must have the same power that was given to the apostles and to other New Testament Christians if we do the work that they did.

We remember that Jesus said, "He that believeth on me, the works that I do shall he do also; and greater works than these shall he do; because I go unto my Father" (John 14:12). We have a supernatural task. It would be unspeakable folly, it would be sinful presumption to set out to do the miraculous work of God without the power of God. The command of God to win souls is a great encouragement to seek the power of the Holy Spirit. Jesus everywhere connected the two. He gave the promise of the Father to the apostles but commanded them that they should not depart from Jerusalem but tarry until they were endued with power from on high. He promised them in Acts 1:8, "But ye shall receive power, after that the Holy Ghost is come upon you: and ye shall be witnesses unto me both in Jerusalem, and in all Judæa, and in Samaria, and unto the uttermost part of the earth." How boldly every one of us ought to bring these commands before God and acknowledge our utter helplessness to do the will of God without the power of God.

Then we should be made all the more bold when we ask to be filled with the Spirit, since those very words are a command of the Scriptures. Ephesians 5:18 says, "And be not drunk with wine, where-in is excess; but be filled with the Spirit." We are *commanded* to be filled with the Spirit. There can be no doubt, therefore, that the full-ness of the Spirit is in the will of God for every Christian. Here is one matter, then, about which we can pray with all boldness. God wants us to be filled with the Holy Spirit. Yea, He has even commanded us to be filled with the Holy Spirit. Let us then claim our blessing, enter into our inheritance. Let us call for our equipment.

II. How Believingly, Expectantly, We Should Pray for the Power of Pentecost!

The one hundred and twenty waiting in the Upper Room were filled with the Holy Spirit at Pentecost, after ten days of tarrying and continuing in prayer and supplication. I believe that many Christians wait much longer than needed and tarry and plead when they ought to believe God and take the blessing sooner.

I know that there is a false teaching on this matter. I know that many Bible teachers insist that no one ought ever to tarry and wait before God and plead for His power. Some men say one should simply surrender and believe that he has God's power and go on about his business. But the sad truth is that most of the Bible teachers who do not favor waiting on God in prevailing prayer for the fullness of the Holy Spirit do not themselves show that revival power, that soul-winning power, which is the mark of New Testament Christianity. They themselves, who talk so glibly about simply surrendering and believing, do not appear to have the fullness of God upon them.

No, there is no clear Bible doctrine that, not only for the power of the Holy Spirit but also for many other things, God wants us to wait upon Him, plead with Him, continue in prayer and supplication until the blessing comes. So Jacob wrestled all night with the angel of God before meeting Esau (Gen. 32:24). So the widow prevailed and pleaded before the unjust judge in the parable of Jesus in Luke 18:1–8. So the disciples waited in the Upper Room for ten days preceding Pentecost and the pouring out of the Holy Ghost upon them. No one has a right to discourage people from persistent prayer for Holy Spirit power. No one has a right to promise shortcuts that do not involve some measure of deep concern and heart-searching and pleading, before one is filled with the Holy Spirit. If it is right to pray, it is right to keep on praying until the answer comes. If it is right to ask God for the enduement of power from on high, it is right to plead and continue in prayer and supplication, as did the disciples.

Yet on the other hand, there is a clear teaching throughout the Bible that bold and undoubting faith can put an end to all the problems in prayer. "Therefore I say unto you, What things soever ye desire, when ye pray, believe that ye receive them, and ye shall have them," said Jesus (Mark 11:24). Again, He said, "If thou canst believe, all things are possible to him that believeth" (Mark 9:23). The more boldly we come in prayer for God's power, then, and the more assured we are that we are praying in the will of God, that He wants to give what we seek, the sooner should we expect His blessing. Oh, dear friend, come boldly when you come to ask for the fullness of power!

Let the Word of God strengthen your faith here. In I John 5:14, 15 we are told, "And this is the confidence that we have in him, that, if we ask any thing according to his will, he heareth us: And if we know that he hear us, whatsoever we ask, we know that we have the petitions that we desired of him." What a blessed ground of confidence! We know that we are asking in the will of God when we want the power to win souls for His purposes and plans only and according to His Word. We know that we are asking a thing that God is pleased to give. And if we know that we ask anything according to His will, we know that He hears us.

In Isaiah 45:11 is a startling verse upon which I believe I have preached only twice in my life, and that, rather timidly. Here it is: "Thus saith the LORD, the Holy One of Israel, and his Maker, Ask me of things to come concerning my sons, and concerning the work of my hands command ye me."

Perhaps it would be wrong to command God about our own needs. Certainly it would be wrong to be ordering God about in any matter where it was not clearly, beyond any doubt, in His precious will and for His own glory. But concerning the work of His hands, concerning the work that honors Him alone and work that He has left us to do in His power, the Scripture says, "Command ye me." This reminds us of Joshua's commanding the sun to stand still. The prayers of Elijah and Elisha were often boldly commanding. Where there is an absolute certainty of the will of God, then there is properly a boldness in prayer.

Dr. F. B. Meyer once had the following to say about claiming the power of the Holy Spirit:

> As once you obtained forgiveness and salvation by faith, so now claim and receive the Spirit's fullness. Fulfill the conditions already named, wait quietly and definitely before God in prayer; for He gives the Holy Spirit to them that ask Him; then reverently appropriate this glorious gift, and rise from your knees, and go on your way reckoning that God has kept His word and that you are filled with the Spirit. Trust Him day by day to fill you and keep you filled. There may not be at first the sound of rushing wind, or the coronet of fire, or the sensible feeling of His presence. Do not look for these, any more than the young convert should look to feeling as an evidence of acceptance. But BELIEVE in spite of feeling that you are filled. Say over and over, "I thank Thee, O my God, that Thou has kept Thy word with me, though as yet I am not aware of any special change." And the feeling will sooner or later break in upon your consciousness, and you will rejoice with exceeding joy, and all the fruits of the Spirit will begin to show themselves.

I do not think I could say that Dr. Meyer exactly expresses my mind on this matter. Jesus said about the man who was begging for bread for others, picturing the Christian waiting on God for soul-winning power, in Luke 11:8; "I say unto you, Though he will not rise and give him, because he is his friend, yet because of his *importunity* he will rise and give him as many as he needeth." The law of getting soul-winning power is "importunity." But Christ meant importunity with faith, importunity with expectancy, importunity that takes the blessing that God wants to give. However trembling your faith as you wait on God, expect God to give you the power to win souls, the power of Pentecost, and believe that He does and will give the blessing He promised.

III. Should One Witness While Waiting?

Some who read this are conscious of the great need to be filled with the Holy Spirit. It may be there are ministers, earnest men of God, who know that their preaching is a failure because it is not endued with power from on high. There are other earnest lay Christians who know that they ought to win souls and who perhaps have tried to win souls but found themselves powerless. Now the honest question comes: Shall such a Christian continue his efforts to win souls while he waits upon God for the fullness of power? Or should he turn away from all efforts of soul winning until he is assured that the anointing of God he seeks is upon him?

Usually, it seems to me, we should go on with our earnest efforts to win souls, even as we plead and wait on God continually for His power. Our earnest, prayerful, tearful, compassionate efforts to win souls are the best evidence that we really want to be filled with the Holy Spirit. We already have the command to win souls, to try to reach every creature with the Gospel. The command is, "Let him that heareth say, Come" (Rev. 22:17). The Scripture does not say that if one has been filled with the Holy Spirit and has perfect assurance that his words will be powerful, he should say, "Come." No, the simple, plain command to every Christian is, "Let him that heareth say, Come." So unless there is clear leading to the contrary from God, I think a Christian ought to maintain steadily every effort possible to get people to Jesus Christ, even while his heart cries out for the fullness of the Spirit, or for a new enduement of power from on high.

I think there are occasions when Christians are so manifestly unprepared to speak for God that they would do well to feel their utter helplessness and not try to speak for God until they first wait before Him and have His assurance that He will speak through them.Before Pentecost those who gathered in the Upper Room "continued with one accord in prayer and supplication" (Acts 1:14), and we do not suppose that they went out among the people to preach or witness during those ten days. It was a time of great emergency. They were utterly inadequate to face the multitudes that had crucified the Lord Jesus, until they should be wonderfully endued with power from on high. And occasionally people face such emergencies today.

Dr. R. A. Torrey, in a letter to Rev. A. M. Hills, quoted in the book *Holiness and Power* (pp. 337,338), says, "At last I was led to the place where I said that I would never enter the pulpit again until I had been baptized with the Holy Ghost and knew it, or until God in some way told me to go. I obtained the blessing in less than a week. If I had understood the Bible as I do now, there need not have passed any days."

But I believe that the case of D. L. Moody is one that more of us might pattern after. He came to have a great longing to be filled with the Holy Spirit. Yet there was in his life some of the power of the Spirit even then, some anointing, some fullness, because he was having people saved. Anyone who wins souls does it by the power of the Holy Spirit, the power of Pentecost. Winning souls is a supernatural business, the work of the Holy Spirit; and in Moody's life the Holy Spirit was working in a limited degree. Some were being saved, though he well knew that his power was only a tiny fraction of what it ought to be. So Moody waited on God day in and day out, while he preached and prayed between times. For about two years he prayed while he worked, and his heart cried out to God continually, whether in his long, secret sessions of prayer or as he went about his visitation. And one day in New York City the fullness of blessing came upon him!

Many Christians have some of the power of the Holy Spirit, have been somewhat filled with the Spirit, but need to wait on God continually until He does His work more perfectly and more powerfully in them, anointing them and filling them with soul-winning power. Usually one should keep on praying and keep on trying to win souls.

My own experience has been that many times, after long waiting and heart-searching and pleading with God, I did not know the fullness of His power until I stood up to preach before a great audience or until I faced some hardhearted sinner and spoke to him in the power of God. How many times as I began to speak I was sure that the breath of Heaven was upon me and that supernatural power was in the words I used. So it is usually right for a Christian to go on obeying the plain commands of God to try to win souls, even while he pleads and prays for the fullness of power.

In a number of cases in the Bible the fullness of the Spirit seemed to come especially at a time of need. The power of the Holy Spirit seems to have come afresh upon Stephen even as he sat in the

Sanhedrin, accused and tried for his life (Acts 6:15; Acts 7:55). Saul, also called Paul the apostle, seemed to have been suddenly filled with the Holy Ghost when he stood before Sergius Paulus and was confronted by Elymas the sorcerer, seeking to turn the deputy from the faith (Acts 13:9). One familiar with the Old Testament will remember that there are often such statements as, "The Spirit of God came upon Azariah..." (II Chron. 15:1); or "The Spirit of God came upon Zechariah..." (II Chron. 24:20). In the Book of Judges the Holy Spirit seemed to come just as there was need for His power upon the judges. (See Judges 11:29; Judges 13:25; Judges 14:6,19; Judges 15:14.) So one who keeps on waiting on God, as he keeps on trying to win souls, is likely to find that the fullness of power comes upon him just when that power is needed most in some soul-winning opportunity.

And it seems to me that this very truth is implied in the way Jesus gave the Great Commission in Matthew 28:19,20. We are to go and make disciples in all nations; to baptize them and teach them to go and make other disciples and observe all that Jesus commanded the apostles. And the blessed promise applies, "And, lo, I am with you alway, even unto the end of the world." That word "lo" seems to imply a blessed surprise! When we suddenly need the Saviour to be manifested by the power of the Holy Spirit in us, then He is present, and we will suddenly find Him there! There is the idea of "behold!" One who keeps on praying and expecting will find the fullness of power upon him when he needs it for the Lord's work, surely. The Saviour is always with the obedient Christian, but surely here is a promise of *His particular power for soul winning*, as we continue honestly working at soul winning. So usually it is wise to keep on witnessing while you wait on God for His power.

IV. Should Christians Expect a Sudden Crisis and Definite Manifestations and Strong Emotions When Filled With the Holy Spirit?

It is most natural for people to want some outward sign as evidence of their acceptance before God. The carnal nature thinks people are saved if they are baptized, that people are saved who are confirmed in the church, or that one's sins are forgiven if the priest, after the confessional, says so. The carnal nature likes to believe that a departed loved one is better off after masses are said for his soul. Even Christians like to have some outward sign. Multitudes of people doubt their salvation because they did not, at conversion, shout aloud, did not feel some great ecstasy, because they were not powerfully moved by emotions of joy and assurance. In this they are wrong. It is true there is much joy in serving God, and it is wonderfully sweet to know that one is born again, that his sins are forgiven, that he is accepted, for Jesus' dear sake, by the heavenly Father. But emotion is not enough evidence. Emotions change, and then where is one's assurance? Many who think they are saved today and then think they are lost tomorrow and then think they have committed the unpardonable sin day after tomorrow, are misled because they are relying upon the evidence of their feeling instead of on the plain statements of the Word of God and upon the all-sufficient sacrifice which Jesus made to pay for their sins.

It is easy, then, to see why people want to talk in tongues or want to feel something like fire go through them, burning out the dross, or want to feel electricity coming in at their heads and going out at their fingers and toes or want to fall "under the power" as an evidence that they are filled with the Holy Spirit. Actually, no such evidences, no such manifestations are promised in the Scripture to those filled with the Holy Spirit.

At Pentecost there was the sound of a rushing mighty wind that filled all the house. There were tongues of fire sitting upon the people, and those who were filled with the Spirit spoke in the languages of those assembled together so that sinners heard them speak in their own tongues in which they were born. But it is wise to remember that these manifestations were not promised to the disciples when Jesus told them to tarry in Jerusalem until they be endued with power from on high. These outward manifestations were incidental. The disciples were waiting for power, and it was power from Heaven that they received, soul-winning power. The power itself was sufficient evidence for them. The proof that they were filled with the Holy Spirit was in the three thousand conversions that day.

The same group prayed again, and in Acts 4:31 we are told that they were filled again with the Spirit. This time there were no tongues, no sound of a rushing mighty wind, no tongues like as a fire sitting on them. This time there was an earthquake; "The place was shaken where they were assembled together." But again the manifestation of the trembling building was not important. "They spake the word of God with boldness," and many were saved as the result of this powerful visitation of the Holy Spirit. And most of the times when we find people filled with the Holy Spirit in the New Testament, or even in the Old Testament, we have no outward evidence or manifestation mentioned, except that those filled with the Spirit spoke for God in great power.

D. L. Moody, when he was filled with the Holy Spirit on Wall Street, New York City, had a crisis experience, a conscious flooding of his soul with the power and joy of the Lord. We do not know that there were any physical manifestations, any physical miracles attending the coming of the Holy Spirit in greater power upon Moody, but certainly there was a tremendous manifestation of emotion in his own soul. However, it is not hard to understand why that might be true in Moody's case. He had recently gone through the great Chicago fire. His work was destroyed; the building where he spoke was burned; his people, scattered; the great and prosperous city had become, for a season, a wilderness. Moody had come to see that his bustling energy and constant activity were not sufficient. He was feeling more and more his inadequacy for the work to which God had called him. He had no education. The future looked dark. He had a great burden of soul. We thank God that D. L. Moody received a sweet assurance from God, a great manifestation of God's power in his emotions. Yet Moody himself never missed the significant thing. He almost never spoke about his feelings or emotions in that sacred hour. He said, "I cannot describe it; I seldom refer to it." He knew that there was no need to reproduce that same emotion in the lives of Christians. What people needed was power, and if they had the power then God Himself could decide whether they needed any particular emotion or miracle or outward manifestation. Moody says, "I went to preaching again. The sermons were not different, I did not present any new truths, and yet hundreds were converted" (*The Life of D. L. Moody* by his son, p. 149). The important thing with Moody, as it ought to be with us, was the soul-winning power.

What emotions went through the heart of Saul, when he was first filled with the Holy Spirit and made into a soul winner, as described in Acts 9:17–20? We do not know. The Bible does not say.

What emotions, what feeling, what joy, what kind of manifestations went through the hearts of the Christians at Samaria when Peter and John laid their hands on them and they received the Holy Ghost, as told in Acts 8:17? We do not know; the Bible does not say! And so it is in most of the cases in the Bible. People filled with the Holy Spirit simply received power from on high, and that was enough. That fulfills the blessed promise of God in Acts 1:8: "But ye shall receive power, after that the Holy Ghost is come upon you: and ye shall be witnesses unto me...."

I think that if being filled with the Spirit should mean an utter revolution in the way a man lives, in the way he thinks, in his plans, then it is likely that the coming of the Holy Spirit upon him would bring a great emotional crisis and tremendous feelings. It is likely that in such a case a man would know the very day and hour when he was first filled with the Holy Spirit.

In salvation it is the same way. I have seen hundreds of drunkards saved. I have seen men in one moment changed from wicked, profane or even criminal men, into saints of God. I have known people who were saved when they were under the influence of liquor and who seemed to be almost instantly sobered by trusting in Christ. Such people very naturally know exactly when they were converted. Yet I find that when children are reared in Christian homes and won to Christ when they are five or six years old, they are not so apt to remember the exact date they were saved.

I was converted when I was about nine years old. I do not know the day, nor the month, nor even for certain the year. In fact, I was not sure even at the time that I was saved, and I did not get perfect assurance until three years later. When I was saved, I did not quit smoking, for I had never smoked. I did not quit cursing, for I had never cursed. I did not quit drinking, for I had never drunk. I was a well-disciplined, carefully reared son of a preacher. There was a definite time when I trusted Christ for my salvation, but the change was not so radical as to bring a tremendous emotional upset and definite manifestations never to be forgotten. In fact, I did not even weep when I came to trust Christ as my Saviour, and my father did not believe that I was old enough to know what I was doing. So I could never tell anybody that I had felt as light as a feather, that my life was radically changed in outward habits. Actually, I know to this very day that I was saved then only because the Word of God makes it clear that one who trusts in Christ is saved. I did in my boyish heart turn to Jesus Christ and trust Him. I do not remember the exact date, though I know the place. But God's Word says I am saved.

In the Southwestern Baptist Theological Seminary, Dr. J. M. Price once remarked to a large class in which I sat that many Christian workers did not know exactly when they had trusted in Christ. One student boldly said that he believed one who could not name the day when he was converted had never been converted, had never trusted Christ for salvation. Thereupon Dr. Price took a vote; and we found that of this class, all of them fundamental in doctrine, all of them assured that they had trusted in Christ and were cleansed by His blood alone, one-fourth did not know when they had first trusted Christ! These preachers and Christian workers had come out of the most devout Christian homes. Many of them had been saved as small children. Many of them had been taught to pray from the time they could talk. They had trusted Christ but there was no great crisis of outward manifestations and of change in habits and thoughts and companions. No one had marked down in the Bible the date they were converted. So they did not remember the date, and some of them did not remember clearly any experience except that they knew that they were now trusting in Christ for salvation.

And that helps us to see how that there may be a difference in the emotions and the manifestations that may accompany the fullness of the Holy Spirit in one person or another. If a cold and prayerless Christian were suddenly set on fire for soul winning, there would be tremendous decisions of the will involved, a giving up of certain sins, a turning from selfish plans. In such a case one might well remember a definite experience, a great climax of self-renunciation and then the flood tides of God's blessing and power. But for Christians who are already surrendered to the will of God as far as they know it, Christians who are already living separated and holy lives, Christians who are already earnestly concerned about soul winning and are willing to win souls at any cost, there usually would not be a great manifestation, either in the feelings and emotions or in any other way, except a consciousness of God's presence and particularly His power upon their efforts to win souls.

In my own experience of long years as a soul winner, several times stand out in my memory when I laid self upon the altar afresh for power. I remember the time in the Pacific Garden Mission in Chicago and in the University of Chicago where I was doing graduate work, when I definitely turned from the teaching profession and gave myself to the Lord for His ministry. I remember the time in 1926 when I gave up the pastorate, gave up a regular salary, gave up my life insurance, and started out to be an evangelist at any cost in the world. And near the same time I faced clearly the problem of giving up the friends of a lifetime by taking a stand plainly against evolutionary teaching in Christian colleges and opposing some who were in high denominational positions. Then there was the crisis time when again in 1940 I felt I must go again into full-time evangelistic work, leaving a blessed ministry in Dallas, Texas. In a Y.M.C.A. room in St. Paul, Minnesota, I waited on God long to make sure that every motive was surrendered to God, that I would wholly do His will, whatever the outcome. Again, some years later in the South Side of Chicago I waited on God far into the night and felt led to make a holy vow that I would give myself to live or die, at any cost, to help restore large union revival campaigns in America. But in none of these cases do I recall great emotional flood tides. I felt that God was with me and would give me grace. I felt that I could wholly trust Him. I did not know the outcome. I was sure that souls would be saved in great numbers, as they have been. And that is about as well as I can describe those times.

And yet I think that I was first filled with the Holy Spirit, perhaps, when I was fifteen years old. I found the second chapter of Acts in the Bible. For days I read it and reread it and meditated upon it and walked among the clouds. Oh, what a thrill to think of three thousand people saved in one day! At fifteen I won my first soul. I can remember spending some time in fasting and prayer when a revival campaign in the little cow town nearby had had no conversions in some days. After my fasting and prayer I had great rejoicing when the flood tides of God's blessings broke over the community and many were saved.

Later when I was a college student and gospel singer, and then a college teacher, I won hundreds of souls to Christ. Many, many times I have earnestly sought and have been assured of a new breath of Heaven upon me, a new enduement of power from on high. But I cannot definitely name the time or the place when I was first filled with the Holy Spirit. However, I have the evidence; thank God, thousands of souls have turned from darkness to light as I have told them the way. I need again more and more to be filled with the Holy Spirit. But I will not demand any special crisis of emotional experience, and I will not be disappointed if I do not have it. Oh, if God will give me hundreds or even thousands of sinners turning to Christ in a revival campaign, I will know that I am filled anew with the Spirit of God.

Yesterday I talked with my brother, Evangelist Bill Rice, on this very matter. He has the power of God upon him and wins many hundreds of souls. Some people feel that his success is largely because of his Western stories or his colorful speech; but I know better. I know how he entered the ministry against opposition of some very near to him. I know how he preached the Gospel when it literally meant going hungry and seeing his wife go without necessary food and clothes. I know that he preached when he was threatened with death; preached boldly and plainly even when wicked people came into the church and raised a gun to shoot him. I know how Bill would not be sidetracked from his burden for souls when he attended Moody Bible Institute. He had to hold revivals though the authorities thought he was too young and immature. He had to preach the Gospel though it involved poverty and temptation and strain beyond words to express. From the very beginning Bill has preached boldly against sin. From the very beginning he has worked hard at soul winning. From the very beginning he has suffered the loss of friends and much else just to please the dear Lord. So when the fullness of the Spirit came upon him there was no need for any great crisis of emotions. There was simply need for power on his ministry, power to win souls. And that power came!

Oh, dear reader, never mind what sights and sounds and feelings and ecstasies some claim. If God wants to send them, then let them come. If they do not come, then it does not matter. The thing that matters is the power of God upon us to win souls. And that, praise God, we can have and will have when the Spirit comes upon us.

V. So You Do Not Agree With This Book?

How could anyone write this many pages on the most controversial of all Bible doctrines and expect every reader to concur heartily? I have no hope that every reader will at once see all the truths taught here nor agree at once with every position taken. Yet for you, dear doubter, I have an earnest word. You may not believe that it is ever necessary for a Christian to tarry and wait on God for the fullness of the Spirit. You may believe that the baptism of the Holy Spirit refers only to what a Christian gets when he is saved. You may think that the teaching here given borders on fanaticism. But whatever it be about this teaching with which you do not agree, there are certain great responsibilities that you still have. There are certain facts that you must face.

First, you will need to bear in mind that, in the main, the position taken here, that every Christian can be filled with the Holy Spirit for soul-winning power and that this is a distinct experience separate from salvation and that this fullness of the Spirit comes in answer to prevailing prayer and for the purpose of soul-winning power—I say that general thesis is exactly the doctrinal position of all the greatest soul winners down through the centuries. Spurgeon believed this. So did Charles G. Finney. So did D. L. Moody and R. A. Torrey and J. Wilbur Chapman. So did Jonathan Edwards. So did A. T. Pierson. So did A. B. Earle, Baptist evangelist who won over 150,000 souls. So did George W. Truett and L. R. Scarborough, mighty Texans.

I say the Plymouth Brethren and the Darby teaching, denying the Moody-Torrey position, has never produced a single great evangelist comparable to the other soul winners mentioned. Those who have won great multitudes of souls have believed in the fullness of the Spirit as a special enduement of power from on high, given for soul-winning power to those who waited on God and gave themselves wholly to Him for His work. Fads of ultradispensational teaching have been brought in, and the old-time teaching of Moody and Torrey has been displaced in some quarters, but every honest Christian has to face the testimony of the great soul winners down through the centuries. All of them believed in a definite enduement of power for soul winning which, they taught, is available for every Christian who pays God's price for power.

Second, dear unconvinced Christian, if you do not agree with me in doctrine, you must still give an account to God. Never mind the theory. Never mind the terminology. What does it matter whether one speaks of the fullness of the Spirit (which term I prefer) or the baptism of the Spirit or the gift of the Spirit or the anointing of the Spirit? Never mind whether you prefer to speak of the deeper life or of holiness or consecration. It is not words that are important, but power. Do you have the power of Pentecost? Do you win many souls for Christ? Do you bear the "much fruit" promised? Do you reproduce New Testament results in your daily life? If not, you are a disobedient Christian. You are not carrying out the Great Commission. If you do not daily live a victorious, soul-winning life, a life of testimony in the power of the Spirit, then you are falling short of your duty and have missed your Christian inheritance. Suppose you do not agree with the detailed teaching given here. The command of Ephesians 5:18, God's plain command, is still for you: "Be not drunk with wine, wherein is excess; but be filled with the Spirit." You are definitely commanded not to be drunk. You are definitely commanded to be filled with the Spirit. There is no excuse for any Christian to violate this plain command of God. If you are not filled with the Holy Spirit, you are living in disobedience and sin.

You do not agree with Dr. Torrey, you say? You do not agree with D. L. Moody, nor Chapman, nor Finney? Never mind about the terminology, the technical points of doctrine; do you have what these men had?

A Spirit-filled soul winner ministered in Philadelphia some years ago, and on the golf course two beloved men of God walked with him and talked together of spiritual things. He had preached on the fullness of the Spirit just as I do. He also had preached to the unsaved, and God had graciously moved the hearts of sinners to turn to Christ as He had moved Christians to forsake their lukewarmness and earnestly set out to win souls. One of these beloved brethren said to him, "I do not believe in all you have said about the Holy Spirit, but I surely believe in what you have!" Do you have what the great soul winners have? I am not so much concerned about the technical outline of doctrine, the terminology that one may use about the Holy Spirit. (However, the kind of doctrine that does not bring the right kind of results must not be true doctrine. The kind of doctrine that does not bring revival is not Bible truth on this matter of the Holy Spirit.) But every reader still must face the clear question: are you filled with the Holy Spirit?

In the book *Why God Used D. L. Moody* by Dr. R. A. Torrey, Torrey tells how Moody insisted again and again that Torrey preach on "The Baptism With the Holy Ghost." Then Torrey says:

> Once he had some teachers at Northfield—fine men, all of them, but they did not believe in a definite baptism with the Holy Ghost for the individual. They believed that every child of God was baptized with the Holy Ghost, and they did not believe in any special baptism with the Holy Ghost for the individual. Mr. Moody came to me and said: "Torrey, will you come up to my house after the meeting tonight? And I will get those men to come, and I want you to talk this thing out with them." Of course, I very readily consented, and Mr. Moody and I talked for a long time, but they did not altogether see eye to eye with us. And when they went, Mr. Moody signaled me to remain for a few moments. Mr. Moody sat there with his chin on his breast, as he so often sat when he was in deep thought; then he looked up and said: "Oh, why will they split hairs? Why don't they see that this is just the one thing that they themselves need? They are good teachers, they are wonderful teachers, and I am so glad to have them here, but why will they not see that the baptism with the Holy Ghost is just the one touch that they themselves need?"

I maintain that no Bible teacher has a right to be dogmatic on this matter if he himself does not have the power of God upon him—wonderful, revival, soul-winning power on his ministry. Many who quibble about terms need, just as Moody said these Bible teachers at Northfield conference needed, the fullness of the Spirit upon them.

Dr. W. H. Houghton, in the introduction to the little book *Why God Used D. L. Moody*, says, "The tragedy is that so many are technically correct and spiritually powerless." If you "know" that you are technically correct on this matter and still if you do not have the tremendous power of the Spirit of God upon you, then what good is it to be technically correct? And what makes you think that you know so much better than all the great soul winners of history what is really technically correct?

And now may the breath of Heaven come upon all who read and ponder these words and who wait upon God for His fullness. Christians, claim your blessing! Enter into your inheritance! The "holy Spirit of promise" (Eph 1:13) is ready to fill you. "The promise is unto you, and to your children, and to all that are afar off, even as many as the Lord our God shall call" (Acts 2:39).

INDEX TO SUBJECTS

Down Graded Gospel

INDEX TO SCRIPTURES

ACTS

For a complete list of available books, write to:
Sword of the Lord Publishers
P. O. Box 1099
Murfreesboro, Tennessee 37133.

(800) 251-4100
(615) 893-6700
FAX (615) 848-6943
www.swordofthelord.com

To be set apart I may have
to deny myself.
Gloria
Stinkem